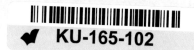

Collins easy learning

Complete French

Grammar + Verbs + Vocabulary

Je suis
content de te voir.
As-tu vu le
nouveau film?
le cerveau

Published by Collins
An imprint of HarperCollins Publishers
Westerhill Road
Bishopbriggs
Glasgow G64 2QT

Second edition 2016

ISBN 978-0-00-814172-1

10 9 8 7 6 5 4 3 2 1

www.collinsdictionary.com
www.collins.co.uk/languagesupport

Typeset by Davidson Publishing Solutions, Glasgow

Printed in Italy by GRAFICA VENETA S.p.A.

A catalogue record for this book is available from the British Library.

If you would like to comment on any aspect of this book, please contact us at the given address or online.

E-mail: dictionaries@harpercollins.co.uk
www.facebook.com/collinsdictionary
@collinsdict

Acknowledgements
We would like to thank those authors and publishers who kindly gave permission for copyright material to be used in the Collins Corpus. We would also like to thank Times Newspapers Ltd for providing valuable data.

MANAGING EDITOR
Maree Airlee

CONTRIBUTORS
Laurence Larroche
Maggie Seaton

FOR THE PUBLISHER
Craig Balfour
Gerry Breslin
Hannah Dove
Chloe Osborne

BASED ON:
Collins Easy Learning French Grammar
Collins Easy Learning French Verbs
Collins Easy Learning French Vocabulary

Contents

Foreword for language teachers

The *Easy Learning Complete French* is designed to be used with both young and adult learners, as a group reference book to complement your course book during classes, or as a recommended text for self-study and homework/coursework.

The text specifically targets learners from beginner to intermediate or GCSE level, and therefore its structural content and vocabulary have been matched to the relevant specifications up to and including Higher GCSE.

The approach aims to develop knowledge and understanding of grammar and your learners' ability to apply it by:

- defining parts of speech at the start of each major section with examples in English to clarify concepts
- minimizing the use of grammar terminology and providing clear explanations of terms both within the text and in the **Glossary**
- illustrating all points with examples (and their translations) based on topics and contexts which are relevant to beginner and intermediate course content

The text helps you develop positive attitudes to grammar learning in your classes by:

- giving clear, easy-to-follow explanations
- prioritizing content according to relevant specifications for the levels
- sequencing points to reflect course content, e.g. verb tenses
- highlighting useful **Tips** to deal with common difficulties
- summarizing **Key points** at the end of sections to consolidate learning

In addition to fostering success and building a thorough foundation in French grammar, the optional **Grammar Extra** sections will encourage and challenge your learners to further their studies to higher and advanced levels.

The blue pages in the middle section of the book contain **Verb Tables** and a **Verb Index** which students can use as a reference in their work.

Finally the **Vocabulary** section in the last part of the book provides thematic vocabulary lists which can either be used for self-study or as an additional teaching resource.

Introduction for students

Whether you are starting to learn French for the very first time, brushing up on topics you have studied in class, or revising for your GCSE exams, the *Easy Learning Complete French* is here to help. This easy-to-use guide takes you through all the basics you will need to speak and understand modern, everyday French.

Newcomers can sometimes struggle with the technical terms they come across when they start to explore the grammar of a new language. The *Easy Learning Complete French* explains how to get to grips with all the parts of speech you will need to know, using simple language and cutting out jargon.

The text is divided into sections, each dealing with a particular area of grammar. Each section can be studied individually, as numerous cross-references in the text point you to relevant points in other sections of the book for further information.

Every major section begins with an explanation of the area of grammar covered on the following pages. For quick reference, these definitions are also collected together on pages viii–xii in a glossary of essential grammar terms.

> **What is a verb?**
> A **verb** is a 'doing' word which describes what someone or something does, what someone or something is, or what happens to them, for example, *be*, *sing*, *live*.

Each grammar point in the text is followed by simple examples of real French, complete with English translations, helping you understand the rules. Underlining has been used in examples throughout the text to highlight the grammatical point being explained.

➤ If you are talking about a part of your body, you usually use a word like *my* or *his* in English, but in French you usually use the definite article.

Tourne la tête à gauche.	Turn your head to the left.
Il s'est cassé le bras.	He's broken his arm.
J'ai mal à la gorge.	I've got a sore throat.

In French, as with any foreign language, there are certain pitfalls which have to be avoided. **Tips** and **Information** notes throughout the text are useful reminders of the things that often trip learners up.

Tip

If you are in doubt as to which form of *you* to use, it is safest to use **vous** and you will not offend anybody.

Key points sum up all the important facts about a particular area of grammar, to save you time when you are revising and help you focus on the main grammatical points.

Key points

- ✔ With masculine singular nouns → use **un**.
- ✔ With feminine singular nouns → use **une**.
- ✔ With plural nouns → use **des**.
- ✔ **un**, **une** and **des** → change to **de** or **d'** in negative sentences.
- ✔ The indefinite article is not usually used when you say what jobs people do, or in exclamations with **quel**.

If you think you would like to continue with your French studies to a higher level, check out the **Grammar Extra** sections. These are intended for advanced students who are interested in knowing a little more about the structures they will come across beyond GCSE.

Grammar Extra!

If you want to use an adjective after **quelque chose**, **rien**, **quelqu'un** and **personne**, you link the words with **de**.

quelqu'un d'important	someone important
quelque chose d'intéressant	something interesting
rien d'amusant	nothing funny

The blue pages in the middle of the book contain **Verb Tables**, where 115 important French verbs (both regular and irregular) are declined in full. Examples show you how to use these verbs in a sentence. You can look up any common verbs in the **Verb Index** on pages 436–446 to find either the conjugation of the verb itself, or a cross-reference to a model verb, which will show you the patterns that verb follows.

Finally the **Vocabulary** section at the end of the book is divided into 50 topics, followed by a list of supplementary vocabulary.

Glossary of Grammar Terms

ABSTRACT NOUN a word used to refer to a quality, idea, feeling or experience, rather than a physical object, for example, *size, reason, happiness*. Compare with **concrete noun**.

ADJECTIVE a 'describing' word that tells you more about a person or thing, such as their appearance, colour, size or other qualities, for example, *pretty, blue, big*.

ADVERB a word usually used with verbs, adjectives or other adverbs that gives more information about when, where, how or in what circumstances something happens, for example, *quickly, happily, now*.

AGREE (to) to change word endings according to whether you are referring to masculine, feminine, singular or plural people or things.

AGREEMENT changing word endings according to whether you are referring to masculine, feminine, singular or plural people or things.

APOSTROPHE s an ending ('s) added to a noun to show who or what someone or something belongs to, for example, *Danielle's dog, the doctor's wife, the book's cover*.

ARTICLE a word like *the, a* and *an*, which is used in front of a noun. See also **definite article, indefinite article** and **partitive article**.

AUXILIARY VERB a verb such as *be, have* and *do* when it is used with a main verb to form tenses, negatives and questions.

BASE FORM the form of the verb without any endings added to it, for example, *walk, have, be, go*. Compare with **infinitive**.

CARDINAL NUMBER a number used in counting, for example, *one, seven, ninety*. Compare with **ordinal number**.

CLAUSE a group of words containing a verb.

COMPARATIVE an adjective or adverb with *-er* on the end of it or *more* or *less* in front of it that is used to compare people, things or actions, for example, *slower, less important, more carefully*.

COMPOUND NOUN a word for a living being, thing or idea, which is made up of two or more words, for example, *tin-opener, railway station*.

CONCRETE NOUN a word that refers to an object you can touch with your hand, rather than to a quality or idea, for example, *ball, map, apples*. Compare with **abstract noun**.

CONDITIONAL a verb form used to talk about things that would happen or would be true under certain conditions, for example, *I <u>would</u> help you if I could*. It is also used to say what you would like or need, for example, *<u>Could</u> you give me the bill?*

CONJUGATE (to) to give a verb different endings according to whether you are referring to *I, you, they* and so on, and according to whether you are referring to past, present or future, for example, *I have, she had, they will have*.

CONJUGATION a group of verbs which have the same endings as each other or change according to the same pattern.

CONJUNCTION a word such as *and*, *because* or *but* that links two words or phrases of a similar type or two parts of a sentence, for example, *Diane and I have been friends for years.*; *I left because I was bored.*

CONSONANT a letter of the alphabet which is not a vowel, for example, *b*, *f*, *m*, *s*, *v* etc. Compare with **vowel**.

CONSTRUCTION an arrangement of words together in a phrase or sentence.

DEFINITE ARTICLE the word *the*. Compare with **indefinite article**.

DEMONSTRATIVE ADJECTIVE one of the words *this*, *that*, *these* and *those* used with a noun to point out a particular person or thing, for example, *this woman*, *that dog*.

DEMONSTRATIVE PRONOUN one of the words *this*, *that*, *these* and *those* used instead of a noun to point out people or things, for example, *That looks fun.*

DIRECT OBJECT a noun referring to the person or thing affected by the action described by a verb, for example, *She wrote her name.*; *I shut the window*. Compare with **indirect object**.

DIRECT OBJECT PRONOUN a word such as *me*, *him*, *us* and *them* which is used instead of a noun to stand in for the person or thing most directly affected by the action described by the verb. Compare with **indirect object pronoun**.

EMPHATIC PRONOUN a word used instead of a noun when you want to emphasize something, for example, *Is this for me?*; *'Who broke the window?' – 'He did.'* Also called **stressed pronoun**.

ENDING a form added to a verb, for example, *go → goes*, and to adjectives and nouns depending on whether they refer to masculine, feminine, singular or plural things.

EXCLAMATION a word, phrase or sentence that you use to show you are surprised, shocked, angry and so on, for example, *Wow!*; *How dare you!*; *What a surprise!*

FEMININE a form of noun, pronoun or adjective that is used to refer to a living being, thing or idea that is not classed as masculine.

FUTURE a verb tense used to talk about something that will happen or will be true.

GENDER whether a noun, pronoun or adjective is feminine or masculine.

IMPERATIVE the form of a verb used when giving orders and instructions, for example, *Shut the door!*; *Sit down!*; *Don't go!*

IMPERFECT one of the verb tenses used to talk about the past, especially in descriptions, and to say what was happening or used to happen, for example, *I used to walk to school*; *It was sunny at the weekend.* Compare with **perfect**.

IMPERSONAL VERB one which does not refer to a real person or thing and where the subject is represented by *it*, for example, *It's going to rain*; *It's 10 o'clock.*

INDEFINITE ADJECTIVE one of a small group of adjectives used to talk about people or things in a general way, without saying who or what they are, for example, *several, all, every*.

INDEFINITE ARTICLE the words *a* and *an*. Compare with **definite article**.

INDEFINITE PRONOUN a small group of pronouns such as *everything, nobody* and *something*, which are used to refer to people or things in a general way, without saying exactly who or what they are.

INDIRECT OBJECT a noun used with verbs that take two objects. For example, in *I gave the carrot to the rabbit*, *the rabbit* is the indirect object and *carrot* is the direct object. Compare with **direct object**.

INDIRECT OBJECT PRONOUN a pronoun used instead of a noun to show the person or the thing the action is intended to benefit or harm, for example, *me* in *He gave me a book* and *Can you get me a towel?* Compare with **direct object pronoun**.

INDIRECT QUESTION used to tell someone else about a question and introduced by a verb such as *ask, tell* or *wonder*, for example, *He asked me what the time was; I wonder who he is*.

INFINITIVE the form of the verb with *to* in front of it and without any endings added, for example, *to walk, to have, to be, to go*. Compare with **base form**.

INTERROGATIVE ADJECTIVE a question word used with a noun to ask *who?*, *what?* or *which?* for example, *<u>What</u> instruments do you play?; <u>Which</u> shoes do you like?*

INTERROGATIVE PRONOUN one of the words *who, whose, whom, what* and *which* when they are used instead of a noun to ask questions, for example, *<u>What</u>'s happening?; <u>Who</u>'s coming?*

INVARIABLE used to describe a form which does not change.

IRREGULAR VERB a verb whose forms do not follow a general pattern or the normal rules. Compare with **regular verb**.

MASCULINE a form of noun, pronoun or adjective that is used to refer to a living being, thing or idea that is not classed as feminine.

NEGATIVE a question or statement which contains a word such as *not, never* or *nothing*, and is used to say that something is not happening, is not true or is absent, for example, *I never eat meat; Don't you love me?*

NOUN a 'naming' word for a living being, thing or idea, for example, *woman, desk, happiness, Andrew*.

NUMBER used to say how many things you are referring to or where something comes in a sequence. See also **ordinal number** and **cardinal number**.

OBJECT a noun or pronoun which refers to a person or thing that is affected by the action described by the verb. Compare with **direct object, indirect object** and **subject**.

OBJECT PRONOUN one of the set of pronouns including *me, him* and *them*, which are used instead of the noun as the object of a verb or preposition. Compare with **subject pronoun**.

ORDINAL NUMBER a number used to indicate where something comes in an order or sequence, for example, *first, fifth, sixteenth*. Compare with **cardinal number**.

PART OF SPEECH a word class, for example, *noun, verb, adjective, preposition, pronoun*.

PARTITIVE ARTICLE the words *some* or *any*, used to refer to part of a thing but not all of it, for example, *Have you got any money?; I'm going to buy some bread*.

PASSIVE a form of the verb that is used when the subject of the verb is the person or thing that is affected by the action, for example, *we were told*.

PAST PARTICIPLE a verb form which is used to form perfect and pluperfect tenses and passives, for example, *watched, swum*. Some past participles are also used as adjectives, for example, *a broken watch*.

PERFECT one of the verb tenses used to talk about the past, especially about actions that took place and were completed in the past. Compare with **imperfect**.

PERSON one of the three classes: the first person (*I, we*), the second person (*you* singular and *you* plural), and the third person (*he, she, it* and *they*).

PERSONAL PRONOUN one of the group of words including *I, you* and *they* which are used to refer to yourself, the people you are talking to, or the people or things you are talking about.

PLUPERFECT one of the verb tenses used to describe something that had happened or had been true at a point in the past, for example, *I'd forgotten to finish my homework*.

PLURAL the form of a word which is used to refer to more than one person or thing. Compare with **singular**.

POSSESSIVE ADJECTIVE one of the words *my, your, his, her, its, our* or *their*, used with a noun to show that one person or thing belongs to another.

POSSESSIVE PRONOUN one of the words *mine, yours, hers, his, ours* or *theirs*, used instead of a noun to show that one person or thing belongs to another.

PREPOSITION is a word such as *at, for, with, into* or *from*, which is usually followed by a noun, pronoun or, in English, a word ending in *-ing*. Prepositions show how people and things relate to the rest of the sentence, for example, *She's at home; a tool for cutting grass; It's from David*.

PRESENT a verb form used to talk about what is true at the moment, what happens regularly, and what is happening now, for example, *I'm a student; I travel to college by train; I'm studying languages*.

PRESENT PARTICIPLE a verb form ending in *-ing* which is used in English to form verb tenses, and which may be used as an adjective or a noun, for example, *What are you doing?; the setting sun; Swimming is easy!*

PRONOUN a word which you use instead of a noun, when you do not need or want to name someone or something directly, for example, *it, you, none*.

PROPER NOUN the name of a person, place, organization or thing. Proper nouns are always written with a capital letter, for example, *Kevin, Glasgow, Europe, London Eye*.

QUESTION WORD a word such as *why, where, who, which* or *how* which is used to ask a question.

REFLEXIVE PRONOUN a word ending in *-self* or *-selves*, such as *myself* or *themselves*, which refers back to the subject, for example, *He hurt himself.; Take care of yourself.*

REFLEXIVE VERB a verb where the subject and object are the same, and where the action 'reflects back' on the subject. A reflexive verb is used with a reflexive pronoun such as *myself, yourself, herself*, for example, *I washed myself.; He cut himself.*

REGULAR VERB a verb whose forms follow a general pattern or the normal rules. Compare with **irregular verb**.

RELATIVE PRONOUN a word such as *that, who* or *which*, when it is used to link two parts of a sentence together.

SENTENCE a group of words which usually has a verb and a subject. In writing, a sentence has a capital letter at the beginning and a full stop, question mark or exclamation mark at the end.

SINGULAR the form of a word which is used to refer to one person or thing. Compare with **plural**.

STEM the main part of a verb to which endings are added.

STRESSED PRONOUN used instead of a noun when you want to emphasize something, for example, *Is this for me?; 'Who broke the window?' – 'He did.'* Also called **emphatic pronoun**.

SUBJECT the noun in a sentence or phrase that refers to the person or thing that does the action described by the verb or is in the state described by the verb, for example, *My cat doesn't drink milk*. Compare with **object**.

SUBJECT PRONOUN a pronoun such as *I, he, she* and *they* which is used instead of a noun as the subject of a sentence. Pronouns stand in for nouns when it is clear who is being talked about, for example, *My brother isn't here at the moment. He'll be back in an hour*. Compare with **object pronoun**.

SUBJUNCTIVE a verb form used in certain circumstances to express some sort of feeling, or to show doubt about whether something will happen or whether something is true. It is only used occasionally in modern English, for example, *If I were you, I wouldn't bother.; So be it.*

SUPERLATIVE an adjective or adverb with *-est* on the end of it or *most* or *least* in front of it that is used to compare people, things or actions, for example, *thinnest, most quickly, least interesting*.

SYLLABLE consonant+vowel units that make up the sounds of a word, for example, *ca-the-dral (3 syllables), im-po-ssi-ble (4 syllables)*.

TENSE the form of a verb which shows whether you are referring to the past, present or future.

VERB a 'doing' word which describes what someone or something does, what someone or something is, or what happens to them, for example *be, sing, live*.

VOWEL one of the letters *a, e, i, o* or *u*. Compare with **consonant**.

Nouns

What is a noun?
A **noun** is a 'naming' word for a living being, thing or idea, for example, *woman*, *happiness*, *Andrew*.

Using nouns

➤ In French, all nouns are either masculine or feminine. This is called their gender. Even words for things have a gender.

➤ Whenever you are using a noun, you need to know whether it is masculine or feminine as this affects the form of other words used with it, such as:

- adjectives that describe it
- articles (such as **le** or **une**) that go before it
- pronouns (such as **il** or **elle**) that replace it

⇨ *For more information on* ***Adjectives***, ***Articles*** *or* ***Pronouns***, *see pages 25, 12 and 42.*

➤ You can find information about gender by looking the word up in a dictionary. When you come across a new noun, always learn the word for *the* or *a* that goes with it to help you remember its gender.

- **le** or **un** before a noun tells you it is masculine
- **la** or **une** before a noun tells you it is feminine

➤ We refer to something as singular when we are talking about just one of them, and as plural when we are talking about more than one. The singular is the form of the noun you will usually find when you look a noun up in the dictionary. As in English, nouns in French change their form in the plural.

➤ Adjectives, articles and pronouns are also affected by whether a noun is singular or plural.

Tip
Remember that you have to use the right word for *the*, *a* and so on according to the gender of the French noun.

Nouns

Gender

1 Nouns referring to people

➤ Most nouns referring to men and boys are masculine.

un homme	a man
un roi	a king

➤ Most nouns referring to women and girls are feminine.

une fille	a girl
une reine	a queen

➤ When the same word is used to refer to either men/boys or women/girls, its gender usually changes depending on the sex of the person it refers to.

un camarade	a (male) friend
une camarade	a (female) friend
un Belge	a Belgian (man)
une Belge	a Belgian (woman)

Grammar Extra!

Some words for people have only one possible gender, whether they refer to a male or a female.

un bébé	a (male or female) baby
un guide	a (male or female) guide
une personne	a (male or female) person
une vedette	a (male or female) star

➤ In English, we can sometimes make a word masculine or feminine by changing the ending, for example, *Englishman* and *Englishwoman*, or *prince* and *princess*. In French, very often the ending of a noun changes depending on whether it refers to a man or a woman.

un Anglais	an Englishman
une Anglaise	an Englishwoman
un prince	a prince
une princesse	a princess
un employé	a (male) employee
une employée	a (female) employee

⇨ *For more information on* ***Masculine and feminine forms of words****, see page 7.*

For further explanation of grammatical terms, please see pages viii-xii.

2 Nouns referring to animals

➤ In English we can choose between words like *bull* or *cow*, depending on the sex of the animal we are referring to. In French too there are sometimes separate words for male and female animals.

un taureau	a bull
une vache	a cow

➤ Sometimes, the same word with different endings is used for male and female animals.

un chien	a (male) dog
une chienne	a (female) dog, a bitch

> *Tip*
> When you do not know or care what sex the animal is, you can usually use the masculine form as a general word.

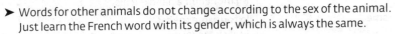

➤ Words for other animals do not change according to the sex of the animal. Just learn the French word with its gender, which is always the same.

un poisson	a fish
une souris	a mouse

3 Nouns referring to things

➤ In English, we call all things – for example, *table, car, book, apple* – 'it'. In French, however, things are either masculine or feminine. As things do not divide into sexes the way humans and animals do, there are no physical clues to help you with their gender in French. Try to learn the gender as you learn the word.

➤ There are lots of rules to help you:

- words ending in **-e** are generally feminine (**une boulangerie** a baker's; **une banque** a bank)
- words ending in a consonant (any letter except *a, e, i, o* or *u*) are generally masculine (**un aéroport** an airport; **un film** a film)

➤ There are some exceptions to these rules, so it is best to check in a dictionary if you are unsure.

Nouns

➤ These endings are often found on masculine nouns.

Masculine ending	Examples
-age	**un village** a village **un voyage** a journey **un étage** a floor **le fromage** cheese BUT: **une image** a picture **une page** a page **la plage** the beach
-ment	**un appartement** a flat **un bâtiment** a building **le ciment** cement **un vêtement** a garment
-oir	**un miroir** a mirror **un couloir** a corridor **le soir** the evening **un mouchoir** a handkerchief
-sme	**le tourisme** tourism **le racisme** racism
-eau	**un cadeau** a present **un chapeau** a hat **un gâteau** a cake **le rideau** the curtain BUT: **la peau** skin **l'eau** water
-eu	**un jeu** a game
-ou	**un chou** a cabbage **le genou** the knee
-ier	**le cahier** the exercise book **un quartier** an area **un escalier** a staircase
-in	**un magasin** a shop **un jardin** a garden **un dessin** a drawing **le vin** the wine BUT: **la fin** the end **une main** a hand

For further explanation of grammatical terms, please see pages viii-xii.

-on	un champignon a mushroom un ballon a ball le citron the lemon BUT: une maison a house la saison the season

➤ The following types of word are also masculine:

- names of the days of the week, and the months and seasons of the year

  le lundi Monday
  septembre prochain next September
  le printemps Spring

- the names of languages

  le français French
  le portugais Portuguese
  Tu apprends le français depuis combien de temps? How long have you been learning French?

- most metric weights and measures

  un gramme a gramme
  un mètre a metre
  un kilomètre a kilometre

- English nouns used in French

  le football football
  un tee-shirt a tee-shirt
  un sandwich a sandwich

➤ These endings are often found on feminine nouns.

Feminine ending	Examples
-ance -anse -ence -ense	**la chance** luck, chance **une danse** a dance **la patience** patience **la défense** defence BUT: **le silence** silence
-ion	**une région** a region **une addition** a bill **une réunion** a meeting **la circulation** traffic BUT: **un avion** a plane
-té -tié	**une spécialité** a speciality **la moitié** half BUT: **un été** a summer **le pâté** pâté

Grammar Extra!

A few words have different meanings depending on whether they are masculine or feminine. These are the most common:

Masculine	Meaning	Example	Feminine	Meaning	Example
un livre	a book	**un livre de poche** a paperback	**une livre**	a pound	**une livre sterling** a pound sterling
un mode	a method	**le mode d'emploi** the directions for use	**la mode**	fashion	**à la mode** in fashion
un poste	a set (*TV/radio*); a post (*job*); an extension (*phone*)	**un poste de professeur** a teaching job	**la poste**	post the post office	**mettre quelque chose à la poste** to post something
un tour	a turn; a walk	**faire un tour** to go for a walk	**une tour**	tower	**la tour Eiffel** the Eiffel Tower

Key points

- ✔ Most nouns referring to men, boys and male animals are masculine; most nouns referring to women, girls and female animals are feminine. The ending of a French noun often changes depending on whether it refers to a male or a female.
- ✔ Generally, words ending in **-e** are feminine and words ending in a consonant are masculine, though there are many exceptions to this rule.
- ✔ These endings are often found on masculine nouns: **-age**, **-ment**, **-oir**, **-sme**, **-eau**, **-eu**, **-ou**, **-ier**, **-in** and **-on**.
- ✔ These endings are often found on feminine nouns: **-ance**, **-anse**, **-ence**, **-ense**, **-ion**, **-té**, **-tié**.
- ✔ Days of the week, months and seasons of the year are masculine. So are languages, most metric weights and measures, and English nouns used in French.

4 Masculine and feminine forms of words

➤ In French there are sometimes very different words for men and women, and for male and female animals, just as in English.

un homme	a man
une femme	a woman
un taureau	a bull
une vache	a cow
un neveu	a nephew
une nièce	a niece

➤ Many masculine French nouns can be made feminine simply by changing the ending. This is usually done by adding an **-e** to the masculine noun to form the feminine.

un ami	a (male) friend
une amie	a (female) friend
un employé	a (male) employee
une employée	a (female) employee
un Français	a Frenchman
une Française	a Frenchwoman

➤ If the masculine singular form already ends in **-e**, no further **e** is added.

un élève	a (male) pupil
une élève	a (female) pupil
un camarade	a (male) friend
une camarade	a (female) friend
un collègue	a (male) colleague
une collègue	a (female) colleague

Tip

If a masculine noun ends in a vowel, its pronunciation does not change when an **-e** is added to form the feminine. For example, **ami** and **amie** (meaning *friend*) are both pronounced the same.

If a masculine noun ends with a consonant that is not pronounced, for example, **-d**, **-s**, **-r** or **-t**, you DO pronounce that consonant when an **-e** is added in the feminine. For example, in **étudiant** (meaning *student*), you cannot hear the **t**; in **étudiante**, you can hear the **t**.

Tip

Some masculine nouns, such as **voisin** (meaning *neighbour*), end in what is called a nasal vowel and an **-n**. With these words, you pronounce the vowel 'through your nose' but DO NOT say the **n**. When an **-e** is added in the feminine – for example, **voisine** – the vowel becomes a normal one instead of a nasal vowel and you DO pronounce the **n**.

5 Some other patterns

➤ Some changes to endings from masculine to feminine are a little more complicated but still fall into a regular pattern.

Masculine ending	Feminine ending	Example	Meaning
-f	-ve	**un veuf/une veuve**	a widower/a widow
-x	-se	**un époux/une épouse**	a husband/a wife
-eur	-euse	**un danseur/ une danseuse**	a (male) dancer/ a (female) dancer
-teur	-teuse -trice	**un chanteur/ une chanteuse** **un acteur/une actrice**	a (male) singer/ a (female) singer an actor/an actress
-an	-anne	**un paysan/ une paysanne**	a (male) farmer/ a (female) farmer
-ien	-ienne	**un Parisien/ une Parisienne**	a (male) Parisian/ a (female) Parisian
-on	-onne	**un lion/une lionne**	a lion/a lioness
-er	-ère	**un étranger/ une étrangère**	a (male) foreigner/ a (female) foreigner
-et	-ette	**le cadet/la cadette**	the youngest (male) child the youngest (female) child
-el	-elle	**un professionnel/ une professionnelle**	a (male) professional/ a (female) professional

Key points

✔ Many masculine French nouns can be made to refer to females by adding an **-e**. If the masculine singular form already ends in **-e**, no further **e** is added.

✔ The pronunciation of feminine nouns is sometimes different from that of the corresponding masculine nouns.

✔ Other patterns include:

-f → **-ve**	**-teur** → **-teuse** or **-trice**	**-er** → **-ère**
-x → **-se**	**-an, -en** and **-on** → **-anne, -enne** and **-onne**	**-et** → **-ette**
-eur → **-euse**		**-el** → **-elle**

For further explanation of grammatical terms, please see pages viii-xii.

Forming plurals

1 Plurals ending in -s

➤ In English we usually make nouns plural by adding an *-s* to the end (*garden* → *gardens*; *house* → *houses*), although we do have some nouns which are irregular and do not follow this pattern (*mouse* → *mice*; *child* → *children*).

Tip

Remember that you have to use **les** with plural nouns in French. Any adjective that goes with the noun has to agree with it, as does any pronoun that replaces it.

➪ *For more information on* ***Adjectives***, ***Articles*** *and* ***Pronouns***, *see pages* 25, 12 *and* 42.

➤ Most French nouns also form their plural by adding an **-s** to their singular form.

un jardin	a garden
des jardins	gardens
une voiture	a car
des voitures	cars
un hôtel	a hotel
des hôtels	hotels

➤ If the singular noun ends in **-s**, **-x** or **-z**, no further **-s** is added in the plural.

un fils	a son
des fils	sons
une voix	a voice
des voix	voices
un nez	a nose
des nez	noses

2 Plurals ending in -x

➤ The following nouns add an **-x** instead of an **-s** in the plural:

- nouns ending in **-eau**

un chapeau	a hat
des chapeaux	hats

- most nouns ending in **-eu**

un jeu	a game
des jeux	games

- a FEW nouns ending in **-ou** (MOST nouns ending in **-ou** add **-s** as usual)

un bijou	a jewel
des bijoux	jewels
un caillou	a pebble
des cailloux	pebbles
un chou	a cabbage
des choux	cabbages
un genou	a knee
des genoux	knees
un hibou	an owl
des hiboux	owls
un joujou	a toy
des joujoux	toys
un pou	a louse
des poux	lice

Tip

Adding an **-s** or **-x** to the end of a noun does not usually change the way the word is pronounced. For example, **professeur** and **professeurs** and **chapeau** and **chapeaux** sound just the same when you say them out loud.

➤ If the singular noun ends in **-al** or **-ail**, the plural usually ends in **-aux**.

un journal	a newspaper
des journaux	newspapers
un animal	an animal
des animaux	animals
un travail	a job
des travaux	jobs

For further explanation of grammatical terms, please see pages viii-xii.

Tip

The plural of **un œil** (*an eye*) is **des yeux** (*eyes*).

3 Plural versus singular

➤ A few words relating to clothing are plural in English but NOT in French.

un slip	pants
un short	shorts
un pantalon	trousers

➤ A few common words are plural in French but NOT in English.

les affaires	business
les cheveux	hair
des renseignements	information

Grammar Extra!

When nouns are made up of two separate words, they are called compound nouns, for example, **les grands-parents** (meaning *grandparents*), **des ouvre-boîtes** (meaning *tin-openers*). The rules for forming the plural of compound nouns are complicated and it is best to check in a dictionary to see what the plural is.

Key points

- ✔ Most French nouns form their plural by adding an **-s** to their singular form. If the singular noun ends in **-s**, **-x** or **-z**, no further **-s** is added in the plural.
- ✔ Most nouns ending in **-eau** or **-eu** add an **-x** in the plural.
- ✔ Most nouns ending in **-ou** take an **-s** in the plural, with a few exceptions.
- ✔ If the singular noun ends in **-al** or **-ail**, the plural usually ends in **-aux**.
- ✔ Adding an **-s** or **-x** to the end of a noun does not generally affect the way the word is pronounced.
- ✔ A few common words are plural in English but not in French, and vice versa.

Articles

What is an article?
In English, an **article** is one of the words *the*, *a*, and *an* which is given in front of a noun.

Different types of article

➤ There are three types of article:

- the definite article: *the* in English. This is used to identify a particular thing or person.

  I'm going to the supermarket.
  That's the woman I was talking to.

- the indefinite article: *a* or *an* in English, *some* or *any* (or no word at all) in the plural. This is used to refer to something unspecific, or that you do not really know about.

  Is there a supermarket near here?
  I need a day off.

- the partitive article: *some* or *any* (or no word at all) in English. This is used to talk about quantities or amounts.

  Can you lend me some sugar?
  Did you buy any wine?
  Do you like chocolate?

For further explanation of grammatical terms, please see pages viii-xii.

The definite article: le, la, l' and les

1 The basic rules

➤ In English we only have <u>one</u> definite article: *the*. In French, there is more than one definite article to choose from. All French nouns are either masculine or feminine and, just as in English, they can be either singular or plural. The word you choose for *the* depends on whether the noun it is used with is masculine or feminine, singular or plural. This may sound complicated, but it is not too difficult.

➪ *For more information on* **Nouns**, *see page 1.*

	with masculine noun	with feminine noun
Singular	le (l')	la (l')
Plural	les	les

Tip

le and **la** change to **l'** when they are used in front of a word starting with a vowel and most words starting with **h**.

➤ **le** is used in front of <u>masculine singular nouns</u>.

<u>le</u> roi the king
<u>le</u> chien the dog
<u>le</u> jardin the garden

➤ **la** is used in front of <u>feminine singular nouns</u>.

<u>la</u> reine the queen
<u>la</u> souris the mouse
<u>la</u> porte the door

➤ **l'** is used in front of <u>singular nouns that start with a vowel</u> (*a*, *e*, *i*, *o*, or *u*), whether they are masculine or feminine.

<u>l'</u>ami (*masculine*) the friend
<u>l'</u>eau (*feminine*) the water
<u>l'</u>étage (*masculine*) the floor

ℹ Note that **l'** is also used in front of most words starting with **h** but some others take **le** or **la** instead.

<u>l'</u>hôpital the hospital
<u>le</u> hamster the hamster
<u>la</u> hi-fi the stereo

> *Tip*
> It is a good idea to learn the article or the gender with the noun when you come across a word for the first time, so that you know whether it is masculine or feminine. A good dictionary will also give you this information.

➤ **les** is used in front of plural nouns, whether they are masculine or feminine and whatever letter they start with.

les chiens	the dogs
les portes	the doors
les amis	the friends
les hôtels	the hotels

Note that you have to make the noun plural too, just as you would in English. In French, as in English, you usually add an **-s**.

➪ *For more information on **Forming plurals**, see page 9.*

> *Tip*
> When **les** is used in front of a word that starts with a consonant, you DO NOT say the **s** on the end of **les**: **les chiens** *the dogs*.
> When **les** is used in front of a word that starts with a vowel, most words starting with **h**, and the French word **y**, you DO pronounce the **s** on the end of **les**. It sounds like the *z* in the English word *zip*: **les amis** *the friends*, **les hôtels** *the hotels*.

2 Using à with le, la, l' and les

➤ The French word **à** is translated into English in several different ways, including *at* or *to*. There are special rules when you use it together with **le** and **les**.

➪ *For more information on the preposition **à**, see page 163.*

➤ When **à** is followed by **le**, the two words become **au**.

au cinéma	to/at the cinema
au professeur	to the teacher

➤ When **à** is followed by **les**, the two words become **aux**.

aux maisons	to the houses
aux étudiants	to the students

➤ When **à** is followed by **la** or **l'**, the words do not change.

à la bibliothèque	to/at the library
à l'hôtel	to/at the hotel

> *Tip*
> **le** and **la** change to **l'** when they are used in front of a word starting with a vowel and most words starting with **h**.

3 Using de with le, la, l' and les

➤ The French word **de** is translated into English in several different ways, including *of* and *from*. There are special rules when you use it together with **le** and **les**.

⇨ *For more information on the preposition **de**, see page 166.*

➤ When **de** is followed by **le**, the two words become **du**.

du cinéma	from/of the cinema
du professeur	from/of the teacher

➤ When **de** is followed by **les**, the two words become **des**.

des maisons	from/of the houses
des étudiants	from/of the students

➤ When **de** is followed by **la** or **l'**, the words do not change.

de la bibliothèque	from/of the library
de l'hôtel	from/of the hotel

> *Tip*
> **le** and **la** change to **l'** when they are used in front of a word starting with a vowel and most words starting with **h**.

Key points

✔ With masculine singular nouns → use **le**.

✔ With feminine singular nouns → use **la**.

✔ With nouns starting with a vowel, most nouns beginning with **h** and the French word **y** → use **l'**.

✔ With plural nouns → use **les**.

✔ **à + le = au**

à + les = aux

de + le = du

de + les = des

4 Using the definite article

➤ The definite article in French (**le**, **la**, **l'** and **les**) is used in more or less the same way as we use *the* in English, but it is also used in French in a few places where you might not expect it.

➤ The definite article is used with words like *prices*, *flu* and *time* that describe qualities, ideas or experiences (called abstract nouns) rather than something that you can touch with your hand. Usually, *the* is missed out in English with this type of word.

Les prix montent.	Prices are rising.
J'ai la grippe.	I've got flu.
Je n'ai pas le temps.	I don't have time.

ℹ Note that there are some set phrases using **avoir**, **avec** or **sans** followed by a noun, where the definite article is NOT used.

avoir faim	to be hungry (*literally*: *to have hunger*)
avec plaisir	with pleasure
sans doute	probably (*literally*: *without doubt*)

➤ You also use the definite article when you are talking about things like *coffee* or *computers* that you can touch with your hand (called concrete nouns) if you are talking generally about that thing. Usually, *the* is missed out in English with this type of word.

Je n'aime pas le café.	I don't like coffee.
Les ordinateurs coûtent très cher.	Computers are very expensive.
Les professeurs ne gagnent pas beaucoup.	Teachers don't earn very much.

For further explanation of grammatical terms, please see pages viii-xii.

➤ If you are talking about a part of your body, you usually use a word like *my* or *his* in English, but in French you usually use the definite article.

Tourne la tête à gauche.	Turn your head to the left.
Il s'est cassé le bras.	He's broken his arm.
J'ai mal à la gorge.	I've got a sore throat.

➤ In French you have to use the definite article in front of the names of countries, continents and regions.

la Bretagne	Brittany
l'Europe	Europe
La France est très belle.	France is very beautiful.
J'ai acheté ce poster au Japon.	I bought this poster in Japan.
Je viens des États-Unis.	I come from the United States.

ℹ Note that if the name of the country comes after the French word **en**, meaning *to* or *in*, you do not use the definite article. **en** is used with the names of countries, continents and regions that are feminine in French.

Je vais en Écosse le mois prochain.	I'm going to Scotland next month.
Il travaille en Allemagne.	He works in Germany.

⇨ *For more information on the preposition* ***en****, see page 168.*

➤ You often use the definite article with the name of school subjects, languages and sports.

Tu aimes les maths?	Do you like maths?
J'apprends le français depuis trois ans.	I've been learning French for three years.
Mon sport préféré, c'est le foot.	My favourite sport is football.

ℹ Note that the definite article is not used after **en**.

Comment est-ce qu'on dit 'fils' en anglais?	How do you say 'fils' in English?
Sophie est nulle en chimie.	Sophie's no good at chemistry.

➤ When you use the verb **parler** (meaning *to speak*) in front of the name of the language, you do not always need to use the definite article in French.

Tu parles espagnol?	Do you speak Spanish?
Il parle bien l'anglais.	He speaks English well.

➤ You use **le** with dates, and also with the names of the days of the week and the seasons when you are talking about something that you do regularly or that is a habit.

Elle part le 7 mai.	She's leaving on the seventh of May.
Je vais chez ma grand-mère le dimanche.	I go to my grandmother's on Sundays.

[i] Note that you do not use the definite article after **en**.

En hiver nous faisons du ski.	In winter we go skiing.

➤ You often find the definite article in phrases that tell you about prices and rates.

6 euros le kilo	6 euros a kilo
3 euros la pièce	3 euros each
On roulait à 100 kilomètres à l'heure.	We were doing 100 kilometres an hour.

Key points

✔ The definite article is used in French with:
- abstract nouns
- concrete nouns (*when you are saying something that is true about a thing in general*)
- parts of the body
- countries, continents and regions
- school subjects, languages and sports
- dates
- days of the week and the seasons (*when you are talking about something that you do regularly or that is a habit*)
- prices and rates

The indefinite article: un, une and des

1 The basic rules

- In English we have the indefinite article *a*, which changes to *an* in front of a word that starts with a vowel. In the plural we say either *some*, *any* or nothing at all.
- In French, you choose from **un**, **une** and **des**, depending on whether the noun is masculine or feminine, and singular or plural.

	with masculine noun	with feminine noun
Singular	un	une
Plural	des	des

- **un** is used in front of masculine singular nouns.

un roi	a king
un chien	a dog
un jardin	a garden

- **une** is used in front of feminine singular nouns.

une reine	a queen
une souris	a mouse
une porte	a door

- **des** is used in front of plural nouns, whether they are masculine or feminine, and whatever letter they start with.

des chiens	(some/any) dogs
des souris	(some/any) mice
des amis	(some/any) friends

Note that **des** is also a combination of **de** + **les** and has other meanings, such as saying who something belongs to or where something is from.

For more information on **des**, *see page 166.*

Tip

When **des** is used in front of a word that starts with a consonant (any letter except *a*, *e*, *i*, *o* or *u*), you DO NOT say the **s** on the end of **des**: **des chiens** *(some/any) dogs*.
When **des** is used in front of a word that starts with a vowel, and most words starting with **h**, you DO pronounce the **s** on the end.
It sounds like the z in the English word *zip*: **des amis** *(some/any) friends*, **des hôtels** *(some/any) hotels*.

2 The indefinite article in negative sentences

➤ In English we use words like *not* and *never* to indicate that something is not happening or is not true. The sentences that these words are used in are called negative sentences.

I don't know him.

I never do my homework on time.

➤ In French, you use word pairs like **ne ... pas** (meaning *not*) and **ne ... jamais** (meaning *never*) to say that something is not happening or not true. When **un**, **une** or **des** is used after this type of expression, it has to be changed to **de**.

Je n'ai pas de vélo.	I don't have a bike.
Nous n'avons pas de cousins.	We don't have any cousins.

➪ *For more information on* ***Negatives****, see page 138.*

Tip

de changes to **d'** in front of a word starting with a vowel and most words starting with **h**.

Je n'ai pas d'ordinateur.	I don't have a computer.
Il n'y a pas d'horloge dans la salle.	There isn't a clock in the room.

Grammar Extra!

There are some very common adjectives, like **beau**, **bon** and **petit**, that can come BEFORE the noun instead of after it. When an adjective comes before a plural noun, **des** changes to **de**.

J'ai reçu de beaux cadeaux.	I got some lovely presents.
Cette région a de très jolis villages.	This area has some very pretty villages.

➪ *For more information on* ***Word order with adjectives****, see page 32.*

3 The meaning of des

➤ **des** can mean different things in English, depending on the sentence. *Some* is often the best word to use.

J'ai un chien, deux chats et des souris.	I've got a dog, two cats and some mice.
Tu veux des chips?	Would you like some crisps?

➤ In questions and negative sentences **des** means *any*, or is not translated at all.

Tu as des frères?	Have you got any brothers?
Il n'y a pas d'œufs.	There aren't any eggs.
Avez-vous des timbres?	Do you have stamps?

Tip

As an English speaker, you will know what sounds right in your own language. The important thing to remember is that **des** can NEVER be missed out in French, even if there is no word in English.

4 Using the indefinite article

➤ The indefinite article is used in French in much the same way as we use *a*, *some* and *any* in English, but there are two places where the indefinite article is NOT used:

- with the adjective **quel** (meaning *what a*), in sentences like

Quel dommage!	What a shame!
Quelle surprise!	What a surprise!
Quelle bonne idée!	What a good idea!

⇨ *For more information on **quel**, see page 148.*

- when you say what jobs people do

Il est professeur.	He's a teacher.
Ma mère est infirmière.	My mother's a nurse.

Tip

When you use **c'est** (to mean *he/she is*), you DO use **un** or **une**. When you use **ce sont** (to mean *they are*), you DO use **des**.

C'est un médecin.	He's/She's a doctor.
Ce sont des acteurs.	They're actors.

⇨ *For more information on **c'est** and **ce sont**, see page 65.*

Key points

✔ With masculine singular nouns → use **un**.
✔ With feminine singular nouns → use **une**.
✔ With plural nouns → use **des**.
✔ **un**, **une** and **des** → change to **de** or **d'** in negative sentences.
✔ The indefinite article is not usually used when you say what jobs people do, or in exclamations with **quel**.

The partitive article: du, de la, de l' and des

1 The basic rules

➤ **du**, **de la**, **de l'** and **des** can all be used to give information about the amount or quantity of a particular thing. They are often translated into English as *some* or *any*.

➤ In French, you choose between **du**, **de la**, **de l'** and **des**, depending on whether the noun is masculine or feminine, singular or plural.

	with masculine noun	with feminine noun
Singular	du (de l')	de la (de l')
Plural	des	des

Tip

de + **le** and **de la** change to **de l'** when they are used in front of a word starting with a vowel, most words starting with **h**, and the French word **y**.

➤ **du** is used in front of masculine singular nouns.

du beurre (some/any) butter
du jus d'orange (some/any) orange juice

ℹ Note that **du** is also a combination of **de** + **le** and has other meanings, such as saying who something belongs to or where something is from.

⇨ *For more information on* **du**, *see page 166.*

➤ **de la** is used in front of feminine singular nouns.

de la viande (some/any) meat
de la margarine (some/any) margarine

➤ **de l'** is used in front of singular nouns that start with a vowel and most nouns starting with **h**, whether they are masculine or feminine.

de l'argent (*masculine*) (some/any) money
de l'eau (*feminine*) (some/any) water
de l'herbe (*feminine*) (some/any) grass

➤ **des** is used in front of plural nouns, whether they are masculine or feminine and whatever letter they start with.

des gâteaux	(some/any) cakes
des lettres	(some/any) letters
des hôtels	(some/any) hotels

Note that **des** is also a combination of **de** + **les** and has other meanings, such as saying who something belongs to or where something is from.

*For more information on **des**, see page 166.*

2 The partitive article in negative sentences

➤ In French, you use word pairs like **ne … pas** (meaning *not*) and **ne … jamais** (meaning *never*) to say that something is not happening or not true. In this type of expression, **du**, **de la**, **de l'** and **des** all change to **de**.

Nous n'avons pas de beurre.	We don't have any butter.
Je ne mange jamais de viande.	I never eat meat.
Il n'y a pas de timbres.	There aren't any stamps.

*For more information on **Negatives**, see page 138.*

Tip

de changes to **d'** in front of a word starting with a vowel and most nouns starting with **h**.

Il n'a pas d'argent.	He doesn't have any money.
Il n'y a pas d'horloge dans la salle.	There isn't a clock in the room.

Grammar Extra!

There are some very common adjectives, like **beau**, **bon** and **petit**, that can come BEFORE the noun instead of after it. When an adjective comes before a plural noun, **des** changes to **de**.

J'ai reçu de beaux cadeaux.	I got some lovely presents.
Cette région a de très jolis villages.	This area has some very pretty villages.

*For more information on **Word order with adjectives**, see page 32.*

3 The meaning of du, de la, de l' and des

➤ **du**, **de la**, **de l'** and **des** are often translated into English as *some* or *any*, but there are times when no word is used in English to translate the French.

Il me doit <u>de l'</u>argent.	He owes me (some) money.
Je vais acheter <u>de la</u> farine et <u>du</u> beurre pour faire un gâteau.	I'm going to buy (some) flour and butter to make a cake.
Est-ce qu'il y a <u>des</u> lettres pour moi?	Are there any letters for me?
Elle ne veut pas <u>de</u> beurre.	She doesn't want any butter.
Je ne prends pas <u>de</u> lait.	I don't take milk.

Tip

Remember that **du**, **de la**, **de l'** and **des** can <u>NEVER</u> be missed out in French, even if there is no word in English.

Key points

✔ With masculine singular nouns → use **du**.

✔ With feminine singular nouns → use **de la**.

✔ With singular nouns starting with a vowel and some nouns beginning with **h** → use **de l'**.

✔ With plural nouns → use **des**.

✔ **du**, **de la**, **de l'** and **des** → change to **de** or **d'** in negative sentences.

Adjectives

What is an adjective?
An **adjective** is a 'describing' word that tells you more about a person or thing, such as their appearance, colour, size or other qualities, for example, *pretty*, *blue*, *big*.

Using adjectives

➤ Adjectives are words like *clever*, *expensive* and *silly* that tell you more about a noun (a living being, thing or idea). They can also tell you more about a pronoun, such as *he* or *they*. Adjectives are sometimes called 'describing words'. They can be used right next to a noun they are describing, or can be separated from the noun by a verb like *be*, *look*, *feel* and so on.

a clever girl
an expensive coat
a silly idea
He's just being silly.

*For more information on **Nouns** and **Pronouns**, see pages 1 and 42.*

➤ In English, the only time an adjective changes its form is when you are making a comparison.

She's cleverer than her brother.
That's the silliest idea I ever heard!

➤ In French, however, most adjectives agree with what they are describing. This means that their endings change depending on whether the person or thing you are referring to is masculine or feminine, and singular or plural.

un mot français	a French word
une chanson française	a French song
des traditions françaises	French traditions

➤ In English we put adjectives BEFORE the noun they describe, but in French you usually put them AFTER it.

un chat noir a black cat

➪ *For further information, see **Word order with adjectives** on page 32.*

Key points

✔ Most French adjectives change their form, according to whether the person or thing they are describing is masculine or feminine, singular or plural.

✔ In French adjectives usually go after the noun they describe.

Making adjectives agree

1 The basic rules

➤ In dictionaries, regular French adjectives are usually shown in the masculine singular form. You need to know how to change them to make them agree with the noun or pronoun that they are describing.

➤ To make an adjective agree with the noun or pronoun it describes, you simply add the following endings in most cases:

	with masculine noun	with feminine noun
Singular	-	-e
Plural	-s	-es

un chat noir a black cat
une chemise noire a black shirt
des chats noirs black cats
des chemises noires black shirts

2 Making adjectives feminine

➤ With most adjectives you add an **-e** to the masculine singular form to make it feminine.

un chat noir a black cat → **une chemise noire** a black shirt
un sac lourd a heavy bag → **une valise lourde** a heavy suitcase

➤ If the adjective already ends in an **-e** in the masculine, you do not add another **-e**.

un sac jaune a yellow bag → **une chemise jaune** a yellow shirt
un garçon sage a good boy → **une fille sage** a good girl

➤ Some changes to endings are a little more complicated but still follow a regular pattern. Sometimes you have to double the consonant as well as adding an **-e**. On the next page there is a table showing these changes.

Masculine ending	Feminine ending	Example	Meaning
-f	-ve	neuf/neuve	new
-x	-se	heureux/heureuse	happy
-er	-ère	cher/chère	dear, expensive
-an -en -on	-anne -enne -onne	paysan/paysanne européen/européenne bon/bonne	farming, country European good, right
-el	-elle	cruel/cruelle	cruel
-eil	-eille	pareil/pareille	similar
-et	-ette -ète	net/nette complet/complète	clear complete, full

un <u>bon</u> repas a good meal → **de <u>bonne</u> humeur** in a good mood
un homme <u>cruel</u> a cruel man → **une remarque <u>cruelle</u>** a cruel remark

Tip

If a masculine adjective ends in a vowel (*a*, *e*, *i*, *o* or *u*), its pronunciation does not change when an **-e** is added to form the feminine. For example, **joli** and **jolie** are both pronounced the same.

If a masculine adjective ends with a consonant that is not pronounced, such as **-d**, **-s** or **-t**, you <u>DO</u> pronounce that consonant when an **-e** is added in the feminine. For example, in **chaud** (meaning *hot, warm*), you cannot hear the **d** when it is said out loud; in the feminine form **chaude**, you can hear the **d** sound.

This is also true when you have to double the consonant before the **-e** is added, for example, **gros** (meaning *big, fat*), where you cannot hear the **s**, and the feminine form **grosse**, where you can hear the **s** sound.

Some masculine adjectives, such as **bon** (meaning *good*) or **italien** (meaning *Italian*), end in what is called a <u>nasal vowel</u> and an **-n**. With these words, you pronounce the vowel 'through your nose' but do not say the **n**. When the consonant is doubled and an **-e** is added in the feminine – **bonne**, **italienne** – the vowel becomes a normal one instead of a nasal vowel and you do pronounce the **n**.

➤ Some very common adjectives have irregular feminine forms.

Masculine form	Feminine form	Meaning
blanc	blanche	white, blank
doux	douce	soft, sweet, mild, gentle
faux	fausse	untrue
favori	favorite	favourite
frais	fraîche	fresh, chilly, cool
gentil	gentille	nice, kind
grec	grecque	Greek
gros	grosse	big, fat
long	longue	long
nul	nulle	useless
roux	rousse	red, red-haired
sec	sèche	dry, dried
turc	turque	Turkish

mon sport favori my favourite sport → **ma chanson favorite** my favourite song
un ami grec a Greek (male) friend → **une amie grecque** a Greek (female) friend

➤ A very small group of French adjectives have an extra masculine singular form that is used in front of words that begin with a vowel (*a*, *e*, *i*, *o* or *u*) and most words beginning with **h**. These adjectives also have an irregular feminine form.

Masculine form in front of a word beginning with a consonant	Masculine form in front of a word beginning with a vowel or most words beginning with h	Feminine form	Meaning
beau	bel	belle	lovely, beautiful, good-looking, handsome
fou	fol	folle	mad
nouveau	nouvel	nouvelle	new
vieux	vieil	vieille	old

un bel appartement a beautiful flat
le Nouvel An New Year
un vieil arbre an old tree

3 Making adjectives plural

➤ With most adjectives you add an **-s** to the masculine singular or feminine singular form to make it plural.

un chat noir a black cat → **des chats noirs** black cats
une valise lourde a heavy suitcase → **des valises lourdes** heavy suitcases

> *Tip*
>
> When an adjective describes a masculine and a feminine noun or pronoun, use the masculine plural form of the adjective.
>
> | | |
> |---|---|
> | **La maison et le jardin sont beaux.** | The house and garden are beautiful. |
> | **Sophie et son petit ami sont très gentils.** | Sophie and her boyfriend are very nice. |

➤ If the masculine singular form already ends in an **-s** or an **-x**, you do not add an **-s**.

un fromage français a French cheese → **des fromages français** French cheeses

un homme dangereux a dangerous man → **des hommes dangereux** dangerous men

➤ If the masculine singular form ends in **-eau** or **-al**, the masculine plural is usually **-eaux** or **-aux**.

le nouveau professeur the new teacher → **les nouveaux professeurs** the new teachers

le rôle principal the main role → **les rôles principaux** the main roles

> *Tip*
>
> Adding an **-s** or an **-x** does not change the pronunciation of a word. For example, **noir** and **noirs** sound just the same, as do **nouveau** and **nouveaux**.
>
> When the **-s** or **-x** ending comes before a word starting with a vowel or most words starting with **h**, you have to pronounce the **s** or **x** on the end of the adjective. It sounds like the *z* in the English word *zip*.
>
> | | |
> |---|---|
> | **les anciens élèves** | the former pupils |
> | **de grands hôtels** | big hotels |

For further explanation of grammatical terms, please see pages viii-xii.

4 Invariable adjectives

➤ A small number of adjectives (mostly relating to colours) do not change in the feminine or plural. They are called invariable because their form NEVER changes, no matter what they are describing. These adjectives are often made up of more than one word – for example, **bleu marine** (meaning *navy blue*), or else come from the names of fruit or nuts – for example, **orange** (meaning *orange*), **marron** (meaning *brown*).

des chaussures marron	brown shoes
une veste bleu marine	a navy blue jacket

Key points

- ✔ To make an adjective agree with a feminine singular noun or pronoun, you usually add **-e** to the masculine singular. If the adjective already ends in an **-e**, no further **-e** is added.
- ✔ Several adjectives ending in a consonant double their consonant as well as adding **-e** in the feminine.
- ✔ **beau**, **fou**, **nouveau** and **vieux** have an irregular feminine form and an extra masculine singular form that is used in front of words that begin with a vowel and most words beginning with **h**: **bel**, **fol**, **nouvel**, **vieil**.
- ✔ To make an adjective agree with a masculine plural noun or pronoun, you usually add **-s** to the masculine singular. If the adjective already ends in an **-s** or an **-x**, no further **-s** is added.
- ✔ If the adjective ends in **-eau** or **-al**, the masculine plural is usually **-eaux** or **-aux**.
- ✔ To make an adjective agree with a feminine plural noun or pronoun, you usually add **-es** to the masculine singular.
- ✔ Some adjectives relating to colours never change their form.

Word order with adjectives

1 The basic rules

➤ When adjectives are used right beside the noun they are describing, they go BEFORE it in English. French adjectives usually go AFTER the noun.

l'heure exacte the right time
la page suivante the following page

➤ Adjectives describing colours, shapes or nationalities always go AFTER the noun.

des cravates rouges red ties
une table ronde a round table
un mot français a French word

➤ Some very common adjectives usually come BEFORE the noun.

beau lovely, beautiful, good-looking, handsome
bon good, right
court short
grand tall, big, long, great
gros big, fat
haut high
jeune young
joli pretty
long long
mauvais bad, poor
meilleur better
nouveau new
petit small, little
premier first
vieux old

une belle journée a lovely day
Bonne chance! Good luck!

➤ There is a small group of common adjectives whose meaning changes depending on whether they come before the noun or go after it.

Adjective	Example before noun	Meaning	Example after noun	Meaning
ancien	**un ancien collègue**	a former colleague	**un fauteuil ancien**	an antique chair
cher	**Chère Julie**	Dear Julie	**une robe chère**	an expensive dress
propre	**ma propre chambre**	my own bedroom	**un mouchoir propre**	a clean handkerchief

For further explanation of grammatical terms, please see pages viii-xii.

Tip

dernier (meaning *last*) and **prochain** (meaning *next*) go AFTER nouns relating to time, for example, **semaine** (meaning *week*) and **mois** (meaning *month*). Otherwise they go BEFORE the noun.

la semaine dernière	last week
la dernière fois que je t'ai vu	the last time I saw you
la semaine prochaine	next week
la prochaine fois que j'y vais	the next time I go there

Grammar Extra!

When certain adjectives are used with certain nouns, they take on a meaning you cannot always guess. You may need to check these in your dictionary and learn them. Here are a few:

mon petit ami	my boyfriend
les petits pois	peas
les grandes vacances	the summer holidays
une grande personne	an adult, a grown-up

2 Using more than one adjective

➤ In French you can use more than one adjective at a time to describe someone or something. If one of the adjectives usually comes BEFORE the noun and the other usually goes AFTER the noun, the word order follows the usual pattern.

une jeune femme blonde	a young blonde woman
un nouveau film intéressant	an interesting new film

➤ If both adjectives usually come AFTER the noun, they are joined together with **et** (meaning *and*).

un homme mince et laid	a thin, ugly man
une personne intelligente et drôle	an intelligent, funny person

Key points

✔ Most French adjectives go after the noun they describe.

✔ Some very common adjectives usually come before the noun: **bon/mauvais**, **court/long**, **grand/petit**, **jeune/nouveau/vieux**, **gros**, **haut**, **beau**, **joli**, **premier**, **meilleur**.

✔ The meaning of some adjectives such as **ancien**, **cher** and **propre** varies according to the position in the sentence.

Comparatives and superlatives of adjectives

1 Making comparisons using comparative adjectives

What is a comparative adjective?
A **comparative adjective** in English is one with *-er* on the end of it or *more* or *less* in front of it, that is used to compare people or things, for example, *slower*, *less important*, *more beautiful*.

➤ In French, to say that something is *easier*, *more expensive* and so on, you use **plus** (meaning *more*) before the adjective.

Cette question est plus facile.	This question is easier.
Cette veste est plus chère.	This jacket is more expensive.

➤ To say something is *less expensive*, *less complicated* and so on, you use **moins** (meaning *less*) before the adjective.

Cette veste est moins chère.	This jacket is less expensive.
un projet moins compliqué	a less complicated plan

➤ To introduce the person or thing you are making the comparison with, use **que** (meaning *than*).

Elle est plus petite que moi.	She's smaller than me.
Cette question est plus facile que la première.	This question is easier than the first one.

➤ To say that something or someone is *as* ... *as* something or someone else, use **aussi ... que**.

Il est aussi inquiet que moi.	He's as worried as me.
Cette ville n'est pas aussi grande que Bordeaux.	This town isn't as big as Bordeaux.

2 Making comparisons using superlative adjectives

What is a superlative adjective?
A **superlative adjective** in English is one with *-est* on the end of it or *most* or *least* in front of it, that is used to compare people or things, for example, *thinnest*, *most beautiful*, *least interesting*.

➤ In French, to say that something or someone is *easiest*, *prettiest*, *most expensive* and so on, you use:

- **le plus** with masculine singular adjectives

For further explanation of grammatical terms, please see pages viii-xii.

- **la plus** with feminine singular adjectives
- **les plus** with plural adjectives (for both masculine and feminine)

le guide le plus utile	the most useful guidebook
la question la plus facile	the easiest question
les plus grands hôtels	the biggest hotels
les plus petites voitures	the smallest cars

➤ To say that something or someone is *the least easy*, *the least pretty*, *the least expensive* and so on, you use:

- **le moins** with masculine singular adjectives
- **la moins** with feminine singular adjectives
- **les moins** with plural adjectives (for both masculine and feminine).

le guide le moins utile	the least useful guidebook
Cette question est la moins facile.	This question is the least easy (*or* the hardest).
les mois les moins agréables	the least pleasant months
les moins belles photos	the least attractive photos

Tip

When the adjective comes AFTER the noun, you repeat the definite article (**le**, **la** or **les**).

les mois les moins agréables	the least pleasant months

When the adjective comes BEFORE the noun, you do not repeat the definite article.

les moins belles photos	the least attractive photos

➪ *For more information on* ***Word order with adjectives****, see page 32.*

➤ In phrases like *the biggest hotel in London* and *the oldest person in the village*, you use **de** to translate *in*.

le plus grand hôtel de Londres	the biggest hotel in London
la personne la plus âgée du village	the oldest person in the village

➪ *For more information on* ***de*** *and* ***du****, see page 166.*

3 Irregular comparative and superlative adjectives

➤ Just as English has some irregular comparative and superlative forms – *better* instead of '*more good*', and *worst* instead of '*most bad*' – French also has a few irregular forms.

Adjective	Meaning	Comparative	Meaning	Superlative	Meaning
bon	good	**meilleur**	better	**le meilleur**	the best
mauvais	bad	**pire** **plus mauvais**	worse	**le pire** **le plus mauvais**	the worst
petit	small	**moindre** **plus petit**	smaller, lesser	**le moindre** **le plus petit**	the smallest, the least, the slightest

J'ai une <u>meilleure</u> idée. I've got a <u>better</u> idea.
Il ne fait pas <u>le moindre</u> effort. He doesn't make the <u>slightest</u> effort.

Tip

Choose the right form of the adjective to match the noun or pronoun, depending on whether it is masculine or feminine, singular or plural. Don't forget to change **le** to **la** or **les** too in superlatives.

Grammar Extra!

bien and its comparative and superlative forms **mieux** and **le mieux** can be both adjectives and adverbs.

Il est <u>bien</u>, ce restaurant. (=*adjective*) This restaurant is good.
Elle va <u>mieux</u> aujourd'hui. (=*adverb*) She's better today.

➪ *For more information on* **Adverbs**, *see page* 152.

Key points

✔ To compare people or things in French you use **plus** + adjective, **moins** + adjective or **aussi ... que**.

✔ *than* in comparatives corresponds to **que**.

✔ French superlatives are formed with **le/la/les plus** + adjective and **le/la/les moins** + adjective.

✔ *in* after superlatives corresponds to **de**.

✔ **bon, mauvais** and **petit** have irregular comparatives and superlatives: **bon/meilleur/le meilleur**, **mauvais/pire/le pire**, **petit/moindre/le moindre**.

Demonstrative adjectives ce, cette, cet and ces

What is a demonstrative adjective?
A **demonstrative adjective** is one of the words *this*, *that*, *these* and *those* used with a noun in English to point out a particular thing or person, for example, *this woman*, *that dog*.

➤ In French you use **ce** to point out a particular thing or person. Like all adjectives in French, **ce** changes its form depending on whether you are referring to a noun that is masculine or feminine, singular or plural.

	Masculine	Feminine	Meaning
Singular	**ce (cet)**	**cette**	this that
Plural	**ces**	**ces**	these those

Tip
cet is used in front of masculine singular nouns which begin with a vowel and most words beginning with **h**.

cet oiseau	this/that bird
cet hôpital	this/that hospital

➤ **ce** comes BEFORE the noun it refers to.

Combien coûte ce manteau?	How much is this/that coat?
Comment s'appelle cette entreprise?	What's this/that company called?
Ces livres sont très intéressants.	These/Those books are very interesting.
Ces couleurs sont jolies.	These/Those colours are pretty.

➤ If you want to emphasize the difference between something that is close to you and something that is further away, you can add:

- **-ci** on the end of the noun for things that are closer

  Prends cette valise-ci. — Take this case.

- **-là** on the end of the noun for things that are further away

Est-ce que tu reconnais cette personne-là?	Do you recognize that person?

Key points

✔ The adjective **ce** corresponds to *this* and *that* in the singular, and *these* and *those* in the plural.

✔ The forms are **ce** and **cette** in the singular, and **ces** in the plural. **cet** is used with masculine singular nouns beginning with a vowel and most words beginning with **h**.

✔ You can add **-ci** on the end of the noun for things that are closer, or **-là** for things that are further away, to emphasize the difference between them.

Possessive adjectives

What is a possessive adjective?
In English a **possessive adjective** is one of the words *my*, *your*, *his*, *her*, *its*, *our* or *their* used with a noun to show that one person or thing belongs to another.

➤ Here are the French possessive adjectives. Like all French adjectives, these agree with the noun they refer to.

with masculine singular noun	with feminine singular noun	with plural noun (masculine or feminine)	Meaning
mon	**ma (mon)**	**mes**	my
ton	**ta (ton)**	**tes**	your
son	**sa (son)**	**ses**	his her its one's
notre	**notre**	**nos**	our
votre	**votre**	**vos**	your
leur	**leur**	**leurs**	their

Tip

You use **mon**, **ton** and **son** with feminine singular nouns in front of words that begin with a vowel and most words beginning with **h**. This makes them easier to say.

<u>mon</u> assiette	my plate
<u>ton</u> histoire	your story
<u>son</u> erreur	his/her mistake
<u>mon</u> autre sœur	my other sister

➤ Possessive adjectives come <u>BEFORE</u> the noun they describe.

Voilà <u>mon</u> mari.	There's my husband.
<u>Mon</u> frère et <u>ma</u> sœur habitent à Glasgow.	My brother and sister live in Glasgow.
Est-ce que <u>tes</u> voisins vendent <u>leur</u> maison?	Are your neighbours selling their house?
Rangez <u>vos</u> affaires.	Put your things away.

Tip

Possessive adjectives agree with what they describe, NOT with the person who owns that thing. For example, **sa** can mean *his*, *her*, *its* and *one's*, but can only ever be used with a feminine singular noun.

Paul cherche sa montre.	Paul's looking for his watch.
Paul cherche ses lunettes.	Paul's looking for his glasses.
Catherine a appelé son frère.	Catherine called her brother.
Catherine a appelé sa sœur.	Catherine called her sister.

➤ The equivalent of *your* in French is **ton/ta/tes** for someone you call **tu**, or **votre/vos** for someone you call **vous**.

➪ *For more information on the difference between* **tu** *and* **vous**, *see page 43.*

ℹ Note that possessive adjectives are not normally used with parts of the body. Use **le**, **la**, **l'** or **les** instead.

J'ai mal à la main.	My hand hurts.

➪ *For more information on* **Articles**, *see page 12.*

Key points

✔ The French possessive adjectives are:
- **mon/ton/son/notre/votre/leur** in the masculine singular
- **ma/ta/sa/notre/votre/leur** in the feminine singular
- **mes/tes/ses/nos/vos/leurs** in the plural

✔ Possessive adjectives come before the noun they refer to. They agree with what they describe, rather than with the person who owns that thing.

✔ You use **mon**, **ton** and **son** with feminine singular nouns when the following word begins with a vowel. You also use them with most words beginning with **h**.

✔ Possessive adjectives are not normally used with parts of the body. Use **le**, **la**, **l'** or **les** instead.

Indefinite adjectives

What is an indefinite adjective?
An **indefinite adjective** is one of a small group of adjectives that are used to talk about people or things in a general way without saying exactly who or what they are, for example, *several*, *all*, *every*.

➤ In French, this type of adjective comes BEFORE the noun it refers to. Here are the most common French indefinite adjectives:

Masculine singular	Feminine singular	Masculine plural	Feminine plural	Meaning
autre	autre	autres	autres	other
chaque	chaque	-	-	every, each
même	même	mêmes	mêmes	same
-	-	quelques	quelques	some, a few
tout	toute	tous	toutes	all, every

J'ai d'autres projets.	I've got other plans.
J'y vais chaque année.	I go every year.
J'ai le même manteau.	I have the same coat.
Il a quelques amis à Paris.	He has some friends in Paris.
Il reste quelques bouteilles.	There are a few bottles left.
Il travaille tout le temps.	He works all the time.

Tip

You can also use **tout** to talk about how often something happens.

tous les jours	every day
tous les deux jours	every other day

i Note that these words can also be used as pronouns, standing in place of a noun instead of being used with one. **chaque** and **quelques** have a slightly different form when they are used in this way.

➪ *For more information on **Pronouns**, see page 42.*

Key points

✔ The most common French indefinite adjectives are **autre**, **chaque**, **même**, **quelques** and **tout**.

✔ They come before the noun when they are used in this way.

Pronouns

What is a pronoun?
A **pronoun** is a word you use instead of a noun, when you do not need or want to name someone or something directly, for example, *it*, *you*, *none*.

➤ There are several different types of pronoun:

- Personal pronouns such as *I*, *you*, *he*, *her* and *they*, which are used to refer to yourself, the person you are talking to, or other people and things. They can be either subject pronouns (*I*, *you*, *he* and so on) or object pronouns (*him*, *her*, *them* and so on).
- Possessive pronouns like *mine* and *yours*, which show who someone or something belongs to.
- Indefinite pronouns like *someone* or *nothing*, which refer to people or things in a general way without saying exactly who or what they are.
- Relative pronouns like *who*, *which* or *that*, which link two parts of a sentence together.
- Demonstrative pronouns like *this* or *those*, which point things or people out.
- Reflexive pronouns, a type of object pronoun that forms part of French reflexive verbs like **se laver** (meaning *to wash*) or **s'appeler** (meaning *to be called*).

⇨ *For more information on* ***Reflexive verbs****, see page 88.*

- The two French pronouns, **en** and **y**, which are used in certain constructions.
- The pronouns **qui?** (meaning *who?*, *whom?*), **que?** (meaning *what?*), **quoi?** (meaning *what?*) and **lequel?** (meaning *which one?*), which are used in asking questions.

⇨ *For more information on* ***Questions****, see page 142.*

➤ Pronouns often stand in for a noun to save repeating it.

I finished my homework and gave it to my teacher.
Do you remember Jack? I saw him at the weekend.

➤ Word order with personal pronouns is usually different in French and English.

For further explanation of grammatical terms, please see pages viii-xii.

Personal pronouns: subject

What is a subject pronoun?
A **subject pronoun** is a word such as *I*, *he*, *she* and *they*, which performs the action expressed by the verb. Pronouns stand in for nouns when it is clear who is being talked about, for example, *My brother isn't here at the moment. He'll be back in an hour.*

1 Using subject pronouns

➤ Here are the French subject pronouns:

Singular	Meaning	Plural	Meaning
je (j')	I	**nous**	we
tu *or* **vous**	you	**vous**	you
il	he it	**ils**	they (*masculine*)
elle	she it	**elles**	they (*feminine*)
on	one (we/you/they)		

Je pars en vacances demain. — I'm going on holiday tomorrow.
Nous habitons à Nice. — We live in Nice.

Tip

je changes to **j'** in front of words beginning with a vowel, most words beginning with **h**, and the French word **y**.

J'arrive! — I'm just coming!
Bon, j'y vais. — Right, I'm off.

2 tu or vous?

➤ In English we have only one way of saying *you*. In French, there are two words: **tu** and **vous**. The word you use depends on:

- whether you are talking to one person or more than one person
- whether you are talking to a friend or family member, or someone else

➤ If you are talking to one person you know well, such as a friend, a young person or a relative, use **tu**.

Tu me prêtes ce CD? — Will you lend me this CD?

➤ If you are talking to one person you do not know so well, such as your teacher, your boss or a stranger, use **vous**.

Vous pouvez entrer.	You may come in.

> ***Tip***
>
> If you are in doubt as to which form of *you* to use, it is safest to use **vous** and you will not offend anybody.

➤ If you are talking to more than one person, you have to use **vous**, no matter how well you know them.

Vous comprenez, les enfants?	Do you understand, children?

ℹ Note that the adjectives you use with **tu** and **vous** have to agree in the feminine and plural forms.

Vous êtes certain, Monsieur Leclerc? (*masculine singular*)	Are you sure, Mr Leclerc?
Vous êtes certains, les enfants? (*masculine plural*)	Are you sure, children?

Grammar Extra!

Any past participles (the form of the verb ending in **-é**, **-i** or **-u** in French) used with **être** in tenses such as the perfect also have to agree in the feminine and plural forms.

Vous êtes partie quand, Estelle? (*feminine singular*)	When did you leave, Estelle?
Estelle et Sophie – vous êtes parties quand? (*feminine plural*)	Estelle and Sophie – when did you leave?

➪ *For more information on the **Past participle**, see page 111.*

3 il/elle and ils/elles

➤ In English we generally refer to things (such as *table*, *book*, *car*) only as *it*. In French, **il** (meaning *he*, *it*) and **elle** (meaning *she*, *it*) are used to talk about a thing, as well as about a person or an animal. You use **il** for masculine nouns and **elle** for feminine nouns.

Il est déjà parti.	He's already left.
Elle est actrice.	She's an actress.
Il mord, ton chien?	Does your dog bite?
Prends cette chaise. Elle est plus confortable.	Take this chair. It's more comfortable.

➤ **il** is also used to talk about the weather, the time and in certain other set phrases, often in the same way as some phrases with *it* in English.

Il pleut.	It's raining.
Il est deux heures.	It's two o'clock.
Il faut partir.	We/You have to go.

➤ **ils** (meaning *they*) and **elles** (meaning *they*) are used in the plural to talk about things, as well as about people or animals. Use **ils** for masculine nouns and **elles** for feminine nouns.

Ils vont appeler ce soir.	They're going to call tonight.
'Où sont Anne et Rachel?' – 'Elles sont à la piscine.'	'Where are Anne and Rachel?' – 'They're at the swimming pool.'
'Est-ce qu'il reste des billets?' – 'Non, ils sont tous vendus.'	'Are there are any tickets left?' – 'No, they're all sold.'
'Tu aimes ces chaussures?' – 'Non, elles sont affreuses!'	'Do you like those shoes?' – 'No, they're horrible!'

➤ If you are talking about a masculine and a feminine noun, use **ils**.

Que font ton père et ta mère quand ils partent en vacances?	What do your father and mother do when they go on holiday?
'Où sont le poivre et la moutarde?' – 'Ils sont déjà sur la table.'	'Where are the pepper and the mustard?' – 'They're already on the table.'

4 on

➤ **on** is frequently used in informal, everyday French to mean *we*.

On va à la plage demain.	We're going to the beach tomorrow.
On y va?	Shall we go?

➤ **on** can also have the sense of *someone* or *they*.

On m'a volé mon porte-monnaie.	Someone has stolen my purse.
On vous demande au téléphone.	There's a phone call for you.

Tip

on is often used to avoid a passive construction in French.

On m'a dit que tu étais malade.	I was told you were ill.

➪ *For more information on the* ***Passive****, see page* 122.

➤ You can also use **on** as we use *you* in English when we mean people in general.

On peut visiter le château en été.	You can visit the castle in the summer.
D'ici on peut voir les côtes françaises.	From here you can see the French coast.

Tip

The form of the verb you use with **on** is the same as the **il/elle** form.

➪ *For more information on **Verbs**, see pages 69–137.*

Key points

- ✔ The French subject pronouns are: **je (j')**, **tu**, **il**, **elle**, **on** in the singular, and **nous**, **vous**, **ils**, **elles** in the plural.
- ✔ To say *you* in French, use **tu** if you are talking to one person you know well or to a young person. Use **vous** if you are talking to one person you do not know so well or to more than one person.
- ✔ **il/ils** (masculine singular/plural) and **elle/elles** (feminine singular/plural) are used to refer to things, as well as to people or animals. **il** is also used in certain set phrases.
- ✔ If there is a mixture of masculine and feminine nouns, use **ils**.
- ✔ **on** can mean *we*, *someone*, *you*, *they*, or people in general. It is often used instead of a passive construction.

Personal pronouns: direct object

What is a direct object pronoun?
A **direct object pronoun** is a word such as *me*, *him*, *us* and *them*, which is used instead of the noun to stand in for the person or thing most directly affected by the action expressed by the verb.

1 Using direct object pronouns

➤ Direct object pronouns stand in for nouns when it is clear who or what is being talked about, and save having to repeat the noun.

I've lost my glasses. Have you seen them?
'Have you met Jo?' – 'Yes, I really like her!'

➤ Here are the French direct object pronouns:

Singular	Meaning	Plural	Meaning
me (m')	me	**nous**	us
te (t')	you	**vous**	you
le (l')	him it	**les**	them (*masculine and feminine*)
la (l')	her it		

Ils vont nous aider. They're going to help us.
Je la vois. I can see her/it.
'Tu aimes les carottes?' – 'Non, je les déteste!' 'Do you like carrots?' – 'No, I hate them!'

Note that you cannot use direct object pronouns after a preposition like **à** or **de**, or when you want to emphasize something.

*For more information on **Emphatic pronouns**, see page 51.*

Tip

me changes to **m'**, **te** to **t'**, and **le/la** to **l'** in front of words beginning with a vowel, most words beginning with **h**, and the French word **y**.

Je t'aime. I love you.
Tu m'entends? Can you hear me?

➤ In orders and instructions telling someone to do something, **moi** is used instead of **me**, and **toi** is used instead of **te**.

Aidez-moi!	Help me!
Assieds-toi.	Sit down.

➤ **le** is sometimes used to refer back to an idea or information that has already been given. The word *it* is often missed out in English.

'Ta chemise est très sale.' – 'Je le sais.'	'Your shirt's very dirty.' – 'I know.'

2 Word order with direct object pronouns

➤ The direct object pronoun usually comes BEFORE the verb.

Je t'aime.	I love you.
Les voyez-vous?	Can you see them?
Elle ne nous connaît pas.	She doesn't know us.

i Note that in orders and instructions telling someone to do something, the direct object pronoun comes AFTER the verb.

Asseyez-vous.	Sit down.

➤ In tenses like the perfect that are formed with **avoir** or **être** and the past participle (the part of the verb that ends in **-é**, **-i** or **-u** in French), the direct object pronoun comes BEFORE the part of the verb that comes from **avoir** or **être**.

Il m'a vu.	He saw me.

➤ When a verb like **vouloir** (meaning *to want*) or **pouvoir** (meaning *to be able to, can*) is followed by another verb in the infinitive (the '*to*' form of the verb), the direct object pronoun comes BEFORE the infinitive.

Il voudrait la revoir.	He'd like to see her again.
Puis-je vous aider?	Can I help you?

Key points

✔ The French direct object pronouns are: **me (m')**, **te (t')**, **le/la (l')** in the singular, and **nous**, **vous**, **les** in the plural.

✔ Except in orders and instructions telling someone to do something, the direct object pronoun comes before the verb.

Personal pronouns: indirect object

What is an indirect object pronoun?
When a verb has two objects (a direct one and an indirect one), the **indirect object pronoun** is used instead of a noun to show the person or thing the action is intended to benefit or harm, for example, *me* in *He gave me a book; Can you get me a towel?*

1 Using indirect object pronouns

➤ It is important to understand the difference between direct and indirect object pronouns in English, as they can have different forms in French:

- an indirect object answers the question *who to/for?* or *to/for what?*
  He gave me a book. → *Who did he give the book to?* → me (=*indirect object pronoun*)
  Can you get me a towel? → *Who can you get a towel for?* → me (=*indirect object pronoun*)
- if something answers the question *what* or *who*, then it is the direct object and NOT the indirect object
  He gave me a book. → *What did he give me?* → a book (=*direct object*)
  Can you get me a towel? → *What can you get me?* → a towel (=*direct object*)

➤ Here are the French indirect object pronouns:

Singular	Meaning	Plural	Meaning
me (m')	me, to me, for me	**nous**	us, to us, for us
te (t')	you, to you, for you	**vous**	you, to you, for you
lui	him, to him, for him her, to her, for her it, to it, for it	**leur**	them, to them, for them (*masculine and feminine*)

Il nous écrit tous les jours. He writes to us every day.
Ils te cachent quelque chose. They're hiding something from you.

> *Tip*
>
> **me** changes to **m'** and **te** to **t'** in front of words beginning with a vowel, most words beginning with **h**, and the French word **y**.
>
> **Il m'a donné un livre.** He gave me a book.
> **Tu m'apportes une serviette?** Can you get me a towel?

➤ The pronouns shown in the table are used instead of the preposition **à** with a noun.

J'écris à Suzanne. I'm writing to Suzanne. → **Je lui écris.** I'm writing to her.
Donne du lait au chat. Give the cat some milk. → **Donne-lui du lait.** Give it some milk.

➤ Some French verbs like **demander à** (meaning *to ask*) and **téléphoner à** (meaning *to phone*) take an indirect object even though English uses a direct object.

Il leur téléphone tous les soirs. He phones them every evening.

➤ On the other hand, some French verbs like **attendre** (meaning *to wait for*), **chercher** (meaning *to look for*) and **regarder** (meaning *to look at*) take a direct object even though English uses an indirect object.

Je les attends devant la gare. I'll wait for them outside the station.

2 Word order with indirect object pronouns

➤ The indirect object pronoun usually comes BEFORE the verb.

Dominique vous écrit une lettre. Dominique's writing you a letter.
Il ne nous parle pas. He doesn't speak to us.
Il ne veut pas me répondre. He won't answer me.

i Note that in orders and instructions telling someone to do something, the indirect object pronoun comes AFTER the verb.

Donne-moi ça! Give me that!

Key points

✔ The French indirect object pronouns are: **me (m')**, **te (t')**, **lui** in the singular, and **nous**, **vous**, **leur** in the plural.

✔ Except in orders and instructions telling someone to do something, the direct object pronoun comes before the verb.

For further explanation of grammatical terms, please see pages viii-xii.

Emphatic pronouns

What is an emphatic pronoun?
An **emphatic pronoun** is used instead of a noun when you want to emphasize something, for example *Is this for me?*

1 Using emphatic pronouns

➤ In French, there is another set of pronouns which you use after prepositions, when you want to emphasize something and in certain other cases. These are called emphatic pronouns or stressed pronouns.

Singular	Meaning	Plural	Meaning
moi	I me	**nous**	we us
toi	you	**vous**	you
lui	he him	**eux**	they (*masculine*) them
elle	she her	**elles**	they (*feminine*) them
soi	oneself (yourself, ourselves)		

Je pense souvent à toi. I often think about you.
C'est pour moi? Is this for me?
Venez avec moi. Come with me.
Il a besoin de nous. He needs us.

➤ **soi** (meaning *oneself*) is used with the subject pronoun **on** and with words like **tout le monde** (meaning *everyone*) or **chacun** (meaning *each one*).

Il faut avoir confiance en soi. You have to have confidence in yourself.
Tout le monde est rentré chez soi. Everyone went home.

2 When to use emphatic pronouns

➤ Emphatic pronouns are used in the following circumstances:

- after a preposition

C'est pour moi? Is this for me?

- for emphasis, especially where a contrast is involved

Toi, tu ressembles à ton père, mais elle non.	You look like your father, she doesn't.
Il m'énerve, lui!	He's getting on my nerves!

- on their own without a verb

'Qui a cassé la fenêtre?' – 'Lui.'	'Who broke the window?' – 'He did.'
'Je suis fatiguée.' – 'Moi aussi.'	'I'm tired.' – 'Me too.'

- after **c'est** and **ce sont** (meaning *it is*)

C'est toi, Simon?	Is that you, Simon?
Ce sont eux.	It's them.

➪ *For more information on* **c'est** *and* **ce sont***, see page 65.*

- in comparisons

Tu es plus jeune que moi.	You're younger than me.
Il est moins grand que toi.	He's smaller than you (are).

- when the subject of the sentence is made up of two pronouns, or of a pronoun and a noun

Mon père et elle ne s'entendent pas.	My father and she don't get on.

Grammar Extra!

You can add **-même** or **-mêmes** to the emphatic pronouns when you particularly want to emphasize something. These forms correspond to English *myself*, *ourselves* and so on.

Form with -même	Meaning
moi-même	myself
toi-même	yourself
lui-même	himself, itself
elle-même	herself, itself
soi-même	oneself (yourself, ourselves)
nous-mêmes	ourselves
vous-même **vous-mêmes**	yourself yourselves
eux-mêmes	themselves (*masculine*)
elles-mêmes	themselves (*feminine*)

Je l'ai fait moi-même.	I did it myself.
Elle l'a choisi elle-même.	She chose it herself.

Key points

✔ The French emphatic pronouns are: **moi**, **toi**, **lui**, **elle**, **soi** in the singular, and **nous**, **vous**, **eux**, **elles** in the plural.

✔ They are used:

- after a preposition
- for emphasis
- on their own without a verb
- after **c'est** and **ce sont**
- in comparisons
- when the subject of the sentence is made up of two pronouns, or of a pronoun and a noun

✔ You can add **-même** or **-mêmes** to the emphatic pronouns when you particularly want to emphasize something.

Possessive pronouns

What is a possessive pronoun?
A **possessive pronoun** is one of the words *mine, yours, hers, his, ours* or *theirs*, which are used instead of a noun to show that one person or thing belongs to another, for example, *Ask Carole if this pen is hers*.

➤ Here are the French possessive pronouns:

Masculine singular	Feminine singular	Masculine plural	Feminine plural	Meaning
le mien	**la mienne**	**les miens**	**les miennes**	mine
le tien	**la tienne**	**les tiens**	**les tiennes**	yours
le sien	**la sienne**	**les siens**	**les siennes**	his hers
le nôtre	**la nôtre**	**les nôtres**	**les nôtres**	ours
le vôtre	**la vôtre**	**les vôtres**	**les vôtres**	yours
le leur	**la leur**	**les leurs**	**les leurs**	theirs

Ces CD-là, ce sont les miens. — Those CDs are mine.
Heureusement que tu as tes clés. J'ai oublié les miennes. — It's lucky you've got your keys. I forgot mine.

Tip

In French, possessive pronouns agree with what they describe, NOT with the person who owns that thing. For example, **le sien** can mean *his* or *hers*, but can only be used to replace a masculine singular noun.

'C'est le vélo de Paul?' – 'Oui, c'est le sien.' — 'Is that Paul's bike?' – 'Yes, it's his.'
'C'est le vélo d'Isabelle?' – 'Oui, c'est le sien.' — 'Is that Isabelle's bike?' – 'Yes, it's hers.'

Grammar Extra!

Remember that **à** with the definite article **le** becomes **au**, and **à** with **les** becomes **aux**, so:

à + le mien → au mien
à + les miens → aux miens
à + les miennes → aux miennes

Tu préfères ce manteau <u>au mien</u>?	Do you prefer this coat to mine?

Remember that **de** with the definite article **le** becomes **du**, and **de** with **les** becomes **des**, so:

de + le mien → du mien
de + les miens → des miens
de + les miennes → des miennes

J'ai oublié mes clés. J'ai besoin <u>des tiennes</u>.	I've forgotten my keys. I need yours.

➪ *For more information on **Articles**, see page 12.*

Key points

- ✔ The French possessive pronouns are **le mien**, **le tien**, **le sien** for singular subject pronouns, and **le nôtre**, **le vôtre** and **le leur** for plural subject pronouns. Their forms change in the feminine and the plural.
- ✔ In French, the pronoun you choose has to agree with the noun it replaces, and <u>not</u> with the person who owns that thing.

en and y

➤ **en** and **y** do not usually refer to people. How we translate them into English depends on where **en** and **y** are found in French.

1 en

➤ **en** is used with verbs and phrases normally followed by **de** to avoid repeating the same word.

Si tu as un problème, tu peux m'en parler.	If you've got a problem, you can talk to me about it. (*en replaces de in parler de quelque chose*)
Est-ce que tu peux me prêter ce livre? J'en ai besoin.	Can you lend me that book? I need it. (*en replaces de in avoir besoin de quelque chose*)
Il a un beau jardin et il en est très fier.	He's got a beautiful garden and is very proud of it. (*en replaces de in être fier de quelque chose*)

➤ **en** can also replace the partitive article (**du**, **de la**, **de l'**, **des**).

Je n'ai pas d'argent. Tu en as?	I haven't got any money. Have you got any?
'Tu peux me prêter des timbres?' – 'Non, je dois en acheter.'	'Can you lend me some stamps?' – 'No, I have to buy some.'

➪ *For more information on the **Partitive article**, see page 22.*

➤ **en** is also used:
- as a preposition
- with the present participle of verbs

➪ *For more information on **Prepositions** and the **Present participle**, see pages 162 and 125.*

➤ When **en** is used with **avoir**, with **il y a** or with numbers, it is often not translated in English but can NEVER be missed out in French.

'Est-ce que tu as un dictionnaire?' – 'Oui, j'en ai un.'	'Have you got a dictionary?' – 'Yes, I've got one.'
'Combien d'élèves y a-t-il dans ta classe?' – 'Il y en a trente.'	'How many pupils are there in your class?' – 'There are thirty.'
J'en veux deux.	I want two (of them).

2 y

➤ **y** is used with verbs and phrases normally followed by **à** to avoid repeating the same word.

'Je pensais à l'examen.' – 'Mais arrête d'y penser!'	'I was thinking about the exam.' – 'Well, stop thinking about it!' (*y replaces à in penser à quelque chose*)
'Je ne m'attendais pas à ça.' – 'Moi, je m'y attendais.'	'I wasn't expecting that.' – 'Well, I was expecting it.' (*y replaces à in s'attendre à quelque chose*)

➤ **y** can also mean *there*. It can be used to replace phrases that would use prepositions such as **dans** (meaning *in*) and **sur** (meaning *on*).

Elle y passe tout l'été.	She spends the whole summer there.
Regarde dans le tiroir. Je pense que les clés y sont.	Look in the drawer. I think the keys are in there.

3 Word order with en and y

➤ **en** and **y** usually come BEFORE the verb.

J'en veux.	I want some.
Elle en a parlé avec lui.	She talked to him about it.
En êtes-vous content?	Are you pleased with it/them?
Comment fait-on pour y aller?	How do you get there?
N'y pense plus.	Don't think about it any more.

➤ In orders and instructions telling someone to do something, **en** or **y** come AFTER the verb and are attached to it with a hyphen (-).

Prenez-en.	Take some.
Restez-y.	Stay there.

Tip

The final **-s** of **-er** verbs is usually dropped in the **tu** form used for orders and instructions. When an **-er** verb in the **tu** form is used before **en** or **y**, however, the **-s** is not dropped, to make it easier to say.

Donne des bonbons à ton frère.	Give some sweets to your brother.
Donnes-en à ton frère.	Give some to your brother.
Va dans ta chambre!	Go to your room!
Vas-y!	Go on!

➪ *For more information on the **Imperative**, see page 85.*

➤ **en** and **y** come AFTER other direct or indirect object pronouns.

Donnez-leur-en.	Give them some.
Il m'en a parlé.	He spoke to me about it.

➪ *For more information on* **Direct object pronouns** *and* **Indirect object pronouns**, *see pages 47 and 49.*

Key points

✔ **en** is used with verbs and expressions normally followed by **de** to avoid repeating the same word.

✔ **en** can also replace the partitive article.

✔ When **en** is used with **avoir** and **il y a** or with numbers, it is often not translated in English but can never be missed out in French.

✔ **y** is used with verbs and expressions normally followed by **à** to avoid repeating the same word.

✔ **y** can also mean *there* and may replace expressions that would be used with **dans** and **sur** or some other preposition indicating a place.

✔ **en** and **y** usually come before the verb, except in orders and instructions telling someone to do something, when **en** or **y** follows the verb and is attached to it with a hyphen.

✔ **en** and **y** come after other direct or indirect object pronouns.

Using different types of pronoun together

➤ Sometimes you find a direct object pronoun and an indirect object pronoun in the same sentence.

He gave me *(indirect object)* them *(direct object)*.

He gave them *(direct object)* to me *(indirect object)*.

➤ When this happens in French, you have to put the indirect and direct object pronouns in a certain order.

Indirect	Direct	Indirect	
me	le	lui	en
te	la	leur	y
nous	les		
vous			

Dominique vous l'envoie demain. Dominique's sending it to you tomorrow.

Il te les a montrés? Has he shown them to you?

Je les lui ai lus. I read them to him/her.

Ne la leur donne pas. Don't give it to them.

Elle ne m'en a pas parlé. She didn't speak to me about it.

Key points

✔ If a direct and an indirect object pronoun are used in the same sentence, you usually put the indirect object pronoun before the direct object pronoun.

✔ With **lui** and **leur**, this order is reversed and you put the direct object pronoun before the indirect object pronoun.

Indefinite pronouns

What is an indefinite pronoun?
An **indefinite pronoun** is one of a small group of pronouns such as *everything*, *nobody* and *something* which are used to refer to people or things in a general way without saying exactly who or what they are.

➤ Here are the most common French indefinite pronouns:

- **chacun** (*masculine singular*)/**chacune** (*feminine singular*) each, everyone

Nous avons chacun donné dix euros.	We each gave ten euros.
Chacun fait ce qu'il veut.	Everyone does what they like.
Toutes les villas ont chacune leur piscine.	Each villa has its own swimming pool.

- **personne** nobody/no one, anybody/anyone

Il n'y a personne à la maison.	There's no one at home.
Elle ne veut voir personne.	She doesn't want to see anybody.

⇨ *For more information on* ***Negatives****, see page 138.*

Tip

You can use **personne** on its own to answer a question.

Qui connaît la réponse? Personne.	Who knows the answer? No one.

If the sentence contains a verb you have to use **ne** with it.

Personne n'est venu.	Nobody came.

- **quelque chose** something, anything

J'ai quelque chose pour toi.	I've got something for you.
Avez-vous quelque chose à déclarer?	Do you have anything to declare?

- **quelqu'un** somebody/someone, anybody/anyone

Il y a quelqu'un à la porte.	There's someone at the door.
Quelqu'un a vu mon parapluie?	Has anybody seen my umbrella?

- **rien** nothing, anything

Elle n'a rien dit.	She didn't say anything.
Rien n'a changé.	Nothing's changed.

⇨ *For more information on* ***Negatives****, see page 138.*

Tip

You can use **rien** on its own to answer a question.

'Qu'est-ce tu as acheté?' – 'Rien.'	'What did you buy?' – 'Nothing.'

If the sentence contains a verb you have to use **ne** with it.

Il n'a rien mangé.	He's eaten nothing.

- **tout** everything

Il organise tout.	He's organizing everything.
Tout va bien?	Is everything OK?

- **tous** (*masculine plural*)/**toutes** (*feminine plural*) all

Je les connais tous.	I know them all.
Elles sont toutes arrivées?	Are they all here?

➤ You can use **quelque chose de/rien de** and **quelqu'un de/personne de** with adjectives if you want to say *nothing interesting*, *something new* and so on.

rien d'intéressant	nothing interesting

Key points

✔ **rien** and **personne** can be used on their own to answer questions, but need to be used with **ne** when there is a verb in the sentence.

✔ **quelque chose/rien** and **quelqu'un/personne** can be followed by **de** + adjective.

Relative pronouns: qui, que, lequel, auquel, duquel

What is a relative pronoun?
In English a **relative pronoun** is one of the words *who*, *which* and *that* (and the more formal *whom*) which can be used to introduce information that makes it clear which person or thing is being talked about, for example, *The man who has just come in is Ann's boyfriend; The vase that you broke was quite valuable.*
Relative pronouns can also introduce further information about someone or something, for example, *Peter, who is a brilliant painter, wants to study art; Jane's house, which was built in 1890, needs a lot of repairs.*

➤ In French, the relative pronouns are **qui**, **que**, **lequel**, **auquel**, and **duquel**.

1 qui and que

➤ **qui** and **que** can both refer to people or things.

	Relative pronoun	Meaning
Subject	**qui**	who which that
Direct object	**que**	who, whom which that

Mon frère, qui a vingt ans, est à l'université.	My brother, who's twenty, is at university.
Est-ce qu'il y a un bus qui va au centre-ville?	Is there a bus that goes to the town centre?
Les amis que je vois le plus sont Léa et Mehdi.	The friends (that) I see most are Léa and Mehdi.
Voilà la maison que nous voulons acheter.	That's the house (which) we want to buy.

Tip
que changes to **qu'** in front of a word beginning with a vowel and most words beginning with **h**.

For further explanation of grammatical terms, please see pages viii-xii.

➤ **qui** is also used after a preposition such as **à**, **de** or **pour** to talk about people.

la personne à qui il parle	the person he is speaking to
les enfants pour qui j'ai acheté des bonbons	the children I bought sweets for

Tip

In English we often miss out the object pronouns *who*, *which* and *that*. For example, we can say both *the friends that I see most*, or *the friends I see most*, and *the house which we want to buy*, or *the house we want to buy*. In French you can NEVER miss out **que** or **qui** in this way.

2 lequel, laquelle, lesquels, lesquelles

➤ **lequel** (meaning *which*) is used after a preposition such as **à**, **de** or **pour** to talk about things. It has to agree with the noun it replaces.

	Masculine	Feminine	Meaning
Singular	**lequel**	**laquelle**	which
Plural	**lesquels**	**lesquelles**	which

le livre pour lequel elle est connue	the book she is famous for
la table sur laquelle j'ai mis mon sac	the table I put my bag on

➤ Remember that **à** and **de** combine with the definite article **le** to become **au** and **du**, and with **les** to become **aux** and **des**. **lequel/lesquels/lesquelles** combine with **à** and **de** as shown in the table. **laquelle** doesn't change.

	+ lequel	+ laquelle	+ lesquels	+ lesquelles	Meaning
à	**auquel**	**à laquelle**	**auxquels**	**auxquelles**	to which
de	**duquel**	**de laquelle**	**desquels**	**desquelles**	of which

➪ *For more information on **à** and **de**, see pages 14 and 15.*

Grammar Extra!

dont means *whose*, *of whom*, *of which*, *about which* and so on. It can refer to people or things, but its form NEVER changes.

la femme dont la voiture est en panne	the woman whose car has broken down
les films dont tu parles	the films you're talking about

Key points

- ✔ **qui** and **que** can both refer to people or things: **qui** is the subject of the part of the sentence it is found in; **que** is the object.
- ✔ In English we often miss out the object pronouns *who*, *which* and *that*, but in French you can never miss out **que** or **qui**.
- ✔ After a preposition you use **qui** if you are referring to people, and **lequel** if you are referring to things – **lequel** agrees with the noun it replaces.
- ✔ **à + lequel → auquel**
  à + lesquels → auxquels
  à + lesquelles → auxquelles
- ✔ **de + lequel → duquel**
  de + lesquels → desquels
  de + lesquelles → desquelles

Demonstrative pronouns: ce, cela/ça, ceci, celui

What is a demonstrative pronoun?
In English a **demonstrative pronoun** is one of the words *this*, *that*, *these*, and *those* used instead of a noun to point people or things out, for example, *That looks fun*.

1 ce

➤ **ce** is usually used with the verb **être** (meaning *to be*) in the expressions **c'est** (meaning *it's*, *that's*), **c'était** (meaning *it was*, *that was*), **ce sont** (meaning *it's*, *that's*) and so on.

C'est moi.	It's me.
C'était mon frère.	That was my brother.
Ce sont eux.	It's them.

Tip

ce becomes **c'** when it is followed by a part of the verb that starts with **e** or **é**.

ce becomes **ç'** when it is followed by a part of the verb that starts with **a**.

Ç'a été difficile.	It was difficult.

Note that after **c'est** and **ce sont** and so on you have to use the emphatic form of the pronoun, for example, **moi** instead of **je**, **eux** instead of **ils** and so on.

C'est moi.	It's me.

➪ *For more information on* **Emphatic pronouns**, *see page* 51.

➤ **ce** is used:

- with a noun or a question word to identify a person or thing

Qui est-ce?	Who is it?, Who's this/that?
Ce sont des professeurs.	They're teachers.
Qu'est-ce que c'est?	What's this/that?
C'est un ouvre-boîte.	It's a tin-opener.

- with an adjective to refer to a statement, idea and so on that cannot be classed as either masculine or feminine

C'est très intéressant.	That's/It's very interesting.
C'est dangereux.	That's/It's dangerous.
Ce n'est pas grave.	It doesn't matter.

- for emphasis

C'est moi qui ai téléphoné.	It was me who phoned.
Ce sont les enfants qui ont fait le gâteau.	It was the children who made the cake.

2 cela, ça and ceci

➤ **cela** and **ça** mean *it*, *this* or *that*. Both refer to a statement, an idea or an object. **ça** is used instead of **cela** in everyday, informal French.

Ça ne fait rien.	It doesn't matter.
Écoute-moi ça!	Listen to this!
Cela dépend.	That/It depends.
Je n'aime pas cela.	I don't like that.
Donne-moi ça!	Give me that!

Tip

ça and **cela** are used in a more general way than **il** and **elle**, which are usually linked to a noun that has already been mentioned.

Alors, ma nouvelle voiture, elle te plaît?	So, do you like my new car?
Ça te plaît d'aller à l'étranger?	Do you like going abroad?

➤ **ceci** means *this* and is not as common as **cela** and **ça**. It is used to talk about something that has not yet been mentioned.

Lisez ceci.	Read this.

➤ **ceci** is also used to hand or show someone something.

Prends ceci. Tu en auras besoin.	Take this. You'll need it.

3 celui, celle, ceux, celles

➤ **celui** and **celle** mean *the one*; **ceux** and **celles** mean *the ones*. The form you choose depends on whether the noun it is replacing is masculine or feminine, and singular or plural.

	Masculine	Feminine	Meaning
Singular	celui	celle	the one
Plural	ceux	celles	the ones

➤ **celui** and its other forms are used before:

- **qui**, **que** or **dont**

'Quelle robe préférez-vous?' – '<u>Celle qui</u> est en vitrine.'	'Which dress do you like best?' – 'The one in the window.'
Prends <u>ceux que</u> tu préfères.	Take the ones you like best.
<u>celui dont</u> je t'ai parlé	the one I told you about
<u>celui qui</u> est proche de la fontaine	the one near the fountain

➤ **celui** and its other forms can be used with **de** to show who something belongs to. In English, we would use 's.

Je n'ai pas d'appareil photo mais je peux emprunter <u>celui de</u> ma sœur.	I haven't got a camera but I can borrow my sister'<u>s</u>.
Comparez vos réponses à <u>celles de</u> votre voisin.	Compare your answers with your neighbour'<u>s</u>.

➤ You can add the endings **-ci** and **-là** to **celui** and its other forms to emphasize the difference between something that is close to you and something that is further away.

- use **-ci** for something that is closer to you
- use **-là** for something that is further away

	Masculine	Feminine	Meaning
Singular	celui-ci celui-là	celle-ci celle-là	this, this one that, that one
Plural	ceux-ci ceux-là	celles-ci celles-là	these, these ones those, those ones

On prend quel fromage? <u>Celui-ci</u> ou <u>celui-là</u>?	Which cheese shall we get? This one or that one?
Ces chemises ont deux poches mais <u>celles-là</u> n'en ont pas.	These shirts have two pockets but those have none.

Key points

✔ **ce** is often found in the expressions **c'est**, **ce sont** and so on.

✔ **ce** is also used:
- to identify a person or thing
- to refer to a statement, idea and so on that cannot be classed as either masculine or feminine
- for emphasis

✔ **cela** and **ça** mean *it*, *this* or *that*; **ceci** means *this*, but is not as common.

✔ **celui** and **celle** mean *the one*; **ceux** and **celles** mean *the ones*. They are often found with the endings **-ci** and **-là** and are used to distinguish between things which are close and things which are further away.

Verbs

What is a verb?
A **verb** is a 'doing' word which describes what someone or something does, what someone or something is, or what happens to them, for example, *be*, *sing*, *live*.

The three conjugations

➤ Verbs are usually used with a noun, with a pronoun such as *I*, *you* or *she*, or with somebody's name. They can relate to the present, the past and the future; this is called their tense.

➪ *For more information on **Nouns** and **Pronouns**, see pages 1 and 42.*

➤ Verbs are either:

- regular; their forms follow the normal rules
- irregular; their forms do not follow the normal rules

➤ Regular English verbs have a base form (the form of the verb without any endings added to it, for example, *walk*). The base form can have *to* in front of it, for example, *to walk*. This is called the infinitive. You will find one of these forms when you look a verb up in your dictionary.

➤ French verbs also have an infinitive, which ends in **-er**, **-ir** or **-re**, for example, **donner** (meaning *to give*), **finir** (meaning *to finish*), **attendre** (meaning *to wait*). Regular French verbs belong to one of these three verb groups, which are called conjugations. We will look at each of these three conjugations in turn on the next few pages.

➤ English verbs have other forms apart from the base form and infinitive: a form ending in *-s* (*walks*), a form ending in *-ing* (*walking*), and a form ending in *-ed* (*walked*).

➤ French verbs have many more forms than this, which are made up of endings added to a stem. The stem of a verb can usually be worked out from the infinitive.

➤ French verb endings change, depending on who you are talking about: **je** (*I*), **tu** (*you*), **il/elle/on** (*he/she/one*) in the singular, or **nous** (*we*), **vous** (*you*) and **ils/elles** (*they*) in the plural. French verbs also have different forms depending on whether you are referring to the present, future or past.

➤ Some verbs in French do not follow the normal rules, and are called irregular verbs. These include some very common and important verbs like **avoir** (meaning *to have*), **être** (meaning *to be*), **faire** (meaning *to do, to make*) and **aller** (meaning *to go*). There is information on many of these irregular verbs in the following sections.

➪ *For* ***Verb tables****, see supplement.*

Key points

✔ French verbs have different forms depending on what noun or pronoun they are used with, and on their tense.

✔ They are made up of a stem and an ending. The stem is usually based on the infinitive.

✔ Regular verbs fit into one of three patterns or conjugations: **-er**, **-ir**, or **-re** verbs.

✔ Irregular verbs do not follow the normal rules.

The present tense

What is the present tense?
The **present tense** is used to talk about what is true at the moment, what happens regularly and what is happening now, for example, *I'm a student*, *I travel to college by train*, *I'm studying languages*.

➤ You use a verb in the present tense to talk about:

- things that are happening now
  It's raining.
  The phone's ringing.
- things that happen all the time or at certain intervals, or things that you do as a habit
  It always snows in January.
  I play football on Saturdays.
- things that are true at the present time:
  She's not very well.
  It's a beautiful house.

➤ There is more than one way to express the present tense in English. For example, you can say either *I give*, *I am giving*, or occasionally *I do give*. In French you use the same form (**je donne**) for all of these.

➤ In English you can also use the present tense to talk about something that is going to happen in the near future. You can do the same in French.

Je vais en France le mois prochain.	I'm going to France next month.
Nous prenons le train de dix heures.	We're getting the ten o'clock train.

Tip

Although English sometimes uses parts of the verb *to be* to form the present tense of other verbs (for example, *I am listening*, *she's talking*), French NEVER uses the verb **être** in this way.

The present tense: regular -er (first conjugation) verbs

- If an infinitive in French ends in **-er**, it means the verb belongs to the first conjugation, for example, **donner**, **aimer**, **parler**.
- To know which form of the verb to use in French, you need to work out what the stem of the verb is and then add the correct ending. The stem of **-er** verbs in the present tense is formed by taking the infinitive and chopping off **-er**.

Infinitive	**Stem** (without **-er**)
donner (*to give*)	**donn-**
aimer (*to like, to love*)	**aim-**
parler (*to speak, to talk*)	**parl-**

- Now you know how to find the stem of a verb, you can add the correct ending. Which one you choose will depend on whether you are referring to **je**, **tu**, **il**, **elle**, **on**, **nous**, **vous**, **ils** or **elles**.

⇨ *For more information on* **Pronouns**, *see page 42.*

- Here are the present tense endings for **-er** verbs:

Pronoun	**Ending**	**Add to stem, e.g. donn-**	**Meanings**
je (j')	**-e**	**je donne**	I give I am giving
tu	**-es**	**tu donnes**	you give you are giving
il **elle** **on**	**-e**	**il donne** **elle donne** **on donne**	he/she/it/one gives he/she/it/one is giving
nous	**-ons**	**nous donnons**	we give we are giving
vous	**-ez**	**vous donnez**	you give you are giving
ils **elles**	**-ent**	**ils donnent** **elles donnent**	they give they are giving

Marie regarde la télé. — Marie is watching TV.
Le train arrive à deux heures. — The train arrives at 2 o'clock.

Tip

je changes to **j'** in front of a word starting with a vowel (*a*, *e*, *i*, *o* or *u*), most words starting with **h**, and the French word **y**.

Note that there are a few regular **-er** verbs that are spelled slightly differently from the way you might expect.

➪ *For more information on **Spelling changes in -er verbs**, see page 78.*

Key points

- ✔ Verbs ending in **-er** belong to the first conjugation and form their present tense stem by losing the **-er** from the infinitive.
- ✔ The present tense endings for -**er** verbs are: **-e**, **-es**, **-e**, **-ons**, **-ez**, **-ent**.

The present tense: regular -ir (second conjugation) verbs

➤ If an infinitive ends in **-ir**, it means the verb belongs to the second conjugation, for example, **finir**, **choisir**, **remplir**.

➤ The stem of **-ir** verbs in the present tense is formed by taking the infinitive and chopping off **-ir**.

Infinitive	**Stem** (without **-ir**)
finir (*to finish*)	**fin-**
choisir (*to choose*)	**chois-**
remplir (*to fill, to fill in*)	**rempl-**

➤ Now add the correct ending, depending on whether you are referring to **je**, **tu**, **il**, **elle**, **on**, **nous**, **vous**, **ils** or **elles**.

➪ *For more information on **Pronouns**, see page 42.*

➤ Here are the present tense endings for **-ir** verbs:

Pronoun	**Ending**	**Add to stem, e.g. fin-**	**Meanings**
je (j')	**-is**	**je finis**	I finish I am finishing
tu	**-is**	**tu finis**	you finish you are finishing
il **elle** **on**	**-it**	**il finit** **elle finit** **on finit**	he/she/it/one finishes he/she/it/one is finishing
nous	**-issons**	**nous finissons**	we finish we are finishing
vous	**-issez**	**vous finissez**	you finish you are finishing
ils **elles**	**-issent**	**ils finissent** **elles finissent**	they finish they are finishing

Le cours finit à onze heures. The lesson finishes at eleven o'clock.
Je finis mes devoirs. I'm finishing my homework.

> *Tip*
> **je** changes to **j'** in front of a word starting with a vowel, most words starting with **h**, and the French word **y**.

➤ The **nous** and **vous** forms of **-ir** verbs have an extra syllable.

tu fi|nis (*two syllables*)
vous fi|ni|ssez (*three syllables*)

Key points

✔ Verbs ending in **-ir** belong to the second conjugation and form their present tense stem by losing the **-ir** from the infinitive.

✔ The present tense endings for **-ir** verbs are:
-is, -is, -it, -issons, -issez, -issent.

✔ Remember the extra syllable in the **nous** and **vous** forms.

The present tense: regular -re (third conjugation) verbs

➤ If an infinitive ends in **-re**, it means the verb belongs to the third conjugation, for example, **attendre**, **vendre**, **entendre**.

➤ The stem of **-re** verbs in the present tense is formed by taking the infinitive and chopping off **-re**.

Infinitive	Stem (without -re)
attendre (*to wait*)	**attend-**
vendre (*to sell*)	**vend-**
entendre (*to hear*)	**entend-**

➤ Now add the correct ending, depending on whether you are referring to **je**, **tu**, **il**, **elle**, **on**, **nous**, **vous**, **ils** or **elles**.

➪ *For more information on* ***Pronouns****, see page 42.*

➤ Here are the present tense endings for **-re** verbs:

Pronoun	Ending	Add to stem, e.g. attend-	Meanings
je (j')	**-s**	**j'attends**	I wait I am waiting
tu	**-s**	**tu attends**	you wait you are waiting
il **elle** **on**	**-**	**il attend** **elle attend** **on attend**	he/she/it/one waits he/she/it/one is waiting
nous	**-ons**	**nous attendons**	we wait we are waiting
vous	**-ez**	**vous attendez**	you wait you are waiting
ils **elles**	**-ent**	**ils attendent** **elles attendent**	they wait they are waiting

J'attends ma sœur. — I'm waiting for my sister.

Chaque matin nous attendons le train ensemble. — Every morning we wait for the train together.

Tip

je changes to **j'** in front of a word starting with a vowel, most words starting with **h**, and the French word **y**.

Key points

✔ Verbs ending in **-re** belong to the third conjugation and form their present tense stem by losing the **-re** from the infinitive.

✔ The present tense endings for **-re** verbs are:
-s, -s, -, -ons, -ez, -ent.

The present tense: spelling changes in -er verbs

➤ Learning the patterns shown on pages 72–73 means you can now work out the forms of most **-er** verbs. A few verbs, though, involve a small spelling change. This is usually to do with how a word is pronounced. In the tables below the form(s) with the irregular spelling is/are underlined.

1 Verbs ending in -cer

➤ With verbs such as **lancer** (meaning *to throw*), which end in **-cer**, **c** becomes **ç** before an **a** or an **o**. This is so the letter **c** is still pronounced as in the English word *ice*.

Pronoun	Example verb: lancer
je	lance
tu	lances
il elle on	lance
nous	<u>lançons</u>
vous	lancez
ils elles	lancent

2 Verbs ending in -ger

➤ With verbs such as **manger** (meaning *to eat*), which end in **-ger**, **g** becomes **ge** before an **a** or an **o**. This is so the letter **g** is still pronounced like the **s** in the English word *leisure*.

Pronoun	Example verb: manger
je	mange
tu	manges
il elle on	mange
nous	<u>mangeons</u>
vous	mangez
ils elles	mangent

For further explanation of grammatical terms, please see pages viii-xii.

3 Verbs ending in -eler

➤ With verbs such as **appeler** (meaning *to call*), which end in **-eler**, the **l** doubles before **-e**, **-es** and **-ent**. The double consonant (**ll**) affects the pronunciation of the word. In **appeler**, the first **e** sounds like the vowel sound at the end of the English word *teacher*, but in **appelle** the first **e** sounds like the one in the English word *pet*.

Pronoun	Example verb: appeler
j'	appelle
tu	appelles
il elle on	appelle
nous	appelons
vous	appelez
ils elles	appellent

➤ The exceptions to this rule are **geler** (meaning *to freeze*) and **peler** (meaning *to peel*), which change in the same way as **lever** (*see page 80*).

➤ Verbs like this are sometimes called '1, 2, 3, 6 verbs' because they change in the first person singular (**je**), second person singular (**tu**), and third person singular and plural (**il/elle/on** and **ils/elles**).

4 Verbs ending in -eter

➤ With verbs such as **jeter** (meaning *to throw*), which end in **-eter**, the **t** doubles before **-e**, **-es** and **-ent**. The double consonant (**tt**) affects the pronunciation of the word. In **jeter**, the first **e** sounds like the vowel sound at the end of the English word *teacher*, but in **jette** the first **e** sounds like the one in the English word *pet*.

Pronoun	Example verb: jeter
je	jette
tu	jettes
il elle on	jette
nous	jetons
vous	jetez
ils elles	jettent

➤ The exceptions to this rule include **acheter** (meaning *to buy*), which changes in the same way as **lever**.

➤ Verbs like this are sometimes called '1, 2, 3, 6 verbs'.

5 Verbs ending in -yer

➤ With verbs such as **nettoyer** (meaning *to clean*), which end in **-yer**, the **y** changes to **i** before **-e**, **-es** and **-ent**.

Pronoun	Example verb: nettoyer
je	nettoie
tu	nettoies
il elle on	nettoie
nous	nettoyons
vous	nettoyez
ils elles	nettoient

➤ Verbs ending in **-ayer**, such as **payer** (meaning *to pay*) and **essayer** (meaning *to try*), can be spelled with either a **y** or an **i**. So **je paie** and **je paye**, for example, are both correct.

➤ Verbs like this are sometimes called '1, 2, 3, 6 verbs'.

6 Changes involving accents

➤ With verbs such as **lever** (meaning *to raise*), **peser** (meaning *to weigh*) and **acheter** (meaning *to buy*), **e** changes to **è** before the consonant + **-e**, **-es** and **-ent**. The accent changes the pronunciation too. In **lever** the first **e** sounds like the vowel sound at the end of the English word *teacher*, but in **lève** and so on the first **e** sounds like the one in the English word *pet*.

Pronoun	Example verb: lever
je	lève
tu	lèves
il elle on	lève
nous	levons
vous	levez
ils elles	lèvent

For further explanation of grammatical terms, please see pages viii-xii.

➤ With verbs such as **espérer** (meaning *to hope*), **régler** (meaning *to adjust*) and **préférer** (meaning *to prefer*), **é** changes to **è** before the consonant + **-e**, **-es** and **-ent**.

Pronoun	**Example verb: espérer**
j'	**espère**
tu	**espères**
il **elle** **on**	**espère**
nous	**espérons**
vous	**espérez**
ils **elles**	**espèrent**

➤ Verbs like this are sometimes called '1, 2, 3, 6 verbs'.

Key points

✔ In verbs ending in **-cer** and **-ger**:
c → **ç** and **g** → **ge** in the **nous** form.

✔ In verbs ending in **-eler** and **-eter**:
l → **ll** and **t** → **tt** in all but the **nous** and **vous** forms.

✔ In verbs ending in **-yer**:
y → **i** in all but the **nous** and **vous** forms (optional in **-ayer** verbs).

The present tense: irregular verbs

➤ Some verbs in French do not follow the normal rules. These verbs include some very common and important verbs like **avoir** (meaning *to have*), **être** (meaning *to be*), **faire** (meaning *to do*, *to make*) and **aller** (meaning *to go*). The present tense of these four verbs is given in full below.

➪ *For **Verb tables**, see supplement.*

1 The present tense of avoir

Pronoun	**avoir**	**Meaning:** *to have*
j'	**ai**	I have
tu	**as**	you have
il **elle** **on**	**a**	he/she/it/one has
nous	**avons**	we have
vous	**avez**	you have
ils **elles**	**ont**	they have

J'<u>ai</u> deux sœurs.	I have two sisters.
Il <u>a</u> les yeux bleus.	He has blue eyes.
Elle <u>a</u> trois ans.	She's three.
Qu'est-ce qu'il y <u>a</u>?	What's the matter?

2 The present tense of être

Pronoun	**être**	**Meaning:** *to be*
je	**suis**	I am
tu	**es**	you are
il **elle** **on**	**est**	he/she/it/one is
nous	**sommes**	we are
vous	**êtes**	you are
ils **elles**	**sont**	they are

Je <u>suis</u> heureux.	I'm happy.
Mon père <u>est</u> instituteur.	My father's a primary school teacher.
Il <u>est</u> deux heures.	It's two o'clock.

3 The present tense of faire

Pronoun	faire	**Meaning:** *to do, to make*
je	fais	I do/make I am doing/making
tu	fais	you do/make you are doing/making
il elle on	fait	he/she/it/one does/makes he/she/it/one is doing/making
nous	faisons	we do/make we are doing/making
vous	faites	you do/make you are doing/making
ils elles	font	they do/make they are doing/making

Je fais un gâteau. I'm making a cake.
Qu'est-ce que tu fais? What are you doing?
Il fait chaud. It's hot.
Ça ne fait rien. It doesn't matter.

4 The present tense of aller

Pronoun	aller	**Meaning:** *to go*
je	vais	I go I am going
tu	vas	you go you are going
il elle on	va	he/she/it/one goes he/she/it/one is going
nous	allons	we go we are going
vous	allez	you go you are going
ils elles	vont	they go they are going

Je vais à Londres. I'm going to London.
'Comment allez-vous?' – 'Je vais bien.' 'How are you?' – 'I'm fine.'
'Comment ça va?' – 'Ça va bien.' 'How are you?' – 'I'm fine.'

5 Irregular -ir verbs

➤ Many irregular verbs that end in **-ir**, such as **partir** (meaning *to go*) and **tenir** (meaning *to hold*), have a common pattern in the singular. The **je** and **tu** forms often end in **-s**, and the **il/elle/on** form often ends in **-t**.

Pronoun	partir	tenir
je	**pars**	**tiens**
tu	**pars**	**tiens**
il/elle/on	**part**	**tient**

Je pars demain. I'm leaving tomorrow.
Elle tient le bébé. She is holding the baby.

⇨ *For* ***Verb tables****, see supplement.*

Key points

✔ Some very important French verbs are irregular, including **avoir**, **être**, **faire** and **aller**. They are worth learning in full.

✔ The **-s**, **-s**, **-t** pattern occurs frequently in irregular **-ir** verbs.

The imperative

What is the imperative?
An **imperative** is a form of the verb used when giving orders and instructions, for example, *Shut the door!; Sit down!; Don't go!*

1 Using the imperative

➤ In French, there are two forms of the imperative that are used to give instructions or orders to someone. These correspond to **tu** and **vous**.

➪ *For more information on the difference between **tu** and **vous**, see page 43.*

➤ There is also a form of the imperative that corresponds to **nous**. This means the same as *let's* in English. It is not used as often as the **tu** and **vous** forms.

2 Forming the present tense imperative

➤ For regular verbs, the imperative is the same as the **tu**, **nous** and **vous** forms of the present tense, except that you do not say the pronouns **tu**, **nous** and **vous**. Also, in the **tu** form of **-er** verbs like **donner**, the final **-s** is dropped.

Pronoun	**-er verbs: donner**	**Meaning**	**-ir verbs: finir**	**Meaning**	**-re verbs: attendre**	**Meaning**
tu	**donne**	give	**finis**	finish	**attends**	wait
nous	**donnons**	let's give	**finissons**	let's finish	**attendons**	let's wait
vous	**donnez**	give	**finissez**	finish	**attendez**	wait

Donne-moi ça! — Give me that!
Finissez vos devoirs et allez vous coucher. — Finish your homework and go to bed.
Attendons le bus. — Let's wait for the bus.

Tip
When a **tu** imperative comes before **en** or **y**, the final **-s** is kept to make the words easier to pronounce. The **s** is pronounced like the *z* in the English word *zip*:

Vas-y! — Go on!
Donnes-en à ton frère. — Give some to your brother.

3 Where to put the object pronoun

➤ An object pronoun is a word like **la** (meaning *her/it*), **me/moi** (meaning *me*) or **leur** (meaning *to them*) that is used instead of a noun as the object of a sentence. In orders and instructions, the position of these object pronouns in the sentence changes depending on whether you are telling someone TO DO something or NOT TO DO something.

➪ *For more information on **Object pronouns**, see page 47.*

➤ If you are telling someone NOT TO DO something, you put the object pronouns BEFORE the verb.

Ne me dérange pas.	Don't disturb me.
Ne leur parlons pas.	Let's not speak to them.
Ne le regardez pas.	Don't look at him/it.

➤ If you are telling someone TO DO something, you put the object pronouns AFTER the verb and join the two words with a hyphen. The word order is the same as in English.

Excusez-moi.	Excuse me.
Aide-nous.	Help us.
Attendons-la.	Let's wait for her/it.

➤ Orders and instructions telling someone to do something may contain direct object and indirect object pronouns. When this happens, the pronouns go in this order:

DIRECT		INDIRECT
le		**moi**
la	BEFORE	**toi**
les		**lui**
		nous
		vous
		leur

Prête-les moi!	Lend them to me! *or* Lend me them!
Donnez-la-nous!	Give it to us! *or* Give us it!

➪ *For imperatives using **Reflexive verbs**, see page 90.*

4 Imperative forms of irregular verbs

➤ **avoir** (meaning *to have*), **être** (meaning *to be*), **savoir** (meaning *to know*) and **vouloir** (meaning *to want*) have irregular imperative forms.

Pronoun	avoir	être	savoir	vouloir
tu	aie	sois	sache	veuille
nous	ayons	soyons	sachons	veuillons
vous	ayez	soyez	sachez	veuillez

Sois sage. — Be good.
Veuillez fermer la porte. — Please shut the door.

Key points

✔ The imperative has three forms: **tu**, **nous** and **vous**.
✔ The forms are the same as the **tu**, **nous** and **vous** forms of the present tense, except that the final **-s** is dropped in the **tu** form of **-er** verbs.
✔ Object pronouns go before the verb when you are telling someone not to do something, but after the verb with a hyphen when you are telling someone to do something.
✔ **avoir**, **être**, **savoir** and **vouloir** have irregular imperative forms.

Reflexive verbs

What is a reflexive verb?
A **reflexive verb** is one where the subject and object are the same, and where the action 'reflects back' on the subject. It is used with a reflexive pronoun such as *myself*, *yourself* and *herself* in English, for example, *I washed myself*; *He shaved himself*.

1 Using reflexive verbs

➤ In French, reflexive verbs are much more common than in English, and many are used in everyday French. They are shown in dictionaries as **se** plus the infinitive (**se** means *himself*, *herself*, *itself*, *themselves* or *oneself*). **se** is called a reflexive pronoun.

Tip
se changes to **s'** in front of a word starting with a vowel, most words starting with **h**, and the French word **y**.

➤ Reflexive verbs are often used to describe things you do (to yourself) every day or that involve a change of some sort (going to bed, sitting down, getting angry, going to sleep). Some of the most common French reflexive verbs are listed here:

s'amuser	to play, to enjoy oneself
s'appeler	to be called
s'arrêter	to stop
s'asseoir	to sit down
se baigner	to go swimming
se coucher	to go to bed
se dépêcher	to hurry
s'habiller	to get dressed
s'intéresser à quelque chose	to be interested in something
se laver	to wash, to have a wash
se lever	to get up, to rise, to stand up
se passer	to take place, to happen, to go
se promener	to go for a walk
se rappeler	to remember
se réveiller	to wake up
se trouver	to be (situated)

For further explanation of grammatical terms, please see pages viii-xii.

Qu'est-ce qui <u>se passe</u>?	What's happening?
Le soleil <u>se lève</u> à cinq heures.	The sun rises at five o'clock.
<u>Asseyez-vous</u>!	Sit down!

i Note that **se** and **s'** are very rarely translated as *himself* and so on in English.

➤ Some French verbs can be used with a reflexive pronoun or without a reflexive pronoun, for example, the verbs **appeler** and **s'appeler**, and **arrêter** and **s'arrêter**. Sometimes, however, their meaning may change.

<u>Appelle</u> le chien.	<u>Call</u> the dog.
Je <u>m'appelle</u> Jacques.	I'<u>m called</u> Jacques.
Il <u>arrête</u> le moteur.	He <u>switches off</u> the engine.
Elle <u>s'arrête</u> devant une vitrine.	She <u>stops</u> in front of a shop window.

2 Forming the present tense of reflexive verbs

➤ To use a reflexive verb in French, you need to decide which reflexive pronoun to use. The forms shown in brackets in the table are used before a word starting with a vowel, most words starting with **h**, or the French word **y**.

Subject pronoun	Reflexive pronoun	Meaning
je	me (m')	myself
tu	te (t')	yourself
il elle on	se (s')	himself herself itself oneself
nous	nous	ourselves
vous	vous	yourself (*singular*) yourselves (*plural*)
ils elles	se (s')	themselves

Je <u>me lève</u> tôt.	I get up early.
Elle <u>s'habille</u>.	She's getting dressed.
Ils <u>s'intéressent</u> beaucoup aux animaux.	They're very interested in animals.

➤ The present tense forms of a reflexive verb work in just the same way as an ordinary verb, except that the reflexive pronoun is used as well.

Reflexive forms	Meaning
je me lave	I wash (myself)
tu te laves	you wash (yourself)
il se lave **elle se lave** **on se lave**	he washes (himself) she washes (herself) it washes (itself) one washes (oneself)
nous nous lavons	we wash (ourselves)
vous vous lavez	you wash (yourself) (*singular*) you wash (yourselves) (*plural*)
ils se lavent **elles se lavent**	they wash (themselves)

➤ Some reflexive verbs, such as **s'asseoir** (meaning *to sit down*), are irregular. Some of these irregular verbs are shown in the **Verb tables**.

➪ *For **Verb tables**, see supplement.*

3 Where to put the reflexive pronoun

➤ In the present tense, the reflexive pronoun almost always comes <u>BEFORE</u> the verb.

Je <u>me</u> couche tôt.	I go to bed early.
Comment <u>t'</u>appelles-tu?	What's your name?

➤ When telling someone <u>NOT TO DO</u> something, you put the reflexive pronoun <u>BEFORE</u> the verb as usual.

Ne <u>te</u> lève pas.	Don't get up.
Ne <u>vous</u> habillez pas.	Don't get dressed.

➤ When telling someone <u>TO DO</u> something, you put the reflexive pronoun <u>AFTER</u> the verb and join the two words with a hyphen.

Lève-<u>toi</u>!	Get up!
Dépêchez-<u>vous</u>!	Hurry up!
Habillons-<u>nous</u>.	Let's get dressed.

Tip

When you are telling someone TO DO something, **te** or **t'** changes to **toi**.

Assieds-toi.	Sit down.

When you are telling someone NOT TO DO something, **te** or **t'** is used, not **toi**.

Ne te lève pas.	Don't get up.

⇨ *For more information on the* ***Imperative****, see page 85.*

4 *Each other and one another*

➤ We use *each other* in English when we are talking about two people, and *one another* when we are talking about three or more people. The French reflexive pronouns **nous**, **vous** and **se** can all mean two or more people.

Nous nous parlons tous les jours.	We speak to each other every day.
On se voit demain?	Shall we see each other tomorrow?
Les trois pays se ressemblent beaucoup.	The three countries are really like one another.

Key points

✔ A reflexive verb is made up of a reflexive pronoun and a verb.

✔ The reflexive pronouns are: **me, te, se, nous, vous, se** (**m', t', s', nous, vous, s'** before a vowel, most words beginning with **h** and the French word **y**).

✔ The reflexive pronoun comes before the verb, except when you are telling someone to do something.

The imperfect tense

What is the imperfect tense?
The **imperfect tense** is one of the verb tenses used to talk about the past, especially in descriptions, and to say what used to happen, for example, *I used to walk to school*; *It was sunny at the weekend*.

1 Using the imperfect tense

➤ The imperfect tense is used:

- to describe what things were like and how people felt in the past

  I was very sad when she left.

  It was pouring with rain.

- to say what used to happen or what you used to do regularly in the past

  We used to get up very early in those days.

  I never used to like milk.

- to indicate things that were happening or something that was true when something else took place

  I was watching TV when the phone rang.

  As we were looking out of the window, we saw someone walk across the lawn.

ℹ Note that if you want to talk about an event or action that took place and was completed in the past, you use the perfect tense.

➪ *For more information on the **Perfect tense**, see page 111.*

➤ You can often recognize an imperfect tense in English because it uses a form like *were looking* or *was raining*. The words *used to* also show an imperfect tense.

Tip

Remember that you NEVER use the verb **être** to translate *was* or *were* in forms like *was raining* or *were looking* and so on. You change the French verb ending instead.

2 Forming the imperfect tense of -er verbs

➤ To form the imperfect tense of **-er** verbs, you use the same stem of the verb as for the present tense. Then you add the correct ending, depending on whether you are referring to **je**, **tu**, **il**, **elle**, **on**, **nous**, **vous**, **ils** or **elles**.

Pronoun	Ending	Add to stem, e.g. donn-	Meanings
je (j')	**-ais**	**je donnais**	I gave I was giving I used to give
tu	**-ais**	**tu donnais**	you gave you were giving you used to give
il **elle** **on**	**-ait**	**il donnait** **elle donnait** **on donnait**	he/she/it/one gave he/she/it/one was giving he/she/it/one used to give
nous	**-ions**	**nous donnions**	we gave we were giving we used to give
vous	**-iez**	**vous donniez**	you gave you were giving you used to give
ils **elles**	**-aient**	**ils donnaient** **elles donnaient**	they gave they were giving they used to give

Il portait toujours un grand chapeau noir. — He always wore a big black hat.

Nous habitions à Paris à cette époque. — We were living in Paris at that time.

Pour gagner un peu d'argent, je donnais des cours de français. — To earn a little money I used to give French lessons.

Tip

je changes to **j'** in front of a word starting with a vowel, most words starting with **h**, and the French word **y**.

3 Forming the imperfect tense of -ir verbs

➤ To form the imperfect tense of **-ir** verbs, you use the same stem of the verb as for the present tense. Then you add the correct ending, depending on whether you are referring to **je**, **tu**, **il**, **elle**, **on**, **nous**, **vous**, **ils** or **elles**.

Pronoun	Ending	Add to stem, e.g. fin-	Meanings
je (j')	**-issais**	**je fin<u>issais</u>**	I finished I was finishing I used to finish
tu	**-issais**	**tu fin<u>issais</u>**	you finished you were finishing you used to finish
il **elle** **on**	**-issait**	**il fin<u>issait</u>** **elle fin<u>issait</u>** **on fin<u>issait</u>**	he/she/it/one finished he/she/it/one was finishing he/she/it/one used to finish
nous	**-issions**	**nous fin<u>issions</u>**	we finished we were finishing we used to finish
vous	**-issiez**	**vous fin<u>issiez</u>**	you finished you were finishing you used to finish
ils **elles**	**-issaient**	**ils fin<u>issaient</u>** **elles fin<u>issaient</u>**	they finished they were finishing they used to finish

Il <u>finissait</u> souvent ses devoirs avant le dîner. — He often finished his homework before dinner.

Cet après-midi-là ils <u>choisissaient</u> une bague de fiançailles. — That afternoon they were choosing an engagement ring.

4 Forming the imperfect tense of -re verbs

➤ To form the imperfect tense of **-re** verbs, you use the same stem of the verb as for the present tense. Then you add the correct ending, depending on whether you are referring to **je**, **tu**, **il**, **elle**, **on**, **nous**, **vous**, **ils** or **elles**. These endings are the same as for **-er** verbs.

Pronoun	Ending	Add to stem, e.g. attend-	Meanings
je (j')	-ais	**j'attendais**	I waited I was waiting I used to wait
tu	-ais	**tu attendais**	you waited you were waiting you used to wait
il elle on	-ait	**il attendait** **elle attendait** **on attendait**	he/she/it/one waited he/she/it/one was waiting he/she/it/one used to wait
nous	-ions	**nous attendions**	we waited we were waiting we used to wait
vous	-iez	**vous attendiez**	you waited you were waiting you used to wait
ils elles	-aient	**ils attendaient** **elles attendaient**	they waited they were waiting they used to wait

Christine m'attendait tous les soirs à la sortie. — Christine used to wait for me every evening at the exit.

Je vivais seule après mon divorce. — I was living alone after my divorce.

5 Spelling changes in -er verbs

➤ As with the present tense, a few **-er** verbs change their spellings slightly when they are used in the imperfect tense. The forms with spelling changes have been underlined in the tables.

➤ With verbs such as **lancer** (meaning *to throw*), which end in **-cer**, **c** becomes **ç** before an **a** or an **o**. This is so that the letter **c** is still pronounced as in the English word *ice*.

Pronoun	Example verb: lancer
je	**lançais**
tu	**lançais**
il elle on	**lançait**
nous	**lancions**
vous	**lanciez**
ils elles	**lançaient**

➤ With verbs such as **manger** (meaning *to eat*), which end in **-ger**, **g** becomes **ge** before an **a** or an **o**. This is so the letter **g** is still pronounced like the s in the English word *leisure*.

Pronoun	Example verb: manger
je	mangeais
tu	mangeais
il elle on	mangeait
nous	mangions
vous	mangiez
ils elles	mangeaient

➤ These verbs follow the 1,2,3,6 pattern. That is, they change in the first, second and third person singular, and in the third person plural.

6 Reflexive verbs in the imperfect tense

➤ The imperfect tense of reflexive verbs is formed just as for ordinary verbs, except that you add the reflexive pronoun (**me**, **te**, **se**, **nous**, **vous**, **se**).

Subject pronoun	Reflexive pronoun	Example with laver	Meaning
je	me (m')	lavais	I washed I was washing I used to wash
tu	te (t')	lavais	you washed you were washing you used to wash
il elle on	se (s')	lavait	he/she/it/one washed he/she/it/one was washing he/she/it/one used to wash
nous	nous	lavions	we washed we were washing we used to wash
vous	vous	laviez	you washed you were washing you used to wash
ils elles	se (s')	lavaient	they washed they were washing they used to wash

Tip

me changes to **m'**, **te** to **t'** and **se** to **s'** before a vowel, most words starting with **h** and the French word **y**.

7 Irregular verbs in the imperfect tense

➤ The only verb that is irregular in the imperfect tense is **être**.

Pronoun	être	Meaning
j'	**étais**	I was
tu	**étais**	you were
il **elle** **on**	**était**	he/she/it/one was
nous	**étions**	we were
vous	**étiez**	you were
ils **elles**	**étaient**	they were

J'étais heureux. — I was happy.

Mon père était instituteur. — My father was a primary school teacher.

Key points

✔ The imperfect tense endings for **-er** and **-re** verbs are: **-ais, -ais, -ait, -ions, -iez, -aient**.

✔ The imperfect tense endings for **-ir** verbs are: **-issais, -issais, -issait, -issions, -issiez, -issaient**.

✔ In verbs ending in **-cer** and **-ger**: **c** → **ç** and **g** → **ge** in all but the **nous** and **vous** forms.

✔ **être** is irregular in the imperfect tense.

The future tense

What is the future tense?
The **future tense** is a verb tense used to talk about something that will happen or will be true.

1 Using the future tense

➤ In English the future tense is often shown by *will* or its shortened form *'ll*.

What will you do?
The weather will be warm and dry tomorrow.
He'll be here soon.
I'll give you a call.

➤ Just as in English, you can use the present tense in French to refer to something that is going to happen in the future.

Je prends le train de dix heures.	I'm taking the ten o'clock train.
Nous allons à Paris la semaine prochaine.	We're going to Paris next week.

➤ In English we often use *going to* followed by an infinitive to talk about something that will happen in the immediate future. You can use the French verb **aller** (meaning *to go*) followed by an infinitive in the same way.

Tu vas tomber si tu continues.	You're going to fall if you carry on.
Il va manquer le train.	He's going to miss the train.

Tip

Remember that French has no direct equivalent of the word *will* in verb forms like *will rain* or *will look* and so on. You change the French verb ending instead to form the future tense.

2 Forming the future tense

➤ To form the future tense in French, you use:

- the infinitive of **-er** and **-ir** verbs, for example, **donner**, **finir**
- the infinitive without the final **e** of **-re** verbs: for example, **attendr-**

➤ Then add the correct ending to the stem, depending on whether you are talking about **je**, **tu**, **il**, **elle**, **on**, **nous**, **vous**, **ils** or **elles**. The endings are the same for **-er**, **-ir** and **-re** verbs.

For further explanation of grammatical terms, please see pages viii-xii.

i Note that apart from the **nous** and **vous** forms, the endings are the same as the present tense of **avoir**.

➪ *For the present tense of **avoir**, see page 82.*

Pronoun	Ending	Add to stem, e.g. donner-, finir-, attendr-	Meanings
je (j')	-ai	je donnerai je finirai j'attendrai	I will give I will finish I will wait
tu	-as	tu donneras tu finiras tu attendras	you will give you will finish you will wait
il elle on	-a	il/elle/on donnera il/elle/on finira il/elle/on attendra	he/she/it/one will give he/she/it/one will finish he/she/it/one will wait
nous	-ons	nous donnerons nous finirons nous attendrons	we will give we will finish we will wait
vous	-ez	vous donnerez vous finirez vous attendrez	you will give you will finish you will wait
ils elles	-ont	ils/elles donneront ils/elles finiront ils/elles attendront	they will give they will finish they will wait

Elle te donnera mon adresse. — She'll give you my address.
Le cours finira à onze heures. — The lesson will finish at eleven o'clock.
Nous t'attendrons devant le cinéma. — We'll wait for you in front of the cinema.

> *Tip*
> **je** changes to **j'** in front of a word starting with a vowel, most words starting with **h**, and the French word **y**.

3 Spelling changes in -er verbs

➤ As with the present and imperfect tenses, a few **-er** verbs change their spellings slightly in the future tense. The forms with spelling changes have been underlined in the tables.

➤ With verbs such as **appeler** (meaning *to call*), which end in **-eler**, the **l** doubles throughout the future tense. The double consonant (**ll**) affects the pronunciation of the word. In **appeler**, the first **e** sounds like the vowel sound at the end of the English word *teacher*, but in **appellerai** the first **e** sounds like the one in the English word *pet*.

Pronoun	Example verb: appeler
j'	appellerai
tu	appelleras
il elle on	appellera
nous	appellerons
vous	appellerez
ils elles	appelleront

➤ The exceptions to this rule are **geler** (meaning *to freeze*) and **peler** (meaning *to peel*), which change in the same way as **lever** (*see page* 101).

➤ With verbs such as **jeter** (meaning *to throw*), that end in **-eter**, the **t** doubles throughout the future tense. The double consonant (**tt**) affects the pronunciation of the word. In **jeter**, the first **e** sounds like the vowel sound at the end of the English word *teacher*, but in **jetterai** the first **e** sounds like the one in the English word *pet*.

Pronoun	Example verb: jeter
je	jetterai
tu	jetteras
il elle on	jettera
nous	jetterons
vous	jetterez
ils elles	jetteront

➤ The exceptions to this rule include **acheter** (meaning *to buy*), which changes in the same way as **lever** (*see page* 101).

➤ With verbs such as **nettoyer** (meaning *to clean*), that end in **-yer**, the **y** changes to **i** throughout the future tense.

Pronoun	Example verb: nettoyer
je	nettoierai
tu	nettoieras
il elle on	nettoiera
nous	nettoierons
vous	nettoierez
ils elles	nettoieront

➤ Verbs ending in **-ayer**, such as **payer** (meaning *to pay*) and **essayer** (meaning *to try*), can be spelled with either a **y** or an **i**. So **je paierai** and **je payerai**, for example, are both correct.

➤ With verbs such as **lever** (meaning *to raise*), **peser** (meaning *to weigh*) and **acheter** (meaning *to buy*), **e** changes to **è** throughout the future tense. In **lever** the first **e** sounds like the vowel sound at the end of the English word *teacher*, but in **lèverai** and so on the first **e** sounds like the one in the English word *pet*.

Pronoun	Example verb: lever
je	lèverai
tu	lèveras
il elle on	lèvera
nous	lèverons
vous	lèverez
ils elles	lèveront

4 Reflexive verbs in the future tense

➤ The future tense of reflexive verbs is formed in just the same way as for ordinary verbs, except that you have to remember to give the reflexive pronoun (**me**, **te**, **se**, **nous**, **vous**, **se**).

Subject pronoun	Reflexive pronoun	Example with laver	Meaning
je	**me (m')**	**laverai**	I will wash
tu	**te (t')**	**laveras**	you will wash
il **elle** **on**	**se (s')**	**lavera**	he/she/it/one will wash
nous	**nous**	**laverons**	we will wash
vous	**vous**	**laverez**	you will wash
ils **elles**	**se (s')**	**laveront**	they will wash

Tip

me changes to **m'**, **te** to **t'** and **se** to **s'** before a vowel, most words starting with **h** and the French word **y**.

5 Irregular verbs in the future tense

➤ There are some verbs that do not use their infinitives as the stem for the future tense, including **avoir**, **être**, **faire** and **aller**, which are shown in full on pages 103–104.

➤ Other irregular verbs include:

Verb	Meaning	je	tu	il/elle/on	nous	vous	ils/elles
devoir	*to have to, must*	**devrai**	**devras**	**devra**	**devrons**	**devrez**	**devront**
pouvoir	*to be able to, can*	**pourrai**	**pourras**	**pourra**	**pourrons**	**pourrez**	**pourront**
savoir	*to know*	**saurai**	**sauras**	**saura**	**saurons**	**saurez**	**sauront**
tenir	*to hold*	**tiendrai**	**tiendras**	**tiendra**	**tiendrons**	**tiendrez**	**tiendront**
venir	*to come*	**viendrai**	**viendras**	**viendra**	**viendrons**	**viendrez**	**viendront**
voir	*to see*	**verrai**	**verras**	**verra**	**verrons**	**verrez**	**verront**
vouloir	*to want*	**voudrai**	**voudras**	**voudra**	**voudrons**	**voudrez**	**voudront**

- **il faut** becomes **il faudra** (meaning *it will be necessary to*).
- **il pleut** becomes **il pleuvra** (meaning *it will rain*).
- This is the future tense of **avoir**:

Pronoun	avoir	Meaning: *to have*
j'	aurai	I will have
tu	auras	you will have
il elle on	aura	he/she/it/one will have
nous	aurons	we will have
vous	aurez	you will have
ils elles	auront	they will have

- This is the future tense of **être**:

Pronoun	être	Meaning: *to be*
je	serai	I will be
tu	seras	you will be
il elle on	sera	he/she/it/one will be
nous	serons	we will be
vous	serez	you will be
ils elles	seront	they will be

- This is the future tense of **faire**:

Pronoun	faire	Meaning: *to do, to make*
je	ferai	I will do/make
tu	feras	you will do/make
il elle on	fera	he/she/it/one will do/make
nous	ferons	we will do/make
vous	ferez	you will do/make
ils elles	feront	they will do/make

➤ This is the future tense of **aller**:

Pronoun	**aller**	**Meaning:** *to go*
j'	**irai**	I will go
tu	**iras**	you will go
il **elle** **on**	**ira**	he/she/it/one will go
nous	**irons**	we will go
vous	**irez**	you will go
ils **elles**	**iront**	they will go

➪ *For **Verb tables**, see supplement.*

Key points

✔ You can use a present tense in French to talk about something that will happen or be true in the future, just as in English.

✔ You can use **aller** with an infinitive to refer to things that will happen in the immediate future.

✔ The stem is the same as the infinitive for **-er**, **-ir** and **-re** verbs, except that the final **-e** of **-re** verbs is lost.

✔ The future tense endings are the same for **-er**, **-ir** and **-re** verbs: **-ai**, **-as**, **-a**, **-ons**, **-ez**, **-ont**.

✔ In verbs ending in **-eler** and **-eter**:
l → **ll** and **t** → **tt** throughout the future tense.

✔ In verbs ending in **-yer**:
y → **i** throughout the future tense (optional in **-ayer** verbs).

✔ Some verbs are irregular in the future tense. It is worth learning these in full.

The conditional

> **What is the conditional?**
> The **conditional** is a verb form used to talk about things that would happen or that would be true under certain conditions, for example, I *would help you if I could*.
> It is also used to say what you would like or need, for example, *Could you give me the bill?*

1 Using the conditional

➤ You can often recognize a conditional in English by the word *would* or its shortened form *'d*.

I would be sad if you left.

If you asked him, he'd help you.

➤ You use the conditional for:

- asking for something formally and politely, especially in shops

  I'd like a kilo of pears, please.

- saying what you would like

  I'd like to go to the United States.

- making a suggestion

  I could come and pick you up.

- giving advice

  You should say you're sorry.

> ***Tip***
> There is no direct French translation of *would* in verb forms like *would be*, *would like*, *would help* and so on. You change the French verb ending instead.

2 Forming the conditional

➤ To form the conditional in French, you have to use:

- the infinitive of **-er** and **-ir** verbs, for example, **donner-**, **finir-**
- the infinitive without the final **e** of **-re** verbs, for example, **attendr-**

➤ Then add the correct ending to the stem, depending on whether you are talking about **je**, **tu**, **il**, **elle**, **on**, **nous**, **vous**, **ils** or **elles**. The endings are the same for all verbs. In fact, they are the same as the **-er** and **-re** endings for the IMPERFECT TENSE, but the stem is the same as the FUTURE TENSE.

⇨ *For more information on the **Imperfect tense** and the **Future tense**, see pages 92 and 98.*

Pronoun	Ending	Add to stem, e.g. donner-, finir-, attendr-	Meanings
je (j')	-ais	**je donnerais** **je finirais** **j'attendrais**	I would give I would finish I would wait
tu	-ais	**tu donnerais** **tu finirais** **tu attendrais**	you would give you would finish you would wait
il elle on	-ait	**il/elle/on donnerait** **il/elle/on finirait** **il/elle/on attendrait**	he/she/it/one would give he/she/it/one would finish he/she/it/one would wait
nous	-ions	**nous donnerions** **nous finirions** **nous attendrions**	we would give we would finish we would wait
vous	-iez	**vous donneriez** **vous finiriez** **vous attendriez**	you would give you would finish you would wait
ils elles	-aient	**ils/elles donneraient** **ils/elles finiraient** **ils/elles attendraient**	they would give they would finish they would wait

J'aimerais aller aux États-Unis. I'd like to go to the United States.

Tip

je changes to **j'** in front of a word starting with a vowel, most words starting with **h**, and the French word **y**.

Note that you have to be careful not to mix up the future tense and the conditional. They look very similar.

FUTURE	CONDITIONAL
je donnerai	**je donnerais**
je finirai	**je finirais**
j'attendrai	**j'attendrais**
j'aimerai	**j'aimerais**
je voudrai	**je voudrais**
je viendrai	**je viendrais**
je serai	**je serais**

3 Spelling changes in -er verbs

➤ As with the future tense, a few **-er** verbs change their spellings slightly in the conditional. The forms with spelling changes have been underlined in the tables below.

➤ With verbs such as **appeler** (meaning *to call*), which end in **-eler**, the **l** doubles throughout the conditional. The double consonant (**ll**) affects the pronunciation of the word. In **appeler**, the first **e** sounds like the vowel sound at the end of the English word *teacher*, but in **appellerais** the first **e** sounds like the one in the English word *pet*.

Pronoun	Example verb: appeler
j'	appellerais
tu	appellerais
il elle on	appellerait
nous	appellerions
vous	appelleriez
ils elles	appelleraient

➤ The exceptions to this rule are **geler** (meaning *to freeze*) and **peler** (meaning *to peel*), which change in the same way as **lever** (*see page 108*).

➤ With verbs such as **jeter** (meaning *to throw*), which end in **-eter**, the **t** doubles throughout the conditional. The double consonant (**tt**) affects the pronunciation of the word. In **jeter**, the first **e** sounds like the vowel sound at the end of the English word *teacher*, but in **jetterais** the first **e** sounds like the one in the English word *pet*.

Pronoun	Example verb: jeter
je	jetterais
tu	jetterais
il elle on	jetterait
nous	jetterions
vous	jetteriez
ils elles	jetteraient

➤ The exceptions to this rule include **acheter** (meaning *to buy*), which changes in the same way as **lever** (*see page 108*).

➤ With verbs such as **nettoyer** (meaning *to clean*), that end in **-yer**, the **y** changes to **i** throughout the conditional.

Pronoun	Example verb: nettoyer
je	nettoierais
tu	nettoierais
il elle on	nettoierait
nous	nettoierions
vous	nettoieriez
ils elles	nettoieraient

➤ Verbs ending in **-ayer**, such as **payer** (meaning *to pay*) and **essayer** (meaning *to try*), can be spelled with either a **y** or an **i**. So **je paierais** and **je payerais**, for example, are both correct.

➤ With verbs such as **lever** (meaning *to raise*), **peser** (meaning *to weigh*) and **acheter** (meaning *to buy*), **e** changes to **è** throughout the conditional. In **lever** the first **e** sounds like the vowel sound at the end of the English word *teacher*, but in **lèverais** and so on the first **e** sounds like the one in the English word *pet*.

Pronoun	Example verb: lever
je	lèverais
tu	lèverais
il elle on	lèverait
nous	lèverions
vous	lèveriez
ils elles	lèveraient

4 Reflexive verbs in the conditional

➤ The conditional of reflexive verbs is formed in just the same way as for ordinary verbs, except that you have to remember to give the reflexive pronoun (**me**, **te**, **se**, **nous**, **vous**, **se**).

Subject pronoun	Reflexive pronoun	Example with laver	Meaning
je	me (m')	laverais	I would wash
tu	te (t')	laverais	you would wash
il elle on	se (s')	laverait	he/she/it would wash
nous	nous	laverions	we would wash
vous	vous	laveriez	you would wash
ils elles	se (s')	laveraient	they would wash

Tip

me changes to **m'**, **te** to **t'** and **se** to **s'** before a vowel, most words starting with **h** and the French word **y**.

5 Irregular verbs in the conditional

➤ The same verbs that are irregular in the future tense are irregular in the conditional, including: **avoir**, **être**, **faire**, **aller**, **devoir**, **pouvoir**, **savoir**, **tenir**, **venir**, **voir**, **vouloir**.

➪ *For more information on **Irregular verbs in the future tense**, see page 102.*

➤ To form the conditional of an irregular verb, use the same stem as for the future tense, for example:

avoir → **aur-**
être → **ser-**

➤ Then add the usual endings for the conditional.

Infinitive	Future stem	Conditional endings	Conditional form
avoir	aur-	-ais, -ais, -ait, -ions, -iez, -aient	j'aurais, tu aurais, il/elle/on aurait, nous aurions, vous auriez, ils/elles auraient
être	ser-	-ais, -ais, -ait, -ions, -iez, -aient	je serais, tu serais, il/elle/on serait, nous serions, vous seriez, ils/elles seraient
faire	fer-	-ais, -ais, -ait, -ions, -iez, -aient	je ferais, tu ferais, il/elle/on ferait, nous ferions, vous feriez, ils/elles feraient
aller	ir-	-ais, -ais, -ait, -ions, -iez, -aient	j'irais, tu irais, il/elle/on irait, nous irions, vous iriez, ils/elles iraient

J'irais si j'avais le temps. — I would go if I had time.
Je voudrais un kilo de poires, s'il vous plaît. — I'd like a kilo of pears, please.
Tu devrais t'excuser. — You should say you're sorry.

Key points

✔ The conditional endings are the same for **-er**, **-ir** and **-re** verbs: **-ais**, **-ais**, **-ait**, **-ions**, **-iez**, **-aient**.

✔ The conditional endings are the same as the endings for the imperfect tense of **-er** and **-re** verbs, but the stem is the same as the stem of the future tense.

✔ In verbs ending in **-eler** and **-eter**: **l** → **ll** and **t** → **tt** throughout the conditional.

✔ In verbs ending in **-yer**: **y** → **i** throughout the conditional (optional in **-ayer** verbs).

✔ The same verbs that are irregular in the future are irregular in the conditional. It is worth learning these in full.

The perfect tense

What is the perfect tense?
The **perfect** is one of the verb tenses used to talk about the past, especially about actions that took place and were completed in the past.

1 Using the perfect tense

➤ You can often recognize a perfect tense in English by a form like *I gave*, *I have finished*.

I gave her my phone number.
I have finished my soup.

Tip

The perfect tense is the tense you will need most to talk about things that have happened or were true in the past. It is used to talk about actions that took place and WERE COMPLETED in the past.
Use the imperfect tense for regular events and in most descriptions.

➪ *For more information on the **Imperfect tense**, see page 92.*

2 Forming the perfect tense

➤ The present, imperfect, future and conditional tenses in French are made up of just one word, for example, **je donne**, **tu finissais**, **il attendra** or **j'aimerais**. The perfect tense has TWO parts to it:

- the present tense of the verb **avoir** (meaning *to have*) or **être** (meaning *to be*)
- a part of the main verb called the past participle, like *given*, *finished* and *done* in English

➤ In other words, the perfect tense in French is like the form *I have done* in English.

➪ *For more information on forming the present tense of **avoir** and **être**, see page 82.*

3 Forming the past participle

➤ To form the past participle of regular verbs, you use the infinitive of the verb:

- For **-er** verbs, you replace the **-er** at the end of the infinitive with **é**.

Infinitive	**Take off -er**	**Add -é**
donner (*to give*)	**donn-**	**donn<u>é</u>**
tomber (*to fall*)	**tomb-**	**tomb<u>é</u>**

- For **-ir** verbs, you replace the **-ir** at the end of the infinitive with **-i**.

Infinitive	**Take off -ir**	**Add -i**
finir (*to finish*)	**fin-**	**fin<u>i</u>**
partir (*to leave, to go*)	**part-**	**part<u>i</u>**

- For **-re** verbs, you replace the **-re** at the end of the infinitive with **-u**.

Infinitive	**Take off -re**	**Add -u**
attendre (*to wait*)	**attend-**	**attend<u>u</u>**
descendre (*to go down, to come down, to get off*)	**descend-**	**descend<u>u</u>**

4 Verbs that form their perfect tense with avoir

➤ Most verbs form their perfect tense with **avoir**, for example **donner**:

Pronoun	**avoir**	**Past participle**	**Meaning**
j'	**ai**	**donné**	I gave I have given
tu	**as**	**donné**	you gave you have given
il **elle** **on**	**a**	**donné**	he/she/it/one gave he/she/it/one has given
nous	**avons**	**donné**	we gave we have given
vous	**avez**	**donné**	you gave you have given
ils **elles**	**ont**	**donné**	they gave they have given

Elle <u>a donné</u> son numéro de téléphone à Claude. — She gave Claude her phone number.
Il <u>a acheté</u> un ordinateur. — He's bought a computer.
Je n'<u>ai</u> pas <u>regardé</u> la télé hier. — I didn't watch TV yesterday.

> *Tip*
> **je** changes to **j'** in front of a word starting with a vowel, most words starting with **h**, and the French word **y**.

➤ The perfect tense of **-ir** verbs like **finir** is formed in the same way, except for the past participle: **j'ai fini**, **tu as fini** and so on.

➤ The perfect tense of **-re** verbs like **attendre** is formed in the same way, except for the past participle: **j'ai attendu**, **tu as attendu** and so on.

5 avoir or être?

➤ MOST verbs form their perfect tense with **avoir**; these include **donner** as shown on page 112.

➤ There are two main groups of verbs which form their perfect tense with **être** instead of **avoir**:

- all reflexive verbs

➪ *For more information on **Reflexive verbs**, see page 88.*

- a group of verbs that are mainly used to talk about movement or a change of some kind, including these ones:

aller	to go
venir	to come
arriver	to arrive, to happen
partir	to leave, to go
descendre	to go down, to come down, to get off
monter	to go up, to come up
entrer	to go in, to come in
sortir	to go out, to come out
mourir	to die
naître	to be born
devenir	to become
rester	to stay
tomber	to fall

Je suis allé au match de football hier.	I went to the football match yesterday.
Il est sorti acheter un journal.	He's gone out to buy a newspaper.
Vous êtes descendu à quelle station?	Which station did you get off at?

Grammar Extra!

Some of the verbs on the previous page take **avoir** when they are used with a direct object, for example:

descendre quelque chose	to get something down, to bring something down, to take something down
monter quelque chose	to go up something, to come up something
sortir quelque chose	to take something out
Est-ce que tu as descendu les bagages?	Did you bring the bags down?
Elle a monté les escaliers.	She went up the stairs.
Elle a sorti son porte-monnaie de son sac.	She took her purse out of her handbag.

➪ *For more information on* ***Direct objects****, see page 47.*

6 Verbs that form their perfect tense with être

➤ When a verb takes **être**, the past participle ALWAYS agrees with the subject of the verb; that is, the endings change in the feminine and plural forms.

	Masculine endings	Examples	Feminine endings	Examples
Singular	-	tombé parti descendu	-e	tombée partie descendue
Plural	-s	tombés partis descendus	-es	tombées parties descendues

Est-ce ton frère est allé à l'étranger?	Did your brother go abroad?
Elle est venue avec nous.	She came with us.
Ils sont partis à six heures.	They left at six o'clock.
Mes cousines sont arrivées hier.	My cousins arrived yesterday. (*The cousins are female.*)

➤ Here are the perfect tense forms of **tomber** in full:

Pronoun	avoir	Past participle	Meaning
je	suis	**tombé** *(masculine)* **tombée** *(feminine)*	I fell/I have fallen
tu	es	**tombé** *(masculine)* **tombée** *(feminine)*	you fell/you have fallen
il	est	**tombé**	he/it fell, he/it has fallen
elle	est	**tombée**	she/it fell, she/it has fallen
on	est	**tombé** *(singular)* **tombés** *(masculine plural)* **tombées** *(feminine plural)*	one fell/one has fallen, we fell/we have fallen
nous	sommes	**tombés** *(masculine)* **tombées** *(feminine)*	we fell/we have fallen
vous	êtes	**tombé** *(masculine singular)* **tombée** *(feminine singular)* **tombés** *(masculine plural)* **tombées** *(feminine plural)*	you fell/you have fallen
ils	sont	**tombés**	they fell/they have fallen
elles	sont	**tombées**	they fell/they have fallen

Grammar Extra!

When **on** means *we*, the past participle can agree with the subject of the sentence, but it is optional.

On est <u>arrivés</u> en retard.	We arrived late. *(masculine)*
On est <u>rentrées</u> toutes les deux à la même heure.	We both came in at the same time. *(feminine)*

➤ The perfect tense of **-ir** verbs like **partir** is formed in the same way, except for the past participle: **je suis parti(e)**, **tu es parti(e)** and so on.

➤ The perfect tense of **-re** verbs like **descendre** is formed in the same way, except for the past participle: **je suis descendu(e)**, **tu es descendu(e)** and so on.

Grammar Extra!

When a verb takes **avoir**, the past participle usually stays in the masculine singular form, as shown in the table for **donner**, and does not change for the feminine or plural forms.

Il a fini sa dissertation.	He's finished his essay.
Elles ont fini leur dissertation.	They've finished their essay.

In one particular case, however, the past participle of verbs with **avoir** does change in the feminine and plural forms. In the sentences above, **dissertation** is the direct object of the verb **finir.** When the direct object comes AFTER the verb, as it does in the examples above, then the past participle doesn't change. If the direct object comes BEFORE the verb, however, the past participle has to change to agree with that direct object.

la dissertation qu'il a finie hier	the essay that he finished yesterday
la dissertation qu'elles ont finie hier	the essay that they finished yesterday

Since object pronouns usually come BEFORE the verb, the past participle changes to agree with the pronoun.

Il a bu son thé? – Oui, il l'a bu.	Did he drink his tea? – Yes, he's drunk it.
Il a bu sa limonade? – Oui, il l'a bue.	Did he drink his lemonade? – Yes, he's drunk it.

Tip

Remember that with verbs taking **être**, it is the subject of the verb that tells you what ending to add to the past participle. Compare this with the rule for verbs taking **avoir** that have a direct object; in their case, it is the direct object coming before the verb that tells you what ending to add to the past participle.

7 The perfect tense of reflexive verbs

➤ Here is the perfect tense of the reflexive verb **se laver** (meaning *to wash (oneself), to have a wash, to get washed*) in full. Remember that all reflexive verbs take **être**, and so the past participle of reflexive verbs usually agrees with the subject of the sentence.

Subject pronoun	Reflexive pronoun	Present tense of être	Past participle	Meaning
je	**me**	**suis**	**lavé** (*masculine*) **lavée** (*feminine*)	I washed myself
tu	**t'**	**es**	**lavé** (*masculine*) **lavée** (*feminine*)	you washed yourself
il	**s'**	**est**	**lavé**	he washed himself one washed oneself
elle	**s'**	**est**	**lavée**	she washed herself
on	**s'**	**est**	**lavé** (*singular*) **lavés** (*masculine plural*) **lavées** (*feminine plural*)	one washed oneself we washed ourselves
nous	**nous**	**sommes**	**lavés** (*masculine*) **lavées** (*feminine*)	we washed ourselves
vous	**vous**	**êtes**	**lavé** (*masculine singular*) **lavée** (*feminine singular*) **lavés** (*masculine plural*) **lavées** (*feminine plural*)	you washed yourself (*singular*) you washed yourselves (*plural*)
ils	**se**	**sont**	**lavés**	they washed themselves
elles	**se**	**sont**	**lavées**	they washed themselves

Tip

When **on** means *we*, the past participle can agree with the subject of the sentence, but it is optional.

On s'est <u>lavées</u> l'une après l'autre. — We washed ourselves one after the other. (*feminine*)

Grammar Extra!

The past participle of reflexive verbs DOES NOT change if the direct object (**la jambe** in the example below) FOLLOWS the verb.

Elle s'est cassé la jambe. — She's broken her leg.

8 Irregular verbs in the perfect tense

➤ Some past participles are irregular. There aren't too many, so try to learn them.

- **avoir** (meaning *to have*) → **eu**
- **devoir** (meaning *to have to, must*) → **dû**
- **dire** (meaning *to say, to tell*) → **dit**
- **être** (meaning *to be*) → **été**
- **faire** (meaning *to do, to make*) → **fait**
- **mettre** (meaning *to put*) → **mis**
- **pouvoir** (meaning *to be able to, can*) → **pu**
- **prendre** (meaning *to take*) → **pris**
- **savoir** (meaning *to know*) → **su**
- **tenir** (meaning *to hold*) → **tenu**
- **venir** (meaning *to come*) → **venu**
- **voir** (meaning *to see*) → **vu**
- **vouloir** (meaning *to want*) → **voulu**

➤ **il pleut** becomes **il a plu** (*it rained*).

➤ **il faut** becomes **il a fallu** (*it was necessary*).

Key points

✔ The perfect tense describes things that happened and were completed in the past. It is not used for things that happened regularly or in descriptions.

✔ The perfect tense is formed with the present tense of **avoir** or **être** and a past participle.

✔ Most verbs take **avoir** in the perfect tense. All reflexive verbs and a small group of verbs referring to movement or change take **être**.

✔ The past participle ends in **-é** for **-er** verbs, in **-i** for **-ir** verbs, and in **-u** for **-re** verbs.

✔ With verbs that take **avoir**, the past participle does not usually change. With verbs that take **être**, including reflexive verbs, the past participle changes in the feminine and plural.

The pluperfect tense

What is the pluperfect tense?
The **pluperfect** is a verb tense which describes something that had happened or had been true at a point in the past, for example, *I'd forgotten to finish my homework*.

1 Using the pluperfect tense

➤ You can often recognize a pluperfect tense in English by a form like *I had arrived*, *you'd fallen*.

Elle avait essayé des dizaines de pulls.	She had tried on dozens of jumpers.
Nous avions déjà commencé à manger quand il est arrivé.	We'd already started eating when he arrived.
J'étais arrivée la première.	I had arrived first.
Mes parents s'étaient couchés tôt.	My parents had gone to bed early.

2 Forming the pluperfect tense

➤ Like the perfect tense, the pluperfect tense in French has two parts to it:

- the imperfect tense of the verb **avoir** (meaning *to have*) or **être** (meaning *to be*)
- the past participle

➤ If a verb takes **avoir** in the perfect tense, then it will take **avoir** in the pluperfect too. If a verb takes **être** in the perfect, then it will take **être** in the pluperfect too.

➪ *For more information on the* ***Imperfect tense*** *and the* ***Perfect tense****, see pages 92 and 111.*

3 Verbs taking avoir

➤ Here are the pluperfect tense forms of **donner** (meaning *to give*) in full.

Pronoun	avoir	Past participle	Meaning
j'	**avais**	**donné**	I had given
tu	**avais**	**donné**	you had given
il **elle** **on**	**avait**	**donné**	he/she/it/one had given
nous	**avions**	**donné**	we had given
vous	**aviez**	**donné**	you had given
ils **elles**	**avaient**	**donné**	they had given

➤ The pluperfect tense of **-ir** verbs like **finir** (meaning *to finish*) is formed in the same way, except for the past participle: **j'avais fini**, **tu avais fini** and so on.

➤ The pluperfect tense of **-re** verbs like **attendre** (meaning *to wait*) is formed in the same way, except for the past participle: **j'avais attendu**, **tu avais attendu** and so on.

4 Verbs taking être

➤ Here are the pluperfect tense forms of **tomber** (meaning *to fall*) in full. When a verb takes **être** in the pluperfect tense, the past participle always agrees with the subject of the verb; that is, the endings change in the feminine and plural forms.

Pronoun	être	Past participle	Meaning
j'	étais	**tombé** (*masculine*) **tombée** (*feminine*)	I had fallen
tu	étais	**tombé** (*masculine*) **tombée** (*feminine*)	you had fallen
il	était	tombé	he/it had fallen
elle	était	tombée	she/it had fallen
on	était	**tombé** (*singular*) **tombés** (*masculine plural*) **tombées** (*feminine plural*)	one had fallen we had fallen
nous	étions	**tombés** (*masculine*) **tombées** (*feminine*)	we had fallen
vous	étiez	**tombé** (*masculine singular*) **tombée** (*feminine singular*) **tombés** (*masculine plural*) **tombées** (*feminine plural*)	you had fallen
ils	étaient	tombés	they had fallen
elles	étaient	tombées	they had fallen

➤ The pluperfect tense of **-ir** verbs like **partir** (meaning *to leave*, *to go*) is formed in the same way, except for the past participle: **j'étais parti(e)**, **tu étais parti(e)** and so on.

➤ The pluperfect tense of **-re** verbs like **descendre** (meaning *to come down*, *to go down*, *to get off*) is formed in the same way, except for the past participle: **j'étais descendu(e)**, **tu étais descendu(e)** and so on.

Tip

When **on** means *we*, the past participle can agree with the subject of the sentence, but it is optional.

On était tombées. — We had fallen. (*feminine*)

5 Reflexive verbs in the pluperfect tense

➤ Reflexive verbs in the pluperfect tense are formed in the same way as in the perfect tense, but with the imperfect tense of the verb **être** (*see page 97*).

➪ *For more information on the **Perfect tense of reflexive verbs**, see page 117.*

6 Irregular verbs in the pluperfect tense

➤ Irregular past participles are the same as for the perfect tense (*see page 118*).

Key points

✔ The pluperfect tense describes things that had happened or were true at a point in the past before something else happened.

✔ It is formed with the imperfect tense of **avoir** or **être** and the past participle.

✔ The rules for agreement of the past participle are the same as for the perfect tense.

The passive

What is the passive?
The **passive** is a form of the verb that is used when the subject of the verb is the person or thing that is affected by the action, for example, *I was given, we were told, it had been made.*

1 Using the passive

➤ In a normal, or *active* sentence, the 'subject' of the verb is the person or thing that carries out the action described by the verb. The 'object' of the verb is the person or thing that the verb 'happens' to.

Ryan *(subject)* hit *(active verb)* me *(object)*.

➤ In English, as in French, you can turn an active sentence round to make a passive sentence.

I *(subject)* was hit *(passive verb)* by Ryan *(agent)*.

➤ Very often, however, you cannot identify who is carrying out the action indicated by the verb.

I was hit in the face.
The trees will be chopped down.
I've been chosen to represent the school.

Tip

There is a very important difference between French and English in sentences containing an indirect object. In English we can quite easily turn a normal (active) sentence with an indirect object into a passive sentence.

Active

Someone *(subject)* gave *(active verb)* me *(indirect object)* a book *(direct object)*.

Passive

I *(subject)* was given *(passive verb)* a book *(direct object)*.

In French, an indirect object can NEVER become the subject of a passive verb.

➪ *For more information on* ***Direct*** *and* ***Indirect objects****, see pages 47 and 49.*

2 Forming the passive

➤ In English we use the verb *to be* with the past participle (*was hit*, *was given*) to form the passive. In French the passive is formed in exactly the same way, using **être** and the past participle. The past participle agrees with the subject of the passive verb; that is, the endings change in the feminine and plural forms.

Elle est encouragée par ses parents.	She is encouraged by her parents.
Vous êtes tous bien payés.	You are all well paid. (*'you' refers to more than one person here*)
Les portes ont été fermées.	The doors have been closed.

➪ *For more information on the* ***Past participle****, see page 111.*

➤ Here is the present tense of the **-er** verb **aimer** (meaning *to like, to love*) in its passive form.

Pronoun	Present tense of être	Past participle	Meaning
je	**suis**	**aimé** (*masculine*) **aimée** (*feminine*)	I am loved
tu	**es**	**aimé** (*masculine*) **aimée** (*feminine*)	you are loved
il	**est**	**aimé**	he/it is loved
elle	**est**	**aimée**	she/it is loved
on	**est**	**aimé** (*singular*) **aimés** (*masculine plural*) **aimées** (*feminine plural*)	one is loved we are loved
nous	**sommes**	**aimés** (*masculine*) **aimées** (*feminine*)	we are loved
vous	**êtes**	**aimé** (*masculine singular*) **aimée** (*feminine singular*) **aimés** (*masculine plural*) **aimées** (*feminine plural*)	you are loved
ils	**sont**	**aimés**	they are loved
elles	**sont**	**aimées**	they are loved

➤ The passive of **-ir** verbs is formed in the same way, except that the past participle is different. For example, **elle est remplie** (meaning *it is full*).

➤ The passive of **-re** verbs is formed in the same way, except that the past participle is different. For example, **il est défendu** (meaning *it is forbidden*).

Grammar Extra!

When **on** means *we*, the past participle can agree with the subject of the sentence, but it is optional.

On est <u>aimés</u> de tout le monde. We're loved by everyone. (*masculine*)

➤ You can form other tenses of the passive by changing the tense of the verb **être**.

Imperfect: **j'étais aimé(e)** I was loved
Future: **tu seras aimé(e)** you will be loved
Perfect: **il a été aimé** he has been loved

⇨ *For more information on the **Imperfect**, **future** and **perfect tenses**, see pages 92, 98 and 111.*

➤ Irregular past participles are the same as for the perfect tense (*see page 118*).

3 <u>Avoiding the passive</u>

➤ Passives are not as common in French as in English. There are <u>two</u> main ways that French speakers express the same idea.

- by using the pronoun **on** (meaning *someone* or *they*) with a normal, active verb

<u>On</u> leur a envoyé une lettre.	They were sent a letter. (*literally*: *Someone sent them a letter*.)
<u>On</u> m'a dit que tu ne venais pas.	I was told that you weren't coming. (*literally*: *They told me you weren't coming*.)

⇨ *For more information on **Pronouns**, see page 42.*

- by using a reflexive verb

Les melons <u>se vendent</u> 2 euros la pièce.	Melons are sold for 2 euros each.

⇨ *For more information on **Reflexive verbs**, see page 88.*

Key points

✔ The present tense of the passive is formed by using the present tense of **être** with the past participle.

✔ The past participle always agrees with the <u>subject</u> of the passive verb.

✔ You can sometimes avoid a passive construction by using a reflexive verb or the pronoun **on**.

The present participle

What is a present participle?
The **present participle** is a verb form ending in *-ing* which is used in English to form verb tenses, and which may be used as an adjective and a noun, for example, *What are you doing?; the setting sun; Swimming is easy!*

1 Using the present participle

➤ Present participles are not as common in French as in English, because they are not used to form tenses. The main uses of the present participle in French are:

- as a verb, on its own, corresponding to the English *-ing* form. It DOES NOT agree with the subject of the verb when it is used in this way.

Habitant près de Paris, je vais assez souvent en ville.	Living close to Paris, I go into town quite often.
les voyageurs descendant à Périgueux	travellers getting off at Périgueux

- as a verb, after the preposition **en**. The present participle DOES NOT agree with the subject of the verb when it is used in this way. The subject of the two parts of the sentence is always the same. **en** can be translated in a number of different ways.

En attendant sa sœur, Richard s'est endormi.	While waiting for his sister, Richard fell asleep.
Appelle-nous en arrivant chez toi.	Call us when you get home.
En appuyant sur ce bouton, on peut imprimer ses documents.	By pressing this button, you can print your documents.
Il s'est blessé en essayant de sauver un chat.	He hurt himself trying to rescue a cat.

➪ *For more information on the preposition* ***en****, see page 168.*

- as an adjective, like in English. As with all adjectives in French, the ending DOES change in the feminine and plural forms.

le soleil couchant	the setting sun
l'année suivante	the following year
Ces enfants sont énervants.	Those children are annoying.
des chaises pliantes	folding chairs

Tip

The French present participle is NEVER used to translate English verb forms like *I was walking*, *we are leaving*.

⇨ *For more information on the* ***Imperfect tense*** *and the* ***Present tense****, see pages 92 and 71.*

➤ English verbs describing movement that are followed by an adverb such as *out* or *down*, or a preposition such as *across* or *up* are often translated by a verb + **en** + present participle.

Il est sorti en courant.	He ran out. (*literally*: *He came out running*.)
J'ai traversé la rue en boîtant.	I limped across the street. (*literally*: *I crossed the street limping*.)

2 Forming the present participle

➤ To form the present participle of regular **-er**, **-ir** and **-re** verbs, you use the **nous** form of the present tense and replace the **-ons** ending with **-ant**.

nous form of present tense	**Take off -ons**	**Add -ant**
donnons	**donn-**	**donnant**
lançons	**lanç-**	**lançant**
mangeons	**mange-**	**mangeant**
finissons	**finiss-**	**finissant**
partons	**part-**	**partant**
attendons	**attend-**	**attendant**
descendons	**descend-**	**descendant**

3 Irregular verbs

➤ Three verbs have an irregular present participle:

avoir (meaning *to have*) → **ayant**
être (meaning *to be*) → **étant**
savoir (meaning *to know*) → **sachant**

Key points

✔ Present participles are never used to form tenses in French, but they can be used as verbs, either on their own or after **en**.

✔ They can also be used as adjectives, in which case they agree with the noun they describe.

✔ They are formed by taking the **nous** form of the present tense and replacing the **-ons** ending with **-ant**. The exceptions are **avoir, être** and **savoir**.

Impersonal verbs

What is an impersonal verb?
An **impersonal verb** is one that does not refer to a real person or thing and where the subject is represented by *it*, for example, *It's going to rain; It's ten o'clock.*

➤ Impersonal verbs are only used with **il** (meaning *it*) and in the infinitive. They are called impersonal verbs because **il** does not really refer to a real person, animal or thing, just like *it* and *there* in English in the examples below.

Il pleut.	It's raining.
Il va pleuvoir.	It's going to rain.
Il y a un problème.	There's a problem.
Il pourrait y avoir un problème.	There could be a problem.

➤ There are also some very common verbs that can be used in this way in addition to their normal meanings, for example, **avoir**, **être** and **faire**.

Infinitive	Expression	Meaning
avoir + noun	**il y a**	there is (*singular*) there are (*plural*)
être + time	**il est**	it is
faire + noun	**il fait jour** **il fait nuit**	it's daylight it's dark
falloir + noun	**il faut**	we/you *etc*. need it takes
falloir + infinitive	**il faut**	we/you *etc*. have to
manquer	**il manque**	there is ... missing (*singular*) there are ... missing (*plural*)
paraître	**il paraît que**	it appears that it seems that
rester + noun	**il reste**	there is ... left (*singular*) there are ... left (*plural*)
sembler	**il semble que**	it appears that it seems that
valoir mieux + infinitive	**il vaut mieux**	it would be better to

Il y a quelqu'un à la porte.	There's somebody at the door.
Il est deux heures.	It's two o'clock.
Il faut partir.	I've/We've *etc*. got to go.
Il manque cent euros.	100 euros are missing.
Il reste du pain.	There's some bread left.
Il vaut mieux ne rien dire.	It would be better to say nothing.

➤ Several impersonal verbs relate to the weather.

Infinitive	Expression	Meaning
faire + adjective	**il fait beau** **il fait mauvais**	the weather's lovely the weather's bad
faire + noun	**il fait du vent** **il fait du soleil**	it's windy it's sunny
geler	**il gèle**	it's freezing
neiger	**il neige**	it's snowing
pleuvoir	**il pleut**	it's raining

Grammar Extra!

There is another group of useful expressions that start with an impersonal **il**. These are followed by a form of the verb called the subjunctive.

il faut que
Il faut que je parte. — I've got to go.

il est nécessaire que
Il est nécessaire que le comité prenne une décision rapidement. — The committee has to take a decision quickly.

il est possible que
Il est possible qu'il vienne. — He might come.

il est dommage que
Il est dommage que tu ne l'aies pas vu. — It's a shame you didn't see him.

➪ *For more information on the* ***Subjunctive****, see page 129.*

Key points

✔ Impersonal verbs can only be used in the infinitive and the **il** form.

✔ **il faut**, **il y a**, **il est** and **il fait** with expressions relating to the weather are very common.

The subjunctive

What is the subjunctive?
The **subjunctive** is a verb form that is used in certain circumstances to express some sort of feeling, or to show there is doubt about whether something will happen or whether something is true. It is only used occasionally in modern English, for example, *If I were you, I wouldn't bother.; So be it.*

1 Using the subjunctive

➤ In French the subjunctive is used after certain verbs and conjunctions when two parts of a sentence have different subjects.

I'm afraid he won't come back.
(The subject of the first part of the sentence is 'I'; the subject of the second part of the sentence is 'he'.)

➤ Sometimes, in a sentence like *We want her to be happy*, you use the infinitive of the verb in English (*to be*). This is NOT possible in French when there is a different subject in the two parts of the sentence (*we* and *her*). You have to use a subjunctive for the second verb.

Nous voulons être heureux. We want to be happy.
(No change of subject, so you can just use an infinitive – ***être*** *– in French.)*

Nous voulons qu'elle soit heureuse. We want her to be happy.
(Subject changes from ***nous*** *to* ***elle****, so you have to use a subjunctive –* ***soit*** *– in French.)*

➤ You can only use the infinitive instead of the subjunctive in French with impersonal verbs.

Il faut que tu viennes à l'heure. *(using subjunctive)* → **Il faut venir à l'heure.** *(using infinitive)*
You have to come on time.

Il vaut mieux que tu restes chez toi. *(using subjunctive)* → **Il vaut mieux rester chez toi.** *(using infinitive)*
It's better that you stay at home.

2 Coming across the subjunctive

➤ The subjunctive has several tenses but you are only likely to come across the present subjunctive.

➤ You may see a subjunctive after certain verbs that you use when you are:

- wishing something: **vouloir que** and **désirer que** (meaning *to wish that, to want*), **aimer que** (meaning *to like that*), **aimer mieux que** and **préférer que** (meaning *to prefer that*)
- fearing something: **avoir peur que** (meaning *to be afraid that*)
- giving your opinion: **croire que** (meaning *to think that*)

- saying how you feel: **regretter que** (meaning *to be sorry that*), **être content que** (meaning *to be pleased that*), **être surpris que** (meaning *to be surprised that*) and so on

  Je suis content que vous les aimiez. — I'm pleased you like them.
  J'ai peur qu'il ne revienne pas. — I'm afraid he won't come back.

➤ You may see a subjunctive after certain verbal expressions starting with **il**, such as **il faut que** (meaning *it is necessary that*) and **il vaut mieux que** (meaning *it is better that*).

Il faut que je vous parle. — I need to speak to you.

➪ *For a list of some expressions requiring the subjunctive, see page 128.*

3 Forming the present subjunctive of -er verbs

➤ To form the stem of the present subjunctive you take the infinitive and chop off **-er**, just as for the present tense. Then you add the correct ending, depending on whether you are referring to **je, tu, il, elle, on, nous, vous, ils** or **elles.**

➤ For **-er** verbs the endings are the same as for the ordinary present tense, apart from the **nous** and **vous** forms, which have an extra **i**, as in the imperfect tense.

Pronoun	Ending	Add to stem, e.g. donn-	Meanings
je (j')	**-e**	**je donne**	I give
tu	**-es**	**tu donnes**	you give
il **elle** **on**	**-e**	**il donne** **elle donne** **on donne**	he/she/it/one gives
nous	**-ions**	**nous donnions**	we give
vous	**-iez**	**vous donniez**	you give
ils **elles**	**-ent**	**ils donnent** **elles donnent**	they give

> ***Tip***
> **je** changes to **j'** in front of a word starting with a vowel, most words starting with **h**, and the French word **y**.

4 Forming the present subjunctive of -ir verbs

➤ To form the stem of the present subjunctive you take the infinitive and chop off **-ir**, just as for the present tense. Then you add the correct ending, depending on whether you are referring to to **je, tu, il, elle, on, nous, vous, ils** or **elles.**

Pronoun	Ending	Add to stem, e.g. fin-	Meanings
je (j')	-isse	je finisse	I finish
tu	-isses	tu finisses	you finish
il elle on	-isse	il finisse elle finisse on finisse	he/she/it/one finishes
nous	-issions	nous finissions	we finish
vous	-issiez	vous finissiez	you finish
ils elles	-issent	ils finissent elles finissent	they finish

Tip

je changes to **j'** in front of a word starting with a vowel, most words starting with **h**, and the French word **y**.

5 Forming the present subjunctive of -re verbs

➤ To form the stem of the present subjunctive you take the infinitive and chop off **-re**, just as for the present tense. Then you add the correct ending, depending on whether you are referring to **je, tu, il, elle, on, nous, vous, ils** or **elles.**

Pronoun	Ending	Add to stem, e.g. attend-	Meanings
je (j')	-e	j'attende	I wait
tu	-es	tu attendes	you wait
il elle on	-e	il attende elle attende on attende	he/she/it/one waits
nous	-ions	nous attendions	we wait
vous	-iez	vous attendiez	you wait
ils elles	-ent	ils attendent elles attendent	they wait

Tip

je changes to **j'** in front of a word starting with a vowel, most words starting with **h**, and the French word **y**.

6 Irregular verbs in the subjunctive

➤ Some important verbs have irregular subjunctive forms.

Verb	Meaning	je (j')	tu	il/elle/on	nous	vous	ils/elles
aller	*to go*	**aille**	**ailles**	**aille**	**allions**	**alliez**	**aillent**
avoir	*to have*	**aie**	**aies**	**ait**	**ayons**	**ayez**	**aient**
devoir	*to have to, must*	**doive**	**doives**	**doive**	**devions**	**deviez**	**doivent**
dire	*to say, to tell*	**dise**	**dises**	**dise**	**disions**	**disiez**	**disent**
être	*to be*	**sois**	**sois**	**soit**	**soyons**	**soyez**	**soient**
faire	*to do, to make*	**fasse**	**fasses**	**fasse**	**fassions**	**fassiez**	**fassent**
pouvoir	*to be able to, can*	**puisse**	**puisses**	**puisse**	**puissions**	**puissiez**	**puissent**
prendre	*to take*	**prenne**	**prennes**	**prenne**	**prenions**	**preniez**	**prennent**
(**apprendre** and **comprendre** also behave like this – **j'apprenne, tu apprennes** and so on)							
savoir	*to know*	**sache**	**saches**	**sache**	**sachions**	**sachiez**	**sachent**
venir	*to come*	**vienne**	**viennes**	**vienne**	**venions**	**veniez**	**viennent**
vouloir	*to want to*	**veuille**	**veuilles**	**veuille**	**voulions**	**vouliez**	**veuillent**

Key points

✔ After certain verbs you have to use a subjunctive in French when there is a different subject in the two clauses. These verbs mostly relate to wishing, fearing, and saying what you think, what you feel and that you are uncertain. A subjunctive is also found after certain verbal expressions that start with **il**.

✔ The stem of the present tense subjunctive is the same as the stem used for the ordinary present tense.

✔ The present tense subjunctive endings for **-er** and **-re** verbs are: **-e**, **-es**, **-e**, **-ions**, **-iez** and **-ent**.

✔ The present tense subjunctive endings for **-ir** verbs are: **-isse**, **-isses**, **-isse**, **-issions**, **-issiez** and **-issent**.

Verbs followed by an infinitive

1 Linking two verbs together

➤ Many verbs in French can be followed by another verb in the infinitive. The infinitive is the form of the verb that is found in the dictionary, such as **donner** (meaning *to give*), **finir** (meaning *to finish*) and **attendre** (meaning *to wait*).

➤ There are three main ways that verbs can be linked together:

- with no linking word

  Vous voulez attendre? — Would you like to wait?
- with the preposition **à**

  J'apprends à nager. — I'm learning to swim.
- with the preposition **de**

  Essayez de venir. — Try to come.

⇨ *For more information on* ***Prepositions after adjectives****, and on* ***Prepositions after verbs****, see pages 183 and 178.*

2 Verbs followed by an infinitive with no preposition

➤ A number of verbs and groups of verbs can be followed by an infinitive with no preposition. The following important group of verbs are all very irregular, but they crop up so frequently that they are worth learning in full:

- **devoir** (*to have to, must, to be due to*)

  Tu dois être fatiguée. — You must be tired.

  Elle doit partir. — She has to leave.

  Le nouveau centre commercial doit ouvrir en mai. — The new shopping centre is due to open in May.
- **pouvoir** (*can, may*)

  Je peux t'aider, si tu veux. — I can help you, if you like.

  Puis-je venir vous voir samedi? — May I come and see you on Saturday?
- **savoir** (*to know how to, can*)

  Tu sais conduire? — Can you drive?

  Je sais faire les omelettes. — I know how to make omelettes.
- **vouloir** (*to want*)

  Élise veut rester un jour de plus. — Élise wants to stay one more day.

  Ma voiture ne veut pas démarrer. — My car won't start.

  Voulez-vous boire quelque chose? — Would you like something to drink?

  Je voudrais acheter un ordinateur. — I'd like to buy a computer.

➤ **falloir** (meaning *to be necessary*) and **valoir mieux** (meaning *to be better*) are only used in the infinitive and with **il**.

Il faut prendre une décision.	We/you *etc*. have to make a decision.
Il vaut mieux téléphoner avant.	It's better to ring first.

➪ *For more information on* ***Impersonal verbs****, see page 127.*

➤ The following common verbs can also be followed by an infinitive without a preposition:

adorer	to love
aimer	to like, to love
aimer mieux	to prefer
désirer	to want
détester	to hate
envoyer	to send
espérer	to hope
faire	to make
laisser	to let
préférer	to prefer
sembler	to seem

J'espère te voir la semaine prochaine.	I hope to see you next week.
Ne me fais pas rire!	Don't make me laugh!
Je préfère manger à la cantine.	I prefer to eat in the canteen.

➤ Some of these verbs combine with infinitives to make set phrases with a special meaning.

aller chercher quelque chose	to go and get something
laisser tomber quelque chose	to drop something
vouloir dire quelque chose	to mean something

Va chercher ton papa!	Go and get your dad!
Paul a laissé tomber le vase.	Paul dropped the vase.
Qu'est-ce que ça veut dire?	What does that mean?

➤ Verbs that relate to seeing or hearing, such as **voir** (meaning *to see*), **regarder** (meaning *to watch, to look at*), **écouter** (meaning *to listen to*) and **entendre** (meaning *to hear*) can be followed by an infinitive.

Il nous a vus arriver.	He saw us arrive.
On entend chanter les oiseaux.	You can hear the birds singing.

➤ Verbs that relate to movement of some kind and do not have a direct object, such as **aller** (meaning *to go*) and **venir** (meaning *to come*), can be followed by an infinitive.

Je <u>vais voir</u> Nicolas ce soir.	I'm going to see Nicolas tonight.
<u>Viens voir</u>!	Come and see!

3 Verbs followed by <u>à</u> + infinitive

➤ There are some common verbs that can be followed by **à** and an infinitive.

s'amuser <u>à</u> faire quelque chose	to have fun doing something
apprendre <u>à</u> faire quelque chose	to learn to do something
commencer <u>à</u> faire quelque chose	to begin to do something
continuer <u>à</u> faire quelque chose	to go on doing something
s'habituer <u>à</u> faire quelque chose	to get used to doing something

J'apprends <u>à</u> skier.	I'm learning to ski.
Il a commencé <u>à</u> pleuvoir.	It began to rain.

➤ Some verbs can be followed by a person's name or by a noun relating to a person, and then by **à** and an infinitive. Sometimes you need to put **à** in front of the person too.

aider quelqu'un <u>à</u> faire quelque chose	to help someone do something
apprendre <u>à</u> quelqu'un <u>à</u> faire quelque chose	to teach someone to do something
inviter quelqu'un <u>à</u> faire quelque chose	to invite someone to do something

4 Verbs followed by <u>de</u> + infinitive

➤ There are some common verbs that can be followed by **de** and an infinitive.

arrêter <u>de</u> faire quelque chose, s'arrêter <u>de</u> faire quelque chose	to stop doing something
continuer <u>de</u> faire quelque chose	to go on doing something
décider <u>de</u> faire quelque chose	to decide to do something
se dépêcher <u>de</u> faire quelque chose	to hurry to do something
essayer <u>de</u> faire quelque chose	to try to do something
s'excuser <u>de</u> faire quelque chose	to apologize for doing something
finir <u>de</u> faire quelque chose	to finish doing something
oublier <u>de</u> faire quelque chose	to forget to do something
proposer <u>de</u> faire quelque chose	to suggest doing something
refuser <u>de</u> faire quelque chose	to refuse to do something
suggérer <u>de</u> faire quelque chose	to suggest doing something

J'ai décidé de lui écrire.	I decided to write to her.
Je leur ai suggéré de partir de bonne heure.	I suggested that they set off early.

➤ The following verbs meaning asking or telling are also followed by **de** and an infinitive. Sometimes you need to put **à** in front of the person you are asking or telling.

commander à quelqu'un de faire quelque chose	to order someone to do something
demander à quelqu'un de faire quelque chose	to ask someone to do something
dire à quelqu'un de faire quelque chose	to tell someone to do something
empêcher quelqu'un de faire quelque chose	to prevent someone from doing something
interdire à quelqu'un de faire quelque chose	to forbid someone to do something
remercier quelqu'un de faire quelque chose	to thank someone for doing something

Grammar Extra!

If it is important to emphasize that something is going on at a particular time, you can use the phrase **être en train de faire quelque chose**.

Il est en train de travailler. Est-ce que vous pouvez rappeler plus tard?	He's working. Can you call back later?

If you want to say you have just done something, you can use the phrase **venir de faire quelque chose**. In English you use the PAST tense, but in French you use the PRESENT tense.

Élisabeth vient de partir. Élisabeth has just left.

Key points

✔ Many French verbs can be followed by another verb in the infinitive.

✔ The two verbs may be linked by nothing at all, or by the preposition **à** or **de**.

✔ The construction in French does not always match the English exactly. It's best to learn these constructions when you learn a new verb.

Other uses of the infinitive

➤ The infinitive can be used in many other ways:

- after certain adjectives

  content de happy to
  prêt à ready to

  Il est toujours prêt à rendre service. He's always ready to help.

- after certain prepositions

  Pour aller à la gare? How do you get to the station?
  Il est parti sans dire au revoir. He left without saying goodbye.

- after certain set phrases involving a verb plus a noun

  avoir envie de faire quelque chose to feel like doing something
  avoir besoin de faire quelque chose to need to do something
  avoir peur de faire quelque chose to be frightened of doing something

  J'ai besoin de changer de l'argent. I need to change some money.

- in instructions that are aimed at the general public – for example, on signs or in cookery books

  Ajouter le sel et le poivre, et bien mélanger. Add the salt and pepper, and mix well.
  Conserver au frais. Keep refrigerated.

- as the subject or object of a sentence, when the infinitive corresponds to the *-ing* form in English used as a noun

  Fumer n'est pas bon pour la santé. Smoking isn't good for your health.
  J'adore lire. I love reading.

Tip

You can use the verb **faire** with an infinitive to refer to something you are having done by someone else.

Je dois faire réparer ma voiture. I have to get my car repaired.

Key points

✔ Infinitives are found after certain adjectives, prepositions and set phrases, and in instructions to the general public.

✔ They can also function like nouns, as the subject or object of another verb.

Negatives

What is a negative?
A **negative** question or statement is one which contains a word such as *not*, *no*, *never* or *nothing* and is used to say that something is not happening, is not true or is absent.

1 Using negatives

➤ In English we use words like *not*, *no*, *nothing* and *never* to show a negative.

I'm not very pleased.
Dan never rang me.
Nothing ever happens here!
There's no milk left.

➤ *Not* is often combined with certain English verbs – for example, *can't*, *won't*, *didn't*, *hasn't*.

He isn't joking.
She didn't say.

➤ In French, if you want to make something negative, you generally use a pair of words, for example, **ne ... pas** (meaning *not*). The verb goes in the middle.

ne ... pas	not
ne ... rien	nothing, not ... anything
ne ... personne	nobody, no one, not ... anybody, not ... anyone
ne ... jamais	never, not ... ever
ne ... plus	no longer, no more, not ... any longer, not ... any more

Je ne fume pas.	I don't smoke.
Ne changez rien.	Don't change anything.
Je ne vois personne.	I can't see anybody.
Elle n'arrive jamais à l'heure.	She never arrives on time.
Il ne travaille plus ici.	He's no longer working here.

Tip

ne changes to **n'** in front of a word that starts with a vowel, most words beginning with **h** and the French word **y**.

For further explanation of grammatical terms, please see pages viii-xii.

➤ In English, *did* is often used to make a statement negative.

I went to his party. → I did<u>n't</u> go to his party.

We saw David at the weekend. → We did<u>n't</u> see David at the weekend.

ℹ Note that the French verb **faire** is <u>NEVER</u> used in this way.

➤ **non plus** is the equivalent of English *neither* in phrases like *me neither*, *neither do I* and so on.

'Je n'aime pas les hamburgers.' – 'Moi <u>non plus</u>.'	'I don't like hamburgers.' – 'Me neither.'
Il n'y va pas et moi <u>non plus</u>.	He isn't going and neither am I.

➤ The French word **ne** is missed out when negatives are used without a verb to answer a question.

'Qui a téléphoné?' – '<u>Personne</u>.'	'Who rang?' – 'Nobody.'
'Qu'est-ce que tu fais cet après-midi?' – '<u>Rien</u>.'	'What are you doing this afternoon?' – 'Nothing.'

Tip

In everyday conversation French native speakers often miss out the word **ne**. Be careful about doing this yourself in formal situations.

Je peux pas venir ce soir.	I can't come tonight.
Il me l'a pas dit.	He didn't tell me.

Grammar Extra!

Sometimes you will find two of these negative expressions combined.

Ils ne font jamais rien d'intéressant.	They never do anything interesting.
Je ne connais plus personne à Nice.	I don't know anyone in Nice any more.

2 Word order with negatives

➤ Negative expressions in French 'sandwich' the verb in the present tense and in other tenses that consist of just one word. **ne** goes before the verb and the other half of the expression comes after the verb.

Il <u>ne</u> boit <u>jamais</u> d'alcool.	He never drinks alcohol.
Il <u>ne</u> pleuvait <u>pas</u>.	It wasn't raining.

➤ In the perfect tense and other tenses that consist of two or more words such as the pluperfect, there are two possibilities:

- **ne ... pas**, **ne ... rien**, **ne ... plus** and **ne ... jamais** follow the pattern: **ne (n')** + **avoir** or **être** + **pas/rien/plus/jamais** + past participle

Elle n'a pas fait ses devoirs.	She hasn't done her homework.
Je n'ai rien dit.	I didn't say anything.
Pierre n'est pas encore arrivé.	Pierre isn't here yet.

- **ne ... personne** follows the pattern:
ne (n') + **avoir** + past participle + **personne**

Je n'ai vu personne.	I didn't see anybody.

➪ *For more information on the **Perfect tense**, see page 111.*

➤ A negative sentence may also contain a pronoun such as **te**, **le**, **lui** and so on that is the direct or indirect object of the verb, or a reflexive pronoun. If so, **ne** comes before the pronoun.

Je ne t'entends pas.	I can't hear you.
Ne lui parle pas!	Don't speak to him/her!
Tu ne te souviens pas de lui?	Don't you remember him?
Il ne se lève jamais avant midi.	He never gets up before midday.

➪ *For more information on **Direct** and **Indirect object pronouns** and on **Reflexive pronouns**, see pages 47, 49 and 89.*

➤ When a verb is in the infinitive, **ne ... pas**, **ne ... rien**, **ne ... plus** and **ne ... jamais** come together before the infinitive.

Il essayait de ne pas rire.	He was trying not to laugh.
J'ai peur de ne pas réussir.	I'm afraid of not succeeding.

Tip

After these negative expressions, **un**, **une** and **des** (the indefinite article) and **du**, **de la**, **de l'** and **des** (the partitive article) change to **de**.

Il ne reste plus de biscuits.	There aren't any biscuits left.

➪ *For more information on the **Indefinite article** and the **Partitive article**, see pages 19 and 22.*

3 non and pas

➤ **non** (meaning *no*) is the usual negative answer to a question. It can also correspond to *not* in English.

'Tu veux nous accompagner?' – '<u>Non</u>, merci.'	'Do you want to come with us?' – '<u>No</u> thanks.'
Tu viens ou <u>non</u>?	Are you coming or <u>not</u>?
J'espère que <u>non</u>.	I hope <u>not</u>.

➤ **pas** is generally used when a distinction is being made, or for emphasis. It, too, often corresponds to *not* in English.

'Qui veut m'aider?' – '<u>Pas</u> moi!'	'Who wants to help me?' – '<u>Not</u> me!'
'Est-il de retour?' – '<u>Pas</u> encore.'	'Is he back?' – '<u>Not</u> yet.'
'Tu as froid?' – '<u>Pas</u> du tout.'	'Are you cold?' – '<u>Not</u> at all.'
<u>Pas</u> question!	<u>No</u> way!

Key points

✔ Negatives indicate when something is not happening or is not true. French uses set expressions or word pairs to indicate this.

✔ The two parts of these negative expressions 'sandwich' the verb in tenses consisting of only one word.

✔ **ne** comes before any object pronouns or reflexive pronouns.

✔ Before infinitives, **ne ... pas, ne ... rien, ne ... plus** and **ne ... jamais** come together.

✔ The articles **un, une, des, du, de la** and **de l'** change to **de** after negatives.

Questions

What is a question?
A **question** is a sentence which is used to ask someone about something and which normally has the verb in front of the subject. A question word such as *why*, *where*, *who*, *which* or *how* is used to ask a question.

How to ask a question in French

1 The basic rules

➤ There are four ways of asking questions in French:
- by making your voice go up at the end of the sentence
- by using the phrase **est-ce que**
- by changing round the order of words in a sentence
- by using a question word

2 Asking a question by making your voice go up

➤ If you are expecting the answer *yes* or *no*, there is a very straightforward way of asking a question. You can keep word order just as it would be in a normal sentence (subject then verb), but turn it into a question by making your voice go up at the end of the sentence. So to turn the sentence **Vous aimez la France** (meaning *You like France)* into a question, all you need to do is to add a question mark and make your voice go up at the end.

Vous (*subject*) **aimez** (*verb*) **la France?**	Do you like France?
On part tout de suite.	We're leaving right away.
On part tout de suite?	Are we leaving right away?
C'est vrai.	That's true.
C'est vrai?	Is that true?
Tes parents sont en vacances.	Your parents on holiday.
Tes parents sont en vacances?	Are your parents on holiday?

Tip
French speakers use this way of asking a question in ordinary, everyday conversations.

For further explanation of grammatical terms, please see pages viii-xii.

3 Asking a question by using est-ce que

➤ The phrase **est-ce que** is used to ask a question. Word order stays just the same as it would in an ordinary sentence. **Est-ce que** comes before the subject, and the verb comes after the subject. So to turn the sentence **Tu connais Marie** (meaning *You know Marie*) into a question, all you need to do is to add **est-ce que**.

Est-ce que tu *(subject)* **connais** *(verb)* **Marie?**	Do you know Marie?
Est-ce que vous allez en ville?	Are you going into town?
Est-ce que ta sœur est vraiment heureuse?	Is your sister really happy?

4 Asking a question by changing word order

➤ In ordinary sentences, the verb comes AFTER its subject. In this type of question, the verb is put BEFORE the subject. This change to normal word order is called inversion. You can do this when the subject is a pronoun such as **vous** or **il**. When you change the word order (or invert) in this way, you add a hyphen (-) between the verb and the pronoun.

Vous *(subject)* **aimez** *(verb)* **la France.**	You like France.
Aimez *(verb)***-vous** *(subject)* **la France?**	Do you like France?
Il écrit bien.	He writes well.
Écrit-il bien?	Does he write well?
On part tout de suite.	We're leaving right away.
Partez-vous tout de suite?	Are you leaving right away?

➪ *For more information on* ***Pronouns****, see page 42.*

> ***Tip***
>
> This is quite a formal way of asking a question.

➤ In the perfect tense and other tenses that consist of two or more words such as the pluperfect, the part of the verb that comes from **avoir** or **être** is the one that goes before the pronoun.

As-tu vu mon sac?	Have you seen my bag?
Est-elle restée longtemps?	Did she stay long?

➪ *For more information on the* ***Perfect tense****, see page 111.*

➤ When the verb ends in a vowel in the **il/elle** form, **-t-** is inserted before the pronoun to make the words easier to say.

Aime-t-il les chiens?	Does he like dogs?
A-t-elle assez d'argent?	Does she have enough money?

Tip

Unlike English there are two ways in French of answering *yes* to a question or statement. **oui** is the word you use to reply to an ordinary question.

'Tu l'as fait?' – 'Oui.'	'Have you done it?' – 'Yes.'
'Elle est belle, n'est-ce pas?' – 'Oui.'	'She's beautiful, isn't she?' – 'Yes.'

si is the word you use to reply to a question or statement that contains a negative expression like **ne ... pas**.

'Tu ne l'as pas fait?' – 'Si.'	'Haven't you done it?' – 'Yes (I have).'
'Elle n'est pas très belle.' – 'Mais si!'	'She isn't very beautiful.' – 'Yes, she is!'

Grammar Extra!

You can also form a question in this way with a noun or a person's name. If you do this, the noun or name comes first, then you add an extra pronoun after the verb and link them with a hyphen.

Jean-Pierre *(subject)* **est**(*verb*)**-il** *(pronoun)* **là?**	Is Jean-Pierre there?
La pièce dure-t-elle longtemps?	Does the play last long?

In less formal French, the pronoun may come before the verb, and the noun or name may come at the end of the sentence.

Il est là, Jean-Pierre?	Is Jean-Pierre there?
Elle dure longtemps, la pièce?	Does the play last long?

5 Asking a question by using a question word

➤ A question word is a word like *when* or *how* that is used to ask for information. The most common French question words are listed on pages 146-150.

➤ You can use a question word with one of the methods described above:

- you can make your voice go up at the end of the sentence. If you do this, the question word goes at the END of the sentence.

- you can use **est-ce que**. If you do this, the question word goes at the START of the sentence.
- you can change word order so that the verb comes before the subject. If you do this, the question word goes at the START of the sentence.

Vous arrivez quand?	
Quand est-ce que vous arrivez?	When do you arrive?
Quand arrivez-vous?	
Tu prends quel train?	
Quel train est-ce que tu prends?	What train are you getting?
Quel train prends-tu?	
Ils vont où?	
Où est-ce qu'ils vont?	Where are they going?
Où vont-ils?	

➪ *For more information on **Negatives**, see page 138.*

Key points

✔ You ask a question in French by making your voice go up at the end of the sentence, by using **est-ce que**, by changing normal word order, or by using a question word.

✔ When you put the verb in front of the subject, you join the two words with a hyphen. A **-t-** is used in the **il/elle** form if the verb ends in a vowel.

✔ You use **oui** to answer *yes* to an ordinary question, but **si** if there is a negative in the question or statement.

Question words

1 Common question words

➤ Listed below are some very common question words. **que**, **quel**, **qui**, **quoi** and **lequel** are explained on pages 147–150.

- **combien** + *verb*? how much?, how many?
  combien de + *noun*? how much?, how many?

Combien coûte cet ordinateur?	How much does this computer cost?
C'est combien, ce pantalon?	How much are these trousers?
Tu en veux combien? Deux?	How many do you want? Two?
Combien de personnes vas-tu inviter?	How many people are you going to invite?

- **comment?** how?

Comment va-t-elle?	How is she?
Comment tu t'appelles?	What's your name?

> *Tip*
> **pardon** and **comment** are also used to ask someone to repeat something, and are the same as *Pardon?* in English. **quoi** can mean the same thing, but is informal, and is the same as *What?* in English.

- **où?** where?

Où allez-vous?	Where are you going?
D'où viens-tu?	Where are you from?

> *Tip*
> Be careful not to mix up **où**, which means *where*, and **ou** (without an accent), which means *or*.

- **pourquoi?** why?

Pourquoi est-ce qu'il ne vient pas avec nous?	Why isn't he coming with us?

- **quand?** when?

Quand est-ce que tu pars en vacances?	When are you going on holiday?
Depuis quand est-ce que vous le connaissez?	How long have you known him?

2 qui?, que? and quoi?

➤ In questions, **qui**, **que** and **quoi** are all pronouns. Which of them you choose depends on:

- whether you are referring to people or to things
- whether you are referring to the subject or object of the verb (the subject is the person or thing that is carrying out the action described by the verb; the object is the person or thing that 'receives' the action)
- whether the word you use will come after a preposition such as **à**, **de** or **en**

*For more information on **Pronouns** and **Prepositions**, see pages 42 and 62.*

➤ **qui?** and **que?** have longer forms, as shown in the table below. There is a difference in word order between the longer and shorter forms.

➤ **qui?** is used for talking about people, and means *who?* or *whom?* in English. You can use *whom?* in formal English to refer to the object of verb, though most people use *who?*. **qui?** can be used after a preposition.

Who? Whom?	Referring to people	Meaning	Examples	Meaning
Subject	**qui?** **qui est-ce qui?**	who?	**Qui vient?** **Qui est-ce qui vient?**	Who's coming?
Object	**qui?** **qui est-ce que?**	who? whom?	**Qui vois-tu?** **Qui est-ce que tu vois?**	Who/Whom can you see?
After prepositions	**qui?** **qui est-ce que?**	who? whom?	**De qui est-ce qu'il parle?** **Pour qui est ce livre?** **À qui avez-vous écrit?**	Who's he talking about? Who's this book for? Who did you write to?, To whom did you write?

> *Tip*
>
> **que** changes to **qu'** before a vowel, most words beginning with **h**, and the French word **y**.

*For more information on **que** and **qui**, see page 62.*

➤ **à qui** is the usual way of saying *whose* in questions.

À qui est ce sac? Whose is this bag?

➪ *For more information on using **à** to show possession, see page 165.*

➤ **que?** and **quoi?** are used for talking about things, and mean *what?* in English. **que?** cannot be used after a preposition; you have to use **quoi?** instead.

What?	Referring to things	Meaning	Examples	Meaning
Subject	**qu'est-ce qui?**	what?	**Qu'est-ce qui se passe?** **Qu'est-ce qui t'inquiète?**	What's happening? What's worrying you?
Object	**qu'est-ce que?** **que?**	what?	**Qu'est-ce que vous faites?** **Que faites-vous?**	What are you doing?
After prepositions	**quoi?**	what?	**À quoi penses-tu?** **De quoi parlez-vous?**	What are you thinking about? What are you talking about?

Tip

It is possible to finish an English sentence with a preposition such as *about* or *of*, even though some people think this is not good grammar.
Who did you write to?
What are you talking about?
It is NEVER possible to end a French sentence with a preposition.

3 quel?, quelle?, quels? and quelles?

➤ **quel?** (meaning *who?*, *which?* or *what?*) can be used with a noun (as an adjective) or can replace a noun (as a pronoun). Compare this with **que?** (and its longer forms) and **quoi?**, which also mean *what?*, but are NEVER used with nouns.

➪ *For more information on **Adjectives** and **Pronouns**, see pages 25 and 42.*

➤ **quel**, **quelle**, **quels** and **quelles** are all forms of the same word. The form that you choose depends on whether you are referring to something that is masculine or feminine, singular or plural.

	Masculine	Feminine	Meaning
Singular	**quel?**	**quelle?**	who? what? which?
Plural	**quels?**	**quelles?**	who? what? which?

<u>Quel</u> est ton chanteur préféré? Who's your favourite singer?
<u>Quel</u> vin recommandez-vous? Which wine do you recommend?
<u>Quelle</u> est ta couleur préférée? What's your favourite colour?
<u>Quelle</u> heure est-il? What time is it?
<u>Quels</u> sont tes chanteurs préférés? Who are your favourite singers?
Vous jouez de <u>quels</u> instruments? What instruments do you play?
<u>Quelles</u> sont tes couleurs préférées? What are your favourite colours?
<u>Quelles</u> chaussures te plaisent le plus? Which shoes do you like best?

➪ *For more information on how **quel** in used in exclamations, see page 21.*

4 lequel?, laquelle?, lesquels? and lesquelles?

➤ In questions **lequel**, **laquelle**, **lesquels** and **lesquelles** (meaning *which one/ ones?*) are all forms of the same pronoun, and are used to replace nouns. The form that you choose depends on whether you are referring to something that is masculine or feminine, singular or plural.

	Masculine	Feminine	Meaning
Singular	**lequel?**	**laquelle?**	which? which one?
Plural	**lesquels?**	**lesquelles?**	which? which ones?

'J'ai choisi un livre.' – '<u>Lequel</u>?' 'I've chosen a book.' – 'Which one?'
<u>Laquelle</u> de ces valises est à Bruno? Which of these cases is Bruno's?

'Tu te souviens de mes amis?' – '<u>Lesquels</u>?'	'Do you remember my friends?' – 'Which ones?'
<u>Lesquelles</u> de vos sœurs sont mariées?	Which of your sisters are married?

➪ *For more information on* ***lequel****, see page 63.*

5 n'est-ce pas? and non?

➤ English speakers often use an expression like *isn't it?*, *don't they?*, *weren't we?* or *will you?* tagged on to the end of a sentence to turn it into a question. French uses **n'est-ce pas?** instead. This useful little phrase never changes, so is very easy to use. You use it in questions when you expect the person you are talking to to agree with you.

Il fait chaud, <u>n'est-ce pas</u>?	It's warm, <u>isn't it</u>?
Tu parles français, <u>n'est-ce pas</u>?	You speak French, <u>don't you</u>?
Vous n'oublierez pas, <u>n'est-ce pas</u>?	You won't forget, <u>will you</u>?

➤ It is very common to use **non** (meaning *no*) in the same way in spoken French. **hein?** means the same as *eh?* in English, and is only used in very informal conversations.

Il fait chaud, <u>non</u>?	It's warm, isn't it?
Il fait chaud, <u>hein</u>?	It's warm, eh?

Key points

✔ In questions **qui?** means *who?*; **que?** and **quoi?** mean *what?*

✔ **qui est-ce qui?** (*subject*) and **qui est-ce que?** (*object*) are longer forms of **qui?** Both mean *who?* The word order is different from **qui**.

✔ **qu'est-ce qui?** (*subject*) and **qu'est-ce que?** (*object*) are longer forms of **que?** Both mean *what?* The word order is different from **que**.

✔ **qui?** (for people) and **quoi?** (for things) can be used after prepositions.

✔ **quel?** is both an adjective and a pronoun. It means *who?*, *what?* or *which?* in questions, and is used with a noun or replaces a noun.

✔ **lequel?** is a pronoun; it means *which?* or *which one?* in questions.

✔ **n'est-ce pas?** or **non?** can be tagged on to the end of sentences to turn them into questions.

Grammar Extra!

All the questions in the previous section are the actual words that someone uses when they are asking a question, and so they all end with a question mark. These are called direct questions. When you are telling someone else about a question that is being asked, you use an indirect question. Indirect questions never end with a question mark, and they are always introduced by a verb such as *to ask*, *to tell*, *to wonder*, *to know* and so on.

He asked me what the time was. (His actual question was *What is the time?*)
Tell me which way to go. (Your actual question was *Which way do I go?*)

Word order in indirect questions is generally the same as in English: *question word* + *subject* + *verb*.

Dites-moi quel *(question word)* **autobus** *(subject)* **va** *(verb)* **à la gare.**	Tell me which bus goes to the station.
Il m'a demandé combien d'argent j'avais.	He asked me how much money I had.
Je me demande s'il viendra ou pas.	I wonder if he'll come or not.

When the subject of the question is a noun and NOT a pronoun like **je** or **il**, the subject and verb that come after the question word are often swapped round.

Je me demande où (*question word*) **sont** (*verb*) **mes clés** (*subject*).	I wonder where my keys are.
Demande-lui qui est venu.	Ask him who came.

Adverbs

What is an adverb?
An **adverb** is a word usually used with verbs, adjectives or other adverbs that gives more information about when, how, where, or in what circumstances something happens, for example, *quickly*, *happily*, *now*.

How adverbs are used

➤ In general, adverbs are used together with:

- verbs (*act quickly*, *speak strangely*, *smile cheerfully*)
- adjectives (*rather ill*, *a lot better*, *deeply sorry*)
- other adverbs (*really fast*, *too quickly*, *very well*)

➤ Adverbs can also relate to the whole sentence; they often tell you what the speaker is thinking or feeling.

Fortunately, Jan had already left.
Actually, I don't think I'll come.

How adverbs are formed

1 The basic rules

➤ Adverbs in French NEVER change their form, no matter what they refer to.

Il est très beau.	He's very handsome.
Elles sont très belles.	They're very beautiful.
J'y vais souvent.	I often go there.
Nous y allons souvent.	We often go there.

i Note that there is one exception to this rule. The word **tout** changes in certain phrases, for example, **tout seul** (meaning *all alone*).

Il est arrivé tout seul.	He arrived on his own.
Elle est souvent toute seule.	She's often on her own.

➤ Many English adverbs end in *-ly*, which is added to the end of the adjective (*quick* → *quickly*; *sad* → *sadly*; *frequent* → *frequently*). In French, many adverbs end in **-ment**. This is usually added to the end of the feminine singular form of the adjective.

For further explanation of grammatical terms, please see pages viii-xii.

Masculine adjective	Feminine adjective	Adverb	Meaning
heureux	**heureuse**	**heureusement**	fortunately
doux	**douce**	**doucement**	gently, slowly
seul	**seule**	**seulement**	only

➤ The adverb ending **-ment** is added to the masculine not the feminine form of the adjective if the masculine ends in **-é**, **-i** or **-u**.

Masculine adjective	Feminine adjective	Adverb	Meaning
désespéré	**désespérée**	**désespérément**	desperately
vrai	**vraie**	**vraiment**	truly
absolu	**absolue**	**absolument**	absolutely

➤ If the adjective ends in **-ant**, the adverb ends in **-amment**. If the adjective ends in **-ent**, the adverb ends in **-emment**. The first vowel in the **-emment** and **-amment** endings is pronounced in the same way in both – like the *a* in the English word *cat*.

courant → **couramment** (*fluently*)

récent → **récemment** (*recently*)

i Note that an exception to this rule is the adverb **lentement** (meaning *slowly*), which comes from the adjective **lent** (meaning *slow*).

2 Irregular adverbs

➤ There are a number of common irregular adverbs.

Adjective	Meaning	Adverb	Meaning
bon	good	**bien**	well
gentil	nice, kind	**gentiment**	nicely, kindly
mauvais	bad	**mal**	badly
meilleur	better, best	**mieux**	better
petit	small	**peu**	little
pire	worse	**pis**	worse

Elle travaille bien. She works well.

C'est un emploi très mal payé. It's a very badly paid job.

3 Adjectives used as adverbs

➤ Certain adjectives are used as adverbs, mostly in set phrases:

- **bon** good

  sentir bon to smell nice

- **cher** expensive
  coûter cher to be expensive
  payer cher to pay a lot
- **droit** straight
  aller tout droit to go straight on
- **dur** hard
  travailler dur to work hard
- **fort** loud
  parler plus fort to speak up
- **mauvais** bad
  sentir mauvais to smell

4 Adverbs made up of more than one word

➤ Adverbs can be made up of several words instead of just one. Here are some common ones:

bien sûr	of course
c'est-à-dire	that is
d'abord	first
d'habitude	usually
de temps en temps	from time to time
en général	usually
en retard	late
tout de suite	straight away

Key points

✔ With the exception of **tout**, French adverbs do not change their form.

✔ The ending **-ment** is usually added to the feminine singular form of the corresponding adjective.

✔ If the masculine singular adjective ends in **-é**, **-i** or **-u**, the **-ment** ending is added to that.

✔ If the adjective ends in **-ant** or **-ent**, the adverb ends in **-amment** or **-emment** (apart from **lentement**).

Comparatives and superlatives of adverbs

1 Comparative adverbs

What is a comparative adverb?
A **comparative adverb** is one which, in English, has *-er* on the end of it or *more* or *less* in front of it, for example, *earlier*, *later*, *sooner*, *more/less frequently*.

➤ Adverbs can be used to make comparisons in French, just as they can in English. The comparative (*more often, faster*) of adverbs is formed using the same phrases as for adjectives.

- **plus ... (que)** more ... (than)
  Tu marches plus vite que moi. You walk faster than me.
  Elle chante plus fort que les autres. She's singing louder than the others.
- **moins ... (que)** less ... (than)
  Parle moins vite! Don't speak so fast! (*literally*: *Speak less fast!*)
  Nous nous voyons moins souvent qu'avant. We see each other less often than before.
- **aussi ... que** as ... as
  Je parle français aussi bien que toi! I can speak French as well as you!
  Viens aussi vite que possible. Come as quickly as possible.

⇨ *For more information on* ***Comparative adjectives****, see page 34.*

2 Superlative adverbs

What is a superlative adverb?
A **superlative adverb** is one which, in English, has *-est* on the end of it or *most* or *least* in front of it, for example, *soonest*, *fastest*, *most/least frequently*.

➤ The superlative of adverbs (*the most, the fastest*) is formed using the same phrases as for adjectives, except that **le** NEVER changes to **la** or **les** in the feminine and plural with adverbs as it does with adjectives.

- **le plus ... (que)** the most ... (that)
  Marianne parle le plus vite. Marianne speaks fastest.
- **le moins ... (que)** the least ... (that)
  C'est Gordon qui a mangé le moins. Gordon ate the least.

⇨ *For more information on* ***Superlative adjectives****, see page 34.*

3 Adverbs with irregular comparatives and superlatives

➤ Some of the most common adverbs have irregular comparative and superlative forms.

Adverb	Meaning	Comparative	Meaning	Superlative	Meaning
beaucoup	a lot	**plus**	more	**le plus**	(the) most
bien	well	**mieux**	better	**le mieux**	(the) best
mal	badly	**pis** **plus mal**	worse	**le pis** **le plus mal**	(the) worst
peu	little	**moins**	less	**le moins**	(the) least

C'est lui qui danse <u>le mieux</u>. He dances best.

Key points

✔ Comparatives of adverbs are formed in the same way as comparatives of adjectives, using **plus ... (que)**, **moins ... (que)** and **aussi ... que**.

✔ Superlatives of adverbs are formed in the same way as superlatives of adjectives, using **le plus ... (que)** and **le moins ... (que)**. **le** never changes in the feminine and plural.

✔ Unlike adjectives, adverbs do not change their form to agree with the verb, adjective or other adverb they relate to.

Some common adverbs

➤ Here are some common adverbs that do not end in **-ment**:

alors	then, so, at that time
après	afterwards
après-demain	the day after tomorrow
aujourd'hui	today
assez	enough, quite
aussi	also, too, as
avant-hier	the day before yesterday
beaucoup	a lot, much
bientôt	soon
cependant	however
dedans	inside
dehors	outside
déjà	already, before
demain	tomorrow
depuis	since
derrière	behind
devant	in front
encore	still, even, again
enfin	at last
ensemble	together
ensuite	then
environ	about
hier	yesterday
ici	here
jamais	never, ever

Tip

jamais can sometimes be used without **ne** to mean *never* or *ever*.

'Est-ce que tu vas souvent au cinéma?' – 'Non, <u>jamais</u>.'	'Do you go to the cinema a lot?' – 'No, <u>never</u>.'
As-tu <u>jamais</u> revu ton père?	Did you <u>ever</u> see your father again?

➪ *For more information on* ***Negatives****, see page 138.*

là	there, here
là-bas	over there
loin	far, far off, a long time ago

longtemps	a long time
maintenant	now, nowadays
même	even
moins	less
où	where
parfois	sometimes
partout	everywhere
peu	not much, not very

Tip

Be careful not to confuse **peu**, which means *not much* or *not very*, with **un peu**, which means *a little* or *a bit*.

Il voyage peu.	He doesn't travel much.
Elle est un peu timide.	She's a bit shy.

peut-être	perhaps
plus	more
presque	nearly
puis	then
quelquefois	sometimes
si	so
soudain	suddenly
souvent	often
surtout	especially, above all
tard	late
tôt	early
toujours	always, still
tout	all, very
très	very
trop	too much, too
vite	quick, fast, soon

Tip

vite and **rapide** can both mean *fast* or *quick*. Remember, though, that **vite** is an adverb and **rapide** is an adjective.

une voiture rapide	a fast car
Il roule trop vite.	He drives too fast.

For further explanation of grammatical terms, please see pages viii-xii.

➤ Some of the adverbs listed on pages 157 and 158 can be followed by **de** and used in front of a noun to talk about quantities or numbers of things or people:

- **assez de** enough
  Nous n'avons pas assez de temps. We don't have enough time.
- **beaucoup de** a lot of
  Elle fait beaucoup de fautes. She makes a lot of mistakes.
- **trop de** too much, too many
  J'ai mangé trop de fromage. I've eaten too much cheese.

➤ Several of the adverbs listed on pages 157 and 158 can also be used as prepositions: **après**, **avant**, **devant**, **derrière** and **depuis**.

➪ *For more information on **Prepositions**, see page 162.*

➤ The question words **combien** (meaning *how much*, *how many*), **comment** (meaning *how*), **pourquoi** (meaning *why*) and **quand** (meaning *when*) are described on page 146.

➤ **pas**, **plus** and **jamais** are used in negative word pairs.

➪ *For more information on **Negatives**, see page 138.*

Key points

✔ Many very common adverbs do not end in **-ment**. They are worth learning.

✔ Several adverbs can be followed by **de** + noun and used to talk about quantities and numbers.

Word order with adverbs

1 Adverbs with verbs

➤ In English, adverbs can come in different places in a sentence.

I'm never coming back.
See you soon!
Suddenly the phone rang.
I'd really like to come.

➤ In French, the rules are more fixed. When an adverb goes with a verb that consists of just one word, such as a verb in the present tense or the imperfect tense, it generally goes AFTER that verb.

Il neige toujours en janvier.	It always snows in January.
Je pensais souvent à toi.	I often used to think about you.

➤ When an adverb goes with a verb that consists of more than one word, such as a verb in the perfect tense, it generally comes BETWEEN the part of the verb that comes from **avoir** or **être** and the past participle.

Il a trop mangé.	He's eaten too much.
Ils sont déjà partis.	They've already gone.

➪ *For more information on the **Perfect tense**, see page 111.*

➤ The rule above covers most adverbs that tell you about quantity or time (apart from a few listed later), and some very common ones telling you how something is done.

beaucoup	a lot, much
bien	well
bientôt	soon
déjà	already, before
encore	still, even, again
enfin	at last
mal	badly
mieux	better
peu	not much, not very
rarement	rarely
souvent	often
toujours	always, still
trop	too much, too
vraiment	really

➤ Some adverbs FOLLOW the past participle of verbs that consist of more than one word. This rule covers most adverbs that tell you how or where something is done, and a few adverbs that tell you about time.

aujourd'hui	today
demain	tomorrow
hier	yesterday
loin	far, far off, a long time ago
longtemps	a long time
partout	everywhere
quelquefois	sometimes
tôt	early
tard	late
vite	quick, fast, soon

On les a vus partout.	We saw them everywhere.
Elle est revenue hier.	She came back yesterday.

2 Adverbs with adjectives and other adverbs

➤ When an adverb goes with an adjective, it generally comes just BEFORE that adjective.

Ils ont une très belle maison.	They have a very nice house.
une femme bien habillée	a well-dressed woman

➤ When an adverb goes with another adverb, it generally comes just BEFORE that adverb.

C'est trop tard.	It's too late.
Fatima travaille beaucoup plus vite.	Fatima works much faster.

Key points

✔ Adverbs follow verbs that consist of just one word.

✔ They generally go before the past participle of verbs that consist of two words when they relate to quantity or time.

✔ They generally go after the past participle of verbs that consist of two words when they relate to how or where something is done.

✔ When used with an adjective or another adverb, they generally come just before it.

Prepositions

What is a preposition?
A **preposition** is a word such as *at*, *for*, *with*, *into* or *from*, which is usually followed by a noun, pronoun or, in English, a word ending in *-ing*. Prepositions show how people and things relate to the rest of the sentence, for example, *She's <u>at</u> home.*; *a tool <u>for</u> cutting grass*; *it's <u>from</u> David*.

Using prepositions

➤ Prepositions are used in front of nouns and pronouns (such as *me*, *him*, *the man* and so on), and show the relationship between the noun or pronoun and the rest of the sentence. Some prepositions can be used before verb forms ending in *-ing* in English.

I showed my ticket <u>to</u> the inspector.
Come <u>with</u> me.
This brush is really good <u>for</u> cleaning shoes.

⇨ *For more information on **Nouns** and **Pronouns**, see pages 1 and 42.*

➤ Prepositions are also used after certain adjectives and verbs and link them to the rest of the sentence.

Je suis très contente <u>de</u> te voir.	I'm very happy to see you.
Tu aimes jouer <u>au</u> tennis?	Do you like playing tennis?

➤ In English it is possible to finish a sentence with a preposition such as *for*, *about* or *on*, even though some people think this is not good grammar. You can <u>NEVER</u> end a French sentence with a preposition.

Le café au lait, c'est <u>pour</u> qui?	Who's the white coffee <u>for</u>?
<u>De</u> quoi parlez-vous?	What are you talking <u>about</u>?

Tip
The French preposition is not always the direct equivalent of the preposition that is used in English. It is often difficult to give just one English equivalent for French prepositions, as the way they are used varies so much between the two languages.

à, de and en

1 à

➤ Be careful not to confuse the preposition **à** with the **il/elle/on** form of the verb **avoir: il a** (meaning *he has*) and so on.

> *Tip*
> When **à** is followed by **le**, the two words become **au**. Similarly, when **à** is followed by **les**, the two words become **aux**.
>
> ⇨ *For more information on* ***Articles****, see page 12.*

➤ **à** can mean *at*.

Les melons se vendent à 2 euros pièce.	Melons are selling at 2 euros each.
Nous roulions à 100 km à l'heure.	We were driving at 100 km an hour
J'ai lancé une pierre à Chantal.	I threw a stone at Chantal.
Je suis à la maison.	I'm at home.

ℹ Note that **à la maison** can also mean *to the house*.

Je rentre à la maison.	I'm going back to the house *or* back home.

➤ **à** can mean *in*.

Nous habitons à la campagne.	We live in the country.
Mon père est à Londres.	My father is in London.
Restez au lit.	Stay in bed.
Jean est entré, un livre à la main.	Jean came in with a book in his hand.

> *Tip*
> **à** is used to mean *in* with the names of towns and cities, and **au** (*singular*) or **aux** (*plural*) with the names of countries that are masculine in French.
>
> | | |
> |---|---|
> | **J'habite au Mexique.** | I live in Mexico. |
> | **Elle est aux États-Unis.** | She's in the States. |

➤ **à** can mean *to*.

Je vais au cinéma ce soir.	I'm going to the cinema tonight.
Donne le ballon à ton frère.	Give the ball to your brother.

Tip

à is used to mean *to* with the names of towns and cities, and **au** (*singular*) or **aux** (*plural*) with the names of countries that are masculine in French.

Je vais assez souvent à Paris.	I go to Paris quite often.
Il va aux États-Unis la semaine prochaine.	He's going to the States next week.

➤ **à** is also used with **de** to mean *from ... to ...*

le trajet de Londres à Paris	the journey from London to Paris
La banque est ouverte de 9 heures à midi.	The bank is open from 9 to 12.
Je suis en vacances du 21 juin au 5 juillet.	I'm on holiday from 21 June to 5 July.

➤ **à** can mean *on*.

Il y a deux beaux tableaux au mur.	There are two beautiful paintings on the wall.
Le bureau se trouve au premier étage.	The office is on the first floor.
Qu'est-ce qu'il y a à la télé ce soir?	What's on TV tonight?

ℹ Note that **à** and **sur** can both mean *on* in English. **sur** usually means on the top of something. **sur la télé** means *on top of the TV set*, but **à la télé** means *broadcast on TV*. Both can be translated as *on the TV* in English. **sur le mur** means *on top of the wall*, but **au mur** means *hanging on the wall*.

➤ **à** is often used to describe:

- what someone looks like or is wearing

la femme au chapeau vert	the woman with the green hat
un garçon aux yeux bleus	a boy with blue eyes

- how something is done

fait à la main	hand-made
laver à la machine	to machine-wash

- what a type of food is made of

une tarte aux poires	a pear tart
un sandwich au jambon	a ham sandwich

- how you travel

On y va à pied?	Shall we walk?
Il est venu à vélo.	He came on his bike.

Tip

Apart from **à vélo** and **à cheval** (meaning *on horseback*), the prepositions **en** and **par** are used with most other means of transport.

➤ **à** can also show what something is used for.

une boîte aux lettres	a letter box
une machine à laver	a washing machine
une tasse à café	a coffee cup

i Note that **une tasse à café** means a *coffee cup*, but **une tasse de café** means *a cup of coffee*. In the same way, **un verre à vin** means *a wine glass* but **un verre de vin** means *a glass of wine*.

➤ **à** is used with times, centuries and the names of festivals.

à trois heures	at three o'clock
au vingtième siècle	in the twentieth century
à Noël	at Christmas
à Pâques	at Easter

➤ **à** is used to talk about distances and rates.

La maison est à 6 kilomètres d'ici.	The house is 6 kilometres from here.
C'est à deux minutes de chez moi.	It's two minutes from my place.
Je suis payé à l'heure.	I'm paid by the hour.

➤ **à** shows who owns something, or whose turn it is.

Ce cahier est à Paul.	This notebook is Paul's.
C'est à toi?	Is this yours?
C'est à qui de nettoyer la salle de bains?	Whose turn is it to clean the bathroom?

➤ If you want to say where something hurts, you use **à**.

J'ai mal à la tête.	I've got a headache.
J'ai mal aux jambes.	My legs ache.
J'ai mal à la gorge.	I've got a sore throat.

➤ **à** is used with certain adjectives.

Son écriture est difficile à lire.	His/Her writing is difficult to read.
Je suis prêt à tout.	I'm ready for anything.

➪ *For more information about* ***Prepositions after adjectives****, see page 183.*

➤ **à** is used with certain verbs.

s'intéresser à quelque chose	to be interested in something
penser à quelque chose	to think about something

➪ *For more information about* ***Prepositions after verbs****, see page 178.*

➤ Finally, some common ways of saying goodbye contain **à**.

À bientôt!	See you soon!
À demain!	See you tomorrow!
À samedi!	See you Saturday!
À tout à l'heure!	See you later!

2 de

➤ **de** is used as part of the partitive article,, which is usually the equivalent of *some* or *any* in English.

➪ *For more information on the* ***Partitive article****, see page 22.*

Tip

When **de** is followed by **le**, the two words become **du**. Similarly, when **de** is followed by **les**, the two words become **des**.

➪ *For more information on* ***Articles****, see page 12.*

➤ **de** can mean *from*.

Je viens d'Édimbourg.	I'm from Edinburgh.
une lettre de Rachid	a letter from Rachid
Je la vois de temps en temps.	I see her from time to time.

Tip

de changes to **d'** in front of a word starting with a vowel, most words starting with **h**, and the French word **y**.

➤ **de** is also used with **à** to mean *from ... to ...*

le trajet de Londres à Paris	the journey from London to Paris
La banque est ouverte de 9 heures à midi.	The bank is open from 9 to 12.
Je suis en vacances du 21 juin au 5 juillet.	I'm on holiday from 21 June to 5 July.

➤ **de** often shows who or what something belongs to.

un ami de la famille	a friend of the family
les fenêtres de la maison	the windows of the house
la voiture de Marie-Pierre	Marie-Pierre's car

➤ **de** can indicate what something contains, when it usually corresponds to *of* in English.

une boîte d'allumettes	a box of matches
deux bouteilles de vin	two bottles of wine
une tasse de café	a cup of coffee

ℹ Note that **une tasse de café** means *a cup of coffee* but **une tasse à café** means *a coffee cup*. In the same way, **un verre à vin** means *a wine glass* but **un verre de vin** means *a glass of wine*.

➤ **de** can describe what material something is made of.

une robe de coton	a cotton dress
une porte de bois	a wooden door

Tip

en can also be used to say what something is made of, and is used when it is important to stress the material.

un bracelet en or	a gold bracelet

➤ You can use **de** to say what something is used for.

un sac de couchage	a sleeping bag
un terrain de foot	a football pitch
un arrêt de bus	a bus stop

➤ **de** is found after superlatives (*the most…*, *the biggest*, *the least* … and so on).

la plus belle ville du monde	the most beautiful city in the world
le film le moins intéressant du festival	the least interesting film in the festival

➪ *For more information on* ***Superlative adjectives****, see page 34.*

➤ **de** is used in phrases to talk about quantities.

Elle fait <u>beaucoup de</u> fautes.	She makes a lot of mistakes.
<u>Combien de</u> personnes as-tu invitées?	How many people have you invited?

➤ **de** is used with certain adjectives.

Je suis très surpris <u>de</u> te voir.	I'm very surprised to see you.
Il est triste <u>de</u> partir.	He's sad to be leaving.

➪ *For more information on **Prepositions after adjectives**, see page 183.*

Grammar Extra!

If you want to use an adjective after **quelque chose**, **rien**, **quelqu'un** and **personne**, you link the words with **de**.

quelqu'un <u>d'</u>important	someone important
quelque chose <u>d'</u>intéressant	something interesting
rien <u>d'</u>amusant	nothing funny

➤ **de** is found after certain verbs.

dépendre <u>de</u> quelque chose	to depend on something
parler <u>de</u> quelque chose	to talk about something

➪ *For more information on **Prepositions after verbs**, see page 178.*

3 <u>en</u>

ℹ Note that **en** is never followed by an article such as **le**, **du** or **des**.

➤ **en** is used to talk about a place. It can be the equivalent of the English *to* or *in*.

Je vais <u>en</u> ville.	I'm going <u>to</u> town.
Il a un appartement <u>en</u> ville.	He has a flat <u>in</u> town.
Nous allons <u>en</u> France cet été.	We're going <u>to</u> France this summer.
Nous habitons <u>en</u> France.	We live <u>in</u> France.

> ***Tip***
> **en** is used with the names of countries that are feminine in French. Use **à** with the names of towns and cities, and **au** or **aux** with masculine countries.

➤ **en** is used to talk about years and months, and to say how long something will take, when it is the equivalent of *in/within*:

en 1923	in 1923
en janvier	in January
Je le ferai en trois jours.	I'll do it in three days.

Grammar Extra!

en and **dans** can both be used in French to talk about a length of time, but the meaning is very different.

Je le ferai dans trois jours.	I'll do it in three days.
Je le ferai en trois jours.	I'll do it in three days.

Though both can be translated in the same way, the first sentence means that you'll do it in three days' time; the second means that it will take three days for you to do it.

➤ **en** is used with the names of the seasons, except for spring.

en été	in summer
en automne	in autumn
en hiver	in winter
BUT: **au printemps**	in spring

➤ **en** is used for most means of transport.

Je suis venu en voiture.	I came by car.
C'est plus rapide en train.	It's quicker by train.
Il est allé en Italie en avion.	He flew to Italy.

> *Tip*
>
> The prepositions **à** and **par** are also used with means of transport.

➤ Use **en** to say what language something is in.

une lettre écrite en espagnol	a letter written in Spanish
Dis-le en anglais.	Say it in English.

➤ **en** can be used to say what something is made of when you particularly want to stress the material.

un bracelet en or	a bracelet made of gold, a gold bracelet
un manteau en cuir	a coat made of leather, a leather coat

Tip

de can also be used to say what something is made of.

une porte de bois	a wooden door

➤ **en** often describes the situation or state that something or someone is in.

Je suis en vacances.	I'm on holiday.
La voiture est en panne.	The car's broken down.
Tu es toujours en retard!	You're always late!

➤ **en** is found before present participles, the form of the verb that ends in *-ing* in English and **-ant** in French.

Je fais mes devoirs en regardant la télé.	I do my homework while watching TV.
Il m'a vu en passant devant la porte.	He saw me as he came past the door.

⇨ *For more information on the **Present participle**, see page 125.*

Key points

✔ **à**, **de** and **en** are very frequent prepositions which you will use all the time.

✔ Each of them has several possible meanings, which depend on the context they are used in.

Some other common prepositions

i Note that some of these words are also adverbs, for example, **avant**, **depuis**.

⇨ *For more information on the **Adverbs**, see page 152.*

➤ The following prepositions are also frequently used in French:

- **après** after

après le déjeuner	after lunch
après son départ	after he had left
la troisième maison après la mairie	the third house after the town hall
Après vous!	After you!

i Note that where English uses a verb in the perfect tense following *after*, French uses the infinitive **avoir** or **être** and a past participle.

Nous viendrons après avoir fait la vaisselle.	We'll come after we've done the dishes.

- **avant** before

Il est arrivé avant toi.	He arrived before you.
Tournez à gauche avant la poste.	Turn left before the post office.

i Note that where English uses a verb ending in *-ing* after *before*, French uses **de** followed by the infinitive.

Je préfère finir mes devoirs avant de manger.	I prefer to finish my homework before eating.

- **avec** with

avec mon père	with my father
une chambre avec salle de bain	a room with its own bathroom
Ouvre-la avec un couteau.	Open it with a knife.

- **chez**

Elle est chez Pierre.	She's at Pierre's house.
Elle va chez Pierre.	She's going to Pierre's house.
Je reste chez moi ce week-end.	I'm staying at home this weekend.
Je vais rentrer chez moi.	I'm going home.
Ils habitent près de chez moi.	They live near my house.

> ### *Tip*
> **chez** is also used with the name of jobs or professions to indicate a shop or place of business.
>
> | | |
> |---|---|
> | **Je vais chez le médecin.** | I'm going to the doctor's. |

- **contre** against

Ne mets pas ton vélo contre le mur.	Don't put your bike against the wall.

- **dans** in, into

Il est dans sa chambre.	He's in his bedroom.
Nous passons une semaine dans les Alpes.	We're spending a week in the Alps.
dans deux mois	in two months' time
Il est entré dans mon bureau.	He came into my office.

Grammar Extra!

dans and **en** can both be used in French to talk about a length of time, but the meaning is very different.

Je le ferai dans trois jours.	I'll do it in three days.
Je le ferai en trois jours.	I'll do it in three days.

Though both can be translated in the same way, the first sentence means that you'll do it in three days' time; the second means that it will take three days for you to do it.

- **depuis** since, for

Elle habite Paris depuis 1998.	She's been living in Paris since 1998.
Elle habite Paris depuis cinq ans.	She's been living in Paris for five years.

i Note that French uses the present tense with **depuis** to talk about actions that started in the past and are still going on.

Il est en France depuis le mois de septembre.	He's been in France since September. (*and he is still there*)

If you are saying how long something has NOT happened for, you use the perfect tense with **depuis**.

Nous ne l'avons pas vu depuis un mois.	We haven't seen him for a month.

➪ *For more information on the* ***Present tense*** *and the* ***Perfect tense****, see pages 71 and 111.*

- **derrière** behind

derrière la porte	behind the door

- **devant** in front of

Il est assis devant moi.	He's sitting in front of me.

- **entre ... et** between ... and

Il est assis entre son père et son oncle.	He's sitting between his father and his uncle.
Le bureau est fermé entre 13 et 14 heures.	The office is closed between 1 and 2 p.m.

- **jusque** as far as, until

Je te raccompagne jusque chez toi.	I'll go with you as far as your house.
Jusqu'où vas-tu?	How far are you going?
Jusqu'ici nous n'avons pas eu de problèmes.	Up to now we've had no problems.
Je reste jusqu'à la fin du mois.	I'm staying until the end of the month.

> *Tip*
>
> **jusque** changes to **jusqu'** before a word beginning with a vowel, most words starting with **h**, and the French word **y**.

- **par** by, with, per

deux par deux	two by two
par le train	by train
par la poste	by post
par e-mail	by email
Son nom commence par un H.	His name begins with H.
Prenez trois cachets par jour.	Take three tablets per day.
Le voyage coûte quatre cents euros par personne.	The trip costs four hundred euros per person.
Nous nous voyons une fois par mois.	We see each other once a month.
Il est tombé par terre.	He fell down.
Il y a beaucoup de touristes par ici.	There are a lot of tourists around here.

Tip

The prepositions **à** and **en** are also used with means of transport.

- **pendant** during, for

Ça s'est passé pendant l'été.	It happened during the summer.
Il n'a pas pu travailler pendant plusieurs mois.	He couldn't work for several months.

Tip

French uses the perfect tense with **pendant** to talk about actions in the past that are completed.

Nous avons habité pendant dix ans en Écosse.	We lived in Scotland for ten years. (*but don't any more*)

You can also miss out **pendant**.

Nous avons habité dix ans en Écosse.	We lived in Scotland for ten years.

pendant is also used to talk about something that will happen in the future.

Je serai à New York pendant un mois.	I'll be in New York for a month.

➪ *For more information on the* ***Perfect tense****, see page 111.*

- **pour** for (*who or what something is for, and where something or someone is going*)

C'est un cadeau pour toi.	It's a present for you.
Nous voudrions une chambre pour deux nuits.	We'd like a room for two nights.
le train pour Bordeaux	the train for Bordeaux

ℹ Note that **pour** can also be used with infinitives, when it has the meaning of *in order to*.

Elle téléphone pour savoir à quelle heure on arrivera.	She's ringing to find out what time we'll get there.
Pour aller à Nice, s'il vous plaît?	Which way is it to Nice, please?

- **sans** without

Elle est venue <u>sans</u> son frère.	She came without her brother.
un café <u>sans</u> sucre	a coffee without sugar
un pull <u>sans</u> manches	a sleeveless sweater

ℹ Note that **sans** can also be used before infinitives in French. In English a verb form ending in *-ing* is used after *without*.

Elle est partie <u>sans dire</u> au revoir.	She left <u>without saying</u> goodbye.

- **sauf** except

Tout le monde vient <u>sauf</u> lui.	Everyone's coming except him.

- **sous** under

<u>sous</u> la table	under the table
<u>sous</u> terre	underground

- **sur** on

Pose-le <u>sur</u> le bureau.	Put it down on the desk.
Ton sac est <u>sur</u> la table.	Your bag is on the table.
Vous verrez l'hôpital <u>sur</u> votre gauche.	You'll see the hospital on your left.
un livre <u>sur</u> la politique	a book on politics

ℹ Note that **à** and **sur** can both mean *on* in English. **sur** usually means on the top of something. **sur la télé** means *on top of the TV set*, but **à la télé** means *broadcast on TV*. Both can be translated as *on the TV* in English. **sur le mur** means *on top of the wall*, but **au mur** means *hanging on the wall*.

Tip

With numbers and measurements **sur** can also mean *in*, *out of* and *by*.

une personne <u>sur</u> dix	one person <u>in</u> ten
J'ai eu quatorze <u>sur</u> vingt en maths.	I got 14 <u>out of</u> 20 in maths.
La pièce fait quatre mètres <u>sur</u> deux.	The room measures four metres <u>by</u> two.

- **vers** towards (*a place*), at about

Il allait <u>vers</u> la gare.	He was going towards the station.
Je rentre chez moi <u>vers</u> cinq heures.	I go home at about 5 o'clock.

➤ **voici** (meaning *this is, here is*) and **voilà** (meaning *there is, that is*) are two very useful prepositions that French speakers often use to point things out.

<u>Voici</u> mon frère et <u>voilà</u> ma sœur.	This is my brother and that's my sister.
<u>Voici</u> ton sac.	Here's your bag.
Le <u>voici</u>!	Here he/it is!
Tiens! <u>Voilà</u> Paul.	Look! There's Paul.
Tu as perdu ton stylo? En <u>voilà</u> un autre.	Have you lost your pen? Here's another one.
Les <u>voilà</u>!	There they are!

Prepositions consisting of more than one word

➤ Prepositions can also be made up of several words instead of just one.

au bord de	at the edge of, at the side of
au bout de	after
à cause de	because of
au-dessous de	below
au-dessus de	above
au fond de	at the bottom of, at the end of
au milieu de	in the middle of

Au bout d'un moment, il s'est endormi.	After a while, he fell asleep.
Nous ne pouvons pas sortir à cause du mauvais temps.	We can't go out because of the bad weather.
J'ai garé la voiture au bord de la route.	I parked the car by the side of the road.
Mon porte-monnaie est au fond de mon sac.	My purse is at the bottom of my bag.
Place le vase au milieu de la table.	Put the vase in the middle of the table.

Prepositions after verbs

➤ Some French verbs can be followed by an infinitive (the *to* form of the verb) and linked to it by either **de** or **à**, or no preposition at all. This is also true of verbs and their objects: the person or thing that the verb 'happens' to.

➪ *For more information on **Verbs followed by an infinitive**, see page 133.*

> ***Tip***
> The preposition that is used in French is not always the same as the one that is used in English. Whenever you learn a new verb, try to learn which preposition can be used after it too.

➤ The lists in this section concentrate on those French verbs that involve a different construction from the one that is used in English.

1 Verbs that are followed by à + object

➤ **à** is often the equivalent of the English word *to* when it is used with an indirect object after verbs like *send*, *give* and *say*.

dire quelque chose à quelqu'un	to say something to someone
donner quelque chose à quelqu'un	to give something to someone
écrire quelque chose à quelqu'un	to write something to someone
envoyer quelque chose à quelqu'un	to send something to someone
montrer quelque chose à quelqu'un	to show something to someone

➪ *For more information on **Indirect objects**, see page 49.*

> ***Tip***
> There is an important difference between French and English with this type of verb. In English, you can say either *to give something to someone* or *to give someone something*; to *show something to someone* or *to show someone something*.
> You can NEVER miss out **à** in French in the way that you can sometimes miss out *to* in English.

➤ Here are some verbs taking **à** in French that have a different construction in English.

croire <u>à</u> quelque chose	to believe <u>in</u> something
s'intéresser <u>à</u> quelqu'un/quelque chose	to be interested <u>in</u> someone/something
jouer <u>à</u> quelque chose	to play something (*sports, games*)
obéir <u>à</u> quelqu'un	to obey someone
penser <u>à</u> quelqu'un/quelque chose	to think <u>about</u> someone/something
répondre <u>à</u> quelqu'un	to answer someone
téléphoner <u>à</u> quelqu'un	to phone someone

Tip

When you are using **jouer** to talk about sports and games, you use **à**. When you are using **jouer** to talk about musical instruments, you use **de**.

jouer <u>au</u> tennis	to play tennis
jouer <u>aux</u> échecs	to play chess
jouer <u>de</u> la guitare	to play the guitar
jouer <u>du</u> piano	to play the piano

➤ **plaire** followed by **à** is a common way of saying you like something.

plaire <u>à</u> quelqu'un	to please someone (*literally*)
Ton cadeau me plaît beaucoup.	I like your present a lot.
Ce film plaît beaucoup aux jeunes.	This film is very popular with young people.

Grammar Extra!

manquer à works quite differently from its English equivalent, *to miss*. The English object is the French subject, and the English subject is the French object.

manquer <u>à</u> quelqu'un	to be missed by someone (*literally*)
Tu (*subject*) **me** (*object*) **manques.**	I (*subject*) miss you (*object*).
Mon pays (*subject*) **me** (*object*) **manque beaucoup.**	I (*subject*) miss my country (*object*) very much.

➤ There are also some verbs where you can put a direct object before **à**. The verb **demander** is the most common.

demander quelque chose <u>à</u> quelqu'un	to ask someone something, to ask someone for something

⇨ *For more information on **Direct objects**, see page 47.*

i Note that **demander** in French does NOT mean *to demand*. It means *to ask something* or *to ask for something*. If you want to say *demand* in French, use **exiger**.

Nous avons demandé notre chemin à un chauffeur de taxi.	We asked a taxi driver the way.
J'exige des excuses!	I demand an apology!

2 Verbs that are followed by de + object

➤ Here are some verbs taking **de** in French that have a different construction in English.

changer de quelque chose	to change something (*one's shoes and so on*)
dépendre de quelqu'un/ quelque chose	to depend on someone/something
s'excuser de quelque chose	to apologize for something
jouer de quelque chose	to play something
parler de quelque chose	to talk about something
se servir de quelque chose	to use something
se souvenir de quelqu'un/ quelque chose	to remember someone/something

Tip

When you are using **jouer** to talk about sports and games, you use **à**. When you are using **jouer** to talk about musical instruments, you use **de**.

jouer au tennis	to play tennis
jouer aux échecs	to play chess
jouer de la guitare	to play the guitar
jouer du piano	to play the piano

➤ Some common phrases using **avoir** also contain **de**.

avoir besoin de quelque chose	to need something
avoir envie de quelque chose	to want something
avoir peur de quelque chose	to be afraid of something

➤ There are also some verbs where you can put a direct object before **de**. **remercier** is the most common.

remercier quelqu'un de quelque chose to thank someone for something

⇨ *For more information on **Direct objects**, see page 47.*

Grammar Extra!

The verb **se tromper de quelque chose** is often the equivalent of *to get the wrong* ...

Je me suis trompé de numéro.	I got the wrong number.
Je me suis trompé de maison.	I got the wrong house.

3 Verbs taking a direct object in French but not in English

➤ In English there are a few verbs that are followed by *for*, *on*, *in*, *to* or *at* which, in French, are not followed by a preposition such as **à** or **de**. Here are the most common:

attendre quelqu'un/quelque chose	to wait <u>for</u> sb/sth
chercher quelqu'un/quelque chose	to look <u>for</u> sb/sth
demander quelqu'un/quelque chose	to ask <u>for</u> sb/sth
écouter quelqu'un/quelque chose	to listen <u>to</u> sb/sth
espérer quelque chose	to hope <u>for</u> sth
payer quelque chose	to pay <u>for</u> sth
regarder quelqu'un/quelque chose	to look <u>at</u> sb/sth

i Note that **attendre** does <u>NOT</u> mean *to attend* in English. It means *to wait for*. If you want to say that you attend something, use **assister à quelque chose.**

Je t'attends devant la gare.	I'll wait for you in front of the station.
Vous allez assister au concert?	Are you going to attend the concert?

➤ **habiter** can be used with or without a preposition:

- **habiter** is mostly used <u>without a preposition</u> when you are talking about living in a house, a flat and so on

Nous habitons un petit appartement en ville.	We live in a small flat in town.

- use **habiter** <u>with à</u> when you are talking about a town or city, and **au** (*singular*) or **aux** (*plural*) with the names of countries that are masculine in French

Nous habitons <u>à</u> Liverpool.	We live in Liverpool.
Nous habitons <u>aux</u> États-Unis.	We live in the United States.

- use **habiter** <u>with en</u> when you are talking about feminine countries

Nous habitons <u>en</u> Espagne.	We live in Spain.

Key points

- ✔ French prepositions after verbs are often not the ones that are used in English. French verbs often have a different construction from English verbs.
- ✔ French verbs are usually linked to their objects by **de**, **à** or nothing at all.
- ✔ You can never miss out **à** in French in the way that you can miss out *to* in English constructions like *to give someone something*.

For further explanation of grammatical terms, please see pages viii-xii.

Prepositions after adjectives

- Just like verbs, some French adjectives can be linked to what follows by either **à** or **de**.
- An adjective followed by **de** or **à** can be followed by a noun, a pronoun or an infinitive.
- Some adjectives that can be followed by **de** are used to say how you feel, that you are certain about something, or that it is necessary or important to do something. These are the most common:

certain	certain
content	happy
désolé	sorry
enchanté	delighted
heureux	happy
important	important
malheureux	unhappy
nécessaire	necessary
sûr	sure
triste	sad

Tu es <u>sûr de</u> pouvoir venir?	Are you sure you can come?
<u>Enchanté de</u> faire votre connaissance.	Delighted to meet you.
Il est <u>nécessaire de</u> réserver.	You have to book.

Grammar Extra!

- Some adjectives, such as **facile** (meaning *easy*), **intéressant** (meaning *interesting*) or **impossible** (meaning *impossible*), can be followed by either **à** or **de**. **de** tends to be used when you are saying something that is generally true. **à** tends to be used when you are saying something about someone or something in particular.

Il est difficile <u>de</u> prendre une décision.	It's difficult to make a decision.
<u>Il</u> est difficile <u>à</u> connaître.	He's difficult to get to know.
<u>Son accent</u> est difficile <u>à</u> comprendre.	His accent is difficult to understand.

Conjunctions

What is a conjunction?
A **conjunction** is a word such as *and*, *but*, *or*, *so*, *if* and *because*, that links two words or phrases of a similar type, or two parts of a sentence, for example, *Diane and I have been friends for years; I left because I was bored*.

et, mais, ou, parce que and si

➤ **et**, **mais**, **ou**, **parce que** and **si** are the most common conjunctions that you need to know in French.

- **et** and

toi et moi	you and me
Il pleut et il fait très froid.	It's raining and it's very cold.

- **mais** but

C'est cher mais de très bonne qualité.	It's expensive, but very good quality.

i Note that **mais** is also commonly found in front of **oui** and **si**.

'Tu viens ce soir?' – 'Mais oui!'	'Are you coming tonight?' – 'Definitely!'
'Il n'a pas encore fini?' – 'Mais si!'	'Hasn't he finished yet?' – 'He certainly has!'

- **ou** or

Tu préfères le vert ou le bleu?	Do you like the green one or the blue one?
Donne-moi ça ou je me fâche!	Give me that or I'll get cross!

Tip
Be careful not to confuse **ou** (meaning *or*) with **où** (meaning *where*).

- **parce que** because

Je ne peux pas sortir parce que j'ai encore du travail à faire.	I can't go out because I've still got work to do.

For further explanation of grammatical terms, please see pages viii-xii.

> **Tip**
>
> **parce que** changes to **parce qu'** before a word beginning with a vowel, most words starting with **h**, and the French word **y**.
>
> | | |
> |---|---|
> | **Il ne vient pas <u>parce qu</u>'il n'a pas de voiture.** | He isn't coming <u>because</u> he doesn't have a car. |

- si if

Je me demande <u>si</u> elle ment.	I wonder <u>if</u> she's lying.
<u>Si</u> j'étais à ta place, je ne l'inviterais pas.	<u>If</u> I were you, I wouldn't invite him.

> **Tip**
>
> **si** changes to **s'** before **il** or **ils**.
>
> | | |
> |---|---|
> | **<u>S'</u>il ne pleut pas, on mangera dehors.** | <u>If</u> it doesn't rain, we'll eat outside. |

Some other common conjunctions

➤ Here are some other common French conjunctions:

- **car** because

  Il faut prendre un bus pour y accéder car il est interdit d'y monter en voiture. You need to take a bus to get there because cars are prohibited.

🛈 Note that **car** is used in formal language or in writing. The normal way of saying *because* is **parce que**.

- **comme** as

  Comme il pleut, je prends la voiture. As it's raining, I'm taking the car.

- **donc** so

  J'ai raté le train, donc je serai en retard. I missed the train, so I'll be late.

- **lorsque** when

  J'allais composer ton numéro lorsque tu as appelé. I was about to dial your number when you called.

- **quand** when

  Je ne sors pas quand il pleut. I don't go out when it rains.

🛈 Note that when **quand** and **lorsque** are used to talk about something that will happen in the future, the French verb has to be in the future tense even though English uses a verb in the present tense.

Quand je serai riche, j'achèterai une belle maison. When I'm rich, I'll buy a nice house.

⇨ *For more information on the* ***Present tense*** *and the* ***Future tense****, see pages 71 and 98.*

➤ French, like English, also has conjunctions which have more than one part. Here are the most common:

- **ne ... ni ... ni** neither ... nor

  Je n'aime ni les lentilles ni les épinards. I like neither lentils nor spinach.

🛈 Note that the **ne** part of this expression goes just before the verb.

- **ou ... ou, ou bien ... ou bien** either ... or

  Ou il est malade ou il ment. Either he's sick or he's lying.

  Ou bien il m'évite ou bien il ne me reconnaît pas. Either he's avoiding me or else he doesn't recognize me.

The conjunction que

➤ When **que** is used to join two parts of a sentence, it means *that*.

Il dit qu'il m'aime.	He says that he loves me.
Elle sait que vous êtes là.	She knows that you're here.

> *Tip*
> In English you could say both *He says he loves me* and *He says that he loves me*, or *She knows you're here* and *She knows that you're here*. You can NEVER leave out **que** in French in the same way.

➤ **que** is also used when you are comparing two things or two people. In this case, it means *as* or *than*.

Ils n'y vont pas aussi souvent que nous.	They don't go as often as us.
Les melons sont plus chers que les bananes.	Melons are more expensive than bananas.

➪ *For more information on* ***Comparative adjectives****, see page* 34.

➤ Some words which give you information about when something happens, can also be conjunctions if you put **que** after them. **pendant que** (meaning *while*) is the most common of these.

Christian a téléphoné pendant que Chantal prenait son bain.	Christian phoned while Chantal was in the bath.

ⓘ Note that when **pendant que** (meaning *while*), **quand** (meaning *when*) and **lorsque** (meaning *when*) are used to talk about something that will happen in the future, the French verb has to be in the future tense even though English uses a verb in the present tense.

Pendant que je serai en France, j'irai les voir.	I'll go and visit them while I'm in France.

➪ *For more information on the* ***Present tense*** *and the* ***Future tense****, see pages* 71 *and* 98.

Grammar Extra!

que can replace another conjunction to avoid having to repeat it.

Quand tu seras plus grand et que tu auras une maison à toi, ...	When you're older and you have a house of your own, ...
Comme il pleut et que je n'ai pas de parapluie, ...	As it's raining and I don't have an umbrella, ...

Numbers

1	**un (une)**
2	**deux**
3	**trois**
4	**quatre**
5	**cinq**
6	**six**
7	**sept**
8	**huit**
9	**neuf**
10	**dix**
11	**onze**
12	**douze**
13	**treize**
14	**quatorze**
15	**quinze**
16	**seize**
17	**dix-sept**
18	**dix-huit**
19	**dix-neuf**
20	**vingt**
21	**vingt et un (une)**
22	**vingt-deux**
30	**trente**
40	**quarante**
50	**cinquante**
60	**soixante**
70	**soixante-dix**
71	**soixante et onze**
72	**soixante-douze**
80	**quatre-vingts**
81	**quatre-vingt-un (-une)**
90	**quatre-vingt-dix**
91	**quatre-vingt-onze**
100	**cent**
101	**cent un (une)**
300	**trois cents**
301	**trois cent un (une)**
1000	**mille**
2000	**deux mille**
1,000,000	**un million**

1st	**premier (1er), première (1re)**
2nd	**deuxième (2e *or* 2ème) *or* second(e) ($2^{nd(e)}$)**
3rd	**troisième (3e *or* 3ème)**
4th	**quatrième (4e *or* 4ème)**
5th	**cinquième (5e *or* 5ème)**
6th	**sixième (6e *or* 6ème)**
7th	**septième (7e *or* 7ème)**
8th	**huitième (8e *or* 8ème)**
9th	**neuvième (9e *or* 9ème)**
10th	**dixième (10e *or* 10ème)**
11th	**onzième (11e *or* 11ème)**
12th	**douzième (12e *or* 12ème)**
13th	**treizième (13e *or* 13ème)**
14th	**quatorzième (14e *or* 14ème)**
15th	**quinzième (15e *or* 15ème)**
16th	**seizième (16e *or* 16ème)**
17th	**dix-septième (17e *or* 17ème)**
18th	**dix-huitième (18e *or* 18ème)**
19th	**dix-neuvième (19e *or* 19ème)**
20th	**vingtième (20e *or* 20ème)**
21st	**vingt et unième (21e *or* 21ème)**
22nd	**vingt-deuxième (22e *or* 22ème)**
30th	**trentième (30e *or* 30ème)**
100th	**centième (100e *or* 100ème)**
101st	**cent unième (101e *or* 101ème)**
1000th	**millième (1000e *or* 1000ème)**
1/2	**un demi**
1/3	**un tiers**
2/3	**deux tiers**
1/4	**un quart**
1/5	**un cinquième**
0.5	**zéro virgule cinq (0,5)**
3.4	**trois virgule quatre (3,4)**
10%	**dix pour cent**
100%	**cent pour cent**

EXEMPLES	EXAMPLES
Il habite au dix.	He lives at number ten.
à la page dix-neuf	on page nineteen
au chapitre sept	in chapter seven
Il habite au cinquième (étage).	He lives on the fifth floor.
Il est arrivé troisième.	He came in third.
échelle au vingt-cinq millième	scale one to twenty-five thousand

L'HEURE	THE TIME
Quelle heure est-il?	What time is it?
Il est...	It's...
une heure	one o'clock
une heure dix	ten past one
une heure et quart	quarter past one
une heure et demie	half past one
deux heures moins vingt	twenty to two
deux heures moins le quart	quarter to two
À quelle heure?	At what time?
à minuit	at midnight
à midi	at midday, at noon
à une heure (de l'après-midi)	at one o'clock (in the afternoon)
à huit heures (du soir)	at eight o'clock (in the evening)
à 11h15 *or* **onze heures quinze**	at 11.15 *or* eleven fifteen
à 20h45 *or* **vingt heures quarante-cinq**	at 20.45 *or* twenty forty-five

LA DATE	THE DATE
LES JOURS DE LA SEMAINE	**DAYS OF THE WEEK**
lundi	Monday
mardi	Tuesday
mercredi	Wednesday
jeudi	Thursday
vendredi	Friday
samedi	Saturday
dimanche	Sunday
Quand?	**When?**
lundi	on Monday
le lundi	on Mondays
tous les lundis	every Monday
mardi dernier	last Tuesday
vendredi prochain	next Friday
samedi en huit	a week on Saturday
samedi en quinze	two weeks on Saturday

i Note that days of the week are NOT written with a capital letter in French.

LES MOIS	MONTHS OF THE YEAR
janvier	January
février	February
mars	March
avril	April
mai	May
juin	June
juillet	July
août	August
septembre	September
octobre	October
novembre	November
décembre	December

Quand?	When?
en février	in February
le 1er décembre	on December 1st
le premier décembre	on December first
en 1998	in 1998
en mille neuf cent quatre-vingt-dix-huit	in nineteen ninety-eight

Quel jour sommes-nous? Nous sommes le…	What day is it? It's…
lundi 26 février *or* **lundi vingt-six février**	Monday 26 February *or* Monday twenty-sixth of February
dimanche 1er octobre *or* **dimanche premier octobre**	Sunday 1st October *or* Sunday the first of October

i Note that months of the year are NOT written with a capital letter in French.

VOCABULAIRE	USEFUL VOCABULARY
Quand?	**When?**
aujourd'hui	today
ce matin	this morning
cet après-midi	this afternoon
ce soir	this evening
Souvent?	**How often?**
tous les jours	every day
tous les deux jours	every other day
une fois par semaine	once a week
deux fois par semaine	twice a week
une fois par mois	once a month
Ça s'est passé quand?	**When did it happen?**
le matin	in the morning
le soir	in the evening
hier	yesterday
hier soir	yesterday evening
avant-hier	the day before yesterday
il y a une semaine	a week ago
il y a quinze jours	two weeks ago
l'an dernier *or* l'année dernière	last year
Ça va se passer quand?	**When is it going to happen?**
demain	tomorrow
demain matin	tomorrow morning
après-demain	the day after tomorrow
dans deux jours	in two days
dans une semaine	in a week
dans quinze jours	in two weeks
le mois prochain	next month
l'an prochain *or* l'année prochaine	next year

Some common difficulties

General problems

➤ You can't always translate French into English and English into French word for word. While occasionally it is possible to do this, often it is not. For example:

- English phrasal verbs (verbs followed by a preposition or adverb), for example, *to run away*, *to fall down*, are often translated by ONE word in French.

continuer	to go on
tomber	to fall down
rendre	to give back

☞ *For more information on **Verbs**, see pages 69–137.*

- Sentences which contain a verb and preposition in English, might NOT contain a preposition in French.

payer quelque chose	to pay for something
regarder quelqu'un/quelque chose	to look at somebody/something
écouter quelqu'un/quelque chose	to listen to somebody/something

- Similarly, sentences which contain a verb and preposition in French, might NOT contain a preposition in English.

obéir à quelqu'un/quelque chose	to obey somebody/something
changer de quelque chose	to change something
manquer de quelque chose	to lack something

- The same French preposition may be translated into English in different ways.

parler de quelque chose	to talk about something
sûr de quelque chose	sure of something
voler quelque chose à quelqu'un	to steal something from someone
croire à quelque chose	to believe in something

☞ *For more information on **Prepositions**, see page 162.*

- A word which is singular in English may not be in French.

les bagages	luggage
ses cheveux	his/her hair

- Similarly, a word which is singular in French may not be in English.

un short	shorts
mon pantalon	my trousers

➪ *For more information on* ***Nouns****, see page 1.*

- In English, you can use 's to show who or what something belongs to; in French, you have to use **de**.

la voiture de mon frère	my brother's car
la chambre des enfants	the children's bedroom

➪ *For more information on the preposition* ***de****, see page 166.*

Specific problems

1 -ing

➤ The *-ing* ending in English is translated in a number of different ways in French:

- *to be ...-ing* is translated by a verb consisting of one word.

Il part demain.	He's leaving tomorrow.
Je lisais un roman.	I was reading a book.

➪ *For more information on* ***Verbs****, see pages 69–137.*

ℹ Note that when you are talking about somebody's or something's physical position, you use a past participle.

Elle est assise là-bas.	She's sitting over there.
Il était couché par terre.	He was lying on the ground.

➪ *For more information on the* ***Past participle****, see page 111.*

➤ *-ing* can also be translated by:

- an infinitive

J'aime aller au cinéma.	I like going to the cinema.
Arrêtez de vous disputer!	Stop arguing!
Avant de partir...	Before leaving...

➪ *For more information on* ***Infinitives****, see page 133.*

- a present participle

<u>Étant</u> plus timide que moi, elle...	Being shyer than me, she...

➪ *For more information on the **Present participle**, see page 125.*

- a noun

<u>Le ski</u> me maintient en forme.	<u>Skiing</u> keeps me fit.

➪ *For more information on **Nouns**, see page 1.*

2 to be

➤ The verb *to be* is generally translated by **être**.

Il <u>est</u> tard.	It<u>'s</u> late.
Ce n'<u>est</u> pas possible!	It<u>'s</u> not possible!

➤ When you are talking about the physical position of something, **se trouver** may be used.

Où <u>se trouve</u> la gare?	Where<u>'s</u> the station?

➤ In certain set phrases which describe how you are feeling or a state you are in, the verb **avoir** is used.

avoir chaud	to be warm
avoir froid	to be cold
avoir faim	to be hungry
avoir soif	to be thirsty
avoir peur	to be afraid
avoir tort	to be wrong
avoir raison	to be right

➤ When you are describing what the weather is like, use the verb **faire**.

Quel temps <u>fait</u>-il?	What<u>'s</u> the weather like?
Il <u>fait</u> beau.	It<u>'s</u> lovely.
Il <u>fait</u> mauvais.	It<u>'s</u> miserable.
Il <u>fait</u> du vent.	It<u>'s</u> windy.

➤ When you are talking about someone's age, use the verb **avoir**.

Quel âge <u>as</u>-tu?	How old <u>are</u> you?
J'<u>ai</u> quinze ans.	I<u>'m</u> fifteen.

➤ When talking about your health, use the verb **aller**.

Comment <u>allez</u>-vous?	How <u>are</u> you?
Je <u>vais</u> très bien.	I<u>'m</u> very well.

3 it is, it's

➤ *it is* and *it's* are usually translated by **il est** or **elle est** when referring to a noun.

'Où est mon parapluie?' – 'Il est là, dans le coin.'	'Where's my umbrella?' – 'It's there, in the corner.'
Descends la valise si elle n'est pas trop lourde.	Bring the case down if it isn't too heavy.

➤ When you are talking about the time, use **il est**.

'Quelle heure est-il?' – 'Il est sept heures et demie.'	'What time is it?' – 'It's half past seven.'

➤ When you are describing what the weather is like, use the verb **faire**.

Il fait beau.	It's lovely.
Il fait mauvais.	It's miserable.
Il fait du vent.	It's windy.

➤ If you want to say, for example, *it is difficult to do something* or *it is easy to do something*, use **il est**.

Il est difficile de répondre à cette question.	It is difficult to answer this question.

➤ In ALL other phrases and constructions, use **c'est**.

C'est moi qui ne l'aime pas.	It's me who doesn't like him.
C'est Charles qui l'a dit.	It's Charles who said so.
C'est ici que je les ai achetés.	It's here that I bought them.
C'est parce que la poste est fermée que...	It's because the post office is closed that...

4 there is, there are

➤ Both *there is* and *there are* are translated by **il y a**.

Il y a quelqu'un à la porte.	There is someone at the door.
Il y a cinq livres sur la table.	There are five books on the table.

5 can, to be able

➤ If you want to talk about someone's physical ability to do something, use **pouvoir**.

Pouvez-vous faire dix kilomètres à pied?	Can you walk ten kilometres?

➤ If you want to say that *you know how to do something*, use **savoir**.

Elle ne sait pas nager.	She can't swim.

➤ When *can* is used with verbs to do with what you can see or hear, you do NOT use **pouvoir** in French.

Je ne vois rien.	I can't see anything.
Il les entendait.	He could hear them.

6 to

➤ The preposition *to* is generally translated by **à**.

Donne le livre à Patrick.	Give the book to Patrick.

➪ *For more information on the preposition **à**, see page 163.*

➤ When you are talking about the time, use **moins**.

dix heures moins cinq	five to ten
à sept heures moins le quart	at a quarter to seven

➤ If you want to say *(in order) to*, use **pour**.

Je l'ai fait pour vous aider.	I did it to help you.
Il va en ville pour acheter un cadeau.	He's going into town to buy a present.

The Alphabet

➤ The French alphabet is pronounced differently from the way it is pronounced in English. Use the list below to help you sound out the letters.

A, a	[ɑ]	(ah)	like 'a' in 'la'
B, b	[be]	(bay)	
C, c	[se]	(say)	
D, d	[de]	(day)	
E, e	[ə]	(uh)	like 'e' in 'le'
F, f	[ɛf]	(eff)	
G, g	[ʒe]	(jay)	
H, h	[aʃ]	(ash)	
I, i	[i]	(ee)	
J, j	[ʒi]	(jee)	
K, k	[ka]	(ka)	
L, l	[ɛl]	(ell)	
M, m	[ɛm]	(emm)	
N, n	[ɛn]	(enn)	
O, o	[o]	(oh)	
P, p	[pe]	(pay)	
Q, q	[ky]	(ku)	like 'u' in 'une'
R, r	[ɛr]	(air)	
S, s	[ɛs]	(ess)	
T, t	[te]	(tay)	
U, u	[y]	(u)	like 'u' in 'une'
V, v	[ve]	(vay)	
W, w	[dubləve]	(doobla-vay)	
X, x	[iks]	(eex)	
Y, y	[igrɛk]	(ee-grek)	
Z, z	[zɛd]	(zed)	

For further explanation of grammatical terms, please see pages viii-xii.

Main Index

Verb Tables

VERB TABLES

Introduction

The **Verb Tables** in the following section contain 115 tables of French verbs (some regular and some irregular) in alphabetical order. Each table shows you the following forms: **Present, Present Subjunctive, Perfect, Imperfect, Future, Conditional, Past Historic, Pluperfect, Imperative** and the **Present** and **Past Participles**. For more information on these tenses and how they are formed you should look at the section on Verbs on pages 69–137.

In order to help you use the verbs shown in the Verb Tables correctly, there are also a number of example phrases at the bottom of each page to show the verb as it is used in context.

In French there are both **regular** (their forms follow the normal rules) and **irregular** verbs (their forms do not follow the normal rules). The regular verbs in these tables are:

donner (regular **-er** verb, page 274)
finir (regular **-ir** verb, page 304)
attendre (regular **-re** verb, page 226)

The irregular verbs are shown in full.

The **Verb Index** at the end of this section contains over 2000 verbs, each of which is cross-referred to one of the verbs given in the Verb Tables. The table shows the patterns that the verb listed in the index follows.

acheter (to buy)

PRESENT

j'	**achète**
tu	**achètes**
il/elle/on	**achète**
nous	**achetons**
vous	**achetez**
ils/elles	**achètent**

PRESENT SUBJUNCTIVE

j'	**achète**
tu	**achètes**
il/elle/on	**achète**
nous	**achetions**
vous	**achetiez**
ils/elles	**achètent**

PERFECT

j'	**ai acheté**
tu	**as acheté**
il/elle/on	**a acheté**
nous	**avons acheté**
vous	**avez acheté**
ils/elles	**ont acheté**

IMPERFECT

j'	**achetais**
tu	**achetais**
il/elle/on	**achetait**
nous	**achetions**
vous	**achetiez**
ils/elles	**achetaient**

PRESENT PARTICIPLE

achetant

PAST PARTICIPLE

acheté

EXAMPLE PHRASES

Nous n'**achetons** jamais de chips. We never buy crisps.

Qu'est-ce que tu **as acheté**? What did you buy?

N'**achète** rien pour moi. Don't buy anything for me.

Il faut que j'**achète** un cadeau pour son anniversaire. I must buy a present for his birthday.

Ses parents lui **achetaient** des bonbons. His parents bought him sweets.

acheter

FUTURE

j'	**achèterai**
tU	**achèteras**
il/elle/on	**achètera**
nous	**achèterons**
vous	**achèterez**
ils/elles	**achèteront**

CONDITIONAL

j'	**achèterais**
tu	**achèterais**
il/elle/on	**achèterait**
nous	**achèterions**
vous	**achèteriez**
ils/elles	**achèteraient**

PAST HISTORIC

j'	**achetai**
tu	**achetas**
il/elle/on	**acheta**
nous	**achetâmes**
vous	**achetâtes**
ils/elles	**achetèrent**

PLUPERFECT

j'	**avais acheté**
tu	**avais acheté**
il/elle/on	**avait acheté**
nous	**avions acheté**
vous	**aviez acheté**
ils/elles	**avaient acheté**

IMPERATIVE

achète / achetons / achetez

EXAMPLE PHRASES

J'**achèterai** des gâteaux à la pâtisserie. I'll buy some cakes at the cake shop.
Elle **acheta** la robe rouge. She bought the red dress.
Si j'étais riche j'**achèterais** un voilier. If I were rich, I'd buy a yacht.
Il lui **avait acheté** une liseuse, mais elle ne voulait pas s'en servir.
He'd bought her an e-reader, but she didn't want to use it.

je/j' = I **tu** = you **il** = he/it **elle** = she/it **on** = we/one **nous** = we **vous** = you **ils/elles** = they

acquérir (to acquire)

PRESENT

j'	**acquiers**
tu	**acquiers**
il/elle/on	**acquiert**
nous	**acquérons**
vous	**acquérez**
ils/elles	**acquièrent**

PRESENT SUBJUNCTIVE

j'	**acquière**
tu	**acquières**
il/elle/on	**acquière**
nous	**acquérions**
vous	**acquériez**
ils/elles	**acquièrent**

PERFECT

j'	**ai acquis**
tu	**as acquis**
il/elle/on	**a acquis**
nous	**avons acquis**
vous	**avez acquis**
ils/elles	**ont acquis**

IMPERFECT

j'	**acquérais**
tu	**acquérais**
il/elle/on	**acquérait**
nous	**acquérions**
vous	**acquériez**
ils/elles	**acquéraient**

PRESENT PARTICIPLE

acquérant

PAST PARTICIPLE

acquis

EXAMPLE PHRASES

Nous **acquérons** de nouvelles connaissances tous les jours. We acquire new knowledge every day.

Les mauvaises habitudes s'**acquièrent** facilement. One easily acquires bad habits.

Elle **a acquis** la nationalité française en 2003. She acquired French nationality in 2003.

Il faut qu'il **acquière** de l'expérience avant que nous puissions lui offrir un travail. He has to gain some experience before we can offer him a job.

acquérir

FUTURE

j'	**acquerrai**
tu	**acquerras**
il/elle/on	**acquerra**
nous	**acquerrons**
vous	**acquerrez**
ils/elles	**acquerront**

CONDITIONAL

j'	**acquerrais**
tu	**acquerrais**
il/elle/on	**acquerrait**
nous	**acquerrions**
vous	**acquerriez**
ils/elles	**acquerraient**

PAST HISTORIC

j'	**acquis**
tu	**acquis**
il/elle/on	**acquit**
nous	**acquîmes**
vous	**acquîtes**
ils/elles	**acquirent**

PLUPERFECT

j'	**avais acquis**
tu	**avais acquis**
il/elle/on	**avait acquis**
nous	**avions acquis**
vous	**aviez acquis**
ils/elles	**avaient acquis**

IMPERATIVE

acquiers / acquérons / acquérez

EXAMPLE PHRASES

Elle **acquit** soudain la certitude qu'il lui avait toujours menti. She suddenly felt certain that he'd always lied to her.

Tu **acquerrais** un peu d'expérience si tu travaillais cet été. You'd gain some experience if you worked this summer.

Il **avait** mystérieusement **acquis** une superbe voiture de sport. He had mysteriously acquired a beautiful sportscar.

Le tableau **avait acquis** beaucoup de valeur. The painting had risen a lot in value.

aller (to go)

PRESENT

je	**vais**
tu	**vas**
il/elle/on	**va**
nous	**allons**
vous	**allez**
ils/elles	**vont**

PRESENT SUBJUNCTIVE

j'	**aille**
tu	**ailles**
il/elle/on	**aille**
nous	**allions**
vous	**alliez**
ils/elles	**aillent**

PERFECT

je	**suis allé(e)**
tu	**es allé(e)**
il/elle/on	**est allé(e)**
nous	**sommes allé(e)s**
vous	**êtes allé(e)(s)**
ils/elles	**sont allé(e)s**

IMPERFECT

j'	**allais**
tu	**allais**
il/elle/on	**allait**
nous	**allions**
vous	**alliez**
ils/elles	**allaient**

PRESENT PARTICIPLE
allant

PAST PARTICIPLE
allé

EXAMPLE PHRASES

Vous **allez** souvent au cinéma? Do you often go to the cinema?
Je **suis allé** à Londres. I went to London.
Est-ce que tu **es** déjà **allé** en Allemagne? Have you ever been to Germany?
Va voir s'ils sont arrivés. Go and see whether they have arrived.
Il faut que j'**aille** la chercher à la gare. I have to go and get her at the station.
J'**allais** tous les jours à l'école à pied. I would walk to school every day.

je/j' = I **tu** = you **il** = he/it **elle** = she/it **on** = we/one **nous** = we **vous** = you **ils/elles** = they

aller

FUTURE

j'	**irai**
tu	**iras**
il/elle/on	**ira**
nous	**irons**
vous	**irez**
ils/elles	**iront**

CONDITIONAL

j'	**irais**
tu	**irais**
il/elle/on	**irait**
nous	**irions**
vous	**iriez**
ils/elles	**iraient**

PAST HISTORIC

j'	**allai**
tu	**allas**
il/elle/on	**alla**
nous	**allâmes**
vous	**allâtes**
ils/elles	**allèrent**

PLUPERFECT

j'	**étais allé(e)**
tu	**étais allé(e)**
il/elle/on	**était allé(e)**
nous	**étions allé(e)s**
vous	**étiez allé(e)(s)**
ils/elles	**étaient allé(e)s**

IMPERATIVE

va / allons / allez

EXAMPLE PHRASES

J'**irai** en ville demain. I'll go into town tomorrow.

Ils **allèrent** la voir à l'hôpital. They went to see her at the hospital.

J'**irais** au théâtre avec toi s'il restait des places. I'd go to the theatre with you if there were any tickets left.

Nous **étions allés** à Paris en avion mais nous étions rentrés par le train. We'd flown to Paris, but we'd come back by train.

je/j' = I **tu** = you **il** = he/it **elle** = she/it **on** = we/one **nous** = we **vous** = you **ils/elles** = they

s'amuser (to play; to enjoy oneself)

PRESENT

je	**m'amuse**
tu	**t'amuses**
il/elle/on	**s'amuse**
nous	**nous amusons**
vous	**vous amusez**
ils/elles	**s'amusent**

PRESENT SUBJUNCTIVE

je	**m'amuse**
tu	**t'amuses**
il/elle/on	**s'amuse**
nous	**nous amusions**
vous	**vous amusiez**
ils/elles	**s'amusent**

PERFECT

je	**me suis amusé(e)**
tu	**t'es amusé(e)**
il/elle/on	**s'est amusé(e)**
nous	**nous sommes amusé(e)s**
vous	**vous êtes amusé(e)(s)**
ils/elles	**se sont amusé(e)s**

IMPERFECT

je	**m'amusais**
tu	**t'amusais**
il/elle/on	**s'amusait**
nous	**nous amusions**
vous	**vous amusiez**
ils/elles	**s'amusaient**

PRESENT PARTICIPLE
s'amusant

PAST PARTICIPLE
amusé

EXAMPLE PHRASES

Les enfants **s'amusent** dehors. The children are playing outside.

On **s'est** bien **amusés** à cette soirée. We really enjoyed ourselves at that party.

Amuse-toi bien au parc accrobranche. Have fun at the treetop adventure park.

J'ai peur que personne ne **s'amuse** cet après-midi. I'm scared nobody enjoys themselves this afternoon.

Ils **s'amusaient** à sauter dans les flaques d'eau. They had fun jumping in the puddles.

---

je/j' = I **tu** = you **il** = he/it **elle** = she/it **on** = we/one **nous** = we **vous** = you **ils/elles** = they

s'amuser

FUTURE

je	**m'amuserai**
tu	**t'amuseras**
il/elle/on	**s'amusera**
nous	**nous amuserons**
vous	**vous amuserez**
ils/elles	**s'amuseront**

CONDITIONAL

je	**m'amuserais**
tu	**t'amuserais**
il/elle/on	**s'amuserait**
nous	**nous amuserions**
vous	**vous amuseriez**
ils/elles	**s'amuseraient**

PAST HISTORIC

je	**m'amusai**
tu	**t'amusas**
il/elle/on	**s'amusa**
nous	**nous amusâmes**
vous	**vous amusâtes**
ils/elles	**s'amusèrent**

PLUPERFECT

je	**m'étais amusé(e)**
tu	**t'étais amusé(e)**
il/elle/on	**s'était amusé(e)**
nous	**nous étions amusé(e)s**
vous	**vous étiez amusé(e)(s)**
ils/elles	**s'étaient amusé(e)s**

IMPERATIVE

amuse-toi / amusons-nous / amusez-vous

EXAMPLE PHRASES

Je suis sûr qu'ils **s'amuseront** comme des fous. I'm sure they'll have a whale of a time.

Ils **s'amusèrent** à dessiner un monstre. They had fun drawing a monster.

Tu **t'amuserais** bien si tu venais avec nous. You'd have fun if you came with us.

Je **m'étais** bien **amusé** à leur mariage. I'd really enjoyed myself at their wedding.

apercevoir (to see)

PRESENT

j'	**aperçois**
tu	**aperçois**
il/elle/on	**aperçoit**
nous	**apercevons**
vous	**apercevez**
ils/elles	**aperçoivent**

PRESENT SUBJUNCTIVE

j'	**aperçoive**
tu	**aperçoives**
il/elle/on	**aperçoive**
nous	**apercevions**
vous	**aperceviez**
ils/elles	**aperçoivent**

PERFECT

j'	**ai aperçu**
tu	**as aperçu**
il/elle/on	**a aperçu**
nous	**avons aperçu**
vous	**avez aperçu**
ils/elles	**ont aperçu**

IMPERFECT

j'	**apercevais**
tu	**apercevais**
il/elle/on	**apercevait**
nous	**apercevions**
vous	**aperceviez**
ils/elles	**apercevaient**

PRESENT PARTICIPLE
apercevant

PAST PARTICIPLE
aperçu

EXAMPLE PHRASES

J'**aperçois** une lumière là-bas. I can see a light over there.
Je l'**ai aperçue** hier au marché. I saw her yesterday at the market.
Ils ont marché longtemps, jusqu'à ce qu'ils **aperçoivent** une maison. They walked for a long time, until they saw a house.
Je les **apercevais** de temps en temps en allant travailler. I saw them from time to time on my way to work.

je/j' = I **tu** = you **il** = he/it **elle** = she/it **on** = we/one **nous** = we **vous** = you **ils/elles** = they

apercevoir

FUTURE		CONDITIONAL	
j'	**apercevrai**	j'	**apercevrais**
tu	**apercevras**	tu	**apercevrais**
il/elle/on	**apercevra**	il/elle/on	**apercevrait**
nous	**apercevrons**	nous	**apercevrions**
vous	**apercevrez**	vous	**apercevriez**
ils/elles	**apercevront**	ils/elles	**apercevraient**

PAST HISTORIC		PLUPERFECT	
j'	**aperçus**	j'	**avais aperçu**
tu	**aperçus**	tu	**avais aperçu**
il/elle/on	**aperçut**	il/elle/on	**avait aperçu**
nous	**aperçûmes**	nous	**avions aperçu**
vous	**aperçûtes**	vous	**aviez aperçu**
ils/elles	**aperçurent**	ils/elles	**avaient aperçu**

IMPERATIVE

not used

EXAMPLE PHRASES

Va jusqu'à l'arrêt du bus et tu **apercevras** le magasin au coin de la rue.
Go up to the bus stop and you'll see the shop on the street corner.

Ils **aperçurent** une silhouette au loin. They saw a shadow in the distance.

Il l'**avait aperçue** une ou deux fois chez les Duval il y avait très longtemps.
He'd seen her once or twice at the Duvals' a long time before.

Je ne me souvenais pas de l'endroit où je l'**avais aperçu**. I couldn't remember where I'd seen him.

appeler (to call)

PRESENT

j'	**appelle**
tu	**appelles**
il/elle/on	**appelle**
nous	**appelons**
vous	**appelez**
ils/elles	**appellent**

PRESENT SUBJUNCTIVE

j'	**appelle**
tu	**appelles**
il/elle/on	**appelle**
nous	**appelions**
vous	**appeliez**
ils/elles	**appellent**

PERFECT

j'	**ai appelé**
tu	**as appelé**
il/elle/on	**a appelé**
nous	**avons appelé**
vous	**avez appelé**
ils/elles	**ont appelé**

IMPERFECT

j'	**appelais**
tu	**appelais**
il/elle/on	**appelait**
nous	**appelions**
vous	**appeliez**
ils/elles	**appelaient**

PRESENT PARTICIPLE
appelant

PAST PARTICIPLE
appelé

EXAMPLE PHRASES

Louise! Descends: maman t'**appelle**. Louise! Go downstairs – Mum's calling you.
Comment tu t'**appelles**? What's your name?
Elle **a appelé** le médecin. She called the doctor.
Appelle-moi sur mon portable. Call me on my mobile.
Il faut que je l'**appelle** après dîner. I must call her after dinner.
Elle **appelait** souvent le soir. She often called in the evening.

je/j' = I **tu** = you **il** = he/it **elle** = she/it **on** = we/one **nous** = we **vous** = you **ils/elles** = they

appeler

FUTURE

j'	**appellerai**
tu	**appelleras**
il/elle/on	**appellera**
nous	**appellerons**
vous	**appellerez**
ils/elles	**appelleront**

CONDITIONAL

j'	**appellerais**
tu	**appellerais**
il/elle/on	**appellerait**
nous	**appellerions**
vous	**appelleriez**
ils/elles	**appelleraient**

PAST HISTORIC

j'	**appelai**
tu	**appelas**
il/elle/on	**appela**
nous	**appelâmes**
vous	**appelâtes**
ils/elles	**appelèrent**

PLUPERFECT

j'	**avais appelé**
tu	**avais appelé**
il/elle/on	**avait appelé**
nous	**avions appelé**
vous	**aviez appelé**
ils/elles	**avaient appelé**

IMPERATIVE

appelle / appelons / appelez

EXAMPLE PHRASES

Je t'**appellerai** demain. I'll call you tomorrow.

On **appela** mon nom et je me levai. My name was called and I stood up.

Je l'**appellerais** si j'étais sûr de ne pas le déranger. I'd call him if I was sure not to disturb him.

Elle m'**avait appelé** mais je ne l'avais pas entendue. She had called me but I hadn't heard her.

appuyer (to lean/press)

PRESENT		PRESENT SUBJUNCTIVE	
j'	**appuie**	j'	**appuie**
tu	**appuies**	tu	**appuies**
il/elle/on	**appuie**	il/elle/on	**appuie**
nous	**appuyons**	nous	**appuyions**
vous	**appuyez**	vous	**appuyiez**
ils/elles	**appuient**	ils/elles	**appuient**

PERFECT		IMPERFECT	
j'	**ai appuyé**	j'	**appuyais**
tu	**as appuyé**	tu	**appuyais**
il/elle/on	**a appuyé**	il/elle/on	**appuyait**
nous	**avons appuyé**	nous	**appuyions**
vous	**avez appuyé**	vous	**appuyiez**
ils/elles	**ont appuyé**	ils/elles	**appuyaient**

PRESENT PARTICIPLE
appuyant

PAST PARTICIPLE
appuyé

EXAMPLE PHRASES

Elle **a appuyé** son vélo contre le mur. She leaned her bike against the wall.
Appuie sur le bouton rouge. Press the red button.
N'**appuie** pas trop fort. Don't press too hard.
Appuyez bien sur le couvercle. Press well on the lid.
Il faut que tu **appuies** fort. You have to press hard.

je/j' = I **tu** = you **il** = he/it **elle** = she/it **on** = we/one **nous** = we **vous** = you **ils/elles** = they

appuyer

FUTURE	
j'	**appuierai**
tu	**appuieras**
il/elle/on	**appuiera**
nous	**appuierons**
vous	**appuierez**
ils/elles	**appuieront**

CONDITIONAL	
j'	**appuierais**
tu	**appuierais**
il/elle/on	**appuierait**
nous	**appuierions**
vous	**appuieriez**
ils/elles	**appuieraient**

PAST HISTORIC	
j'	**appuyai**
tu	**appuyas**
il/elle/on	**appuya**
nous	**appuyâmes**
vous	**appuyâtes**
ils/elles	**appuyèrent**

PLUPERFECT	
j'	**avais appuyé**
tu	**avais appuyé**
il/elle/on	**avait appuyé**
nous	**avions appuyé**
vous	**aviez appuyé**
ils/elles	**avaient appuyé**

IMPERATIVE

appuie / appuyons / appuyez

EXAMPLE PHRASES

J'**appuierai** trois fois sur la sonnette. I'll press the bell three times.

Il **appuya** longtemps mais la colle ne tenait pas. He pressed for a long time but the glue didn't hold.

Si j'étais toi, j'**appuierais** plus fort. If I were you, I would press harder.

Elle n'**avait** pas **appuyé** assez fort et la cloche n'avait pas sonné. She hadn't pressed hard enough and the bell hadn't rung.

arriver (to arrive; to happen)

PRESENT

j'	**arrive**
tu	**arrives**
il/elle/on	**arrive**
nous	**arrivons**
vous	**arrivez**
ils/elles	**arrivent**

PRESENT SUBJUNCTIVE

j'	**arrive**
tu	**arrives**
il/elle/on	**arrive**
nous	**arrivions**
vous	**arriviez**
ils/elles	**arrivent**

PERFECT

je	**suis arrivé(e)**
tu	**es arrivé(e)**
il/elle/on	**est arrivé(e)**
nous	**sommes arrivé(e)s**
vous	**êtes arrivé(e)(s)**
ils/elles	**sont arrivé(e)s**

IMPERFECT

j'	**arrivais**
tu	**arrivais**
il/elle/on	**arrivait**
nous	**arrivions**
vous	**arriviez**
ils/elles	**arrivaient**

PRESENT PARTICIPLE

arrivant

PAST PARTICIPLE

arrivé

EXAMPLE PHRASES

J'**arrive** à l'école à huit heures. I arrive at school at 8 o'clock.

Qu'est-ce qui **est arrivé** à Aurélie? What happened to Aurélie?

N'**arrivez** pas en retard demain. Don't arrive late tomorrow.

Il faut que j'**arrive** à jouer cet air pour la leçon de demain. I'll have to be able to play this tune for tomorrow's lesson.

Il m'**arrivait** de dormir jusqu'à midi. I sometimes slept till midday.

arriver

FUTURE	
j'	**arriverai**
tu	**arriveras**
il/elle/on	**arrivera**
nous	**arriverons**
vous	**arriverez**
ils/elles	**arriveront**

CONDITIONAL	
j'	**arriverais**
tu	**arriverais**
il/elle/on	**arriverait**
nous	**arriverions**
vous	**arriveriez**
ils/elles	**arriveraient**

PAST HISTORIC	
j'	**arrivai**
tu	**arrivas**
il/elle/on	**arriva**
nous	**arrivâmes**
vous	**arrivâtes**
ils/elles	**arrivèrent**

PLUPERFECT	
j'	**étais arrivé(e)**
tu	**étais arrivé(e)**
il/elle/on	**était arrivé(e)**
nous	**étions arrivé(e)s**
vous	**étiez arrivé(e)(s)**
ils/elles	**étaient arrivé(e)s**

IMPERATIVE

arrive / arrivons / arrivez

EXAMPLE PHRASES

Arriveras-tu à l'heure pour ton rendez-vous? Will you be on time for your appointment?

La réunion était finie depuis longtemps quand il **arriva**. The meeting had finished long before he arrived.

Je n'arriverais jamais à faire tout ce travail sans ton aide. I would never be able to get all this work done without your help.

Le prof n'**était** pas encore **arrivé**. The teacher hadn't arrived yet.

s'asseoir (to sit down)

PRESENT

je	**m'assieds/m'assois**
tu	**t'assieds/t'assois**
il/elle/on	**s'assied/s'assoit**
nous	**nous asseyons/nous assoyons**
vous	**vous asseyez/vous assoyez**
ils/elles	**s'asseyent/s'assoient**

PRESENT SUBJUNCTIVE

je	**m'asseye**
tu	**t'asseyes**
il/elle/on	**s'asseye**
nous	**nous asseyions**
vous	**vous asseyiez**
ils/elles	**s'asseyent**

PERFECT

je	**me suis assis(e)**
tu	**t'es assis(e)**
il/elle/on	**s'est assis(e)**
nous	**nous sommes assis(es)**
vous	**vous êtes assis(e(s))**
ils/elles	**se sont assis(es)**

IMPERFECT

je	**m'asseyais**
tu	**t'asseyais**
il/elle/on	**s'asseyait**
nous	**nous asseyions**
vous	**vous asseyiez**
ils/elles	**s'asseyaient**

PRESENT PARTICIPLE
s'asseyant

PAST PARTICIPLE
assis

EXAMPLE PHRASES

Je peux **m'asseoir**? May I sit down?
Je **me suis assise** sur un chewing-gum! I've sat on chewing-gum!
Assieds-toi, Nicole. Sit down Nicole.
Asseyez-vous, les enfants. Sit down children.
On **s'asseyait** toujours l'un à côté de l'autre. We would always sit next to each other.

je/j' = I **tu** = you **il** = he/it **elle** = she/it **on** = we/one **nous** = we **vous** = you **ils/elles** = they

s'asseoir

FUTURE	
je	**m'assiérai**
tu	**t'assiéras**
il/elle/on	**s'assiéra**
nous	**nous assiérons**
vous	**vous assiérez**
ils/elles	**s'assiéront**

CONDITIONAL	
je	**m'assiérais**
tu	**t'assiérais**
il/elle/on	**s'assiérait**
nous	**nous assiérons**
vous	**vous assiérez**
ils/elles	**s'assiéraient**

PAST HISTORIC	
je	**m'assis**
tu	**t'assis**
il/elle/on	**s'assit**
nous	**nous assîmes**
vous	**vous assîtes**
ils/elles	**s'assirent**

PLUPERFECT	
je	**m'étais assis(e)**
tu	**t'étais assis(e)**
il/elle/on	**s'était assis(e)**
nous	**nous étions assis(es)**
vous	**vous étiez assis(e(s))**
ils/elles	**s'étaient assis(es)**

IMPERATIVE

assieds-toi / asseyons-nous / asseyez-vous

EXAMPLE PHRASES

Je **m'assiérai** à côté de toi. I'll sit next to you.

Il **s'assit** en face de moi. He sat down opposite me.

Je ne **m'assiérais** pas là si j'étais toi. I wouldn't sit there if I were you.

Elle ne **s'était** pas encore **assise** quand la fillette l'appela à nouveau.
She hadn't even sat down when the little girl called her once again.

je/j' = I **tu** = you **il** = he/it **elle** = she/it **on** = we/one **nous** = we **vous** = you **ils/elles** = they

atteindre (to reach)

PRESENT		PRESENT SUBJUNCTIVE	
j'	**atteins**	j'	**atteigne**
tu	**atteins**	tu	**atteignes**
il/elle/on	**atteint**	il/elle/on	**atteigne**
nous	**atteignons**	nous	**atteignions**
vous	**atteignez**	vous	**atteigniez**
ils/elles	**atteignent**	ils/elles	**atteignent**

PERFECT		IMPERFECT	
j'	**ai atteint**	j'	**atteignais**
tu	**as atteint**	tu	**atteignais**
il/elle/on	**a atteint**	il/elle/on	**atteignait**
nous	**avons atteint**	nous	**atteignions**
vous	**avez atteint**	vous	**atteigniez**
ils/elles	**ont atteint**	ils/elles	**atteignaient**

PRESENT PARTICIPLE
atteignant

PAST PARTICIPLE
atteint

EXAMPLE PHRASES

Je n'arrive pas à **atteindre** ma valise. I can't reach my suitcase.

Cette Ferrari **atteint** une vitesse de 245 km/h. This Ferrari reaches a speed of 245km/h.

Ils **ont atteint** le sommet en quatre heures et demie. They reached the summit in four and a half hours.

Ils **atteignaient** Paris quand l'accident se produisit. They were nearing Paris when the accident happened.

atteindre

FUTURE

j'	**atteindrai**
tu	**atteindras**
il/elle/on	**atteindra**
nous	**atteindrons**
vous	**atteindrez**
ils/elles	**atteindront**

CONDITIONAL

j'	**atteindrais**
tu	**atteindrais**
il/elle/on	**atteindrait**
nous	**atteindrions**
vous	**atteindriez**
ils/elles	**atteindraient**

PAST HISTORIC

j'	**atteignis**
tu	**atteignis**
il/elle/on	**atteignit**
nous	**atteignîmes**
vous	**atteignîtes**
ils/elles	**atteignirent**

PLUPERFECT

j'	**avais atteint**
tu	**avais atteint**
il/elle/on	**avait atteint**
nous	**avions atteint**
vous	**aviez atteint**
ils/elles	**avaient atteint**

IMPERATIVE

atteins / atteignons / atteignez

EXAMPLE PHRASES

Nous **atteindrons** Rouen dans dix minutes. We'll reach Rouen in ten minutes.

Il **atteignit** sa destination en trois semaines. He reached his destination in three weeks.

Il se rendit compte qu'il n'**atteindrait** jamais son but. He realized that he would never reach his goal.

Le tableau **avait atteint** un prix exorbitant. The painting had reached a prohibitive price.

attendre (to wait)

PRESENT

j'	**attends**
tu	**attends**
il/elle/on	**attend**
nous	**attendons**
vous	**attendez**
ils/elles	**attendent**

PRESENT SUBJUNCTIVE

j'	**attende**
tu	**attendes**
il/elle/on	**attende**
nous	**attendions**
vous	**attendiez**
ils/elles	**attendent**

PERFECT

j'	**ai attendu**
tu	**as attendu**
il/elle/on	**a attendu**
nous	**avons attendu**
vous	**avez attendu**
ils/elles	**ont attendu**

IMPERFECT

j'	**attendais**
tu	**attendais**
il/elle/on	**attendait**
nous	**attendions**
vous	**attendiez**
ils/elles	**attendaient**

PRESENT PARTICIPLE
attendant

PAST PARTICIPLE
attendu

EXAMPLE PHRASES

Tu **attends** depuis longtemps? Have you been waiting long?
Je l'**ai attendu** à la poste. I waited for him at the post office.
Attends-moi! Wait for me!
Elle veut que je l'**attende** dans le hall. She wants me to wait for her in the hall.
Elle **attendait** un bébé. She was expecting a baby.

je/j' = I **tu** = you **il** = he/it **elle** = she/it **on** = we/one **nous** = we **vous** = you **ils/elles** = they

attendre

FUTURE

j'	**attendrai**
tu	**attendras**
il/elle/on	**attendra**
nous	**attendrons**
vous	**attendrez**
ils/elles	**attendront**

CONDITIONAL

j'	**attendrais**
tu	**attendrais**
il/elle/on	**attendrait**
nous	**attendrions**
vous	**attendriez**
ils/elles	**attendraient**

PAST HISTORIC

j'	**attendis**
tu	**attendis**
il/elle/on	**attendit**
nous	**attendîmes**
vous	**attendîtes**
ils/elles	**attendirent**

PLUPERFECT

j'	**avais attendu**
tu	**avais attendu**
il/elle/on	**avait attendu**
nous	**avions attendu**
vous	**aviez attendu**
ils/elles	**avaient attendu**

IMPERATIVE

attends / attendons / attendez

EXAMPLE PHRASES

J'**attendrai** qu'il ne pleuve plus. I'll wait until it's stopped raining.

Nous **attendîmes** en silence. We waited in silence.

Je t'**attendrais** si tu n'étais pas si lente. I'd wait for you if you weren't so slow.

Elle m'**avait attendu** patiemment en jouant sur sa tablette. She had patiently waited for me while playing on her tablet.

avoir (to have)

PRESENT		PRESENT SUBJUNCTIVE	
j'	**ai**	j'	**aie**
tu	**as**	tu	**aies**
il/elle/on	**a**	il/elle/on	**ait**
nous	**avons**	nous	**ayons**
vous	**avez**	vous	**ayez**
ils/elles	**ont**	ils/elles	**aient**

PERFECT		IMPERFECT	
j'	**ai eu**	j'	**avais**
tu	**as eu**	tu	**avais**
il/elle/on	**a eu**	il/elle/on	**avait**
nous	**avons eu**	nous	**avions**
vous	**avez eu**	vous	**aviez**
ils/elles	**ont eu**	ils/elles	**avaient**

PRESENT PARTICIPLE
ayant

PAST PARTICIPLE
eu

EXAMPLE PHRASES

Il **a** les yeux bleus. He's got blue eyes.
Quel âge **as**-tu? How old are you?
Il y **a** beaucoup de monde. There are lots of people.
Il **a eu** un accident. He's had an accident.
J'**avais** faim. I was hungry.

avoir

FUTURE

j'	**aurai**
tu	**auras**
il/elle/on	**aura**
nous	**aurons**
vous	**aurez**
ils/elles	**auront**

CONDITIONAL

j'	**aurais**
tu	**aurais**
il/elle/on	**aurait**
nous	**aurions**
vous	**auriez**
ils/elles	**auraient**

PAST HISTORIC

j'	**eus**
tu	**eus**
il/elle/on	**eut**
nous	**eûmes**
vous	**eûtes**
ils/elles	**eurent**

PLUPERFECT

j'	**avais eu**
tu	**avais eu**
il/elle/on	**avait eu**
nous	**avions eu**
vous	**aviez eu**
ils/elles	**avaient eu**

IMPERATIVE
aie / ayons / ayez

EXAMPLE PHRASES

Cloé **aura** cinq ans au mois d'août. Cloé will be five in August.

J'**eus** soudain l'idée de lui rendre visite. I suddenly thought of paying him a visit.

Je n'**aurais** pas tant mangé si j'avais su qu'il y avait un dessert. I wouldn't have eaten so much if I'd known that there was a pudding.

Paul **avait eu** mal au ventre toute la nuit. Paul had had a sore stomach all night.

je/j' = I **tu** = you **il** = he/it **elle** = she/it **on** = we/one **nous** = we **vous** = you **ils/elles** = they

battre (to beat)

PRESENT

je	**bats**
tu	**bats**
il/elle/on	**bat**
nous	**battons**
vous	**battez**
ils/elles	**battent**

PRESENT SUBJUNCTIVE

je	**batte**
tu	**battes**
il/elle/on	**batte**
nous	**battions**
vous	**battiez**
ils/elles	**battent**

PERFECT

j'	**ai battu**
tu	**as battu**
il/elle/on	**a battu**
nous	**avons battu**
vous	**avez battu**
ils/elles	**ont battu**

IMPERFECT

je	**battais**
tu	**battais**
il/elle/on	**battait**
nous	**battions**
vous	**battiez**
ils/elles	**battaient**

PRESENT PARTICIPLE
battant

PAST PARTICIPLE
battu

EXAMPLE PHRASES

J'ai le cœur qui **bat vite**! My heart's beating fast!
Arrêtez de vous **battre**! Stop fighting!
On les **a battus** deux à un. We beat them two-one.
Bats les cartes s'il te plaît. Shuffle the cards please.
Elle le **battait** toujours au poker. She'd always beat him at poker.

battre

FUTURE	
je	**battrai**
tu	**battras**
il/elle/on	**battra**
nous	**battrons**
vous	**battrez**
ils/elles	**battront**

CONDITIONAL	
je	**battrais**
tu	**battrais**
il/elle/on	**battrait**
nous	**battrions**
vous	**battriez**
ils/elles	**battraient**

PAST HISTORIC	
je	**battis**
tu	**battis**
il/elle/on	**battit**
nous	**battîmes**
vous	**battîtes**
ils/elles	**battirent**

PLUPERFECT	
j'	**avais battu**
tu	**avais battu**
il/elle/on	**avait battu**
nous	**avions battu**
vous	**aviez battu**
ils/elles	**avaient battu**

IMPERATIVE

bats / battons / battez

EXAMPLE PHRASES

Tu ne me **battras** jamais à la course. You'll never beat me at running.

Elle le **battit** au Scrabble®. She beat him at Scrabble®.

Ils se **battraient** tout le temps si je les laissais faire. They'd fight all the time if I let them.

Elle **avait battu** le record du monde du saut à la perche. She'd beaten the world record for the pole vault.

je/j' = I **tu** = you **il** = he/it **elle** = she/it **on** = we/one **nous** = we **vous** = you **ils/elles** = they

boire (to drink)

PRESENT		PRESENT SUBJUNCTIVE	
je	**bois**	je	**boive**
tu	**bois**	tu	**boives**
il/elle/on	**boit**	il/elle/on	**boive**
nous	**buvons**	nous	**buvions**
vous	**buvez**	vous	**buviez**
ils/elles	**boivent**	ils/elles	**boivent**

PERFECT		IMPERFECT	
j'	**ai bu**	je	**buvais**
tu	**as bu**	tu	**buvais**
il/elle/on	**a bu**	il/elle/on	**buvait**
nous	**avons bu**	nous	**buvions**
vous	**avez bu**	vous	**buviez**
ils/elles	**ont bu**	ils/elles	**buvaient**

PRESENT PARTICIPLE
buvant

PAST PARTICIPLE
bu

EXAMPLE PHRASES

Qu'est-ce que tu veux **boire**? What would you like to drink?
Il ne **boit** jamais d'alcool. He never drinks alcohol.
J'**ai bu** un litre d'eau. I drank a litre of water.
Bois ton café avant de partir. Drink your coffee before we leave.
Elle **buvait** un whisky tous les soirs. She had a whisky every night.

boire

FUTURE	
je	**boirai**
tu	**boiras**
il/elle/on	**boira**
nous	**boirons**
vous	**boirez**
ils/elles	**boiront**

CONDITIONAL	
je	**boirais**
tu	**boirais**
il/elle/on	**boirait**
nous	**boirions**
vous	**boiriez**
ils/elles	**boiraient**

PAST HISTORIC	
je	**bus**
tu	**bus**
il/elle/on	**but**
nous	**bûmes**
vous	**bûtes**
ils/elles	**burent**

PLUPERFECT	
j'	**avais bu**
tu	**avais bu**
il/elle/on	**avait bu**
nous	**avions bu**
vous	**aviez bu**
ils/elles	**avaient bu**

IMPERATIVE

bois / buvons / buvez

EXAMPLE PHRASES

Que **boirez**-vous? What will you have to drink?

Il **but** son jus d'orange d'un trait. He drank his orange juice in one gulp.

Je **boirais** bien un cognac. I'd quite like a brandy.

On voyait qu'il **avait bu**. He was obviously drunk.

bouillir (to boil)

PRESENT

je	**bous**
tu	**bous**
il/elle/on	**bout**
nous	**bouillons**
vous	**bouillez**
ils/elles	**bouillent**

PRESENT SUBJUNCTIVE

je	**bouille**
tu	**bouilles**
il/elle/on	**bouille**
nous	**bouillions**
vous	**bouilliez**
ils/elles	**bouillent**

PERFECT

j'	**ai bouilli**
tu	**as bouilli**
il/elle/on	**a bouilli**
nous	**avons bouilli**
vous	**avez bouilli**
ils/elles	**ont bouilli**

IMPERFECT

je	**bouillais**
tu	**bouillais**
il/elle/on	**bouillait**
nous	**bouillions**
vous	**bouilliez**
ils/elles	**bouillaient**

PRESENT PARTICIPLE
bouillant

PAST PARTICIPLE
bouilli

EXAMPLE PHRASES

Tu peux mettre de l'eau à **bouillir**? Can you boil some water?
Faites **bouillir** pendant quelques minutes. Boil for a few minutes.
L'eau **bout**. The water's boiling.
La soupe **a bouilli** trop longtemps. The soup has boiled for too long.
Je **bouillais** d'impatience. I was bursting with impatience.

bouillir

FUTURE

je	**bouillirai**
tu	**bouilliras**
il/elle/on	**bouillira**
nous	**bouillirons**
vous	**bouillirez**
ils/elles	**bouilliront**

CONDITIONAL

je	**bouillirais**
tu	**bouillirais**
il/elle/on	**bouillirait**
nous	**bouillirions**
vous	**bouilliriez**
ils/elles	**bouilliraient**

PAST HISTORIC

je	**bouillis**
tu	**bouillis**
il/elle/on	**bouillit**
nous	**bouillîmes**
vous	**bouillîtes**
ils/elles	**bouillirent**

PLUPERFECT

j'	**avais bouilli**
tu	**avais bouilli**
il/elle/on	**avait bouilli**
nous	**avions bouilli**
vous	**aviez bouilli**
ils/elles	**avaient bouilli**

IMPERATIVE

bous / bouillons / bouillez

EXAMPLE PHRASES

Quand l'eau **bouillira**, la bouilloire sifflera. When the water boils, the kettle will whistle.

Le lait **bouillit** et déborda. The milk boiled over.

L'eau n'**avait** pas encore **bouilli**. The water hadn't boiled yet.

je/j' = I **tu** = you **il** = he/it **elle** = she/it **on** = we/one **nous** = we **vous** = you **ils/elles** = they

commencer (to start; to begin)

PRESENT

je	**commence**
tu	**commences**
il/elle/on	**commence**
nous	**commençons**
vous	**commencez**
ils/elles	**commencent**

PRESENT SUBJUNCTIVE

je	**commence**
tu	**commences**
il/elle/on	**commence**
nous	**commencions**
vous	**commenciez**
ils/elles	**commencent**

PERFECT

j'	**ai commencé**
tu	**as commencé**
il/elle/on	**a commencé**
nous	**avons commencé**
vous	**avez commencé**
ils/elles	**ont commencé**

IMPERFECT

je	**commençais**
tu	**commençais**
il/elle/on	**commençait**
nous	**commencions**
vous	**commenciez**
ils/elles	**commençaient**

PRESENT PARTICIPLE
commençant

PAST PARTICIPLE
commencé

EXAMPLE PHRASES

Les cours **commencent** à neuf heures. Lessons start at nine o'clock.

Tu **as** déjà **commencé** de réviser pour tes examens? Have you started revising for your exams?

Ne **commence** pas à m'embêter. Don't start annoying me.

J'aimerais que tu **commences** à faire les valises. I'd like you to start packing the suitcases.

Son attitude **commençait** à m'énerver. Her attitude had started to annoy me.

je/j' = I **tu** = you **il** = he/it **elle** = she/it **on** = we/one **nous** = we **vous** = you **ils/elles** = they

commencer

FUTURE	
je	**commencerai**
tu	**commenceras**
il/elle/on	**commencera**
nous	**commencerons**
vous	**commencerez**
ils/elles	**commenceront**

CONDITIONAL	
je	**commencerais**
tu	**commencerais**
il/elle/on	**commencerait**
nous	**commencerions**
vous	**commenceriez**
ils/elles	**commenceraient**

PAST HISTORIC	
je	**commençai**
tu	**commenças**
il/elle/on	**commença**
nous	**commençâmes**
vous	**commençâtes**
ils/elles	**commencèrent**

PLUPERFECT	
j'	**avais commencé**
tu	**avais commencé**
il/elle/on	**avait commencé**
nous	**avions commencé**
vous	**aviez commencé**
ils/elles	**avaient commencé**

IMPERATIVE

commence / commençons / commencez

EXAMPLE PHRASES

Nous ne **commencerons** pas sans toi. We won't start without you.

C'est quand les nouveaux voisins arrivèrent que les ennuis **commencèrent**. It's when the new neighbours arrived that the problems started.

Nous **commencerions** une partie de cartes si nous étions sûrs d'avoir le temps de la finir. We'd start a game of cards if we were sure we'd have time to finish it.

Il **avait commencé** à pleuvoir. It had started to rain.

je/j' = I **tu** = you **il** = he/it **elle** = she/it **on** = we/one **nous** = we **vous** = you **ils/elles** = they

conclure (to conclude)

PRESENT		PRESENT SUBJUNCTIVE	
je	**conclus**	je	**conclue**
tu	**conclus**	tu	**conclues**
il/elle/on	**conclut**	il/elle/on	**conclue**
nous	**concluons**	nous	**concluions**
vous	**concluez**	vous	**concluiez**
ils/elles	**concluent**	ils/elles	**concluent**

PERFECT		IMPERFECT	
j'	**ai conclu**	je	**concluais**
tu	**as conclu**	tu	**concluais**
il/elle/on	**a conclu**	il/elle/on	**concluait**
nous	**avons conclu**	nous	**concluions**
vous	**avez conclu**	vous	**concluiez**
ils/elles	**ont conclu**	ils/elles	**concluaient**

PRESENT PARTICIPLE
concluant

PAST PARTICIPLE
conclu

EXAMPLE PHRASES

J'en **conclus** qu'il ne m'a pas dit la vérité. I conclude from this that he didn't tell me the truth.
Ils **ont conclu** un marché. They concluded a deal.
Il en **a conclu** qu'il s'était trompé. He concluded that he had got it wrong.
Il faut que je **conclue** le marché aujourd'hui. I must conclude the deal today.

conclure

FUTURE	
je	**conclurai**
tu	**concluras**
il/elle/on	**conclura**
nous	**conclurons**
vous	**conclurez**
ils/elles	**concluront**

CONDITIONAL	
je	**conclurais**
tu	**conclurais**
il/elle/on	**conclurait**
nous	**conclurions**
vous	**concluriez**
ils/elles	**concluraient**

PAST HISTORIC	
je	**conclus**
tu	**conclus**
il/elle/on	**conclut**
nous	**conclûmes**
vous	**conclûtes**
ils/elles	**conclurent**

PLUPERFECT	
j'	**avais conclu**
tu	**avais conclu**
il/elle/on	**avait conclu**
nous	**avions conclu**
vous	**aviez conclu**
ils/elles	**avaient conclu**

IMPERATIVE

conclus / concluons / concluez

EXAMPLE PHRASES

Je **conclurai** par ces mots... I will conclude with these words...

Elle en **conclut** qu'il était parti. She concluded that he had gone.

Nous n'**avions** encore rien **conclu** quand il est arrivé. We hadn't concluded anything when he arrived.

Ils **avaient conclu** la soirée par une partie de cartes. They had concluded the evening with a game of cards.

conduire (to drive)

PRESENT

je	**conduis**
tu	**conduis**
il/elle/on	**conduit**
nous	**conduisons**
vous	**conduisez**
ils/elles	**conduisent**

PRESENT SUBJUNCTIVE

je	**conduise**
tu	**conduises**
il/elle/on	**conduise**
nous	**conduisions**
vous	**conduisiez**
ils/elles	**conduisent**

PERFECT

j'	**ai conduit**
tu	**as conduit**
il/elle/on	**a conduit**
nous	**avons conduit**
vous	**avez conduit**
ils/elles	**ont conduit**

IMPERFECT

je	**conduisais**
tu	**conduisais**
il/elle/on	**conduisait**
nous	**conduisions**
vous	**conduisiez**
ils/elles	**conduisaient**

PRESENT PARTICIPLE
conduisant

PAST PARTICIPLE
conduit

EXAMPLE PHRASES

Elle **conduit** sa fille à l'école tous les matins. She drives her daughter to school every morning.

Cela fait longtemps que je n'**ai** pas **conduit**. I haven't driven for a long time.

Conduis prudemment. Drive carefully.

J'aimerais que tu me **conduises** à la gare. I'd like you to drive me to the station.

Il **conduisait** lentement quand l'accident est arrivé. He was driving slowly when the accident happened.

conduire

FUTURE

je	**conduirai**
tu	**conduiras**
il/elle/on	**conduira**
nous	**conduirons**
vous	**conduirez**
ils/elles	**conduiront**

CONDITIONAL

je	**conduirais**
tu	**conduirais**
il/elle/on	**conduirait**
nous	**conduirions**
vous	**conduiriez**
ils/elles	**conduiraient**

PAST HISTORIC

je	**conduisis**
tu	**conduisis**
il/elle/on	**conduisit**
nous	**conduisîmes**
vous	**conduisîtes**
ils/elles	**conduisirent**

PLUPERFECT

j'	**avais conduit**
tu	**avais conduit**
il/elle/on	**avait conduit**
nous	**avions conduit**
vous	**aviez conduit**
ils/elles	**avaient conduit**

IMPERATIVE

conduis / conduisons / conduisez

EXAMPLE PHRASES

Je te **conduirai** chez le docteur. I'll drive you to the doctor's.

Elle **conduisit** sans dire un mot. She drove without saying a word.

Je te **conduirais** en ville si j'avais le temps. I'd drive you into town if I had time.

Elle **avait conduit** toute la nuit et elle était épuisée. She'd driven all night and she was exhausted.

connaître (to know)

PRESENT

je	**connais**
tu	**connais**
il/elle/on	**connaît**
nous	**connaissons**
vous	**connaissez**
ils/elles	**connaissent**

PRESENT SUBJUNCTIVE

je	**connaisse**
tu	**connaisses**
il/elle/on	**connaisse**
nous	**connaissions**
vous	**connaissiez**
ils/elles	**connaissent**

PERFECT

j'	**ai connu**
tu	**as connu**
il/elle/on	**a connu**
nous	**avons connu**
vous	**avez connu**
ils/elles	**ont connu**

IMPERFECT

je	**connaissais**
tu	**connaissais**
il/elle/on	**connaissait**
nous	**connaissions**
vous	**connaissiez**
ils/elles	**connaissaient**

PRESENT PARTICIPLE

connaissant

PAST PARTICIPLE

connu

EXAMPLE PHRASES

Je ne **connais** pas du tout cette région. I don't know the area at all.
Vous **connaissez** M. Amiot? Do you know Mr Amiot?
Il n'**a** pas **connu** son grand-père. He never knew his granddad.
Je **connaissais** bien sa mère. I knew his mother well.

je/j' = I **tu** = you **il** = he/it **elle** = she/it **on** = we/one **nous** = we **vous** = you **ils/elles** = they

connaître

FUTURE

je	**connaîtrai**
tu	**connaîtras**
il/elle/on	**connaîtra**
nous	**connaîtrons**
vous	**connaîtrez**
ils/elles	**connaîtront**

CONDITIONAL

je	**connaîtrais**
tu	**connaîtrais**
il/elle/on	**connaîtrait**
nous	**connaîtrions**
vous	**connaîtriez**
ils/elles	**connaîtraient**

PAST HISTORIC

je	**connus**
tu	**connus**
il/elle/on	**connut**
nous	**connûmes**
vous	**connûtes**
ils/elles	**connurent**

PLUPERFECT

j'	**avais connu**
tu	**avais connu**
il/elle/on	**avait connu**
nous	**avions connu**
vous	**aviez connu**
ils/elles	**avaient connu**

IMPERATIVE

connais / connaissons / connaissez

EXAMPLE PHRASES

Je ne la **connaîtrai** jamais bien. I'll never know her well.

Il **connut** d'abord Laura puis il rencontra Claire. First he got to know Laura and then he met Claire.

Nous ne nous **connaîtrions** pas s'il ne nous avait pas présentés. We wouldn't know each other if he hadn't introduced us.

J'aurais gagné si j'**avais connu** la réponse à la dernière question. I would have won if I had known the answer to the last question.

Ils s'**étaient connus** à Rouen. They'd first met in Rouen.

continuer (to continue; to go on)

PRESENT

je	**continue**
tu	**continues**
il/elle/on	**continue**
nous	**continuons**
vous	**continuez**
ils/elles	**continuent**

PRESENT SUBJUNCTIVE

je	**continue**
tu	**continues**
il/elle/on	**continue**
nous	**continuions**
vous	**continuiez**
ils/elles	**continuent**

PERFECT

j'	**ai continué**
tu	**as continué**
il/elle/on	**a continué**
nous	**avons continué**
vous	**avez continué**
ils/elles	**ont continué**

IMPERFECT

je	**continuais**
tu	**continuais**
il/elle/on	**continuait**
nous	**continuions**
vous	**continuiez**
ils/elles	**continuaient**

PRESENT PARTICIPLE
continuant

PAST PARTICIPLE
continué

EXAMPLE PHRASES

Il **continue** de fumer malgré son asthme. He keeps on smoking despite his asthma.

Ils **ont continué** à s'envoyer des textos jusqu'à minuit. They went on texting each other till midnight.

Il faut que tu **continues** à réviser si tu veux réussir à ton examen. You'll have to carry on revising if you want to do well in your exam.

La phrase **continuait** sur la page suivante. The sentence continued on the next page.

continuer

FUTURE

je	**continuerai**
tu	**continueras**
il/elle/on	**continuera**
nous	**continuerons**
vous	**continuerez**
ils/elles	**continueront**

CONDITIONAL

je	**continuerais**
tu	**continuerais**
il/elle/on	**continuerait**
nous	**continuerions**
vous	**continueriez**
ils/elles	**continueraient**

PAST HISTORIC

je	**continuai**
tu	**continuas**
il/elle/on	**continua**
nous	**continuâmes**
vous	**continuâtes**
ils/elles	**continuèrent**

PLUPERFECT

j'	**avais continué**
tu	**avais continué**
il/elle/on	**avait continué**
nous	**avions continué**
vous	**aviez continué**
ils/elles	**avaient continué**

IMPERATIVE

continue / continuons / continuez

EXAMPLE PHRASES

Nous **continuerons** l'histoire demain. We'll continue the story tomorrow.

Ils **continuèrent** à la harceler toute la soirée. They went on harassing her all evening.

Je **continuerais** à regarder ce film si j'avais le temps. I'd carry on watching this film if I had time.

Ils **avaient continué** à lui rendre visite même après leur déménagement. They had carried on visiting her even after they had moved house.

je/j' = I **tu** = you **il** = he/it **elle** = she/it **on** = we/one **nous** = we **vous** = you **ils/elles** = they

coudre (to sew)

PRESENT

je	**couds**
tu	**couds**
il/elle/on	**coud**
nous	**cousons**
vous	**cousez**
ils/elles	**cousent**

PRESENT SUBJUNCTIVE

je	**couse**
tu	**couses**
il/elle/on	**couse**
nous	**cousions**
vous	**cousiez**
ils/elles	**cousent**

PERFECT

j'	**ai cousu**
tu	**as cousu**
il/elle/on	**a cousu**
nous	**avons cousu**
vous	**avez cousu**
ils/elles	**ont cousu**

IMPERFECT

je	**cousais**
tu	**cousais**
il/elle/on	**cousait**
nous	**cousions**
vous	**cousiez**
ils/elles	**cousaient**

PRESENT PARTICIPLE
cousant

PAST PARTICIPLE
cousu

EXAMPLE PHRASES

Tu sais **coudre**? Can you sew?
Ma mère **coud** beaucoup. My mum sews a lot.
J'**ai cousu** toute la soirée hier. I spent all evening yesterday sewing.
Elle **cousait** tous les soirs après dîner. She would sew every night after dinner.

coudre

FUTURE	
je	**coudrai**
tu	**coudras**
il/elle/on	**coudra**
nous	**coudrons**
vous	**coudrez**
ils/elles	**coudront**

CONDITIONAL	
je	**coudrais**
tu	**coudrais**
il/elle/on	**coudrait**
nous	**coudrions**
vous	**coudriez**
ils/elles	**coudraient**

PAST HISTORIC	
je	**cousus**
tu	**cousus**
il/elle/on	**cousut**
nous	**cousûmes**
vous	**cousûtes**
ils/elles	**cousurent**

PLUPERFECT	
j'	**avais cousu**
tu	**avais cousu**
il/elle/on	**avait cousu**
nous	**avions cousu**
vous	**aviez cousu**
ils/elles	**avaient cousu**

IMPERATIVE

couds / cousons / cousez

EXAMPLE PHRASES

Demain, je **coudrai** l'écusson sur ton sweat. Tomorrow, I'll sew the badge on your sweatshirt.

Elle **cousut** rapidement le bouton. She quickly sewed the button on.

Je **coudrais** l'ourlet si j'étais sûr de ce que je faisais. I'd sew the hem if I knew what I was doing.

Je n'**avais** pas bien **cousu** le bouton et je l'avais perdu. I hadn't sewn the button on properly and I'd lost it.

courir (to run)

PRESENT

je	**cours**
tu	**cours**
il/elle/on	**court**
nous	**courons**
vous	**courez**
ils/elles	**courent**

PRESENT SUBJUNCTIVE

je	**coure**
tu	**coures**
il/elle/on	**coure**
nous	**courions**
vous	**couriez**
ils/elles	**courent**

PERFECT

j'	**ai couru**
tu	**as couru**
il/elle/on	**a couru**
nous	**avons couru**
vous	**avez couru**
ils/elles	**ont couru**

IMPERFECT

je	**courais**
tu	**courais**
il/elle/on	**courait**
nous	**courions**
vous	**couriez**
ils/elles	**couraient**

PRESENT PARTICIPLE

courant

PAST PARTICIPLE

couru

EXAMPLE PHRASES

Je ne **cours** pas très vite. I can't run very fast.
J'**ai couru** jusqu'à l'école. I ran all the way to school.
Ne **courez** pas dans le couloir. Don't run in the corridor.
Elle est sortie en **courant**. She ran out.

courir

FUTURE		CONDITIONAL	
je	**courrai**	je	**courrais**
tu	**courras**	tu	**courrais**
il/elle/on	**courra**	il/elle/on	**courrait**
nous	**courrons**	nous	**courrions**
vous	**courrez**	vous	**courriez**
ils/elles	**courront**	ils/elles	**courraient**

PAST HISTORIC		PLUPERFECT	
je	**courus**	j'	**avais couru**
tu	**courus**	tu	**avais couru**
il/elle/on	**courut**	il/elle/on	**avait couru**
nous	**courûmes**	nous	**avions couru**
vous	**courûtes**	vous	**aviez couru**
ils/elles	**coururent**	ils/elles	**avaient couru**

IMPERATIVE

cours / courons / courez

EXAMPLE PHRASES

L' été prochain, nous **courrons** le marathon de Londres. Next summer, we'll run the London marathon.

Il **courut** après elle, mais elle était trop rapide. He ran after her, but she was too fast.

Je **courrais** bien plus vite si je n'étais pas fatigué. I'd run much faster if I wasn't tired.

J'étais essoufflé parce que j'**avais couru**. I was out of breath because I'd been running.

craindre (to fear)

PRESENT

je	**crains**
tu	**crains**
il/elle/on	**craint**
nous	**craignons**
vous	**craignez**
ils/elles	**craignent**

PRESENT SUBJUNCTIVE

je	**craigne**
tu	**craignes**
il/elle/on	**craigne**
nous	**craignions**
vous	**craigniez**
ils/elles	**craignent**

PERFECT

j'	**ai craint**
tu	**as craint**
il/elle/on	**a craint**
nous	**avons craint**
vous	**avez craint**
ils/elles	**ont craint**

IMPERFECT

je	**craignais**
tu	**craignais**
il/elle/on	**craignait**
nous	**craignions**
vous	**craigniez**
ils/elles	**craignaient**

PRESENT PARTICIPLE
craignant

PAST PARTICIPLE
craint

EXAMPLE PHRASES

Tu n'as rien à **craindre**. You've got nothing to fear.
Je **crains** le pire. I fear the worst.
Ne **craignez** rien, ce chien n'est pas méchant. Don't be scared, this dog is harmless.
Il **craignait** qu'elle ne soit partie. He feared that she had gone.

craindre

FUTURE

je	**craindrai**
tu	**craindras**
il/elle/on	**craindra**
nous	**craindrons**
vous	**craindrez**
ils/elles	**craindront**

CONDITIONAL

je	**craindrais**
tu	**craindrais**
il/elle/on	**craindrait**
nous	**craindrions**
vous	**craindriez**
ils/elles	**craindraient**

PAST HISTORIC

je	**craignis**
tu	**craignis**
il/elle/on	**craignit**
nous	**craignîmes**
vous	**craignîtes**
ils/elles	**craignirent**

PLUPERFECT

j'	**avais craint**
tu	**avais craint**
il/elle/on	**avait craint**
nous	**avions craint**
vous	**aviez craint**
ils/elles	**avaient craint**

IMPERATIVE

crains / craignons / craignez

EXAMPLE PHRASES

Je **craignis** qu'il ne se vexe. I feared he might get upset.

Je ne le **craindrais** pas tant s'il n'était pas si irritable. I wouldn't fear him so much if he wasn't so irritable.

Si j'étais toi, je **craindrais** sa colère. If I were you, I'd fear his anger.

Elle **avait craint** sa colère, mais il n'avait rien dit. She had feared his anger, but he didn't say anything.

je/j' = I **tu** = you **il** = he/it **elle** = she/it **on** = we/one **nous** = we **vous** = you **ils/elles** = they

créer (to create)

PRESENT

je	**crée**
tu	**crées**
il/elle/on	**crée**
nous	**créons**
vous	**créez**
ils/elles	**créent**

PRESENT SUBJUNCTIVE

je	**crée**
tu	**crées**
il/elle/on	**crée**
nous	**créions**
vous	**créiez**
ils/elles	**créent**

PERFECT

j'	**ai créé**
tu	**as créé**
il/elle/on	**a créé**
nous	**avons créé**
vous	**avez créé**
ils/elles	**ont créé**

IMPERFECT

je	**créais**
tu	**créais**
il/elle/on	**créait**
nous	**créions**
vous	**créiez**
ils/elles	**créaient**

PRESENT PARTICIPLE
créant

PAST PARTICIPLE
créé

EXAMPLE PHRASES

Ce virus **crée** des difficultés dans le monde entier. This virus is causing problems all over the world.

Il **a créé** une nouvelle recette. He's created a new recipe.

Nous **avons créé** ce parfum spécialement pour cette occasion. We've created this perfume specially for this occasion.

Elle **créait** souvent des disputes entre nous. She would often cause arguments between us.

je/j' = I **tu** = you **il** = he/it **elle** = she/it **on** = we/one **nous** = we **vous** = you **ils/elles** = they

créer

FUTURE

je	**créerai**
tu	**créeras**
il/elle/on	**créera**
nous	**créerons**
vous	**créerez**
ils/elles	**créeront**

CONDITIONAL

je	**créerais**
tu	**créerais**
il/elle/on	**créerait**
nous	**créerions**
vous	**créeriez**
ils/elles	**créeraient**

PAST HISTORIC

je	**créai**
tu	**créas**
il/elle/on	**créa**
nous	**créâmes**
vous	**créâtes**
ils/elles	**créèrent**

PLUPERFECT

j'	**avais créé**
tu	**avais créé**
il/elle/on	**avait créé**
nous	**avions créé**
vous	**aviez créé**
ils/elles	**avaient créé**

IMPERATIVE

crée / créons / créez

EXAMPLE PHRASES

Le gouvernement **créera** deux mille emplois supplémentaires. The government will create an extra two thousand jobs.

Les licenciements créèrent des tensions dans l'entreprise. The redundancies created tensions in the firm.

Elle **avait créé** une crème qui allait révolutionner l'industrie des produits cosmétiques. She had created a cream which was to revolutionize the cosmetics industry.

je/j' = I **tu** = you **il** = he/it **elle** = she/it **on** = we/one **nous** = we **vous** = you **ils/elles** = they

crier (to shout)

PRESENT		PRESENT SUBJUNCTIVE	
je	**crie**	je	**crie**
tu	**cries**	tu	**cries**
il/elle/on	**crie**	il/elle/on	**crie**
nous	**crions**	nous	**criions**
vous	**criez**	vous	**criiez**
ils/elles	**crient**	ils/elles	**crient**

PERFECT		IMPERFECT	
j'	**ai crié**	je	**criais**
tu	**as crié**	tu	**criais**
il/elle/on	**a crié**	il/elle/on	**criait**
nous	**avons crié**	nous	**criions**
vous	**avez crié**	vous	**criiez**
ils/elles	**ont crié**	ils/elles	**criaient**

PRESENT PARTICIPLE
criant

PAST PARTICIPLE
crié

EXAMPLE PHRASES

La maîtresse **crie** tout le temps après nous. The teacher's always shouting after us.
Elle **a crié** au secours. She cried for help.
Ne **crie** pas comme ça! Don't shout!
Je ne veux pas que tu **cries** devant mes copines. I don't want you to shout in front of my friends.
Il **criait** toujours plus fort que moi. He would always shout louder than me.

crier

FUTURE	
je	**crierai**
tu	**crieras**
il/elle/on	**criera**
nous	**crierons**
vous	**crierez**
ils/elles	**crieront**

CONDITIONAL	
je	**crierais**
tu	**crierais**
il/elle/on	**crierait**
nous	**crierions**
vous	**crieriez**
ils/elles	**crieraient**

PAST HISTORIC	
je	**criai**
tu	**crias**
il/elle/on	**cria**
nous	**criâmes**
vous	**criâtes**
ils/elles	**crièrent**

PLUPERFECT	
j'	**avais crié**
tu	**avais crié**
il/elle/on	**avait crié**
nous	**avions crié**
vous	**aviez crié**
ils/elles	**avaient crié**

IMPERATIVE

crie / crions / criez

EXAMPLE PHRASES

Ton père ne **criera** pas si tu lui expliques ce qui s'est passé. Your dad won't shout if you explain to him what happened.

"Attention!", **cria**-t-il. "Watch out!" he shouted.

Elle **crierait** drôlement si tu lui tachais sa robe. She would really shout if you stained her dress.

Il n'**avait** pas **crié** comme ça depuis longtemps. He hadn't shouted like that for a long time.

je/j' = I **tu** = you **il** = he/it **elle** = she/it **on** = we/one **nous** = we **vous** = you **ils/elles** = they

croire (to believe)

PRESENT

je	**crois**
tu	**crois**
il/elle/on	**croit**
nous	**croyons**
vous	**croyez**
ils/elles	**croient**

PRESENT SUBJUNCTIVE

je	**croie**
tu	**croies**
il/elle/on	**croie**
nous	**croyions**
vous	**croyiez**
ils/elles	**croient**

PERFECT

j'	**ai cru**
tu	**as cru**
il/elle/on	**a cru**
nous	**avons cru**
vous	**avez cru**
ils/elles	**ont cru**

IMPERFECT

je	**croyais**
tu	**croyais**
il/elle/on	**croyait**
nous	**croyions**
vous	**croyiez**
ils/elles	**croyaient**

PRESENT PARTICIPLE
croyant

PAST PARTICIPLE
cru

EXAMPLE PHRASES

Je ne te **crois** pas. I don't believe you.
J'**ai cru** que tu n'allais pas venir. I thought you weren't going to come.
Crois-moi, Mme Leblond est très stricte. Believe me, Mrs Leblond is very strict.
Il faut que tu me **croies**. You have to believe me.
Elle **croyait** encore au père Noël. She still believed in Father Christmas.

je/j' = I **tu** = you **il** = he/it **elle** = she/it **on** = we/one **nous** = we **vous** = you **ils/elles** = they

croire

FUTURE

je	**croirai**
tu	**croiras**
il/elle/on	**croira**
nous	**croirons**
vous	**croirez**
ils/elles	**croiront**

CONDITIONAL

je	**croirais**
tu	**croirais**
il/elle/on	**croirait**
nous	**croirions**
vous	**croiriez**
ils/elles	**croiraient**

PAST HISTORIC

je	**crus**
tu	**crus**
il/elle/on	**crut**
nous	**crûmes**
vous	**crûtes**
ils/elles	**crurent**

PLUPERFECT

j'	**avais cru**
tu	**avais cru**
il/elle/on	**avait cru**
nous	**avions cru**
vous	**aviez cru**
ils/elles	**avaient cru**

IMPERATIVE

crois / croyons / croyez

EXAMPLE PHRASES

Elle ne me **croira** pas si je lui dis que j'ai gagné. She won't believe me if I tell her that I won.

Il **crut** que je me moquais de lui. He thought that I was making fun of him.

Elle te **croirait** peut-être si tu lui disais que tu as oublié ton maillot de bain. She might believe you if you tell her that you forgot your swimming costume.

Au début, il ne m'**avait** pas **cru**, mais plus tard il s'était rendu compte que c'était vrai. Initially he hadn't believed me, but later he had realized that it was true.

je/j' = I **tu** = you **il** = he/it **elle** = she/it **on** = we/one **nous** = we **vous** = you **ils/elles** = they

croître (to grow; to increase)

PRESENT

je	**croîs**
tu	**croîs**
il/elle/on	**croît**
nous	**croissons**
vous	**croissez**
ils/elles	**croissent**

PRESENT SUBJUNCTIVE

je	**croisse**
tu	**croisses**
il/elle/on	**croisse**
nous	**croissions**
vous	**croissiez**
ils/elles	**croissent**

PERFECT

j'	**ai crû**
tu	**as crû**
il/elle/on	**a crû**
nous	**avons crû**
vous	**avez crû**
ils/elles	**ont crû**

IMPERFECT

je	**croissais**
tu	**croissais**
il/elle/on	**croissait**
nous	**croissions**
vous	**croissiez**
ils/elles	**croissaient**

PRESENT PARTICIPLE

croissant

PAST PARTICIPLE

crû (*NB:* **crue**, **crus**, **crues**)

EXAMPLE PHRASES

Les ventes **croissent** de 6% par an. Sales are growing by 6% per year.

C'est une plante qui **croît** dans les pays chauds. This plant grows in hot countries.

Le nombre de gens qui partent travailler à l'étranger va **croissant**. An increasing number of people go and work abroad.

croître

FUTURE

je	**croîtrai**
tu	**croîtras**
il/elle/on	**croîtra**
nous	**croîtrons**
vous	**croîtrez**
ils/elles	**croîtront**

CONDITIONAL

je	**croîtrais**
tu	**croîtrais**
il/elle/on	**croîtrait**
nous	**croîtrions**
vous	**croîtriez**
ils/elles	**croîtraient**

PAST HISTORIC

je	**crûs**
tu	**crûs**
il/elle/on	**crût**
nous	**crûmes**
vous	**crûtes**
ils/elles	**crûrent**

PLUPERFECT

j'	**avais crû**
tu	**avais crû**
il/elle/on	**avait crû**
nous	**avions crû**
vous	**aviez crû**
ils/elles	**avaient crû**

IMPERATIVE

croîs/ croissons / croissez

EXAMPLE PHRASES

Les problèmes **crûrent** de jour en jour. Problems increased day after day.

Les dépenses **croîtraient** rapidement si on ne faisait pas attention.
Spending would increase rapidly if we weren't careful.

cueillir (to pick)

PRESENT

je	**cueille**
tu	**cueilles**
il/elle/on	**cueille**
nous	**cueillons**
vous	**cueillez**
ils/elles	**cueillent**

PRESENT SUBJUNCTIVE

je	**cueille**
tu	**cueilles**
il/elle/on	**cueille**
nous	**cueillions**
vous	**cueilliez**
ils/elles	**cueillent**

PERFECT

j'	**ai cueilli**
tu	**as cueilli**
il/elle/on	**a cueilli**
nous	**avons cueilli**
vous	**avez cueilli**
ils/elles	**ont cueilli**

IMPERFECT

je	**cueillais**
tu	**cueillais**
il/elle/on	**cueillait**
nous	**cueillions**
vous	**cueilliez**
ils/elles	**cueillaient**

PRESENT PARTICIPLE
cueillant

PAST PARTICIPLE
cueilli

EXAMPLE PHRASES

Il est interdit de **cueillir** des fleurs sauvages dans la montagne. It's forbidden to pick wild flowers in the mountains.

J'**ai cueilli** quelques fraises dans le jardin. I picked a few strawberries in the garden.

Ne **cueille** pas les fleurs dans le parc. Don't pick the flowers in the park.

J'aimerais que tu me **cueilles** des mûres pour faire de la confiture. I'd like you to pick some blackberries for me to make jam.

cueillir

FUTURE	
je	**cueillerai**
tu	**cueilleras**
il/elle/on	**cueillera**
nous	**cueillerons**
vous	**cueillerez**
ils/elles	**cueilleront**

CONDITIONAL	
je	**cueillerais**
tu	**cueillerais**
il/elle/on	**cueillerait**
nous	**cueillerions**
vous	**cueilleriez**
ils/elles	**cueilleraient**

PAST HISTORIC	
je	**cueillis**
tu	**cueillis**
il/elle/on	**cueillit**
nous	**cueillîmes**
vous	**cueillîtes**
ils/elles	**cueillirent**

PLUPERFECT	
j'	**avais cueilli**
tu	**avais cueilli**
il/elle/on	**avait cueilli**
nous	**avions cueilli**
vous	**aviez cueilli**
ils/elles	**avaient cueilli**

IMPERATIVE

cueille / cueillons / cueillez

EXAMPLE PHRASES

Je **cueillerai** des framboises à la ferme. I'll pick some raspberries at the farm.

Elle **cueillit** des fraises des bois. She picked some wild strawberries.

Je **cueillerais** toutes les fleurs de la terre entière pour toi. I'd pick all the flowers in the whole wide world for you.

Il lui **avait cueilli** un beau bouquet de fleurs. He'd picked a beautiful bunch of flowers for her.

cuire (to cook)

PRESENT		PRESENT SUBJUNCTIVE	
je	**cuis**	je	**cuise**
tu	**cuis**	tu	**cuises**
il/elle/on	**cuit**	il/elle/on	**cuise**
nous	**cuisons**	nous	**cuisions**
vous	**cuisez**	vous	**cuisiez**
ils/elles	**cuisent**	ils/elles	**cuisent**

PERFECT		IMPERFECT	
j'	**ai cuit**	je	**cuisais**
tu	**as cuit**	tu	**cuisais**
il/elle/on	**a cuit**	il/elle/on	**cuisait**
nous	**avons cuit**	nous	**cuisions**
vous	**avez cuit**	vous	**cuisiez**
ils/elles	**ont cuit**	ils/elles	**cuisaient**

PRESENT PARTICIPLE
cuisant

PAST PARTICIPLE
cuit

EXAMPLE PHRASES

Ce gâteau prend environ une heure à **cuire**. This cake takes about an hour to bake.

En général, je **cuis** les légumes à la vapeur. I usually steam vegetables.

Je les **ai cuits** au beurre. I cooked them in butter.

Mon père **cuisait** toujours la viande au barbecue. My dad always barbecued meat.

je/j' = I **tu** = you **il** = he/it **elle** = she/it **on** = we/one **nous** = we **vous** = you **ils/elles** = they

cuire

FUTURE

je	**cuirai**
tu	**cuiras**
il/elle/on	**cuira**
nous	**cuirons**
vous	**cuirez**
ils/elles	**cuiront**

CONDITIONAL

je	**cuirais**
tu	**cuirais**
il/elle/on	**cuirait**
nous	**cuirions**
vous	**cuiriez**
ils/elles	**cuiraient**

PAST HISTORIC

je	**cuisis**
tu	**cuisis**
il/elle/on	**cuisit**
nous	**cuisîmes**
vous	**cuisîtes**
ils/elles	**cuisirent**

PLUPERFECT

j'	**avais cuit**
tu	**avais cuit**
il/elle/on	**avait cuit**
nous	**avions cuit**
vous	**aviez cuit**
ils/elles	**avaient cuit**

IMPERATIVE

cuis / cuisons / cuisez

EXAMPLE PHRASES

Nous **cuirons** les côtelettes sur le gril. We'll grill the chops.

Elle **cuisit** l'omelette et la servit. She cooked the omelette and served it.

Je **cuirais** les crêpes plus longtemps si je n'avais pas peur de les faire brûler. I'd cook the pancakes longer if I wasn't scared of burning them.

Elle **avait cuit** le poisson au four. She'd baked the fish in the oven.

se débrouiller (to manage)

PRESENT

je	**me débrouille**
tu	**te débrouilles**
il/elle/on	**se débrouille**
nous	**nous débrouillons**
vous	**vous débrouillez**
ils/elles	**se débrouillent**

PRESENT SUBJUNCTIVE

je	**me débrouille**
tu	**te débrouilles**
il/elle/on	**se débrouille**
nous	**nous débrouillions**
vous	**vous débrouilliez**
ils/elles	**se débrouillent**

PERFECT

je	**me suis débrouillé(e)**
tu	**t'es débrouillé(e)**
il/elle/on	**s'est débrouillé(e)**
nous	**nous sommes débrouillé(e)s**
vous	**vous êtes débrouillé(e)(s)**
ils/elles	**se sont débrouillé(e)s**

IMPERFECT

je	**me débrouillais**
tu	**te débrouillais**
il/elle/on	**se débrouillait**
nous	**nous débrouillions**
vous	**vous débrouilliez**
ils/elles	**se débrouillaient**

PRESENT PARTICIPLE
se débrouillant

PAST PARTICIPLE
débrouillé

EXAMPLE PHRASES

Elle **se débrouille** bien à l'école. She gets on well at school.

C'était difficile, mais je ne **me suis** pas trop mal **débrouillé**. It was difficult, but I managed OK.

Débrouille-toi tout seul. Sort things out for yourself.

Débrouillez-vous pour arriver à l'heure. Make sure you're on time.

Je **me débrouillais** mieux en français qu'en maths. I got on better in French than in maths.

je/j' = I **tu** = you **il** = he/it **elle** = she/it **on** = we/one **nous** = we **vous** = you **ils/elles** = they

se débrouiller

FUTURE

je	**me débrouillerai**
tu	**te débrouilleras**
il/elle/on	**se débrouillera**
nous	**nous débrouillerons**
vous	**vous débrouillerez**
ils/elles	**se débrouilleront**

CONDITIONAL

je	**me débrouillerais**
tu	**te débrouillerais**
il/elle/on	**se débrouillerait**
nous	**nous débrouillerions**
vous	**vous débrouilleriez**
ils/elles	**se débrouilleraient**

PAST HISTORIC

je	**me débrouillai**
tu	**te débrouillas**
il/elle/on	**se débrouilla**
nous	**nous débrouillâmes**
vous	**vous débrouillâtes**
ils/elles	**se débrouillèrent**

PLUPERFECT

je	**m'étais débrouillé(e)**
tu	**t'étais débrouillé(e)**
il/elle/on	**s'était débrouillé(e)**
nous	**nous étions débrouillé(e)s**
vous	**vous étiez débrouillé(e)(s)**
ils/elles	**s'étaient débrouillé(e)s**

IMPERATIVE

débrouille-toi / débrouillons-nous / débrouillez-vous

EXAMPLE PHRASES

Nous **nous débrouillerons** bien sans toi. We'll manage fine without you.

Il **se débrouilla** tant bien que mal pour préparer le dîner. He just about managed to prepare dinner.

Il **se débrouillerait** bien tout seul s'il était obligé. He would manage fine by himself if he had to.

Comme mes parents étaient partis, je **m'étais débrouillée** toute seule. As my parents were away, I had managed by myself.

je/j' = I **tu** = you **il** = he/it **elle** = she/it **on** = we/one **nous** = we **vous** = you **ils/elles** = they

descendre (to go down; to take down)

PRESENT

je	**descends**
tu	**descends**
il/elle/on	**descend**
nous	**descendons**
vous	**descendez**
ils/elles	**descendent**

PRESENT SUBJUNCTIVE

je	**descende**
tu	**descendes**
il/elle/on	**descende**
nous	**descendions**
vous	**descendiez**
ils/elles	**descendent**

PERFECT

je	**suis descendu(e)**
tu	**es descendu(e)**
il/elle/on	**est descendu(e)**
nous	**sommes descendu(e)s**
vous	**êtes descendu(e)(s)**
ils/elles	**sont descendu(e)s**

IMPERFECT

je	**descendais**
tu	**descendais**
il/elle/on	**descendait**
nous	**descendions**
vous	**descendiez**
ils/elles	**descendaient**

PRESENT PARTICIPLE
descendant

PAST PARTICIPLE
descendu

In the perfect and the pluperfect, use the auxiliary "avoir" when there is a direct object.

EXAMPLE PHRASES

Vous pouvez **descendre** ma valise, s'il vous plaît? Could you get my suitcase down, please?

Reste en bas: je **descends**! Stay downstairs – I'm coming down!

Nous **sommes descendus** à la station Trocadéro. We got off at Trocadéro.

Descendez la rue jusqu'au rond-point. Go down the street to the roundabout.

Il faut que je **descende** chercher quelque chose à la cave. I have to go down to the cellar to get something.

descendre

FUTURE

je	**descendrai**
tu	**descendras**
il/elle/on	**descendra**
nous	**descendrons**
vous	**descendrez**
ils/elles	**descendront**

CONDITIONAL

je	**descendrais**
tu	**descendrais**
il/elle/on	**descendrait**
nous	**descendrions**
vous	**descendriez**
ils/elles	**descendraient**

PAST HISTORIC

je	**descendis**
tu	**descendis**
il/elle/on	**descendit**
nous	**descendîmes**
vous	**descendîtes**
ils/elles	**descendirent**

PLUPERFECT

j'	**étais descendu(e)**
tu	**étais descendu(e)**
il/elle/on	**était descendu(e)**
nous	**étions descendu(e)s**
vous	**étiez descendu(e)(s)**
ils/elles	**étaient descendu(e)s**

IMPERATIVE

descends / descendons / descendez

EXAMPLE PHRASES

Nous **descendrons** dans le Midi au mois de juillet. We'll go down to the south of France in July.

Il **descendit** les escaliers en courant. He ran down the stairs.

Si j'étais toi, je ne **descendrais** pas l'escalier si vite. I wouldn't rush down the stairs if I were you.

Ils **étaient descendus** regarder la télé quand les plombs ont sauté. They had gone down to watch TV when the fuses blew.

devenir (to become)

PRESENT		PRESENT SUBJUNCTIVE	
je	**deviens**	je	**devienne**
tu	**deviens**	tu	**deviennes**
il/elle/on	**devient**	il/elle/on	**devienne**
nous	**devenons**	nous	**devenions**
vous	**devenez**	vous	**deveniez**
ils/elles	**deviennent**	ils/elles	**deviennent**

PERFECT		IMPERFECT	
je	**suis devenu(e)**	je	**devenais**
tu	**es devenu(e)**	tu	**devenais**
il/elle/on	**est devenu(e)**	il/elle/on	**devenait**
nous	**sommes devenu(e)s**	nous	**devenions**
vous	**êtes devenu(e)(s)**	vous	**deveniez**
ils/elles	**sont devenu(e)s**	ils/elles	**devenaient**

PRESENT PARTICIPLE
devenant

PAST PARTICIPLE
devenu

EXAMPLE PHRASES

Ça **devient** de plus en plus difficile. It's becoming more and more difficult.
Il **est devenu** médecin. He became a doctor.
Qu'est-ce qu'elle **est devenue**? What has become of her?
Il ne faut pas que ça **devienne** une corvée. It mustn't become a chore.
Elle **devenait** de plus en plus exigeante. She was becoming more and more demanding.

je/j' = I **tu** = you **il** = he/it **elle** = she/it **on** = we/one **nous** = we **vous** = you **ils/elles** = they

devenir

FUTURE

je	**deviendrai**
tu	**deviendras**
il/elle/on	**deviendra**
nous	**deviendrons**
vous	**deviendrez**
ils/elles	**deviendront**

CONDITIONAL

je	**deviendrais**
tu	**deviendrais**
il/elle/on	**deviendrait**
nous	**deviendrions**
vous	**deviendriez**
ils/elles	**deviendraient**

PAST HISTORIC

je	**devins**
tu	**devins**
il/elle/on	**devint**
nous	**devînmes**
vous	**devîntes**
ils/elles	**devinrent**

PLUPERFECT

j'	**étais devenu(e)**
tu	**étais devenu(e)**
il/elle/on	**était devenu(e)**
nous	**étions devenu(e)s**
vous	**étiez devenu(e)(s)**
ils/elles	**étaient devenu(e)s**

IMPERATIVE

deviens / devenons / devenez

EXAMPLE PHRASES

J'espère qu'elle ne **deviendra** pas comme sa mère. I hope that she won't become like her mother.

Elle **devint** la première femme à traverser l'Atlantique en avion. She became the first woman to fly across the Atlantic.

Si on les nourrissait trop, les poissons rouges **deviendraient** énormes. If we overfed them, the goldfish would become enormous.

Je me demandais ce qu'ils **étaient devenus**. I wondered what had become of them.

devoir (to have to; to owe)

PRESENT

je	**dois**
tu	**dois**
il/elle/on	**doit**
nous	**devons**
vous	**devez**
ils/elles	**doivent**

PRESENT SUBJUNCTIVE

je	**doive**
tu	**doives**
il/elle/on	**doive**
nous	**devions**
vous	**deviez**
ils/elles	**doivent**

PERFECT

j'	**ai dû**
tu	**as dû**
il/elle/on	**a dû**
nous	**avons dû**
vous	**avez dû**
ils/elles	**ont dû**

IMPERFECT

je	**devais**
tu	**devais**
il/elle/on	**devait**
nous	**devions**
vous	**deviez**
ils/elles	**devaient**

PRESENT PARTICIPLE

devant

PAST PARTICIPLE

dû (*NB*: **due**, **dus**, **dues**)

EXAMPLE PHRASES

Je **dois** aller faire les courses ce matin. I have to do the shopping this morning.

À quelle heure est-ce que tu **dois** partir? What time do you have to leave?

J'**ai dû** partir avant la fin du film. I had to leave before the end of the film.

Il **a dû** changer d'avis. He must have changed his mind.

Il **devait** prendre le train pour aller travailler. He had to go to work by train.

devoir

FUTURE		CONDITIONAL	
je	**devrai**	je	**devrais**
tu	**devras**	tu	**devrais**
il/elle/on	**devra**	il/elle/on	**devrait**
nous	**devrons**	nous	**devrions**
vous	**devrez**	vous	**devriez**
ils/elles	**devront**	ils/elles	**devraient**

PAST HISTORIC		PLUPERFECT	
je	**dus**	j'	**avais dû**
tu	**dus**	tu	**avais dû**
il/elle/on	**dut**	il/elle/on	**avait dû**
nous	**dûmes**	nous	**avions dû**
vous	**dûtes**	vous	**aviez dû**
ils/elles	**durent**	ils/elles	**avaient dû**

IMPERATIVE

dois / devons / devez

EXAMPLE PHRASES

Ils **devront** finir leurs devoirs avant de venir. They'll have to finish their homework before they come.

Elle **dut** lui annoncer elle-même la mauvaise nouvelle. She had to tell him the bad news herself.

Tu ne **devrais** pas les déranger tout le temps comme ça. You shouldn't disturb them all the time like that.

Comme il était malade, il **avait dû** arrêter de fumer. As he were ill, he'd had to stop smoking.

je/j' = I **tu** = you **il** = he/it **elle** = she/it **on** = we/one **nous** = we **vous** = you **ils/elles** = they

dire (to say; to tell)

PRESENT

je	**dis**
tu	**dis**
il/elle/on	**dit**
nous	**disons**
vous	**dites**
ils/elles	**disent**

PRESENT SUBJUNCTIVE

je	**dise**
tu	**dises**
il/elle/on	**dise**
nous	**disions**
vous	**disiez**
ils/elles	**disent**

PERFECT

j'	**ai dit**
tu	**as dit**
il/elle/on	**a dit**
nous	**avons dit**
vous	**avez dit**
ils/elles	**ont dit**

IMPERFECT

je	**disais**
tu	**disais**
il/elle/on	**disait**
nous	**disions**
vous	**disiez**
ils/elles	**disaient**

PRESENT PARTICIPLE

disant

PAST PARTICIPLE

dit

EXAMPLE PHRASES

Qu'est-ce qu'elle **dit**? What is she saying?
Comment ça se **dit** en anglais? How do you say that in English?
"Bonjour!", **a**-t-il **dit**. "Hello!" he said.
Ne **dis** pas de bêtises. Don't talk nonsense.
Ils m'**ont dit** que le film était nul. They told me that the film was rubbish.

je/j' = I **tu** = you **il** = he/it **elle** = she/it **on** = we/one **nous** = we **vous** = you **ils/elles** = they

dire

FUTURE

je	**dirai**
tu	**diras**
il/elle/on	**dira**
nous	**dirons**
vous	**direz**
ils/elles	**diront**

CONDITIONAL

je	**dirais**
tu	**dirais**
il/elle/on	**dirait**
nous	**dirions**
vous	**diriez**
ils/elles	**diraient**

PAST HISTORIC

je	**dis**
tu	**dis**
il/elle/on	**dit**
nous	**dîmes**
vous	**dîtes**
ils/elles	**dirent**

PLUPERFECT

j'	**avais dit**
tu	**avais dit**
il/elle/on	**avait dit**
nous	**avions dit**
vous	**aviez dit**
ils/elles	**avaient dit**

IMPERATIVE

dis / disons / dites

EXAMPLE PHRASES

Je lui **dirai** de venir à midi. I'll tell him to come at midday.

"Viens ici!" **dit**-il. Mais le chien refusait de bouger. "Come here!" he said. But the dog refused to move.

On **dirait** qu'il va neiger. It looks like snow.

On ne m'**avait** pas **dit** que tu serais là. I hadn't been told that you'd be there.

je/j' = I **tu** = you **il** = he/it **elle** = she/it **on** = we/one **nous** = we **vous** = you **ils/elles** = they

donner (to give)

PRESENT

je	**donne**
tu	**donnes**
il/elle/on	**donne**
nous	**donnons**
vous	**donnez**
ils/elles	**donnent**

PRESENT SUBJUNCTIVE

je	**donne**
tu	**donnes**
il/elle/on	**donne**
nous	**donnions**
vous	**donniez**
ils/elles	**donnent**

PERFECT

j'	**ai donné**
tu	**as donné**
il/elle/on	**a donné**
nous	**avons donné**
vous	**avez donné**
ils/elles	**ont donné**

IMPERFECT

je	**donnais**
tu	**donnais**
il/elle/on	**donnait**
nous	**donnions**
vous	**donniez**
ils/elles	**donnaient**

PRESENT PARTICIPLE
donnant

PAST PARTICIPLE
donné

EXAMPLE PHRASES

L'appartement **donne** sur la place. The flat overlooks the square.
Est-ce que je t'**ai donné** mon adresse e-mail? Did I give you my email address?
Donne-moi la main. Give me your hand.
Il faut que tu me **donnes** plus de détails. You must give me more details.
Je **donnais** des sucres aux chevaux. I'd give sugar lumps to the horses.

donner

FUTURE

je	**donnerai**
tu	**donneras**
il/elle/on	**donnera**
nous	**donnerons**
vous	**donnerez**
ils/elles	**donneront**

CONDITIONAL

je	**donnerais**
tu	**donnerais**
il/elle/on	**donnerait**
nous	**donnerions**
vous	**donneriez**
ils/elles	**donneraient**

PAST HISTORIC

je	**donnai**
tu	**donnas**
il/elle/on	**donna**
nous	**donnâmes**
vous	**donnâtes**
ils/elles	**donnèrent**

PLUPERFECT

j'	**avais donné**
tu	**avais donné**
il/elle/on	**avait donné**
nous	**avions donné**
vous	**aviez donné**
ils/elles	**avaient donné**

IMPERATIVE

donne / donnons / donnez

EXAMPLE PHRASES

Je te **donnerai** un ticket de métro. I'll give you a tube ticket.

Il lui **donna** un vieux livre. He gave him an old book.

Je lui **donnerais** des nouvelles si j'avais son adresse. I'd give her some news if I had her address.

Je lui **avais donné** mon numéro de téléphone mais il a dû le perdre. I had given him my phone number but he must have lost it.

dormir (to sleep)

PRESENT

je	**dors**
tu	**dors**
il/elle/on	**dort**
nous	**dormons**
vous	**dormez**
ils/elles	**dorment**

PRESENT SUBJUNCTIVE

je	**dorme**
tu	**dormes**
il/elle/on	**dorme**
nous	**dormions**
vous	**dormiez**
ils/elles	**dorment**

PERFECT

j'	**ai dormi**
tu	**as dormi**
il/elle/on	**a dormi**
nous	**avons dormi**
vous	**avez dormi**
ils/elles	**ont dormi**

IMPERFECT

je	**dormais**
tu	**dormais**
il/elle/on	**dormait**
nous	**dormions**
vous	**dormiez**
ils/elles	**dormaient**

PRESENT PARTICIPLE
dormant

PAST PARTICIPLE
dormi

EXAMPLE PHRASES

Nous **dormons** dans la même chambre. We sleep in the same bedroom.
Tu **as** bien **dormi**? Did you sleep well?
Dors bien. Sleep well.
Elle m'a fait une tisane pour que je **dorme** bien. She made me a herbal tea so that I got a good sleep.
À 9 heures, il **dormait** déjà. He was already asleep by nine.

dormir

FUTURE	
je	**dormirai**
tu	**dormiras**
il/elle/on	**dormira**
nous	**dormirons**
vous	**dormirez**
ils/elles	**dormiront**

CONDITIONAL	
je	**dormirais**
tu	**dormirais**
il/elle/on	**dormirait**
nous	**dormirions**
vous	**dormiriez**
ils/elles	**dormiraient**

PAST HISTORIC	
je	**dormis**
tu	**dormis**
il/elle/on	**dormit**
nous	**dormîmes**
vous	**dormîtes**
ils/elles	**dormirent**

PLUPERFECT	
j'	**avais dormi**
tu	**avais dormi**
il/elle/on	**avait dormi**
nous	**avions dormi**
vous	**aviez dormi**
ils/elles	**avaient dormi**

IMPERATIVE
dors / dormons / dormez

EXAMPLE PHRASES

Ce soir, nous **dormirons** sous la tente. Tonight we'll sleep in the tent.

Il était si fatigué qu'il **dormit** toute la journée. He was so tired that he slept all day.

Il **dormirait** mieux s'il buvait moins de café. He'd sleep better if he didn't drink so much coffee.

J'étais épuisé car je n'**avais** pas **dormi** de la nuit. I was exhausted as I hadn't slept all night.

écrire (to write)

PRESENT

j'	**écris**
tu	**écris**
il/elle/on	**écrit**
nous	**écrivons**
vous	**écrivez**
ils/elles	**écrivent**

PRESENT SUBJUNCTIVE

j'	**écrive**
tu	**écrives**
il/elle/on	**écrive**
nous	**écrivions**
vous	**écriviez**
ils/elles	**écrivent**

PERFECT

j'	**ai écrit**
tu	**as écrit**
il/elle/on	**a écrit**
nous	**avons écrit**
vous	**avez écrit**
ils/elles	**ont écrit**

IMPERFECT

j'	**écrivais**
tu	**écrivais**
il/elle/on	**écrivait**
nous	**écrivions**
vous	**écriviez**
ils/elles	**écrivaient**

PRESENT PARTICIPLE

écrivant

PAST PARTICIPLE

écrit

EXAMPLE PHRASES

Elle **écrit** des romans. She writes novels.

Le prof **a écrit** sur le tableau blanc. The teacher wrote on the whiteboard.

Écrivez votre nom en haut de la feuille. Write your name at the top of the page.

Elle aimerait que tu **écrives** plus souvent. She'd like you to write more often.

Il ne nous **écrivait** jamais quand il était en France. He never wrote to us when he was in France.

écrire

FUTURE

j'	**écrirai**
tu	**écriras**
il/elle/on	**écrira**
nous	**écrirons**
vous	**écrirez**
ils/elles	**écriront**

CONDITIONAL

j'	**écrirais**
tu	**écrirais**
il/elle/on	**écrirait**
nous	**écririons**
vous	**écririez**
ils/elles	**écriraient**

PAST HISTORIC

j'	**écrivis**
tu	**écrivis**
il/elle/on	**écrivit**
nous	**écrivîmes**
vous	**écrivîtes**
ils/elles	**écrivirent**

PLUPERFECT

j'	**avais écrit**
tu	**avais écrit**
il/elle/on	**avait écrit**
nous	**avions écrit**
vous	**aviez écrit**
ils/elles	**avaient écrit**

IMPERATIVE

écris / écrivons / écrivez

EXAMPLE PHRASES

Demain, j'**écrirai** une lettre au directeur. Tomorrow, I'll write a letter to the headmaster.

Il **écrivit** un poème à la lueur de la bougie. He wrote a poem by candlelight.

J'**écrirais** plus souvent si j'avais le temps. I'd write more often if I had the time.

Comme il n'**avait** encore rien **écrit** sur sa feuille, il se fit disputer par la maîtresse. As he hadn't written anything on his sheet yet, he was told off by the teacher.

émouvoir (to move)

PRESENT

j'	**émeus**
tu	**émeus**
il/elle/on	**émeut**
nous	**émouvons**
vous	**émouvez**
ils/elles	**émeuvent**

PRESENT SUBJUNCTIVE

j'	**émeuve**
tu	**émeuves**
il/elle/on	**émeuve**
nous	**émeuvions**
vous	**émeuviez**
ils/elles	**émeuvent**

PERFECT

j'	**ai ému**
tu	**as ému**
il/elle/on	**a ému**
nous	**avons ému**
vous	**avez ému**
ils/elles	**ont ému**

IMPERFECT

j'	**émouvais**
tu	**émouvais**
il/elle/on	**émouvait**
nous	**émouvions**
vous	**émouviez**
ils/elles	**émouvaient**

PRESENT PARTICIPLE
émouvant

PAST PARTICIPLE
ému

EXAMPLE PHRASES

Cette histoire m'**émeut** toujours beaucoup. This story always moves me to tears.

Sa fausse gentillesse ne m'**émeut** pas. I won't be moved by his fake kindness.

Ce film nous **a ému**. This film moved us.

Cela m'**émouvait** toujours de les voir se quitter à la fin de l'été. It always moved me to see them part at the end of the summer.

je/j' = I **tu** = you **il** = he/it **elle** = she/it **on** = we/one **nous** = we **vous** = you **ils/elles** = they

émouvoir

FUTURE

j'	**émouvrai**
tu	**émouvras**
il/elle/on	**émouvra**
nous	**émouvrons**
vous	**émouvrez**
ils/elles	**émouvront**

CONDITIONAL

j'	**émouvrais**
tu	**émouvrais**
il/elle/on	**émouvrait**
nous	**émouvrions**
vous	**émouvriez**
ils/elles	**émouvraient**

PAST HISTORIC

j'	**émus**
tu	**émus**
il/elle/on	**émut**
nous	**émûmes**
vous	**émûtes**
ils/elles	**émurent**

PLUPERFECT

j'	**avais ému**
tu	**avais ému**
il/elle/on	**avait ému**
nous	**avions ému**
vous	**aviez ému**
ils/elles	**avaient ému**

IMPERATIVE

émeus / émouvons / émouvez

EXAMPLE PHRASES

Sa franchise l'**émut** vraiment. His frankness really moved her.

Sa lettre l'**avait** beaucoup **émue**. She had been deeply moved by his letter.

s'ennuyer (to be bored)

PRESENT

je	**m'ennuie**
tu	**t'ennuies**
il/elle/on	**s'ennuie**
nous	**nous ennuyons**
vous	**vous ennuyez**
ils/elles	**s'ennuient**

PRESENT SUBJUNCTIVE

je	**m'ennuie**
tu	**t'ennuies**
il/elle/on	**s'ennuie**
nous	**nous ennuyions**
vous	**vous ennuyiez**
ils/elles	**s'ennuient**

PERFECT

je	**me suis ennuyé(e)**
tu	**t'es ennuyé(e)**
il/elle/on	**s'est ennuyé(e)**
nous	**nous sommes ennuyé(e)s**
vous	**vous êtes ennuyé(e)(s)**
ils/elles	**se sont ennuyé(e)s**

IMPERFECT

je	**m'ennuyais**
tu	**t'ennuyais**
il/elle/on	**s'ennuyait**
nous	**nous ennuyions**
vous	**vous ennuyiez**
ils/elles	**s'ennuyaient**

PRESENT PARTICIPLE
s'ennuyant

PAST PARTICIPLE
ennuyé

EXAMPLE PHRASES

Elle **s'ennuie** un peu à l'école. She's a little bored at school.
Je **me suis ennuyé** quand tu étais partie. I got bored when you were away.
Ne **t'ennuie** pas trop cet après-midi. Don't get too bored this afternoon.
Je ne voudrais pas qu'elle **s'ennuie** avec moi. I wouldn't want her to get bored with me.
On ne **s'ennuyait** jamais avec lui. We never got bored with him.

s'ennuyer

FUTURE

je	**m'ennuierai**
tu	**t'ennuieras**
il/elle/on	**s'ennuiera**
nous	**nous ennuierons**
vous	**vous ennuierez**
ils/elles	**s'ennuieront**

CONDITIONAL

je	**m'ennuierais**
tu	**t'ennuierais**
il/elle/on	**s'ennuierait**
nous	**nous ennuierions**
vous	**vous ennuieriez**
ils/elles	**s'ennuieraient**

PAST HISTORIC

je	**m'ennuyai**
tu	**t'ennuyas**
il/elle/on	**s'ennuya**
nous	**nous ennuyâmes**
vous	**vous ennuyâtes**
ils/elles	**s'ennuyèrent**

PLUPERFECT

je	**m'étais ennuyé(e)**
tu	**t'étais ennuyé(e)**
il/elle/on	**s'était ennuyé(e)**
nous	**nous étions ennuyé(e)s**
vous	**vous étiez ennuyé(e)(s)**
ils/elles	**s'étaient ennuyé(e)s**

IMPERATIVE

ennuie-toi / ennuyons-nous / ennuyez-vous

EXAMPLE PHRASES

Il **s'ennuiera** sûrement quand ses copains seront partis. He'll certainly be bored when his friends are away.

Elle **s'ennuya** un peu. She got a little bored.

Tu ne **t'ennuierais** pas tant si tu allais jouer avec les autres. You wouldn't be so bored if you went to play with the others.

Il **s'était ennuyé** pendant les vacances et il était content de retrouver ses copains. He'd got bored during the holidays and he was happy to be with his friends again.

je/j' = I **tu** = you **il** = he/it **elle** = she/it **on** = we/one **nous** = we **vous** = you **ils/elles** = they

entendre (to hear)

PRESENT

j'	**entends**
tu	**entends**
il/elle/on	**entend**
nous	**entendons**
vous	**entendez**
ils/elles	**entendent**

PRESENT SUBJUNCTIVE

j'	**entende**
tu	**entendes**
il/elle/on	**entende**
nous	**entendions**
vous	**entendiez**
ils/elles	**entendent**

PERFECT

j'	**ai entendu**
tu	**as entendu**
il/elle/on	**a entendu**
nous	**avons entendu**
vous	**avez entendu**
ils/elles	**ont entendu**

IMPERFECT

j'	**entendais**
tu	**entendais**
il/elle/on	**entendait**
nous	**entendions**
vous	**entendiez**
ils/elles	**entendaient**

PRESENT PARTICIPLE
entendant

PAST PARTICIPLE
entendu

EXAMPLE PHRASES

Il n'**entend** pas bien. He can't hear very well.

Tu **as entendu** ce que je t'ai dit? Did you hear what I said to you?

Il ne faut pas qu'elle nous **entende**. She mustn't hear us.

Elle n'**entendait** jamais son portable sonner. She never heard her mobile ring.

entendre

FUTURE

j'	**entendrai**
tu	**entendras**
il/elle/on	**entendra**
nous	**entendrons**
vous	**entendrez**
ils/elles	**entendront**

CONDITIONAL

j'	**entendrais**
tu	**entendrais**
il/elle/on	**entendrait**
nous	**entendrions**
vous	**entendriez**
ils/elles	**entendraient**

PAST HISTORIC

j'	**entendis**
tu	**entendis**
il/elle/on	**entendit**
nous	**entendîmes**
vous	**entendîtes**
ils/elles	**entendirent**

PLUPERFECT

j'	**avais entendu**
tu	**avais entendu**
il/elle/on	**avait entendu**
nous	**avions entendu**
vous	**aviez entendu**
ils/elles	**avaient entendu**

IMPERATIVE

entends / entendons / entendez

EXAMPLE PHRASES

Tu les **entendras** sûrement rentrer. You'll certainly hear them come back.
Elle **entendit** les oiseaux chanter. She heard the birds singing.
On **entendrait** moins les voisins si les murs étaient plus épais. We'd hear the neighbours less if the walls were thicker.
Il ne les **avait** pas **entendus** arriver. He hadn't heard them arrive.

entrer (to come in; to go in)

PRESENT

j'	**entre**
tu	**entres**
il/elle/on	**entre**
nous	**entrons**
vous	**entrez**
ils/elles	**entrent**

PRESENT SUBJUNCTIVE

j'	**entre**
tu	**entres**
il/elle/on	**entre**
nous	**entrions**
vous	**entriez**
ils/elles	**entrent**

PERFECT

je	**suis entré(e)**
tu	**es entré(e)**
il/elle/on	**est entré(e)**
nous	**sommes entré(e)s**
vous	**êtes entré(e)(s)**
ils/elles	**sont entré(e)s**

IMPERFECT

j'	**entrais**
tu	**entrais**
il/elle/on	**entrait**
nous	**entrions**
vous	**entriez**
ils/elles	**entraient**

PRESENT PARTICIPLE

entrant

PAST PARTICIPLE

entré

In the perfect and the pluperfect, use the auxiliary "avoir" when there is a direct object.

EXAMPLE PHRASES

Je peux **entrer**? Can I come in?

Ils **sont** tous **entrés** dans la maison. They all went inside the house.

Entrez par la porte de derrière. Come in by the back door.

Essuie-toi les pieds en **entrant**. Wipe your feet as you come in.

je/j' = I **tu** = you **il** = he/it **elle** = she/it **on** = we/one **nous** = we **vous** = you **ils/elles** = they

entrer

FUTURE

j' **entrerai**
tu **entreras**
il/elle/on **entrera**
nous **entrerons**
vous **entrerez**
ils/elles **entreront**

CONDITIONAL

j' **entrerais**
tu **entrerais**
il/elle/on **entrerait**
nous **entrerions**
vous **entreriez**
ils/elles **entreraient**

PAST HISTORIC

j' **entrai**
tu **entras**
il/elle/on **entra**
nous **entrâmes**
vous **entrâtes**
ils/elles **entrèrent**

PLUPERFECT

j' **étais entré(e)**
tu **étais entré(e)**
il/elle/on **était entré(e)**
nous **étions entré(e)s**
vous **étiez entré(e)(s)**
ils/elles **étaient entré(e)s**

IMPERATIVE

entre / entrons / entrez

EXAMPLE PHRASES

Elle **entrera** en sixième à la rentrée. She'll go into first year of high school after the summer.

Comme personne ne répondit, il poussa la porte et **entra**. As nobody answered, he pushed the door and went in.

Je n'**entrerais** pas sans frapper si j'étais toi. I wouldn't go in without knocking if I were you.

Comme j'avais perdu les clés, j'**étais entré** par la fenêtre. As I'd lost the keys, I'd gone in through the window.

envoyer (to send)

PRESENT

j'	**envoie**
tu	**envoies**
il/elle/on	**envoie**
nous	**envoyons**
vous	**envoyez**
ils/elles	**envoient**

PRESENT SUBJUNCTIVE

j'	**envoie**
tu	**envoies**
il/elle/on	**envoie**
nous	**envoyions**
vous	**envoyiez**
ils/elles	**envoient**

PERFECT

j'	**ai envoyé**
tu	**as envoyé**
il/elle/on	**a envoyé**
nous	**avons envoyé**
vous	**avez envoyé**
ils/elles	**ont envoyé**

IMPERFECT

j'	**envoyais**
tu	**envoyais**
il/elle/on	**envoyait**
nous	**envoyions**
vous	**envoyiez**
ils/elles	**envoyaient**

PRESENT PARTICIPLE
envoyant

PAST PARTICIPLE
envoyé

EXAMPLE PHRASES

Ma cousine nous **envoie** toujours des cadeaux pour Noël. My cousin always sends us presents for Christmas.
J'**ai envoyé** une carte postale à ma tante. I sent my aunt a postcard.
Envoie-moi un e-mail. Send me an e-mail.
Il faut que j'**envoie** ce paquet demain. I must send this parcel away tomorrow.
Elle m'**envoyait** toujours une carte pour mon anniversaire. She would always send me a card for my birthday.

je/j' = I **tu** = you **il** = he/it **elle** = she/it **on** = we/one **nous** = we **vous** = you **ils/elles** = they

envoyer

FUTURE

j'	**enverrai**
tu	**enverras**
il/elle/on	**enverra**
nous	**enverrons**
vous	**enverrez**
ils/elles	**enverront**

CONDITIONAL

j'	**enverrais**
tu	**enverrais**
il/elle/on	**enverrait**
nous	**enverrions**
vous	**enverriez**
ils/elles	**enverraient**

PAST HISTORIC

j'	**envoyai**
tu	**envoyas**
il/elle/on	**envoya**
nous	**envoyâmes**
vous	**envoyâtes**
ils/elles	**envoyèrent**

PLUPERFECT

j'	**avais envoyé**
tu	**avais envoyé**
il/elle/on	**avait envoyé**
nous	**avions envoyé**
vous	**aviez envoyé**
ils/elles	**avaient envoyé**

IMPERATIVE

envoie / envoyons / envoyez

EXAMPLE PHRASES

J'**enverrai** Julie te chercher à l'aéroport. I'll send Julie to fetch you at the airport.

Sa mère l'**envoya** chercher du pain. His mother sent him to get some bread.

Je lui **enverrais** un cadeau si j'étais sûr de lui faire plaisir. I'd send her a present if I thought it would make her happy.

Je ne lui **avais** pas **envoyé** mes vœux et elle était très vexée. I hadn't sent her a Christmas card and she was very upset.

espérer (to hope)

PRESENT

j'	**espère**
tu	**espères**
il/elle/on	**espère**
nous	**espérons**
vous	**espérez**
ils/elles	**espèrent**

PRESENT SUBJUNCTIVE

j'	**espère**
tu	**espères**
il/elle/on	**espère**
nous	**espérions**
vous	**espériez**
ils/elles	**espèrent**

PERFECT

j'	**ai espéré**
tu	**as espéré**
il/elle/on	**a espéré**
nous	**avons espéré**
vous	**avez espéré**
ils/elles	**ont espéré**

IMPERFECT

j'	**espérais**
tu	**espérais**
il/elle/on	**espérait**
nous	**espérions**
vous	**espériez**
ils/elles	**espéraient**

PRESENT PARTICIPLE
espérant

PAST PARTICIPLE
espéré

EXAMPLE PHRASES

J'**espère** que tu vas bien. I hope you're well.

Tu penses réussir tes examens? – J'**espère** bien! Do you think you'll pass your exams? – I hope so!

Il **espérait** pouvoir venir. He was hoping he'd be able to come.

Elle **espérait** qu'il n'était pas déjà parti. She was hoping that he hadn't already left.

espérer

FUTURE

j'	**espérerai**
tu	**espéreras**
il/elle/on	**espérera**
nous	**espérerons**
vous	**espérerez**
ils/elles	**espéreront**

CONDITIONAL

j'	**espérerais**
tu	**espérerais**
il/elle/on	**espérerait**
nous	**espérerions**
vous	**espéreriez**
ils/elles	**espéreraient**

PAST HISTORIC

j'	**espérai**
tu	**espéras**
il/elle/on	**espéra**
nous	**espérâmes**
vous	**espérâtes**
ils/elles	**espérèrent**

PLUPERFECT

j'	**avais espéré**
tu	**avais espéré**
il/elle/on	**avait espéré**
nous	**avions espéré**
vous	**aviez espéré**
ils/elles	**avaient espéré**

IMPERATIVE

espère / espérons / espérez

EXAMPLE PHRASES

Il **espéra** qu'ils se reverraient bientôt. He hoped that they would see each other again soon.

Si j'étais toi, je n'**espérerais** pas trop qu'il vienne: tu risques d'être déçu. If I were you, I wouldn't put too much hope in him coming – you could be disappointed.

J'**avais espéré** que tu pourrais venir. I had hoped that you would be able to come.

je/j' = I **tu** = you **il** = he/it **elle** = she/it **on** = we/one **nous** = we **vous** = you **ils/elles** = they

essayer (to try)

PRESENT

j'	**essaie**
tu	**essaies**
il/elle/on	**essaie**
nous	**essayons**
vous	**essayez**
ils/elles	**essaient**

PRESENT SUBJUNCTIVE

j'	**essaie**
tu	**essaies**
il/elle/on	**essaie**
nous	**essayions**
vous	**essayiez**
ils/elles	**essaient**

PERFECT

j'	**ai essayé**
tu	**as essayé**
il/elle/on	**a essayé**
nous	**avons essayé**
vous	**avez essayé**
ils/elles	**ont essayé**

IMPERFECT

j'	**essayais**
tu	**essayais**
il/elle/on	**essayait**
nous	**essayions**
vous	**essayiez**
ils/elles	**essayaient**

PRESENT PARTICIPLE
essayant

PAST PARTICIPLE
essayé

EXAMPLE PHRASES

Elle adorait **essayer** mes vêtements. She loved trying on my clothes.
J'**ai essayé** de t'appeler hier soir. I tried to ring you last night.
Essaie de ne pas t'énerver. Try not to get all worked up.
Il faut que j'**essaie** cette nouvelle recette. I must try this new recipe.
Il **essayait** de la comprendre, mais il n'y arrivait pas. He tried to understand her, but he couldn't.

essayer

FUTURE

j'	**essaierai**
tu	**essaieras**
il/elle/on	**essaiera**
nous	**essaierons**
vous	**essaierez**
ils/elles	**essaieront**

CONDITIONAL

j'	**essaierais**
tu	**essaierais**
il/elle/on	**essaierait**
nous	**essaierions**
vous	**essaieriez**
ils/elles	**essaieraient**

PAST HISTORIC

j'	**essayai**
tu	**essayas**
il/elle/on	**essaya**
nous	**essayâmes**
vous	**essayâtes**
ils/elles	**essayèrent**

PLUPERFECT

j'	**avais essayé**
tu	**avais essayé**
il/elle/on	**avait essayé**
nous	**avions essayé**
vous	**aviez essayé**
ils/elles	**avaient essayé**

IMPERATIVE

essaie / essayons / essayez

EXAMPLE PHRASES

J'**essaierai** d'aller le voir après le travail demain. I'll try to go and see him after work tomorrow.

Ils **essayèrent** de la rattraper. They tried to catch up with her.

Je n'**essaierais** pas de lui parler tout de suite si j'étais toi. I wouldn't try to speak to her right now if I were you.

Elle **avait essayé** la robe, mais elle ne lui allait pas. She'd tried on the dress, but it didn't fit her.

éteindre (to switch off)

PRESENT

j'	**éteins**
tu	**éteins**
il/elle/on	**éteint**
nous	**éteignons**
vous	**éteignez**
ils/elles	**éteignent**

PRESENT SUBJUNCTIVE

j'	**éteigne**
tu	**éteignes**
il/elle/on	**éteigne**
nous	**éteignions**
vous	**éteigniez**
ils/elles	**éteignent**

PERFECT

j'	**ai éteint**
tu	**as éteint**
il/elle/on	**a éteint**
nous	**avons éteint**
vous	**avez éteint**
ils/elles	**ont éteint**

IMPERFECT

j'	**éteignais**
tu	**éteignais**
il/elle/on	**éteignait**
nous	**éteignions**
vous	**éteigniez**
ils/elles	**éteignaient**

PRESENT PARTICIPLE
éteignant

PAST PARTICIPLE
éteint

EXAMPLE PHRASES

N'oubliez pas d'**éteindre** la lumière en sortant. Don't forget to switch off the light when you leave.

Elle n'**éteint** jamais la lumière dans sa chambre. She never switches off her bedroom light.

Tu **as éteint** la lumière dans la salle de bain? Have you switched off the bathroom light?

Karine, **éteins** la télé s'il te plaît. Switch off the TV please, Karine.

éteindre

FUTURE	
j'	**éteindrai**
tu	**éteindras**
il/elle/on	**éteindra**
nous	**éteindrons**
vous	**éteindrez**
ils/elles	**éteindront**

CONDITIONAL	
j'	**éteindrais**
tu	**éteindrais**
il/elle/on	**éteindrait**
nous	**éteindrions**
vous	**éteindriez**
ils/elles	**éteindraient**

PAST HISTORIC	
j'	**éteignis**
tu	**éteignis**
il/elle/on	**éteignit**
nous	**éteignîmes**
vous	**éteignîtes**
ils/elles	**éteignirent**

PLUPERFECT	
j'	**avais éteint**
tu	**avais éteint**
il/elle/on	**avait éteint**
nous	**avions éteint**
vous	**aviez éteint**
ils/elles	**avaient éteint**

IMPERATIVE

éteins / éteignons / éteignez

EXAMPLE PHRASES

J'**éteindrai** tout avant de partir. I'll switch everything off before I leave.

Elle **éteignit** la lumière et s'endormit. She switched off the light and fell asleep.

Il **éteindrait** sa cigarette s'il savait que la fumée te dérange. He'd put out his cigarette if he knew that the smoke bothers you.

Il **avait éteint** son portable en entrant dans le cinéma. He'd switched off his mobile on the way in to the cinema.

être (to be)

PRESENT

je	**suis**
tu	**es**
il/elle/on	**est**
nous	**sommes**
vous	**êtes**
ils/elles	**sont**

PRESENT SUBJUNCTIVE

je	**sois**
tu	**sois**
il/elle/on	**soit**
nous	**soyons**
vous	**soyez**
ils/elles	**soient**

PERFECT

j'	**ai été**
tu	**as été**
il/elle/on	**a été**
nous	**avons été**
vous	**avez été**
ils/elles	**ont été**

IMPERFECT

j'	**étais**
tu	**étais**
il/elle/on	**était**
nous	**étions**
vous	**étiez**
ils/elles	**étaient**

PRESENT PARTICIPLE
étant

PAST PARTICIPLE
été

EXAMPLE PHRASES

Quelle heure **est**-il? – Il **est** dix heures. What time is it? – It's ten o'clock.

Ils ne **sont** pas encore **arrivés**. They haven't arrived yet.

Sois courageux. Be brave.

Je veux que vous **soyez** particulièrement sages aujourd'hui. I want you to behave particularly well today.

Il **était** professeur de maths dans mon lycée. He was a maths teacher in my school.

être

FUTURE

je	**serai**
tu	**seras**
il/elle/on	**sera**
nous	**serons**
vous	**serez**
ils/elles	**seront**

CONDITIONAL

je	**serais**
tu	**serais**
il/elle/on	**serait**
nous	**serions**
vous	**seriez**
ils/elles	**seraient**

PAST HISTORIC

je	**fus**
tu	**fus**
il/elle/on	**fut**
nous	**fûmes**
vous	**fûtes**
ils/elles	**furent**

PLUPERFECT

j'	**avais été**
tu	**avais été**
il/elle/on	**avait été**
nous	**avions été**
vous	**aviez été**
ils/elles	**avaient été**

IMPERATIVE

sois / soyons / soyez

EXAMPLE PHRASES

Je **serai** chez moi à partir de midi. I'll be at home from midday onwards.

Il **fut** tellement vexé qu'il ne lui parla pas de la soirée. He was so upset that he didn't speak to her all evening.

Nous **serions** contents de vous voir si vous aviez le temps de passer. We'd be happy to see you if you had time to drop by.

Nous étions punis parce que nous n'**avions** pas **été** sages. We were punished because we hadn't been good.

faillir (faire qch to nearly do sth)

PRESENT

je	**faillis**
tu	**faillis**
il/elle/on	**faillit**
nous	**faillissons**
vous	**faillissez**
ils/elles	**faillissent**

PRESENT SUBJUNCTIVE

je	**faillisse**
tu	**faillisses**
il/elle/on	**faillisse**
nous	**faillissions**
vous	**faillissiez**
ils/elles	**faillissent**

PERFECT

j'	**ai failli**
tu	**as failli**
il/elle/on	**a failli**
nous	**avons failli**
vous	**avez failli**
ils/elles	**ont failli**

IMPERFECT

je	**faillissais**
tu	**faillissais**
il/elle/on	**faillissait**
nous	**faillissions**
vous	**faillissiez**
ils/elles	**faillissaient**

PRESENT PARTICIPLE

faillissant

PAST PARTICIPLE

failli

EXAMPLE PHRASES

J'**ai failli** tomber. I nearly fell.
Il **a failli** s'énerver. He nearly got angry.
Nous **avons failli** rater notre train. We nearly missed our train.
Ils **ont failli** ne pas venir. They nearly didn't come.

faillir

FUTURE		CONDITIONAL	
je	**faillirai**	je	**faillirais**
tu	**failliras**	tu	**faillirais**
il/elle/on	**faillira**	il/elle/on	**faillirait**
nous	**faillirons**	nous	**faillirions**
vous	**faillirez**	vous	**failliriez**
ils/elles	**failliront**	ils/elles	**failliraient**

PAST HISTORIC		PLUPERFECT	
je	**faillis**	j'	**avais failli**
tu	**faillis**	tu	**avais failli**
il/elle/on	**faillit**	il/elle/on	**avait failli**
nous	**faillîmes**	nous	**avions failli**
vous	**faillîtes**	vous	**aviez failli**
ils/elles	**faillirent**	ils/elles	**avaient failli**

IMPERATIVE

not used

EXAMPLE PHRASES

Il **faillit** s'en aller sans dire au revoir. He nearly left without saying goodbye.

Elle **faillit** pleurer quand ils lui annoncèrent la nouvelle. She nearly cried when they told her the news.

Nous **avions failli** nous perdre en venant vous voir ce jour-là. We had nearly got lost on our way to see you that day.

Ils **avaient failli** se battre, mais la cloche avait sonné au bon moment. They had nearly had a fight, but the bell had rung just at the right time.

faire (to do; to make)

PRESENT

je	**fais**
tu	**fais**
il/elle/on	**fait**
nous	**faisons**
vous	**faites**
ils/elles	**font**

PRESENT SUBJUNCTIVE

je	**fasse**
tu	**fasses**
il/elle/on	**fasse**
nous	**fassions**
vous	**fassiez**
ils/elles	**fassent**

PERFECT

j'	**ai fait**
tu	**as fait**
il/elle/on	**a fait**
nous	**avons fait**
vous	**avez fait**
ils/elles	**ont fait**

IMPERFECT

je	**faisais**
tu	**faisais**
il/elle/on	**faisait**
nous	**faisions**
vous	**faisiez**
ils/elles	**faisaient**

PRESENT PARTICIPLE

faisant

PAST PARTICIPLE

fait

EXAMPLE PHRASES

Qu'est-ce que tu **fais**? What are you doing?

Qu'est-ce qu'il **a fait**? What has he done?

Il s'**est fait** couper les cheveux. He's had his hair cut.

Ne **fais** pas l'idiot. Don't behave like an idiot.

J'aimerais que tu **fasses** la vaisselle plus souvent. I'd like you to wash the dishes more often.

Il ne **faisait** jamais son lit. He would never make his bed.

je/j' = I **tu** = you **il** = he/it **elle** = she/it **on** = we/one **nous** = we **vous** = you **ils/elles** = they

faire

FUTURE

je	**ferai**
tu	**feras**
il/elle/on	**fera**
nous	**ferons**
vous	**ferez**
ils/elles	**feront**

CONDITIONAL

je	**ferais**
tu	**ferais**
il/elle/on	**ferait**
nous	**ferions**
vous	**feriez**
ils/elles	**feraient**

PAST HISTORIC

je	**fis**
tu	**fis**
il/elle/on	**fit**
nous	**fîmes**
vous	**fîtes**
ils/elles	**firent**

PLUPERFECT

j'	**avais fait**
tu	**avais fait**
il/elle/on	**avait fait**
nous	**avions fait**
vous	**aviez fait**
ils/elles	**avaient fait**

IMPERATIVE

fais / faisons / faites

EXAMPLE PHRASES

Demain, nous **ferons** une promenade sur la plage. Tomorrow, we'll go for a walk on the beach.

Il **fit** semblant de ne pas comprendre. He pretended not to understand.

Si je gagnais à la loterie, je **ferais** le tour du monde. If I won the lottery, I would take a trip round the world.

Elle **avait fait** un gâteau. She'd made a cake.

falloir (to be necessary)

PRESENT

il **faut**

PRESENT SUBJUNCTIVE

il **faille**

PERFECT

il **a fallu**

IMPERFECT

il **fallait**

PRESENT PARTICIPLE

not used

PAST PARTICIPLE

fallu

EXAMPLE PHRASES

Il **faut** se dépêcher! We have to hurry up!
Il ne **faut** pas paniquer. Let's not panic.
Il **a fallu** que je lui prête ma voiture. I had to lend her my car.
Il me **fallait** de l'argent. I needed money.

je/j' = I **tu** = you **il** = he/it **elle** = she/it **on** = we/one **nous** = we **vous** = you **ils/elles** = they

falloir

FUTURE

il **faudra**

CONDITIONAL

il **faudrait**

PAST HISTORIC

il **fallut**

PLUPERFECT

il **avait fallu**

IMPERATIVE

not used

EXAMPLE PHRASES

Il **faudra** que tu sois là à 8 heures. You'll have to be there at 8.

Il **fallut** qu'ils partent de très bonne heure. They had to leave very early.

Il **faudrait** t'arrêter de fumer. You should stop smoking.

Il nous **avait fallu** nettoyer toute la maison. We'd had to clean the whole house.

finir (to finish)

PRESENT

je	**finis**
tu	**finis**
il/elle/on	**finit**
nous	**finissons**
vous	**finissez**
ils/elles	**finissent**

PRESENT SUBJUNCTIVE

je	**finisse**
tu	**finisses**
il/elle/on	**finisse**
nous	**finissions**
vous	**finissiez**
ils/elles	**finissent**

PERFECT

j'	**ai fini**
tu	**as fini**
il/elle/on	**a fini**
nous	**avons fini**
vous	**avez fini**
ils/elles	**ont fini**

IMPERFECT

je	**finissais**
tu	**finissais**
il/elle/on	**finissait**
nous	**finissions**
vous	**finissiez**
ils/elles	**finissaient**

PRESENT PARTICIPLE

finissant

PAST PARTICIPLE

fini

EXAMPLE PHRASES

Je **finis** mes cours à 17h. I finish my lessons at 5pm.

J'**ai fini**! I've finished!

Finis ta soupe! Finish your soup!

Il faut que je **finisse** mon livre avant de commencer celui-là. I have to finish my book before I start that one.

Elle **finissait** toujours en retard. She'd always finish late.

je/j' = I **tu** = you **il** = he/it **elle** = she/it **on** = we/one **nous** = we **vous** = you **ils/elles** = they

finir

FUTURE		CONDITIONAL	
je	**finirai**	je	**finirais**
tu	**finiras**	tu	**finirais**
il/elle/on	**finira**	il/elle/on	**finirait**
nous	**finirons**	nous	**finirions**
vous	**finirez**	vous	**finiriez**
ils/elles	**finiront**	ils/elles	**finiraient**

PAST HISTORIC		PLUPERFECT	
je	**finis**	j'	**avais fini**
tu	**finis**	tu	**avais fini**
il/elle/on	**finit**	il/elle/on	**avait fini**
nous	**finîmes**	nous	**avions fini**
vous	**finîtes**	vous	**aviez fini**
ils/elles	**finirent**	ils/elles	**avaient fini**

IMPERATIVE

finis / finissons / finissez

EXAMPLE PHRASES

Je **finirai** mes devoirs demain. I'll finish my homework tomorrow.

Il **finit** son dîner et alla se coucher. He finished his dinner and went to bed.

Si on l'ignorait, elle **finirait** par comprendre. If we ignored her, she'd eventually understand.

Elle n'**avait** pas **fini** de manger quand nous sommes arrivés. She hadn't finished eating when we arrived.

je/j' = I **tu** = you **il** = he/it **elle** = she/it **on** = we/one **nous** = we **vous** = you **ils/elles** = they

fuir (to flee; to leak)

PRESENT		PRESENT SUBJUNCTIVE	
je	**fuis**	je	**fuie**
tu	**fuis**	tu	**fuies**
il/elle/on	**fuit**	il/elle/on	**fuie**
nous	**fuyons**	nous	**fuyions**
vous	**fuyez**	vous	**fuyiez**
ils/elles	**fuient**	ils/elles	**fuient**

PERFECT		IMPERFECT	
j'	**ai fui**	je	**fuyais**
tu	**as fui**	tu	**fuyais**
il/elle/on	**a fui**	il/elle/on	**fuyait**
nous	**avons fui**	nous	**fuyions**
vous	**avez fui**	vous	**fuyiez**
ils/elles	**ont fui**	ils/elles	**fuyaient**

PRESENT PARTICIPLE
fuyant

PAST PARTICIPLE
fui

EXAMPLE PHRASES

J'ai un stylo qui **fuit**. My pen leaks.

Ils **ont fui** leur pays. They fled their country.

Il ne faut pas que tu le **fuies** comme ça. You mustn't run away from him like that.

Le robinet **fuyait**. The tap was dripping.

fuir

FUTURE

je	**fuirai**
tu	**fuiras**
il/elle/on	**fuira**
nous	**fuirons**
vous	**fuirez**
ils/elles	**fuiront**

CONDITIONAL

je	**fuirais**
tu	**fuirais**
il/elle/on	**fuirait**
nous	**fuirions**
vous	**fuiriez**
ils/elles	**fuiraient**

PAST HISTORIC

je	**fuis**
tu	**fuis**
il/elle/on	**fuit**
nous	**fuîmes**
vous	**fuîtes**
ils/elles	**fuirent**

PLUPERFECT

j'	**avais fui**
tu	**avais fui**
il/elle/on	**avait fui**
nous	**avions fui**
vous	**aviez fui**
ils/elles	**avaient fui**

IMPERATIVE

fuis / fuyons / fuyez

EXAMPLE PHRASES

Il **fuira** toujours les responsabilités. He will always run away from responsibilities.

Beaucoup de gens **fuirent** vers le sud. A lot of people fled south.

La machine à laver **fuirait** si on la remplissait trop. The washing machine would leak if we overloaded it.

Ils **avaient fui** leur village et s'étaient réfugiés dans les montagnes. They had fled from their village and had taken refuge in the mountains.

haïr (to hate)

PRESENT

je	**hais**
tu	**hais**
il/elle/on	**hait**
nous	**haïssons**
vous	**haïssez**
ils/elles	**haïssent**

PRESENT SUBJUNCTIVE

je	**haïsse**
tu	**haïsses**
il/elle/on	**haïsse**
nous	**haïssions**
vous	**haïssiez**
ils/elles	**haïssent**

PERFECT

j'	**ai haï**
tu	**as haï**
il/elle/on	**a haï**
nous	**avons haï**
vous	**avez haï**
ils/elles	**ont haï**

IMPERFECT

je	**haïssais**
tu	**haïssais**
il/elle/on	**haïssait**
nous	**haïssions**
vous	**haïssiez**
ils/elles	**haïssaient**

PRESENT PARTICIPLE
haïssant

PAST PARTICIPLE
haï

EXAMPLE PHRASES

Je te **hais**! I hate you!
Ils se **haïssent**. They hate each other.
Il ne faut pas que tu le **haïsses** pour ça. You mustn't hate him for that.
Elle **haïssait** tout le monde. She hated everyone.

haïr

FUTURE

je	**haïrai**
tu	**haïras**
il/elle/on	**haïra**
nous	**haïrons**
vous	**haïrez**
ils/elles	**haïront**

CONDITIONAL

je	**haïrais**
tu	**haïrais**
il/elle/on	**haïrait**
nous	**haïrions**
vous	**haïriez**
ils/elles	**haïraient**

PAST HISTORIC

je	**haïs**
tu	**haïs**
il/elle/on	**haït**
nous	**haïmes**
vous	**haïtes**
ils/elles	**haïrent**

PLUPERFECT

j'	**avais haï**
tu	**avais haï**
il/elle/on	**avait haï**
nous	**avions haï**
vous	**aviez haï**
ils/elles	**avaient haï**

IMPERATIVE

hais / haïssons / haïssez

EXAMPLE PHRASES

Je la **haïrai** toujours. I'll always hate her.

Elle le **haït** pour ce qu'il venait de dire. She hated him for what he'd just said.

Elle me **haïrait** si je n'allais pas voir ses parents avec elle. She'd hate me if I didn't go and see her parents with her.

Elle m'**avait haï** durant toutes ces années et maintenant nous étions les meilleures amies du monde. She had hated me all these years and now we were the best of friends.

je/j' = I **tu** = you **il** = he/it **elle** = she/it **on** = we/one **nous** = we **vous** = you **ils/elles** = they

s'inquiéter (to worry)

PRESENT		PRESENT SUBJUNCTIVE	
je	**m'inquiète**	je	**m'inquiète**
tu	**t'inquiètes**	tu	**t'inquiètes**
il/elle/on	**s'inquiète**	il/elle/on	**s'inquiète**
nous	**nous inquiétons**	nous	**nous inquiétions**
vous	**vous inquiétez**	vous	**vous inquiétiez**
ils/elles	**s'inquiètent**	ils/elles	**s'inquiètent**

PERFECT		IMPERFECT	
je	**me suis inquiété(e)**	je	**m'inquiétais**
tu	**t'es inquiété(e)**	tu	**t'inquiétais**
il/elle/on	**s'est inquiété(e)**	il/elle/on	**s'inquiétait**
nous	**nous sommes inquiété(e)s**	nous	**nous inquiétions**
vous	**vous êtes inquiété(e)(s)**	vous	**vous inquiétiez**
ils/elles	**se sont inquiété(e)s**	ils/elles	**s'inquiétaient**

PRESENT PARTICIPLE
s'inquiétant

PAST PARTICIPLE
inquiété

EXAMPLE PHRASES

Elle **s'inquiète** toujours si je suis en retard. She always worries if I'm late.

Comme je savais où tu étais, je ne **me suis** pas **inquiétée**. As I knew where you were, I didn't worry.

Ne **t'inquiète** pas, je ne rentrerai pas tard. Don't worry, I'll not be late coming home.

Je ne veux pas qu'ils **s'inquiètent**. I don't want them to worry.

Ça **m'inquiétait** un peu que tu ne nous aies pas téléphoné. I was a little worried that you hadn't phoned us.

je/j' = I **tu** = you **il** = he/it **elle** = she/it **on** = we/one **nous** = we **vous** = you **ils/elles** = they

s'inquiéter

FUTURE

je	**m'inquiéterai**
tu	**t'inquiéteras**
il/elle/on	**s'inquiétera**
nous	**nous inquiéterons**
vous	**vous inquiéterez**
ils/elles	**s'inquiéteront**

CONDITIONAL

je	**m'inquiéterais**
tu	**t'inquiéterais**
il/elle/on	**s'inquiéterait**
nous	**nous inquiéterions**
vous	**vous inquiéteriez**
ils/elles	**s'inquiéteraient**

PAST HISTORIC

je	**m'inquiétai**
tu	**t'inquiétas**
il/elle/on	**s'inquiéta**
nous	**nous inquiétâmes**
vous	**vous inquiétâtes**
ils/elles	**s'inquiétèrent**

PLUPERFECT

je	**m'étais inquiété(e)**
tu	**t'étais inquiété(e)**
il/elle/on	**s'était inquiété(e)**
nous	**nous étions inquiété(e)s**
vous	**vous étiez inquiété(e)(s)**
ils/elles	**s'étaient inquiété(e)s**

IMPERATIVE

inquiète-toi / inquiétons-nous / inquiétez-vous

EXAMPLE PHRASES

Mes parents **s'inquiéteront** si j'y vais toute seule. My parents will worry if I go there on my own.

Il **s'inquiéta** pour elle. He worried about her.

Je **m'inquiéterais** moins si tu n'étais pas si loin. I'd worry less if you weren't so far away.

Comme ils savaient qu'elle était avec Vincent, ils ne **s'étaient** pas **inquiétés**. As they knew that she was with Vincent, they hadn't worried.

interdire (to forbid)

PRESENT		PRESENT SUBJUNCTIVE	
j'	**interdis**	j'	**interdise**
tu	**interdis**	tu	**interdises**
il/elle/on	**interdit**	il/elle/on	**interdise**
nous	**interdisons**	nous	**interdisions**
vous	**interdisez**	vous	**interdisiez**
ils/elles	**interdisent**	ils/elles	**interdisent**

PERFECT		IMPERFECT	
j'	**ai interdit**	j'	**interdisais**
tu	**as interdit**	tu	**interdisais**
il/elle/on	**a interdit**	il/elle/on	**interdisait**
nous	**avons interdit**	nous	**interdisions**
vous	**avez interdit**	vous	**interdisiez**
ils/elles	**ont interdit**	ils/elles	**interdisaient**

PRESENT PARTICIPLE
interdisant

PAST PARTICIPLE
interdit

EXAMPLE PHRASES

Je t'**interdis** de toucher à ça. I forbid you to touch this.

Ses parents lui **ont interdit** de sortir. His parents have forbidden him to go out.

Interdisons-leur de regarder la télé ce week-end. Let's ban them from watching TV over the weekend.

Elle nous **interdisait** de jouer avec lui. She forbade us to play with him.

interdire

FUTURE

j'	**interdirai**
tu	**interdiras**
il/elle/on	**interdira**
nous	**interdirons**
vous	**interdirez**
ils/elles	**interdiront**

CONDITIONAL

j'	**interdirais**
tu	**interdirais**
il/elle/on	**interdirait**
nous	**interdirions**
vous	**interdiriez**
ils/elles	**interdiraient**

PAST HISTORIC

j'	**interdis**
tu	**interdis**
il/elle/on	**interdit**
nous	**interdîmes**
vous	**interdîtes**
ils/elles	**interdirent**

PLUPERFECT

j'	**avais interdit**
tu	**avais interdit**
il/elle/on	**avait interdit**
nous	**avions interdit**
vous	**aviez interdit**
ils/elles	**avaient interdit**

IMPERATIVE

interdis / interdisons / interdisez

EXAMPLE PHRASES

Si vous n'êtes pas raisonnables, je vous **interdirai** de sortir du jardin. If you're not sensible, I'll forbid you to leave the garden.

À partir de ce jour, ils nous **interdirent** de la voir. From that day on, they forbade us to see her.

Si ma fille me parlait comme ça, je lui **interdirais** de sortir avec ses copines. If my daughter spoke to me like that, I'd ban her from going out with her friends.

Elle nous **avait interdit** de lui en parler. She had forbidden us to tell him about it.

je/j' = I **tu** = you **il** = he/it **elle** = she/it **on** = we/one **nous** = we **vous** = you **ils/elles** = they

jeter (to throw)

PRESENT

je	**jette**
tu	**jettes**
il/elle/on	**jette**
nous	**jetons**
vous	**jetez**
ils/elles	**jettent**

PRESENT SUBJUNCTIVE

je	**jette**
tu	**jettes**
il/elle/on	**jette**
nous	**jetions**
vous	**jetiez**
ils/elles	**jettent**

PERFECT

j'	**ai jeté**
tu	**as jeté**
il/elle/on	**a jeté**
nous	**avons jeté**
vous	**avez jeté**
ils/elles	**ont jeté**

IMPERFECT

je	**jetais**
tu	**jetais**
il/elle/on	**jetait**
nous	**jetions**
vous	**jetiez**
ils/elles	**jetaient**

PRESENT PARTICIPLE

jetant

PAST PARTICIPLE

jeté

EXAMPLE PHRASES

Ils ne **jettent** jamais rien. They never throw anything away.

Elle **a jeté** son chewing-gum par la fenêtre. She threw her chewing gum out of the window.

Ne **jette** pas de papiers par terre. Don't throw litter on the ground.

Il faut qu'on **jette** tous ces vieux jouets cassés. We'll have to throw away all these old broken toys.

Il **jetait** toujours ses vêtements par terre. He'd always throw his clothes on the floor.

jeter

FUTURE		CONDITIONAL	
je	**jetterai**	je	**jetterais**
tu	**jetteras**	tu	**jetterais**
il/elle/on	**jettera**	il/elle/on	**jetterait**
nous	**jetterons**	nous	**jetterions**
vous	**jetterez**	vous	**jetteriez**
ils/elles	**jetteront**	ils/elles	**jetteraient**

PAST HISTORIC		PLUPERFECT	
je	**jetai**	j'	**avais jeté**
tu	**jetas**	tu	**avais jeté**
il/elle/on	**jeta**	il/elle/on	**avait jeté**
nous	**jetâmes**	nous	**avions jeté**
vous	**jetâtes**	vous	**aviez jeté**
ils/elles	**jetèrent**	ils/elles	**avaient jeté**

IMPERATIVE

jette / jetons / jetez

EXAMPLE PHRASES

Je **jetterai** tout ça à la poubelle. I'll throw all this in the bin.

Il **jeta** sa veste sur la chaise et répondit au téléphone. He threw his jacket on the chair and answered the phone.

Je **jetterais** bien tous ces vieux magazines. I'd quite like to throw all these old magazines away.

Elle jurait qu'elle n'**avait** rien **jeté**. She swore she hadn't thrown anything away.

je/j' = I **tu** = you **il** = he/it **elle** = she/it **on** = we/one **nous** = we **vous** = you **ils/elles** = they

joindre (to join; to contact)

PRESENT

je	**joins**
tu	**joins**
il/elle/on	**joint**
nous	**joignons**
vous	**joignez**
ils/elles	**joignent**

PRESENT SUBJUNCTIVE

je	**joigne**
tu	**joignes**
il/elle/on	**joigne**
nous	**joignions**
vous	**joigniez**
ils/elles	**joignent**

PERFECT

j'	**ai joint**
tu	**as joint**
il/elle/on	**a joint**
nous	**avons joint**
vous	**avez joint**
ils/elles	**ont joint**

IMPERFECT

je	**joignais**
tu	**joignais**
il/elle/on	**joignait**
nous	**joignions**
vous	**joigniez**
ils/elles	**joignaient**

PRESENT PARTICIPLE

joignant

PAST PARTICIPLE

joint

EXAMPLE PHRASES

Où est-ce qu'on peut te **joindre** ce week-end? Where can we contact you this weekend?

Il n'est pas facile à **joindre**. He's not easy to contact.

Je vous **ai joint** un plan de la ville. I have enclosed a map of the town.

joindre

FUTURE

je	**joindrai**
tu	**joindras**
il/elle/on	**joindra**
nous	**joindrons**
vous	**joindrez**
ils/elles	**joindront**

CONDITIONAL

je	**joindrais**
tu	**joindrais**
il/elle/on	**joindrait**
nous	**joindrions**
vous	**joindriez**
ils/elles	**joindraient**

PAST HISTORIC

je	**joignis**
tu	**joignis**
il/elle/on	**joignit**
nous	**joignîmes**
vous	**joignîtes**
ils/elles	**joignirent**

PLUPERFECT

j'	**avais joint**
tu	**avais joint**
il/elle/on	**avait joint**
nous	**avions joint**
vous	**aviez joint**
ils/elles	**avaient joint**

IMPERATIVE

joins / joignons / joignez

EXAMPLE PHRASES

J'espère que vous vous **joindrez** à nous dimanche. I hope you'll join us on Sunday.

Il **joignit** les mains et se mit à prier. He put his hands together and started to pray.

On **avait joint** les deux tables. We'd put the two tables together.

lever (to lift)

PRESENT		PRESENT SUBJUNCTIVE	
je	**lève**	je	**lève**
tu	**lèves**	tu	**lèves**
il/elle/on	**lève**	il/elle/on	**lève**
nous	**levons**	nous	**levions**
vous	**levez**	vous	**leviez**
ils/elles	**lèvent**	ils/elles	**lèvent**

PERFECT		IMPERFECT	
j'	**ai levé**	je	**levais**
tu	**as levé**	tu	**levais**
il/elle/on	**a levé**	il/elle/on	**levait**
nous	**avons levé**	nous	**levions**
vous	**avez levé**	vous	**leviez**
ils/elles	**ont levé**	ils/elles	**levaient**

PRESENT PARTICIPLE
levant

PAST PARTICIPLE
levé

EXAMPLE PHRASES

Je me **lève** tous les matins à sept heures. I get up at seven every day.
Elle **a levé** la main pour répondre à la question. She put her hand up to answer the question.
Levez le doigt! Put your hand up!
Levons notre verre à ta réussite. Let's raise our glasses to your success.

lever

FUTURE

je	**lèverai**
tu	**lèveras**
il/elle/on	**lèvera**
nous	**lèverons**
vous	**lèverez**
ils/elles	**lèveront**

CONDITIONAL

je	**lèverais**
tu	**lèverais**
il/elle/on	**lèverait**
nous	**lèverions**
vous	**lèveriez**
ils/elles	**lèveraient**

PAST HISTORIC

je	**levai**
tu	**levas**
il/elle/on	**leva**
nous	**levâmes**
vous	**levâtes**
ils/elles	**levèrent**

PLUPERFECT

j'	**avais levé**
tu	**avais levé**
il/elle/on	**avait levé**
nous	**avions levé**
vous	**aviez levé**
ils/elles	**avaient levé**

IMPERATIVE

lève / levons / levez

EXAMPLE PHRASES

Je ne **lèverai** pas le petit doigt pour l'aider. I won't lift a finger to help him.

Elle **leva** les yeux et vit qu'il était en train de tricher. She looked up and saw that he was cheating.

Si mon père était encore là, il **lèverait** les bras au ciel. If my dad were still here, he'd throw his arms up in despair.

lire (to read)

PRESENT		PRESENT SUBJUNCTIVE	
je	**lis**	je	**lise**
tu	**lis**	tu	**lises**
il/elle/on	**lit**	il/elle/on	**lise**
nous	**lisons**	nous	**lisions**
vous	**lisez**	vous	**lisiez**
ils/elles	**lisent**	ils/elles	**lisent**

PERFECT		IMPERFECT	
j'	**ai lu**	je	**lisais**
tu	**as lu**	tu	**lisais**
il/elle/on	**a lu**	il/elle/on	**lisait**
nous	**avons lu**	nous	**lisions**
vous	**avez lu**	vous	**lisiez**
ils/elles	**ont lu**	ils/elles	**lisaient**

PRESENT PARTICIPLE
lisant

PAST PARTICIPLE
lu

EXAMPLE PHRASES

Il **lit** beaucoup. He reads a lot.
Vous **avez lu** "Madame Bovary"? Have you read "Madame Bovary"?
Lisez bien les instructions. Read the instructions carefully.
J'aimerais que tu **lises** ce livre. I'd like you to read this book.
Elle lui **lisait** une histoire. She was reading him a story.

lire

FUTURE

je	**lirai**
tu	**liras**
il/elle/on	**lira**
nous	**lirons**
vous	**lirez**
ils/elles	**liront**

CONDITIONAL

je	**lirais**
tu	**lirais**
il/elle/on	**lirait**
nous	**lirions**
vous	**liriez**
ils/elles	**liraient**

PAST HISTORIC

je	**lus**
tu	**lus**
il/elle/on	**lut**
nous	**lûmes**
vous	**lûtes**
ils/elles	**lurent**

PLUPERFECT

j'	**avais lu**
tu	**avais lu**
il/elle/on	**avait lu**
nous	**avions lu**
vous	**aviez lu**
ils/elles	**avaient lu**

IMPERATIVE

lis / lisons / lisez

EXAMPLE PHRASES

Je le **lirai** dans l'avion. I'll read it on the plane.
Il **lut** la lettre à haute voix. He read the letter aloud.
Je **lirais** plus si j'avais le temps. I'd read more if I had time.
La maîtresse s'aperçut qu'il n'**avait** pas **lu** le livre. The teacher realized that he hadn't read the book.

je/j' = I **tu** = you **il** = he/it **elle** = she/it **on** = we/one **nous** = we **vous** = you **ils/elles** = they

manger (to eat)

PRESENT

je	**mange**
tu	**manges**
il/elle/on	**mange**
nous	**mangeons**
vous	**mangez**
ils/elles	**mangent**

PRESENT SUBJUNCTIVE

je	**mange**
tu	**manges**
il/elle/on	**mange**
nous	**mangions**
vous	**mangiez**
ils/elles	**mangent**

PERFECT

j'	**ai mangé**
tu	**as mangé**
il/elle/on	**a mangé**
nous	**avons mangé**
vous	**avez mangé**
ils/elles	**ont mangé**

IMPERFECT

je	**mangeais**
tu	**mangeais**
il/elle/on	**mangeait**
nous	**mangions**
vous	**mangiez**
ils/elles	**mangeaient**

PRESENT PARTICIPLE
mangeant

PAST PARTICIPLE
mangé

EXAMPLE PHRASES

Nous ne **mangeons** pas souvent ensemble. We don't often eat together.
Tu **as** assez **mangé**? Have you had enough to eat?
Mange ta soupe. Eat your soup.
Il faut que je **mange** avant de partir. I have to eat before I leave.
Ils **mangeaient** en regardant la télé. They were eating while watching TV.

manger

FUTURE

je	**mangerai**
tu	**mangeras**
il/elle/on	**mangera**
nous	**mangerons**
vous	**mangerez**
ils/elles	**mangeront**

CONDITIONAL

je	**mangerais**
tu	**mangerais**
il/elle/on	**mangerait**
nous	**mangerions**
vous	**mangeriez**
ils/elles	**mangeraient**

PAST HISTORIC

je	**mangeai**
tu	**mangeas**
il/elle/on	**mangea**
nous	**mangeâmes**
vous	**mangeâtes**
ils/elles	**mangèrent**

PLUPERFECT

j'	**avais mangé**
tu	**avais mangé**
il/elle/on	**avait mangé**
nous	**avions mangé**
vous	**aviez mangé**
ils/elles	**avaient mangé**

IMPERATIVE

mange / mangeons / mangez

EXAMPLE PHRASES

Je **mangerai** plus tard. I'll eat later on.

Il **mangea** rapidement et retourna travailler. He ate quickly and went back to work.

Je **mangerais** bien le reste si je n'avais pas peur de grossir. I'd gladly eat the rest if I wasn't afraid of putting on weight.

Comme ils **avaient** bien **mangé** le midi, ils ont tenu jusqu'au soir. As they had had a good lunch, they kept going until dinner time.

maudire (to curse)

PRESENT

je	**maudis**
tu	**maudis**
il/elle/on	**maudit**
nous	**maudissons**
vous	**maudissez**
ils/elles	**maudissent**

PRESENT SUBJUNCTIVE

je	**maudisse**
tu	**maudisses**
il/elle/on	**maudisse**
nous	**maudissions**
vous	**maudissiez**
ils/elles	**maudissent**

PERFECT

j'	**ai maudit**
tu	**as maudit**
il/elle/on	**a maudit**
nous	**avons maudit**
vous	**avez maudit**
ils/elles	**ont maudit**

IMPERFECT

je	**maudissais**
tu	**maudissais**
il/elle/on	**maudissait**
nous	**maudissions**
vous	**maudissiez**
ils/elles	**maudissaient**

PRESENT PARTICIPLE
maudissant

PAST PARTICIPLE
maudit

EXAMPLE PHRASES

Ils **maudissent** leurs ennemis. They curse their enemies.

Je **maudis** le jour où je l'ai rencontrée. I curse the day I met her.

Elle me **maudissait** en nettoyant mon manteau couvert de boue. She cursed me as she was cleaning my muddy coat.

Ce **maudit** stylo ne marche pas! This blasted pen doesn't work!

maudire

FUTURE	
je	**maudirai**
tu	**maudiras**
il/elle/on	**maudira**
nous	**maudirons**
vous	**maudirez**
ils/elles	**maudiront**

CONDITIONAL	
je	**maudirais**
tu	**maudirais**
il/elle/on	**maudirait**
nous	**maudirions**
vous	**maudiriez**
ils/elles	**maudiraient**

PAST HISTORIC	
je	**maudis**
tu	**maudis**
il/elle/on	**maudit**
nous	**maudîmes**
vous	**maudîtes**
ils/elles	**maudirent**

PLUPERFECT	
j'	**avais maudit**
tu	**avais maudit**
il/elle/on	**avait maudit**
nous	**avions maudit**
vous	**aviez maudit**
ils/elles	**avaient maudit**

IMPERATIVE

maudis / maudissons / maudissez

EXAMPLE PHRASES

Je les **maudirai** jusqu'à ma mort. I'll curse them to the day I die.

Il la **maudit** pour sa stupidité. He cursed her for her stupidity.

Je te **maudirais** si tu arrivais en retard. I'd curse you if you arrived late.

Nous les **avions maudits** de nous avoir laissés les attendre sous la pluie.
We had cursed them for making us wait for them in the rain.

mentir (to lie)

PRESENT

je	**mens**
tu	**mens**
il/elle/on	**ment**
nous	**mentons**
vous	**mentez**
ils/elles	**mentent**

PRESENT SUBJUNCTIVE

je	**mente**
tu	**mentes**
il/elle/on	**mente**
nous	**mentions**
vous	**mentiez**
ils/elles	**mentent**

PERFECT

j'	**ai menti**
tu	**as menti**
il/elle/on	**a menti**
nous	**avons menti**
vous	**avez menti**
ils/elles	**ont menti**

IMPERFECT

je	**mentais**
tu	**mentais**
il/elle/on	**mentait**
nous	**mentions**
vous	**mentiez**
ils/elles	**mentaient**

PRESENT PARTICIPLE
mentant

PAST PARTICIPLE
menti

EXAMPLE PHRASES

Je ne **mens** jamais. I never lie.
Il lui **a menti**. He lied to her.
Ne **mens** pas s'il te plaît. Please don't lie.
Je ne veux pas que tu me **mentes**. I don't want you to lie to me.
Elle savait qu'il **mentait**. She knew that he was lying.

mentir

FUTURE

je	**mentirai**
tu	**mentiras**
il/elle/on	**mentira**
nous	**mentirons**
vous	**mentirez**
ils/elles	**mentiront**

CONDITIONAL

je	**mentirais**
tu	**mentirais**
il/elle/on	**mentirait**
nous	**mentirions**
vous	**mentiriez**
ils/elles	**mentiraient**

PAST HISTORIC

je	**mentis**
tu	**mentis**
il/elle/on	**mentit**
nous	**mentîmes**
vous	**mentîtes**
ils/elles	**mentirent**

PLUPERFECT

j'	**avais menti**
tu	**avais menti**
il/elle/on	**avait menti**
nous	**avions menti**
vous	**aviez menti**
ils/elles	**avaient menti**

IMPERATIVE

mens / mentons / mentez

EXAMPLE PHRASES

Je **mentirai** s'il le faut. I'll lie if I have to.

Il **mentit** pour qu'on le laisse tranquille. He lied so that he'd be left alone.

Elle ne **mentirait** pas si tu ne lui faisais pas aussi peur. She wouldn't lie if you didn't frighten her so much.

Il **avait menti** pour ne pas la contrarier. He had lied in order not to upset her.

je/j' = I **tu** = you **il** = he/it **elle** = she/it **on** = we/one **nous** = we **vous** = you **ils/elles** = they

mettre (to put)

PRESENT		PRESENT SUBJUNCTIVE	
je	**mets**	je	**mette**
tu	**mets**	tu	**mettes**
il/elle/on	**met**	il/elle/on	**mette**
nous	**mettons**	nous	**mettions**
vous	**mettez**	vous	**mettiez**
ils/elles	**mettent**	ils/elles	**mettent**

PERFECT		IMPERFECT	
j'	**ai mis**	je	**mettais**
tu	**as mis**	tu	**mettais**
il/elle/on	**a mis**	il/elle/on	**mettait**
nous	**avons mis**	nous	**mettions**
vous	**avez mis**	vous	**mettiez**
ils/elles	**ont mis**	ils/elles	**mettaient**

PRESENT PARTICIPLE
mettant

PAST PARTICIPLE
mis

EXAMPLE PHRASES

Il **met** du gel dans ses cheveux. He puts gel in his hair.
Où est-ce que tu **as mis** les clés? Where have you put the keys?
Mets ton manteau! Put your coat on!
Il faut que je **mette** le gâteau au four. I have to put the cake in the oven.
Elle **mettait** toujours des heures à s'habiller. She would always take hours to get dressed.

mettre

FUTURE

je	**mettrai**
tu	**mettras**
il/elle/on	**mettra**
nous	**mettrons**
vous	**mettrez**
ils/elles	**mettront**

CONDITIONAL

je	**mettrais**
tu	**mettrais**
il/elle/on	**mettrait**
nous	**mettrions**
vous	**mettriez**
ils/elles	**mettraient**

PAST HISTORIC

je	**mis**
tu	**mis**
il/elle/on	**mit**
nous	**mîmes**
vous	**mîtes**
ils/elles	**mirent**

PLUPERFECT

j'	**avais mis**
tu	**avais mis**
il/elle/on	**avait mis**
nous	**avions mis**
vous	**aviez mis**
ils/elles	**avaient mis**

IMPERATIVE

mets / mettons / mettez

EXAMPLE PHRASES

Je **mettrai** ma robe rose demain. I'll put on my pink dress tomorrow.

Elle **mit** la bouilloire à chauffer. She put the kettle on.

Je **mettrais** une robe si tu en mettais une aussi. I'd put on a dress if you'd put one on too.

J'**avais mis** le livre sur la table. I had put the book on the table.

monter (to go up; to take up)

PRESENT

je	**monte**
tu	**montes**
il/elle/on	**monte**
nous	**montons**
vous	**montez**
ils/elles	**montent**

PRESENT SUBJUNCTIVE

je	**monte**
tu	**montes**
il/elle/on	**monte**
nous	**montions**
vous	**montiez**
ils/elles	**montent**

PERFECT

je	**suis monté(e)**
tu	**es monté(e)**
il/elle/on	**est monté(e)**
nous	**sommes monté(e)s**
vous	**êtes monté(e)(s)**
ils/elles	**sont monté(e)s**

IMPERFECT

je	**montais**
tu	**montais**
il/elle/on	**montait**
nous	**montions**
vous	**montiez**
ils/elles	**montaient**

PRESENT PARTICIPLE

montant

PAST PARTICIPLE

monté

In the perfect and the pluperfect, use the auxiliary "avoir" when there is a direct object.

EXAMPLE PHRASES

Je **monte** ces escaliers cent fois par jour. I go up these stairs a hundred times a day.

Hier, je **suis montée** à cheval pour la première fois. Yesterday, I went horse riding for the first time.

Monte dans la voiture, je t'y emmène. Get into the car, I'll take you there.

Il s'est tordu la cheville en **montant** à une échelle. He twisted his ankle going up a ladder.

monter

FUTURE

je	**monterai**
tu	**monteras**
il/elle/on	**montera**
nous	**monterons**
vous	**monterez**
ils/elles	**monteront**

CONDITIONAL

je	**monterais**
tu	**monterais**
il/elle/on	**monterait**
nous	**monterions**
vous	**monteriez**
ils/elles	**monteraient**

PAST HISTORIC

je	**montai**
tu	**montas**
il/elle/on	**monta**
nous	**montâmes**
vous	**montâtes**
ils/elles	**montèrent**

PLUPERFECT

j'	**étais monté(e)**
tu	**étais monté(e)**
il/elle/on	**était monté(e)**
nous	**étions monté(e)s**
vous	**étiez monté(e)(s)**
ils/elles	**étaient monté(e)s**

IMPERATIVE

monte / montons / montez

EXAMPLE PHRASES

Je **monterai** lui dire bonsoir dans cinq minutes. I'll go up to say goodnight to her in five minutes.

Il **monta** les escaliers en courant et sonna à la porte. He ran up the stairs and rang the bell.

Je **monterais** en haut de la tour si je n'avais pas tant le vertige. I'd go up the tower if I wasn't so scared of heights.

Comme elle était malade, je lui **avais monté** son dîner. As she was ill, I had taken her dinner up to her.

mordre (to bite)

PRESENT

je	**mords**
tu	**mords**
il/elle/on	**mord**
nous	**mordons**
vous	**mordez**
ils/elles	**mordent**

PRESENT SUBJUNCTIVE

je	**morde**
tu	**mordes**
il/elle/on	**morde**
nous	**mordions**
vous	**mordiez**
ils/elles	**mordent**

PERFECT

j'	**ai mordu**
tu	**as mordu**
il/elle/on	**a mordu**
nous	**avons mordu**
vous	**avez mordu**
ils/elles	**ont mordu**

IMPERFECT

je	**mordais**
tu	**mordais**
il/elle/on	**mordait**
nous	**mordions**
vous	**mordiez**
ils/elles	**mordaient**

PRESENT PARTICIPLE
mordant

PAST PARTICIPLE
mordu

EXAMPLE PHRASES

Il ne va pas te **mordre**! He won't bite you!
Attention, il **mord**! Watch out, he bites.
Le chien m'**a mordue**. The dog bit me.
Je me **suis mordu** la langue. I bit my tongue.

je/j' = I **tu** = you **il** = he/it **elle** = she/it **on** = we/one **nous** = we **vous** = you **ils/elles** = they

mordre

FUTURE

je	**mordrai**
tu	**mordras**
il/elle/on	**mordra**
nous	**mordrons**
vous	**mordrez**
ils/elles	**mordront**

CONDITIONAL

je	**mordrais**
tu	**mordrais**
il/elle/on	**mordrait**
nous	**mordrions**
vous	**mordriez**
ils/elles	**mordraient**

PAST HISTORIC

je	**mordis**
tu	**mordis**
il/elle/on	**mordit**
nous	**mordîmes**
vous	**mordîtes**
ils/elles	**mordirent**

PLUPERFECT

j'	**avais mordu**
tu	**avais mordu**
il/elle/on	**avait mordu**
nous	**avions mordu**
vous	**aviez mordu**
ils/elles	**avaient mordu**

IMPERATIVE

mords / mordons / mordez

EXAMPLE PHRASES

Il ne te **mordra** pas. He won't bite you.

Elle lui **mordit** le doigt et partit se cacher. She bit his finger and ran off to hide.

Il ne **mordrait** jamais personne. He would never bite anybody!

Le chien l'**avait mordu** à la jambe. The dog had bitten his leg.

moudre (to grind)

PRESENT

je	**mouds**
tu	**mouds**
il/elle/on	**moud**
nous	**moulons**
vous	**moulez**
ils/elles	**moulent**

PRESENT SUBJUNCTIVE

je	**moule**
tu	**moules**
il/elle/on	**moule**
nous	**moulions**
vous	**mouliez**
ils/elles	**moulent**

PERFECT

j'	**ai moulu**
tu	**as moulu**
il/elle/on	**a moulu**
nous	**avons moulu**
vous	**avez moulu**
ils/elles	**ont moulu**

IMPERFECT

je	**moulais**
tu	**moulais**
il/elle/on	**moulait**
nous	**moulions**
vous	**mouliez**
ils/elles	**moulaient**

PRESENT PARTICIPLE
moulant

PAST PARTICIPLE
moulu

EXAMPLE PHRASES

"Qui va m'aider à **moudre** ce grain?", demanda la petite poule rousse.
"Who will help me to grind this grain?" asked the little red hen.
Il **moud** toujours son café lui-même. He always grinds his coffee himself.
J'**ai moulu** du café pour demain matin. I've ground some coffee for tomorrow morning.
Le meunier **moulait** le blé à la meule. The miller ground the wheat with the millstone.

moudre

FUTURE

je	**moudrai**
tu	**moudras**
il/elle/on	**moudra**
nous	**moudrons**
vous	**moudrez**
ils/elles	**moudront**

CONDITIONAL

je	**moudrais**
tu	**moudrais**
il/elle/on	**moudrait**
nous	**moudrions**
vous	**moudriez**
ils/elles	**moudraient**

PAST HISTORIC

je	**moulus**
tu	**moulus**
il/elle/on	**moulut**
nous	**moulûmes**
vous	**moulûtes**
ils/elles	**moulurent**

PLUPERFECT

j'	**avais moulu**
tu	**avais moulu**
il/elle/on	**avait moulu**
nous	**avions moulu**
vous	**aviez moulu**
ils/elles	**avaient moulu**

IMPERATIVE

mouds / moulons / moulez

EXAMPLE PHRASES

Je **moudrai** du café tout à l'heure. I'll grind some coffee in a moment.

Elle **moulut** un peu de poivre sur le rôti. She ground some pepper over the roast.

Si j'avais le temps je **moudrais** mon café moi-même. If I had time, I'd grind my coffee myself.

Il mesura le café qu'il **avait moulu**. He measured the coffee that he'd ground.

je/j' = I **tu** = you **il** = he/it **elle** = she/it **on** = we/one **nous** = we **vous** = you **ils/elles** = they

mourir (to die)

PRESENT

je	**meurs**
tu	**meurs**
il/elle/on	**meurt**
nous	**mourons**
vous	**mourez**
ils/elles	**meurent**

PRESENT SUBJUNCTIVE

je	**meure**
tu	**meures**
il/elle/on	**meure**
nous	**mourions**
vous	**mouriez**
ils/elles	**meurent**

PERFECT

je	**suis mort(e)**
tu	**es mort(e)**
il/elle/on	**est mort(e)**
nous	**sommes mort(e)s**
vous	**êtes mort(e)(s)**
ils/elles	**sont mort(e)s**

IMPERFECT

je	**mourais**
tu	**mourais**
il/elle/on	**mourait**
nous	**mourions**
vous	**mouriez**
ils/elles	**mouraient**

PRESENT PARTICIPLE

mourant

PAST PARTICIPLE

mort

EXAMPLE PHRASES

On **meurt** de froid ici! We're freezing to death here!

Elle **est morte** en 1998. She died in 1998.

Ils **sont morts**. They're dead.

Je ne veux pas qu'il **meure**. I don't want him to die.

Nous **mourions** de froid. We were freezing to death.

mourir

FUTURE

je	**mourrai**
tu	**mourras**
il/elle/on	**mourra**
nous	**mourrons**
vous	**mourrez**
ils/elles	**mourront**

CONDITIONAL

je	**mourrais**
tu	**mourrais**
il/elle/on	**mourrait**
nous	**mourrions**
vous	**mourriez**
ils/elles	**mourraient**

PAST HISTORIC

je	**mourus**
tu	**mourus**
il/elle/on	**mourut**
nous	**mourûmes**
vous	**mourûtes**
ils/elles	**moururent**

PLUPERFECT

j'	**étais mort(e)**
tu	**étais mort(e)**
il/elle/on	**était mort(e)**
nous	**étions mort(e)s**
vous	**étiez mort(e)(s)**
ils/elles	**étaient mort(e)s**

IMPERATIVE

meurs / mourons / mourez

EXAMPLE PHRASES

Si tu t'en vas, j'en **mourrai** de chagrin. If you go, I'll die of sorrow.

Il **mourut** quelques heures plus tard. He died a few hours later.

Je **mourrais** de honte si tu le lui disais. I'd die of shame if you told him about it.

Nous **étions morts** de peur. We were scared to death.

naître (to be born)

PRESENT

je	**nais**
tu	**nais**
il/elle/on	**naît**
nous	**naissons**
vous	**naissez**
ils/elles	**naissent**

PRESENT SUBJUNCTIVE

je	**naisse**
tu	**naisses**
il/elle/on	**naisse**
nous	**naissions**
vous	**naissiez**
ils/elles	**naissent**

PERFECT

je	**suis né(e)**
tu	**es né(e)**
il/elle/on	**est né(e)**
nous	**sommes né(e)s**
vous	**êtes né(e)(s)**
ils/elles	**sont né(e)s**

IMPERFECT

je	**naissais**
tu	**naissais**
il/elle/on	**naissait**
nous	**naissions**
vous	**naissiez**
ils/elles	**naissaient**

PRESENT PARTICIPLE
naissant

PAST PARTICIPLE
né

EXAMPLE PHRASES

Il a l'air innocent comme l'agneau qui vient de **naître**. He looks as innocent as a newborn lamb.
Quand est-ce que tu **es né**? When were you born?
Je **suis née** le 12 février. I was born on the 12th of February.
Je ne **suis** pas **né** de la dernière pluie. I wasn't born yesterday.

naître

FUTURE

je	**naîtrai**
tu	**naîtras**
il/elle/on	**naîtra**
nous	**naîtrons**
vous	**naîtrez**
ils/elles	**naîtront**

CONDITIONAL

je	**naîtrais**
tu	**naîtrais**
il/elle/on	**naîtrait**
nous	**naîtrions**
vous	**naîtriez**
ils/elles	**naîtraient**

PAST HISTORIC

je	**naquis**
tu	**naquis**
il/elle/on	**naquit**
nous	**naquîmes**
vous	**naquîtes**
ils/elles	**naquirent**

PLUPERFECT

j'	**étais né(e)**
tu	**étais né(e)**
il/elle/on	**était né(e)**
nous	**étions né(e)s**
vous	**étiez né(e)(s)**
ils/elles	**étaient né(é)s**

IMPERATIVE

nais / naissons / naissez

EXAMPLE PHRASES

Le bébé de Delphine **naîtra** en mars. Delphine is going to have a baby in March.

Il **naquit** le 5 juillet 1909. He was born on 5 July 1909.

Ses enfants n'**étaient** pas **nés** en Écosse. Her children weren't born in Scotland.

nettoyer (to clean)

PRESENT		PRESENT SUBJUNCTIVE	
je	**nettoie**	je	**nettoie**
tu	**nettoies**	tu	**nettoies**
il/elle/on	**nettoie**	il/elle/on	**nettoie**
nous	**nettoyons**	nous	**nettoyions**
vous	**nettoyez**	vous	**nettoyiez**
ils/elles	**nettoient**	ils/elles	**nettoient**

PERFECT		IMPERFECT	
j'	**ai nettoyé**	je	**nettoyais**
tu	**as nettoyé**	tu	**nettoyais**
il/elle/on	**a nettoyé**	il/elle/on	**nettoyait**
nous	**avons nettoyé**	nous	**nettoyions**
vous	**avez nettoyé**	vous	**nettoyiez**
ils/elles	**ont nettoyé**	ils/elles	**nettoyaient**

PRESENT PARTICIPLE
nettoyant

PAST PARTICIPLE
nettoyé

EXAMPLE PHRASES

Je ne **nettoie** pas souvent l'écran de mon ordinateur. I don't clean my computer screen very often.

Richard **a nettoyé** tout l'appartement. Richard has cleaned the whole flat.

Nettoie tes chaussures avant de les ranger. Clean your shoes before putting them away.

J'aimerais que vous **nettoyiez** ta chambre. I'd like you to clean your room.

Elle **nettoyait** le sol en écoutant la radio. She was cleaning the floor while listening to the radio.

nettoyer

FUTURE

je	**nettoierai**
tu	**nettoieras**
il/elle/on	**nettoiera**
nous	**nettoierons**
vous	**nettoierez**
ils/elles	**nettoieront**

CONDITIONAL

je	**nettoierais**
tu	**nettoierais**
il/elle/on	**nettoierait**
nous	**nettoierions**
vous	**nettoieriez**
ils/elles	**nettoieraient**

PAST HISTORIC

je	**nettoyai**
tu	**nettoyas**
il/elle/on	**nettoya**
nous	**nettoyâmes**
vous	**nettoyâtes**
ils/elles	**nettoyèrent**

PLUPERFECT

j'	**avais nettoyé**
tu	**avais nettoyé**
il/elle/on	**avait nettoyé**
nous	**avions nettoyé**
vous	**aviez nettoyé**
ils/elles	**avaient nettoyé**

IMPERATIVE

nettoie / nettoyons / nettoyez

EXAMPLE PHRASES

Je **nettoierai** tout ça ce soir. I'll clean everything this evening.

Elle **nettoya** le miroir et s'y regarda longuement. She cleaned the mirror and looked at herself for a long time.

Il **nettoierait** sa chambre tout seul si je l'encourageais à le faire. He'd clean his bedroom himself if I encouraged him to do it.

Quand je suis rentrée , ils **avaient** tout **nettoyé**. When I got back, they'd cleaned everything up.

obéir (to obey)

PRESENT

j'	**obéis**
tu	**obéis**
il/elle/on	**obéit**
nous	**obéissons**
vous	**obéissez**
ils/elles	**obéissent**

PRESENT SUBJUNCTIVE

j'	**obéisse**
tu	**obéisses**
il/elle/on	**obéisse**
nous	**obéissions**
vous	**obéissiez**
ils/elles	**obéissent**

PERFECT

j'	**ai obéi**
tu	**as obéi**
il/elle/on	**a obéi**
nous	**avons obéi**
vous	**avez obéi**
ils/elles	**ont obéi**

IMPERFECT

j'	**obéissais**
tu	**obéissais**
il/elle/on	**obéissait**
nous	**obéissions**
vous	**obéissiez**
ils/elles	**obéissaient**

PRESENT PARTICIPLE
obéissant

PAST PARTICIPLE
obéi

EXAMPLE PHRASES

Je n'**obéis** pas toujours à mes parents. I don't always obey my parents.

Quand je te demande de faire quelque chose, j'aimerais que tu **obéisses**. When I ask you to do something, I'd like you to do it.

Mon chien n'**obéissait** jamais. My dog never obeyed commands.

obéir

FUTURE

j'	**obéirai**
tu	**obéiras**
il/elle/on	**obéira**
nous	**obéirons**
vous	**obéirez**
ils/elles	**obéiront**

CONDITIONAL

j'	**obéirais**
tu	**obéirais**
il/elle/on	**obéirait**
nous	**obéirions**
vous	**obéiriez**
ils/elles	**obéiraient**

PAST HISTORIC

j'	**obéis**
tu	**obéis**
il/elle/on	**obéit**
nous	**obéîmes**
vous	**obéîtes**
ils/elles	**obéirent**

PLUPERFECT

j'	**avais obéi**
tu	**avais obéi**
il/elle/on	**avait obéi**
nous	**avions obéi**
vous	**aviez obéi**
ils/elles	**avaient obéi**

IMPERATIVE

obéis / obéissons / obéissez

EXAMPLE PHRASES

Il n'**obéira** jamais si tu lui parles comme ça. He'll never obey if you speak to him like that.

Ils **obéirent** sans se plaindre. They obeyed without complaining.

Ils ne lui **obéiraient** pas s'ils ne l'aimaient pas. They wouldn't obey her if they didn't like her.

Comme elle n'avait pas le choix, elle **avait obéi** à ses ordres. As she didn't have any choice, she'd obeyed his orders.

offrir (to offer; to give)

PRESENT

j'	**offre**
tu	**offres**
il/elle/on	**offre**
nous	**offrons**
vous	**offrez**
ils/elles	**offrent**

PRESENT SUBJUNCTIVE

j'	**offre**
tu	**offres**
il/elle/on	**offre**
nous	**offrions**
vous	**offriez**
ils/elles	**offrent**

PERFECT

j'	**ai offert**
tu	**as offert**
il/elle/on	**a offert**
nous	**avons offert**
vous	**avez offert**
ils/elles	**ont offert**

IMPERFECT

j'	**offrais**
tu	**offrais**
il/elle/on	**offrait**
nous	**offrions**
vous	**offriez**
ils/elles	**offraient**

PRESENT PARTICIPLE
offrant

PAST PARTICIPLE
offert

EXAMPLE PHRASES

Viens, je t'**offre** à boire. Come on, I'll buy you a drink.
Paul m'**a offert** du parfum pour mon anniversaire. Paul gave me some perfume for my birthday.
Offre-lui des fleurs. Give her some flowers.
Il **offrait** souvent de me raccompagner. He often offered me a lift back.

offrir

FUTURE

j'	**offrirai**
tu	**offriras**
il/elle/on	**offrira**
nous	**offrirons**
vous	**offrirez**
ils/elles	**offriront**

CONDITIONAL

j'	**offrirais**
tu	**offrirais**
il/elle/on	**offrirait**
nous	**offririons**
vous	**offririez**
ils/elles	**offriraient**

PAST HISTORIC

j'	**offris**
tu	**offris**
il/elle/on	**offrit**
nous	**offrîmes**
vous	**offrîtes**
ils/elles	**offrirent**

PLUPERFECT

j'	**avais offert**
tu	**avais offert**
il/elle/on	**avait offert**
nous	**avions offert**
vous	**aviez offert**
ils/elles	**avaient offert**

IMPERATIVE

offre / offrons / offrez

EXAMPLE PHRASES

Je lui **offrirai** une voiture pour ses 21 ans. I'll buy her a car for her 21st birthday.

Il lui **offrit** de l'aider. He offered to help her.

S'il était plus aimable, je lui **offrirais** de l'aider. If he were more pleasant, I'd offer to help him.

On lui **avait offert** un poste de secrétaire. They had offered her a secretarial post.

je/j' = I **tu** = you **il** = he/it **elle** = she/it **on** = we/one **nous** = we **vous** = you **ils/elles** = they

ouvrir (to open)

PRESENT

j'	**ouvre**
tu	**ouvres**
il/elle/on	**ouvre**
nous	**ouvrons**
vous	**ouvrez**
ils/elles	**ouvrent**

PRESENT SUBJUNCTIVE

j'	**ouvre**
tu	**ouvres**
il/elle/on	**ouvre**
nous	**ouvrions**
vous	**ouvriez**
ils/elles	**ouvrent**

PERFECT

j'	**ai ouvert**
tu	**as ouvert**
il/elle/on	**a ouvert**
nous	**avons ouvert**
vous	**avez ouvert**
ils/elles	**ont ouvert**

IMPERFECT

j'	**ouvrais**
tu	**ouvrais**
il/elle/on	**ouvrait**
nous	**ouvrions**
vous	**ouvriez**
ils/elles	**ouvraient**

PRESENT PARTICIPLE
ouvrant

PAST PARTICIPLE
ouvert

EXAMPLE PHRASES

Est-ce que tu pourrais **ouvrir** la fenêtre? Could you open the window?
Elle **a ouvert** la porte. She opened the door.
La porte s'**est ouverte**. The door opened.
Ouvre la porte, s'il te plaît. Open the door, please.
Ouvrez vos livres à la page 10. Open your books at page 10.
Je me suis coupé en **ouvrant** une boîte de conserve. I cut myself opening a tin.

ouvrir

FUTURE

j'	**ouvrirai**
tu	**ouvriras**
il/elle/on	**ouvrira**
nous	**ouvrirons**
vous	**ouvrirez**
ils/elles	**ouvriront**

CONDITIONAL

j'	**ouvrirais**
tu	**ouvrirais**
il/elle/on	**ouvrirait**
nous	**ouvririons**
vous	**ouvririez**
ils/elles	**ouvriraient**

PAST HISTORIC

j'	**ouvris**
tu	**ouvris**
il/elle/on	**ouvrit**
nous	**ouvrîmes**
vous	**ouvrîtes**
ils/elles	**ouvrirent**

PLUPERFECT

j'	**avais ouvert**
tu	**avais ouvert**
il/elle/on	**avait ouvert**
nous	**avions ouvert**
vous	**aviez ouvert**
ils/elles	**avaient ouvert**

IMPERATIVE

ouvre / ouvrons / ouvrez

EXAMPLE PHRASES

J'**ouvrirai** la fenêtre tout à l'heure. I'll open the window in a moment.

Elle **ouvrit** les yeux et lui sourit. She opened her eyes and smiled at him.

J'**ouvrirais** la fenêtre s'il ne faisait pas si froid. I would open the window if it weren't so cold.

Ils **avaient ouvert** tous leurs cadeaux de Noël. They had opened all their Christmas presents.

je/j' = I **tu** = you **il** = he/it **elle** = she/it **on** = we/one **nous** = we **vous** = you **ils/elles** = they

paraître (to seem)

PRESENT

je	**parais**
tu	**parais**
il/elle/on	**paraît**
nous	**paraissons**
vous	**paraissez**
ils/elles	**paraissent**

PRESENT SUBJUNCTIVE

je	**paraisse**
tu	**paraisses**
il/elle/on	**paraisse**
nous	**paraissions**
vous	**paraissiez**
ils/elles	**paraissent**

PERFECT

j'	**ai paru**
tu	**as paru**
il/elle/on	**a paru**
nous	**avons paru**
vous	**avez paru**
ils/elles	**ont paru**

IMPERFECT

je	**paraissais**
tu	**paraissais**
il/elle/on	**paraissait**
nous	**paraissions**
vous	**paraissiez**
ils/elles	**paraissaient**

PRESENT PARTICIPLE
paraissant

PAST PARTICIPLE
paru

EXAMPLE PHRASES

Gisèle **paraît** plus jeune que son âge. Gisèle doesn't look her age.

Il **paraît** qu'il fait chaud toute l'année là-bas. Apparently it's hot all year round over there.

Il m'**a paru** angoissé. I thought he looked stressed.

Elle **paraissait** fatiguée. She seemed tired.

paraître

FUTURE

je	**paraîtrai**
tu	**paraîtras**
il/elle/on	**paraîtra**
nous	**paraîtrons**
vous	**paraîtrez**
ils/elles	**paraîtront**

CONDITIONAL

je	**paraîtrais**
tu	**paraîtrais**
il/elle/on	**paraîtrait**
nous	**paraîtrions**
vous	**paraîtriez**
ils/elles	**paraîtraient**

PAST HISTORIC

je	**parus**
tu	**parus**
il/elle/on	**parut**
nous	**parûmes**
vous	**parûtes**
ils/elles	**parurent**

PLUPERFECT

j'	**avais paru**
tu	**avais paru**
il/elle/on	**avait paru**
nous	**avions paru**
vous	**aviez paru**
ils/elles	**avaient paru**

IMPERATIVE

parais / paraissons / paraissez

EXAMPLE PHRASES

Cet article **paraîtra** le mois prochain. This article will be published next month.
Il **parut** gêné. He looked embarrassed.
Cela **paraîtrait** étrange si je venais sans mon mari. It would look strange if I came without my husband.
Il **avait paru** pressé de partir. He had seemed in a hurry to leave.

partir (to go; to leave)

PRESENT

je	**pars**
tu	**pars**
il/elle/on	**part**
nous	**partons**
vous	**partez**
ils/elles	**partent**

PRESENT SUBJUNCTIVE

je	**parte**
tu	**partes**
il/elle/on	**parte**
nous	**partions**
vous	**partiez**
ils/elles	**partent**

PERFECT

je	**suis parti(e)**
tu	**es parti(e)**
il/elle/on	**est parti(e)**
nous	**sommes parti(e)s**
vous	**êtes parti(e)(s)**
ils/elles	**sont parti(e)s**

IMPERFECT

je	**partais**
tu	**partais**
il/elle/on	**partait**
nous	**partions**
vous	**partiez**
ils/elles	**partaient**

PRESENT PARTICIPLE
partant

PAST PARTICIPLE
parti

EXAMPLE PHRASES

On **part** en vacances le 15 août. We're going on holiday on the 15th of August.

Elle **est partie** tôt ce matin. She left early this morning.

Ne **partez** pas sans moi. Don't leave without me!

Il faut qu'on **parte** de bonne heure. We have to leave early.

Il **partait** à huit heures tous les matins. He left at eight o'clock every morning.

partir

FUTURE

je	**partirai**
tu	**partiras**
il/elle/on	**partira**
nous	**partirons**
vous	**partirez**
ils/elles	**partiront**

CONDITIONAL

je	**partirais**
tu	**partirais**
il/elle/on	**partirait**
nous	**partirions**
vous	**partiriez**
ils/elles	**partiraient**

PAST HISTORIC

je	**partis**
tu	**partis**
il/elle/on	**partit**
nous	**partîmes**
vous	**partîtes**
ils/elles	**partirent**

PLUPERFECT

j'	**étais parti(e)**
tu	**étais parti(e)**
il/elle/on	**était parti(e)**
nous	**étions parti(e)s**
vous	**étiez parti(e)(s)**
ils/elles	**étaient parti(e)s**

IMPERATIVE

pars / partons / partez

EXAMPLE PHRASES

Nous **partirons** demain. We'll leave tomorrow.

Il **partit** sans rien dire. He left without saying a word.

Je ne **partirais** pas sans dire au revoir. I wouldn't leave without saying goodbye.

Quand je suis arrivée, ils **étaient** déjà **partis**. When I arrived, they had already left.

passer (to pass; to spend)

PRESENT

je	**passe**
tu	**passes**
il/elle/on	**passe**
nous	**passons**
vous	**passez**
ils/elles	**passent**

PRESENT SUBJUNCTIVE

je	**passe**
tu	**passes**
il/elle/on	**passe**
nous	**passions**
vous	**passiez**
ils/elles	**passent**

PERFECT

je	**suis passé(e)**
tu	**es passé(e)**
il/elle/on	**est passé(e)**
nous	**sommes passé(e)s**
vous	**êtes passé(e)(s)**
ils/elles	**sont passé(e)s**

IMPERFECT

je	**passais**
tu	**passais**
il/elle/on	**passait**
nous	**passions**
vous	**passiez**
ils/elles	**passaient**

PRESENT PARTICIPLE
passant

PAST PARTICIPLE
passé

In the perfect and the pluperfect, use the auxiliary "avoir" when there is a direct object.

EXAMPLE PHRASES

Je vais **passer** les vacances chez mes grands-parents. I'm going to spend the holidays at my grandparents' house.
L'histoire se **passe** au Mexique. The story takes place in Mexico.
Il **a passé** son examen en juin. He sat his exam in June.
Elle **est passée** me dire bonjour. She came by to say hello.
Passe-moi le pain, s'il te plaît. Pass me the bread please.
Ils **passaient** leur temps à regarder la télé. They spent their time watching TV.

je/j' = I **tu** = you **il** = he/it **elle** = she/it **on** = we/one **nous** = we **vous** = you **ils/elles** = they

passer

FUTURE

je	**passerai**
tu	**passeras**
il/elle/on	**passera**
nous	**passerons**
vous	**passerez**
ils/elles	**passeront**

CONDITIONAL

je	**passerais**
tu	**passerais**
il/elle/on	**passerait**
nous	**passerions**
vous	**passeriez**
ils/elles	**passeraient**

PAST HISTORIC

je	**passai**
tu	**passas**
il/elle/on	**passa**
nous	**passâmes**
vous	**passâtes**
ils/elles	**passèrent**

PLUPERFECT

j'	**étais passé(e)**
tu	**étais passé(e)**
il/elle/on	**était passé(e)**
nous	**étions passé(e)s**
vous	**étiez passé(e)(s)**
ils/elles	**étaient passé(e)s**

IMPERATIVE

passe / passons / passez

EXAMPLE PHRASES

Je **passerai** te voir ce soir. I'll come to see you tonight.

Elle **passa** la soirée à emballer les cadeaux de Noël. She spent the evening wrapping up the Christmas presents.

Ils **passeraient** plus de temps à jouer dehors s'il faisait moins mauvais. They'd spend more time playing outside if the weather weren't so bad.

Les mois **avaient passé**. Months had passed.

payer (to pay)

PRESENT

je	**paye**
tu	**payes**
il/elle/on	**paye**
nous	**payons**
vous	**payez**
ils/elles	**payent**

PRESENT SUBJUNCTIVE

je	**paye**
tu	**payes**
il/elle/on	**paye**
nous	**payions**
vous	**payiez**
ils/elles	**payent**

PERFECT

j'	**ai payé**
tu	**as payé**
il/elle/on	**a payé**
nous	**avons payé**
vous	**avez payé**
ils/elles	**ont payé**

IMPERFECT

je	**payais**
tu	**payais**
il/elle/on	**payait**
nous	**payions**
vous	**payiez**
ils/elles	**payaient**

PRESENT PARTICIPLE
payant

PAST PARTICIPLE
payé

EXAMPLE PHRASES

Les étudiants **payent** moitié prix. Students pay half price.
Tu l'**as payé** combien? How much did you pay for it?
Il faut que je **paye** l'électricien. I have to pay the electrician.
Il ne **payait** jamais son loyer. He never paid his rent.

payer

FUTURE

je	**payerai**
tu	**payeras**
il/elle/on	**payera**
nous	**payerons**
vous	**payerez**
ils/elles	**payeront**

CONDITIONAL

je	**payerais**
tu	**payerais**
il/elle/on	**payerait**
nous	**payerions**
vous	**payeriez**
ils/elles	**payeraient**

PAST HISTORIC

je	**payai**
tu	**payas**
il/elle/on	**paya**
nous	**payâmes**
vous	**payâtes**
ils/elles	**payèrent**

PLUPERFECT

j'	**avais payé**
tu	**avais payé**
il/elle/on	**avait payé**
nous	**avions payé**
vous	**aviez payé**
ils/elles	**avaient payé**

IMPERATIVE

paye / payons / payez

EXAMPLE PHRASES

Je vous **payerai** demain. I'll pay you tomorrow.

Il **paya** la note et partit. He paid the bill and left.

Je lui ai dit que je la **payerais** la prochaine fois. I told him that I would pay him the next time.

Sa patronne ne l'**avait** pas **payée** depuis deux mois. Her boss hadn't paid her for the last two months.

peindre (to paint)

PRESENT

je	**peins**
tu	**peins**
il/elle/on	**peint**
nous	**peignons**
vous	**peignez**
ils/elles	**peignent**

PRESENT SUBJUNCTIVE

je	**peigne**
tu	**peignes**
il/elle/on	**peigne**
nous	**peignions**
vous	**peigniez**
ils/elles	**peignent**

PERFECT

j'	**ai peint**
tu	**as peint**
il/elle/on	**a peint**
nous	**avons peint**
vous	**avez peint**
ils/elles	**ont peint**

IMPERFECT

je	**peignais**
tu	**peignais**
il/elle/on	**peignait**
nous	**peignions**
vous	**peigniez**
ils/elles	**peignaient**

PRESENT PARTICIPLE

peignant

PAST PARTICIPLE

peint

EXAMPLE PHRASES

Il ne **peint** plus depuis son opération. He hasn't painted since his operation.
On **a peint** l'entrée en bleu clair. We painted the hall light blue.
Ce tableau **a été peint** en 1913. This picture was painted in 1913.
Il **peignait** toujours des paysages. He always painted landscapes.

peindre

FUTURE

je	**peindrai**
tu	**peindras**
il/elle/on	**peindra**
nous	**peindrons**
vous	**peindrez**
ils/elles	**peindront**

CONDITIONAL

je	**peindrais**
tu	**peindrais**
il/elle/on	**peindrait**
nous	**peindrions**
vous	**peindriez**
ils/elles	**peindraient**

PAST HISTORIC

je	**peignis**
tu	**peignis**
il/elle/on	**peignit**
nous	**peignîmes**
vous	**peignîtes**
ils/elles	**peignirent**

PLUPERFECT

j'	**avais peint**
tu	**avais peint**
il/elle/on	**avait peint**
nous	**avions peint**
vous	**aviez peint**
ils/elles	**avaient peint**

IMPERATIVE

peins / peignons / peignez

EXAMPLE PHRASES

Je **peindrai** le plafond demain. I'll paint the ceiling tomorrow.

Il **peignit** les volets en rose. He painted the shutters pink.

Si j'étais toi, je **peindrais** les murs avant de poser le carrelage. If I were you, I would paint the walls before laying the tiles.

Elle n'**avait peint** que la moitié de la pièce. She'd only painted half of the room.

perdre (to lose)

PRESENT

je	**perds**
tu	**perds**
il/elle/on	**perd**
nous	**perdons**
vous	**perdez**
ils/elles	**perdent**

PRESENT SUBJUNCTIVE

je	**perde**
tu	**perdes**
il/elle/on	**perde**
nous	**perdions**
vous	**perdiez**
ils/elles	**perdent**

PERFECT

j'	**ai perdu**
tu	**as perdu**
il/elle/on	**a perdu**
nous	**avons perdu**
vous	**avez perdu**
ils/elles	**ont perdu**

IMPERFECT

je	**perdais**
tu	**perdais**
il/elle/on	**perdait**
nous	**perdions**
vous	**perdiez**
ils/elles	**perdaient**

PRESENT PARTICIPLE
perdant

PAST PARTICIPLE
perdu

EXAMPLE PHRASES

Si tu te **perds**, appelle-moi. Call me if you get lost.
L'Italie **a perdu** un à zéro. Italy lost one-nil.
J'**ai perdu** mon porte-monnaie dans le métro. I lost my purse on the underground.
Ne **perds** pas encore tes gants. Don't lose your gloves again.
Il ne faut pas que je **perde** son adresse. I mustn't lose his address.
Il **perdait** toujours ses affaires. He was always losing his things.

je/j' = I **tu** = you **il** = he/it **elle** = she/it **on** = we/one **nous** = we **vous** = you **ils/elles** = they

perdre

FUTURE

je	**perdrai**
tu	**perdras**
il/elle/on	**perdra**
nous	**perdrons**
vous	**perdrez**
ils/elles	**perdront**

CONDITIONAL

je	**perdrais**
tu	**perdrais**
il/elle/on	**perdrait**
nous	**perdrions**
vous	**perdriez**
ils/elles	**perdraient**

PAST HISTORIC

je	**perdis**
tu	**perdis**
il/elle/on	**perdit**
nous	**perdîmes**
vous	**perdîtes**
ils/elles	**perdirent**

PLUPERFECT

j'	**avais perdu**
tu	**avais perdu**
il/elle/on	**avait perdu**
nous	**avions perdu**
vous	**aviez perdu**
ils/elles	**avaient perdu**

IMPERATIVE

perds / perdons / perdez

EXAMPLE PHRASES

Je **perdrai** forcément contre lui. I'll obviously lose against him.

Il **perdit** patience et se mit à crier. He lost his patience and began to shout.

Tu ne **perdrais** pas tes affaires si tu faisais plus attention. You wouldn't lose your things if you were more careful.

Elle **avait perdu** la mémoire depuis son accident. She had lost her memory after her accident.

plaire (to please)

PRESENT

je	**plais**
tu	**plais**
il/elle/on	**plaît**
nous	**plaisons**
vous	**plaisez**
ils/elles	**plaisent**

PRESENT SUBJUNCTIVE

je	**plaise**
tu	**plaises**
il/elle/on	**plaise**
nous	**plaisions**
vous	**plaisiez**
ils/elles	**plaisent**

PERFECT

j'	**ai plu**
tu	**as plu**
il/elle/on	**a plu**
nous	**avons plu**
vous	**avez plu**
ils/elles	**ont plu**

IMPERFECT

je	**plaisais**
tu	**plaisais**
il/elle/on	**plaisait**
nous	**plaisions**
vous	**plaisiez**
ils/elles	**plaisaient**

PRESENT PARTICIPLE
plaisant

PAST PARTICIPLE
plu

EXAMPLE PHRASES

Le menu ne me **plaît** pas. I don't like the menu.
s'il te **plaît**. please
s'il vous **plaît**. please
Ça t'**a plu**, le film? Did you like the film?
La robe noire me **plaisait** beaucoup. I really liked the black dress.

plaire

FUTURE

je	**plairai**
tu	**plairas**
il/elle/on	**plaira**
nous	**plairons**
vous	**plairez**
ils/elles	**plairont**

CONDITIONAL

je	**plairais**
tu	**plairais**
il/elle/on	**plairait**
nous	**plairions**
vous	**plairiez**
ils/elles	**plairaient**

PAST HISTORIC

je	**plus**
tu	**plus**
il/elle/on	**plut**
nous	**plûmes**
vous	**plûtes**
ils/elles	**plurent**

PLUPERFECT

j'	**avais plu**
tu	**avais plu**
il/elle/on	**avait plu**
nous	**avions plu**
vous	**aviez plu**
ils/elles	**avaient plu**

IMPERATIVE

plais / plaisons / plaisez

EXAMPLE PHRASES

Ce film ne lui **plaira** pas. He won't like this film.

Elle lui **plut** immédiatement. He liked her straight away.

Ça te **plairait** d'aller à la mer? Would you like to go to the seaside?

Cette remarque ne lui **avait** pas **plu**. He hadn't liked that remark.

pleuvoir (to rain)

PRESENT

il **pleut**

PRESENT SUBJUNCTIVE

il **pleuve**

PERFECT

il **a plu**

IMPERFECT

il **pleuvait**

PRESENT PARTICIPLE

pleuvant

PAST PARTICIPLE

plu

EXAMPLE PHRASES

Il **pleut** beaucoup à Glasgow. It rains a lot in Glasgow.

Il **a plu** toute la journée. It rained all day long.

J'ai peur qu'il **pleuve** cet après-midi. I'm afraid it might rain this afternoon.

Il **pleuvait** tellement qu'ils décidèrent de rester chez eux. It rained so much that they decided to stay at home.

pleuvoir

FUTURE

il **pleuvra**

CONDITIONAL

il **pleuvrait**

PAST HISTORIC

il **plut**

PLUPERFECT

il **avait plu**

IMPERATIVE

not used

EXAMPLE PHRASES

J'espère qu'il ne **pleuvra** pas demain. I hope it won't rain tomorrow.

Il **plut** pendant quarante jours et quarante nuits. It rained for forty days and forty nights.

Il **pleuvrait** probablement si je ne prenais pas mon parapluie. It will probably rain if I don't take my umbrella.

Il n'**avait** pas **plu** de tout l'été. It hadn't rained all summer.

pouvoir (to be able)

PRESENT

je	**peux**
tu	**peux**
il/elle/on	**peut**
nous	**pouvons**
vous	**pouvez**
ils/elles	**peuvent**

PRESENT SUBJUNCTIVE

je	**puisse**
tu	**puisses**
il/elle/on	**puisse**
nous	**puissions**
vous	**puissiez**
ils/elles	**puissent**

PERFECT

j'	**ai pu**
tu	**as pu**
il/elle/on	**a pu**
nous	**avons pu**
vous	**avez pu**
ils/elles	**ont pu**

IMPERFECT

je	**pouvais**
tu	**pouvais**
il/elle/on	**pouvait**
nous	**pouvions**
vous	**pouviez**
ils/elles	**pouvaient**

PRESENT PARTICIPLE
pouvant

PAST PARTICIPLE
pu

EXAMPLE PHRASES

Je **peux** vous aider? Can I help you?
J'ai fait tout ce que j'**ai pu**. I did all I could.
Nous avons changé la date du baptême de Clara pour que tu **puisses** venir.
We've changed the date of Clara's christening so that you're able to come.
Elle ne **pouvait** pas s'empêcher de rire. She couldn't help laughing.

pouvoir

FUTURE

je	**pourrai**
tu	**pourras**
il/elle/on	**pourra**
nous	**pourrons**
vous	**pourrez**
ils/elles	**pourront**

CONDITIONAL

je	**pourrais**
tu	**pourrais**
il/elle/on	**pourrait**
nous	**pourrions**
vous	**pourriez**
ils/elles	**pourraient**

PAST HISTORIC

je	**pus**
tu	**pus**
il/elle/on	**put**
nous	**pûmes**
vous	**pûtes**
ils/elles	**purent**

PLUPERFECT

j'	**avais pu**
tu	**avais pu**
il/elle/on	**avait pu**
nous	**avions pu**
vous	**aviez pu**
ils/elles	**avaient pu**

IMPERATIVE

not used

EXAMPLE PHRASES

Je ne **pourrai** pas venir samedi. I won't be able to come on Saturday.
Il ne **put** se souvenir de son nom. He couldn't remember her name.
Je **pourrais** te prêter ma robe si tu voulais. I could lend you my dress if you like.
Il n'**avait** pas **pu** les rejoindre. He hadn't been able to join them.

je/j' = I **tu** = you **il** = he/it **elle** = she/it **on** = we/one **nous** = we **vous** = you **ils/elles** = they

prendre (to take)

PRESENT

je	**prends**
tu	**prends**
il/elle/on	**prend**
nous	**prenons**
vous	**prenez**
ils/elles	**prennent**

PRESENT SUBJUNCTIVE

je	**prenne**
tu	**prennes**
il/elle/on	**prenne**
nous	**prenions**
vous	**preniez**
ils/elles	**prennent**

PERFECT

j'	**ai pris**
tu	**as pris**
il/elle/on	**a pris**
nous	**avons pris**
vous	**avez pris**
ils/elles	**ont pris**

IMPERFECT

je	**prenais**
tu	**prenais**
il/elle/on	**prenait**
nous	**prenions**
vous	**preniez**
ils/elles	**prenaient**

PRESENT PARTICIPLE
prenant

PAST PARTICIPLE
pris

EXAMPLE PHRASES

N'oublie pas de **prendre** ton passeport. Don't forget to take your passport.
Pour qui est-ce qu'il se **prend**? Who does he think he is?
J'ai pris plein de photos. I took lots of pictures.
Prends ton appareil photo. Take your camera.
Il faut que je **prenne** mes affaires de gym. I have to take my gym kit.
Il **prenait** le bus à huit heures le matin. He got the bus at eight in the morning.

je/j' = I **tu** = you **il** = he/it **elle** = she/it **on** = we/one **nous** = we **vous** = you **ils/elles** = they

prendre

FUTURE

je	**prendrai**
tu	**prendras**
il/elle/on	**prendra**
nous	**prendrons**
vous	**prendrez**
ils/elles	**prendront**

CONDITIONAL

je	**prendrais**
tu	**prendrais**
il/elle/on	**prendrait**
nous	**prendrions**
vous	**prendriez**
ils/elles	**prendraient**

PAST HISTORIC

je	**pris**
tu	**pris**
il/elle/on	**prit**
nous	**prîmes**
vous	**prîtes**
ils/elles	**prirent**

PLUPERFECT

j'	**avais pris**
tu	**avais pris**
il/elle/on	**avait pris**
nous	**avions pris**
vous	**aviez pris**
ils/elles	**avaient pris**

IMPERATIVE

prends / prenons / prenez

EXAMPLE PHRASES

Il **prendra** le train de 8h20. He'll take the 8.20 train.

Elle **prit** son sac et partit. She took her bag and left.

Si j'habitais ici, je **prendrais** le bus pour aller travailler. If I lived here, I'd take the bus to work.

Il n'**avait** jamais **pris** l'avion. He'd never travelled by plane.

je/j' = I **tu** = you **il** = he/it **elle** = she/it **on** = we/one **nous** = we **vous** = you **ils/elles** = they

protéger (to protect)

PRESENT

je	**protège**
tu	**protèges**
il/elle/on	**protège**
nous	**protégeons**
vous	**protégez**
ils/elles	**protègent**

PRESENT SUBJUNCTIVE

je	**protège**
tu	**protèges**
il/elle/on	**protège**
nous	**protégions**
vous	**protégiez**
ils/elles	**protègent**

PERFECT

j'	**ai protégé**
tu	**as protégé**
il/elle/on	**a protégé**
nous	**avons protégé**
vous	**avez protégé**
ils/elles	**ont protégé**

IMPERFECT

je	**protégeais**
tu	**protégeais**
il/elle/on	**protégeait**
nous	**protégions**
vous	**protégiez**
ils/elles	**protégeaient**

PRESENT PARTICIPLE
protégeant

PAST PARTICIPLE
protégé

EXAMPLE PHRASES

Ne crains rien, je te **protège**. Don't be scared, I'm looking after you.

Le champ **est protégé** du vent par la colline. The field is sheltered from the wind by the hill.

Protège ton livre de la pluie. Protect your book from the rain.

Je voudrais une tente qui **protège** bien contre le froid. I'd like a tent which protects you from the cold.

Il me **protégeait** contre tous ceux qui m'embêtaient. He protected me from all those who annoyed me.

je/j' = I **tu** = you **il** = he/it **elle** = she/it **on** = we/one **nous** = we **vous** = you **ils/elles** = they

protéger

FUTURE

je	**protégerai**
tu	**protégeras**
il/elle/on	**protégera**
nous	**protégerons**
vous	**protégerez**
ils/elles	**protégeront**

CONDITIONAL

je	**protégerais**
tu	**protégerais**
il/elle/on	**protégerait**
nous	**protégerions**
vous	**protégeriez**
ils/elles	**protégeraient**

PAST HISTORIC

je	**protégeai**
tu	**protégeas**
il/elle/on	**protégea**
nous	**protégeâmes**
vous	**protégeâtes**
ils/elles	**protégèrent**

PLUPERFECT

j'	**avais protégé**
tu	**avais protégé**
il/elle/on	**avait protégé**
nous	**avions protégé**
vous	**aviez protégé**
ils/elles	**avaient protégé**

IMPERATIVE

protège / protégeons / protégez

EXAMPLE PHRASES

Ce manteau te **protégera** bien du froid. This coat will protect you from the cold.

Il se **protégea** le visage avec ses mains. He protected his face with his hands.

Cette crème te **protégerait** mieux les mains. This cream would protect your hands better.

Il **avait** toujours **protégé** sa petite sœur à l'école. He'd always protected his little sister at school.

je/j' = I **tu** = you **il** = he/it **elle** = she/it **on** = we/one **nous** = we **vous** = you **ils/elles** = they

recevoir (to receive)

PRESENT

je	**reçois**
tu	**reçois**
il/elle/on	**reçoit**
nous	**recevons**
vous	**recevez**
ils/elles	**reçoivent**

PRESENT SUBJUNCTIVE

je	**reçoive**
tu	**reçoives**
il/elle/on	**reçoive**
nous	**recevions**
vous	**receviez**
ils/elles	**reçoivent**

PERFECT

j'	**ai reçu**
tu	**as reçu**
il/elle/on	**a reçu**
nous	**avons reçu**
vous	**avez reçu**
ils/elles	**ont reçu**

IMPERFECT

je	**recevais**
tu	**recevais**
il/elle/on	**recevait**
nous	**recevions**
vous	**receviez**
ils/elles	**recevaient**

PRESENT PARTICIPLE

recevant

PAST PARTICIPLE

reçu

EXAMPLE PHRASES

Je ne **reçois** jamais de courrier. I never get any mail.
Elle **a reçu** une lettre de Charlotte. She received a letter from Charlotte.
Recevez, Monsieur, mes salutations. Yours sincerely.
J'attendais que tu **reçoives** l'invitation pour t'emmener choisir un cadeau. I was waiting for you to get the invitation before I took you to choose a present.
Il **recevait** d'étranges messages. He was getting strange messages.

recevoir

FUTURE		CONDITIONAL	
je	**recevrai**	je	**recevrais**
tu	**recevras**	tu	**recevrais**
il/elle/on	**recevra**	il/elle/on	**recevrait**
nous	**recevrons**	nous	**recevrions**
vous	**recevrez**	vous	**recevriez**
ils/elles	**recevront**	ils/elles	**recevraient**

PAST HISTORIC		PLUPERFECT	
je	**reçus**	j'	**avais reçu**
tu	**reçus**	tu	**avais reçu**
il/elle/on	**reçut**	il/elle/on	**avait reçu**
nous	**reçûmes**	nous	**avions reçu**
vous	**reçûtes**	vous	**aviez reçu**
ils/elles	**reçurent**	ils/elles	**avaient reçu**

IMPERATIVE

reçois / recevons / recevez

EXAMPLE PHRASES

Elle **recevra** une réponse la semaine prochaine. She'll get an answer next week.

Il **reçut** une lettre anonyme. He received an anonymous letter.

Tu ne **recevrais** pas autant de monde si ta maison n'était pas aussi grande. You wouldn't entertain so many people if your house weren't so big.

Cela faisait une semaine qu'il n'**avait** pas **reçu** de courrier. He hadn't had any mail for a week.

réfléchir (to think)

PRESENT

je	**réfléchis**
tu	**réfléchis**
il/elle/on	**réfléchit**
nous	**réfléchissons**
vous	**réfléchissez**
ils/elles	**réfléchissent**

PRESENT SUBJUNCTIVE

je	**réfléchisse**
tu	**réfléchisses**
il/elle/on	**réfléchisse**
nous	**réfléchissions**
vous	**réfléchissiez**
ils/elles	**réfléchissent**

PERFECT

j'	**ai réfléchi**
tu	**as réfléchi**
il/elle/on	**a réfléchi**
nous	**avons réfléchi**
vous	**avez réfléchi**
ils/elles	**ont réfléchi**

IMPERFECT

je	**réfléchissais**
tu	**réfléchissais**
il/elle/on	**réfléchissait**
nous	**réfléchissions**
vous	**réfléchissiez**
ils/elles	**réfléchissaient**

PRESENT PARTICIPLE
réfléchissant

PAST PARTICIPLE
réfléchi

EXAMPLE PHRASES

Il est en train de **réfléchir**. He's thinking.
Je vais **réfléchir** à ta proposition. I'll think about your suggestion.
Réfléchissez avant de répondre. Think before answering.
Il faut que j'y **réfléchisse**. I'll have to think about it.

réfléchir

FUTURE

je	**réfléchirai**
tu	**réfléchiras**
il/elle/on	**réfléchira**
nous	**réfléchirons**
vous	**réfléchirez**
ils/elles	**réfléchiront**

CONDITIONAL

je	**réfléchirais**
tu	**réfléchirais**
il/elle/on	**réfléchirait**
nous	**réfléchirions**
vous	**réfléchiriez**
ils/elles	**réfléchiraient**

PAST HISTORIC

je	**réfléchis**
tu	**réfléchis**
il/elle/on	**réfléchit**
nous	**réfléchîmes**
vous	**réfléchîtes**
ils/elles	**réfléchirent**

PLUPERFECT

j'	**avais réfléchi**
tu	**avais réfléchi**
il/elle/on	**avait réfléchi**
nous	**avions réfléchi**
vous	**aviez réfléchi**
ils/elles	**avaient réfléchi**

IMPERATIVE

réfléchis / réfléchissons / réfléchissez

EXAMPLE PHRASES

J'y **réfléchirai** et nous en reparlerons lors de notre prochaine réunion. I'll think about it and we'll talk about it at our next meeting.

Il **réfléchit** longuement avant de parler. He thought for a long time before he spoke.

Si j'étais toi, j'y **réfléchirais** encore un peu. If I were you, I'd give it more thought.

Ils **avaient** bien **réfléchi** et ils avaient décidé de vendre la maison. They had thought it over and they had decided to sell the house.

je/j' = I **tu** = you **il** = he/it **elle** = she/it **on** = we/one **nous** = we **vous** = you **ils/elles** = they

rentrer (to go back; to go in)

PRESENT

je	**rentre**
tu	**rentres**
il/elle/on	**rentre**
nous	**rentrons**
vous	**rentrez**
ils/elles	**rentrent**

PRESENT SUBJUNCTIVE

je	**rentre**
tu	**rentres**
il/elle/on	**rentre**
nous	**rentrions**
vous	**rentriez**
ils/elles	**rentrent**

PERFECT

je	**suis rentré(e)**
tu	**es rentré(e)**
il/elle/on	**est rentré(e)**
nous	**sommes rentré(e)s**
vous	**êtes rentré(e)(s)**
ils/elles	**sont rentré(e)s**

IMPERFECT

je	**rentrais**
tu	**rentrais**
il/elle/on	**rentrait**
nous	**rentrions**
vous	**rentriez**
ils/elles	**rentraient**

PRESENT PARTICIPLE
rentrant

PAST PARTICIPLE
rentré

In the perfect and the pluperfect, use the auxiliary "avoir" when there is a direct object.

EXAMPLE PHRASES

Je **rentre** déjeuner à midi. I go home for lunch.
À quelle heure est-ce qu'elle **est rentrée**? What time did she get in?
Ne **rentre** pas trop tard. Don't come home too late.
Il faut que je **rentre** de bonne heure aujourd'hui. I have to go home early today.
Il ne **rentrait** jamais avant neuf heures le soir. He never came home before nine in the evening.

je/j' = I **tu** = you **il** = he/it **elle** = she/it **on** = we/one **nous** = we **vous** = you **ils/elles** = they

rentrer

FUTURE

je	**rentrerai**
tu	**rentreras**
il/elle/on	**rentrera**
nous	**rentrerons**
vous	**rentrerez**
ils/elles	**rentreront**

CONDITIONAL

je	**rentrerais**
tu	**rentrerais**
il/elle/on	**rentrerait**
nous	**rentrerions**
vous	**rentreriez**
ils/elles	**rentreraient**

PAST HISTORIC

je	**rentrai**
tu	**rentras**
il/elle/on	**rentra**
nous	**rentrâmes**
vous	**rentrâtes**
ils/elles	**rentrèrent**

PLUPERFECT

j'	**étais rentré(e)**
tu	**étais rentré(e)**
il/elle/on	**était rentré(e)**
nous	**étions rentré(e)s**
vous	**étiez rentré(e)(s)**
ils/elles	**étaient rentré(e)s**

IMPERATIVE

rentre / rentrons / rentrez

EXAMPLE PHRASES

Nous ne **rentrerons** pas tard. We won't come home late.

Il **rentra** chez lui en courant. He ran all the way home.

Si je n'avais pas peur de me perdre, je **rentrerais** sans toi. If I weren't afraid I'd get lost, I'd go home without you.

Ils **étaient rentrés** dans le magasin. They'd gone into the shop.

Il **avait** déjà **rentré** la voiture dans le garage. He'd already put the car into the garage.

répondre (to answer)

PRESENT

je	**réponds**
tu	**réponds**
il/elle/on	**répond**
nous	**répondons**
vous	**répondez**
ils/elles	**répondent**

PRESENT SUBJUNCTIVE

je	**réponde**
tu	**répondes**
il/elle/on	**réponde**
nous	**répondions**
vous	**répondiez**
ils/elles	**répondent**

PERFECT

j'	**ai répondu**
tu	**as répondu**
il/elle/on	**a répondu**
nous	**avons répondu**
vous	**avez répondu**
ils/elles	**ont répondu**

IMPERFECT

je	**répondais**
tu	**répondais**
il/elle/on	**répondait**
nous	**répondions**
vous	**répondiez**
ils/elles	**répondaient**

PRESENT PARTICIPLE

répondant

PAST PARTICIPLE

répondu

EXAMPLE PHRASES

Ça ne **répond** pas. There's no reply.

C'est elle qui **a répondu** au téléphone. She answered the phone.

Lisez le texte et **répondez** aux questions. Read the text and answer the questions.

J'attendais que tu **répondes** à ma lettre. I was waiting for you to reply to my letter.

Il ne **répondait** jamais au téléphone le soir. He never answered the phone in the evening.

je/j' = I **tu** = you **il** = he/it **elle** = she/it **on** = we/one **nous** = we **vous** = you **ils/elles** = they

répondre

FUTURE

je **répondrai**
tu **répondras**
il/elle/on **répondra**
nous **répondrons**
vous **répondrez**
ils/elles **répondront**

CONDITIONAL

je **répondrais**
tu **répondrais**
il/elle/on **répondrait**
nous **répondrions**
vous **répondriez**
ils/elles **répondraient**

PAST HISTORIC

je **répondis**
tu **répondis**
il/elle/on **répondit**
nous **répondîmes**
vous **répondîtes**
ils/elles **répondirent**

PLUPERFECT

j' **avais répondu**
tu **avais répondu**
il/elle/on **avait répondu**
nous **avions répondu**
vous **aviez répondu**
ils/elles **avaient répondu**

IMPERATIVE

réponds / répondons / répondez

EXAMPLE PHRASES

Je **répondrai** à son message ce soir. I'll reply to his message this evening.
"Je ne sais pas," **répondit**-elle. "I don't know," she answered.
Il ne te **répondrait** pas comme ça si tu étais plus stricte. He wouldn't answer back like that if you were stricter.
Je n'**avais** pas encore **répondu** à son invitation. I hadn't replied to her invitation yet.

je/j' = I **tu** = you **il** = he/it **elle** = she/it **on** = we/one **nous** = we **vous** = you **ils/elles** = they

résoudre (to solve; to resolve)

PRESENT

je	**résous**
tu	**résous**
il/elle/on	**résout**
nous	**résolvons**
vous	**résolvez**
ils/elles	**résolvent**

PRESENT SUBJUNCTIVE

je	**résolve**
tu	**résolves**
il/elle/on	**résolve**
nous	**résolvions**
vous	**résolviez**
ils/elles	**résolvent**

PERFECT

j'	**ai résolu**
tu	**as résolu**
il/elle/on	**a résolu**
nous	**avons résolu**
vous	**avez résolu**
ils/elles	**ont résolu**

IMPERFECT

je	**résolvais**
tu	**résolvais**
il/elle/on	**résolvait**
nous	**résolvions**
vous	**résolviez**
ils/elles	**résolvaient**

PRESENT PARTICIPLE
résolvant

PAST PARTICIPLE
résolu

EXAMPLE PHRASES

C'est un problème qui sera difficile à **résoudre.** This problem will be difficult to solve.

La violence ne **résout** rien. Violence doesn't solve anything.

J'**ai résolu** le problème. I've solved the problem.

J'aimerais que vous **résolviez** la question aujourd'hui. I'd like you to resolve the question today.

résoudre

FUTURE	
je	**résoudrai**
tu	**résoudras**
il/elle/on	**résoudra**
nous	**résoudrons**
vous	**résoudrez**
ils/elles	**résoudront**

CONDITIONAL	
je	**résoudrais**
tu	**résoudrais**
il/elle/on	**résoudrait**
nous	**résoudrions**
vous	**résoudriez**
ils/elles	**résoudraient**

PAST HISTORIC	
je	**résolus**
tu	**résolus**
il/elle/on	**résolut**
nous	**résolûmes**
vous	**résolûtes**
ils/elles	**résolurent**

PLUPERFECT	
j'	**avais résolu**
tu	**avais résolu**
il/elle/on	**avait résolu**
nous	**avions résolu**
vous	**aviez résolu**
ils/elles	**avaient résolu**

IMPERATIVE

résous / résolvons / résolvez

EXAMPLE PHRASES

Son refus de s'excuser ne **résoudra** pas la querelle. His refusal to apologize won't resolve the quarrel.

Il **résolut** l'énigme en quelques minutes. He solved the riddle in a few minutes.

C'est un problème qui se **résoudrait** rapidement s'il n'y avait pas déjà d'autres problèmes. This problem could be solved quickly if there weren't already other problems.

À la fin de la réunion, nous **avions résolu** la question. By the end of the meeting, we had resolved the question.

rester (to stay)

PRESENT

je	**reste**
tu	**restes**
il/elle/on	**reste**
nous	**restons**
vous	**restez**
ils/elles	**restent**

PRESENT SUBJUNCTIVE

je	**reste**
tu	**restes**
il/elle/on	**reste**
nous	**restions**
vous	**restiez**
ils/elles	**restent**

PERFECT

je	**suis resté(e)**
tu	**es resté(e)**
il/elle/on	**est resté(e)**
nous	**sommes resté(e)s**
vous	**êtes resté(e)(s)**
ils/elles	**sont resté(e)s**

IMPERFECT

je	**restais**
tu	**restais**
il/elle/on	**restait**
nous	**restions**
vous	**restiez**
ils/elles	**restaient**

PRESENT PARTICIPLE

restant

PAST PARTICIPLE

resté

EXAMPLE PHRASES

Cet été, je **reste** en Écosse. I'm staying in Scotland this summer.

Ils ne **sont** pas **restés** très longtemps. They didn't stay very long.

Reste ici! Stay here!

Elle aimerait que Marianne **reste** dormir ce soir. She'd like Marianne to stay for a sleepover tonight.

Il leur **restait** encore un peu d'argent. They still had some money left.

rester

FUTURE	
je	**resterai**
tu	**resteras**
il/elle/on	**restera**
nous	**resterons**
vous	**resterez**
ils/elles	**resteront**

CONDITIONAL	
je	**resterais**
tu	**resterais**
il/elle/on	**resterait**
nous	**resterions**
vous	**resteriez**
ils/elles	**resteraient**

PAST HISTORIC	
je	**restai**
tu	**restas**
il/elle/on	**resta**
nous	**restâmes**
vous	**restâtes**
ils/elles	**restèrent**

PLUPERFECT	
j'	**étais resté(e)**
tu	**étais resté(e)**
il/elle/on	**était resté(e)**
nous	**étions resté(e)s**
vous	**étiez resté(e)(s)**
ils/elles	**étaient resté(e)s**

IMPERATIVE

reste / restons / restez

EXAMPLE PHRASES

Si tu finis les biscuits il n'en **restera** plus pour ce soir. If you finish the biscuits there won't be any left for tonight.

Il **resta** dans sa chambre toute la soirée. He stayed in his bedroom all evening.

Si c'était à moi de choisir, je **resterais** à la maison. If it were my choice, I'd stay home.

Nous **étions restés** à la maison pour regarder le match de football. We'd stayed home to watch the football match.

retourner (to go back; to turn)

PRESENT

je	**retourne**
tu	**retournes**
il/elle/on	**retourne**
nous	**retournons**
vous	**retournez**
ils/elles	**retournent**

PRESENT SUBJUNCTIVE

je	**retourne**
tu	**retournes**
il/elle/on	**retourne**
nous	**retournions**
vous	**retourniez**
ils/elles	**retournent**

PERFECT

je	**suis retourné(e)**
tu	**es retourné(e)**
il/elle/on	**est retourné(e)**
nous	**sommes retourné(e)s**
vous	**êtes retourné(e)(s)**
ils/elles	**sont retourné(e)s**

IMPERFECT

je	**retournais**
tu	**retournais**
il/elle/on	**retournait**
nous	**retournions**
vous	**retourniez**
ils/elles	**retournaient**

PRESENT PARTICIPLE
retournant

PAST PARTICIPLE
retourné

In the perfect and the pluperfect, use the auxiliary "avoir" when there is a direct object.

EXAMPLE PHRASES

J'aimerais bien **retourner** en Italie un jour. I'd like to go back to Italy one day.

Cet été, nous **retournons** en Grèce. We're going back to Greece this summer.

Est-ce que tu **es retournée** à Londres? Have you been back to London?

Zoë, **retourne**-toi! Turn around, Zoë!

Il va falloir que je **retourne** voir le film. I'll have to go back to see the film.

Elle **retournait** rarement dans son pays natal. She rarely went back to her native country.

je/j' = I **tu** = you **il** = he/it **elle** = she/it **on** = we/one **nous** = we **vous** = you **ils/elles** = they

retourner

FUTURE

je	**retournerai**
tu	**retourneras**
il/elle/on	**retournera**
nous	**retournerons**
vous	**retournerez**
ils/elles	**retourneront**

CONDITIONAL

je	**retournerais**
tu	**retournerais**
il/elle/on	**retournerait**
nous	**retournerions**
vous	**retourneriez**
ils/elles	**retourneraient**

PAST HISTORIC

je	**retournai**
tu	**retournas**
il/elle/on	**retourna**
nous	**retournâmes**
vous	**retournâtes**
ils/elles	**retournèrent**

PLUPERFECT

j'	**étais retourné(e)**
tu	**étais retourné(e)**
il/elle/on	**était retourné(e)**
nous	**étions retourné(e)s**
vous	**étiez retourné(e)(s)**
ils/elles	**étaient retourné(e)s**

IMPERATIVE

retourne / retournons / retournez

EXAMPLE PHRASES

Je ne **retournerai** jamais les voir. I'll never go back to see them.

Elle déjeuna rapidement et **retourna** travailler. She had a quick lunch and went back to work.

Il disait qu'il ne **retournerait** jamais vivre avec elle. He said that he would never go back to live with her.

Elle **avait retourné** la carte pour vérifier. She had turned the card over to check.

je/j' = I **tu** = you **il** = he/it **elle** = she/it **on** = we/one **nous** = we **vous** = you **ils/elles** = they

réussir (to be successful)

PRESENT

je	**réussis**
tu	**réussis**
il/elle/on	**réussit**
nous	**réussissons**
vous	**réussissez**
ils/elles	**réussissent**

PRESENT SUBJUNCTIVE

je	**réussisse**
tu	**réussisses**
il/elle/on	**réussisse**
nous	**réussissions**
vous	**réussissiez**
ils/elles	**réussissent**

PERFECT

j'	**ai réussi**
tu	**as réussi**
il/elle/on	**a réussi**
nous	**avons réussi**
vous	**avez réussi**
ils/elles	**ont réussi**

IMPERFECT

je	**réussissais**
tu	**réussissais**
il/elle/on	**réussissait**
nous	**réussissions**
vous	**réussissiez**
ils/elles	**réussissaient**

PRESENT PARTICIPLE
réussissant

PAST PARTICIPLE
réussi

EXAMPLE PHRASES

Il faut se battre pour **réussir** dans la vie. You have to fight to be successful in life.

Tous ses enfants **ont** très bien **réussi**. All her children are very successful.

J'aimerais qu'il **réussisse** à son permis de conduire. I'd like him to pass his driving test.

Elle **réussissait** toujours à me faire rire quand j'étais triste. She always managed to make me laugh when I was sad.

réussir

FUTURE

je	**réussirai**
tu	**réussiras**
il/elle/on	**réussira**
nous	**réussirons**
vous	**réussirez**
ils/elles	**réussiront**

CONDITIONAL

je	**réussirais**
tu	**réussirais**
il/elle/on	**réussirait**
nous	**réussirions**
vous	**réussiriez**
ils/elles	**réussiraient**

PAST HISTORIC

je	**réussis**
tu	**réussis**
il/elle/on	**réussit**
nous	**réussîmes**
vous	**réussîtes**
ils/elles	**réussirent**

PLUPERFECT

j'	**avais réussi**
tu	**avais réussi**
il/elle/on	**avait réussi**
nous	**avions réussi**
vous	**aviez réussi**
ils/elles	**avaient réussi**

IMPERATIVE

réussis / réussissons / réussissez

EXAMPLE PHRASES

Je suis sûr que tu **réussiras** à ton examen. I'm sure you'll pass your exam.

Finalement, elle **réussit** à le convaincre. She eventually managed to convince him.

Je **réussirais** peut-être mes gâteaux si j'avais un four qui marchait. My cakes might turn out fine if I had an oven that worked.

Elle **avait réussi** à battre le record du monde. She had succeeded in beating the world record.

se réveiller (to wake up)

PRESENT

je	**me réveille**
tu	**te réveilles**
il/elle/on	**se réveille**
nous	**nous réveillons**
vous	**vous réveillez**
ils/elles	**se réveillent**

PRESENT SUBJUNCTIVE

je	**me réveille**
tu	**te réveilles**
il/elle/on	**se réveille**
nous	**nous réveillions**
vous	**vous réveilliez**
ils/elles	**se réveillent**

PERFECT

je	**me suis réveillé(e)**
tu	**t'es réveillé(e)**
il/elle/on	**s'est réveillé(e)**
nous	**nous sommes réveillé(e)s**
vous	**vous êtes réveillé(e)(s)**
ils/elles	**se sont réveillé(e)s**

IMPERFECT

je	**me réveillais**
tu	**te réveillais**
il/elle/on	**se réveillait**
nous	**nous réveillions**
vous	**vous réveilliez**
ils/elles	**se réveillaient**

PRESENT PARTICIPLE
se réveillant

PAST PARTICIPLE
réveillé

EXAMPLE PHRASES

Je **me réveille** à sept heures tous les matins. I wake up at seven every morning.
Il **s'est réveillé** en retard. He overslept.
Réveille-toi: il est huit heures! Wake up - it's eight!
Il faut que je **me réveille** à cinq heures demain matin. I have to wake up at five tomorrow morning.
Elle **se réveillait** toujours avant moi. She always woke up before me.

se réveiller

FUTURE

je	**me réveillerai**
tu	**te réveilleras**
il/elle/on	**se réveillera**
nous	**nous réveillerons**
vous	**vous réveillerez**
ils/elles	**se réveilleront**

CONDITIONAL

je	**me réveillerais**
tu	**te réveillerais**
il/elle/on	**se réveillerait**
nous	**nous réveillerions**
vous	**vous réveilleriez**
ils/elles	**se réveilleraient**

PAST HISTORIC

je	**me réveillai**
tu	**te réveillas**
il/elle/on	**se réveilla**
nous	**nous reveillâmes**
vous	**vous réveillâtes**
ils/elles	**se réveillèrent**

PLUPERFECT

je	**m'étais réveill(e)**
tu	**t'étais réveill(e)**
il/elle/on	**s'était réveillé(e)**
nous	**nous étions réveill(e)s**
vous	**vous étiez réveillé(e)(s)**
ils/elles	**s'étaient réveillé(e)s**

IMPERATIVE

réveille-toi / réveillons-nous / réveillez-nous

EXAMPLE PHRASES

Louise ne **se réveillera** probablement pas avant neuf heures. Louise probably won't wake up before nine.

Elle **se réveilla** en sursaut. She woke up with a start.

Je ne **me réveillerais** pas sans mon réveil. I wouldn't wake up without my alarm clock.

Elle ne **s'était** pas **réveillée** quand je l'avais appelée. She hadn't woken up when I had called her.

revenir (to come back)

PRESENT		PRESENT SUBJUNCTIVE	
je	**reviens**	je	**revienne**
tu	**reviens**	tu	**reviennes**
il/elle/on	**revient**	il/elle/on	**revienne**
nous	**revenons**	nous	**revenions**
vous	**revenez**	vous	**reveniez**
ils/elles	**reviennent**	ils/elles	**reviennent**

PERFECT		IMPERFECT	
je	**suis revenu(e)**	je	**revenais**
tu	**es revenu(e)**	tu	**revenais**
il/elle/on	**est revenu(e)**	il/elle/on	**revenait**
nous	**sommes revenu(e)s**	nous	**revenions**
vous	**êtes revenu(e)(s)**	vous	**reveniez**
ils/elles	**sont revenu(e)s**	ils/elles	**revenaient**

PRESENT PARTICIPLE
revenant

PAST PARTICIPLE
revenu

EXAMPLE PHRASES

Je **reviens** dans cinq minutes! I'll be back in five minutes!
Ça me **revient**! It's coming back to me now!
Mon chat n'**est** toujours pas **revenu**. My cat still hasn't come back.
Philippe! **Reviens** immédiatement! Philippe! Come back immediately!
J'aimerais qu'il **revienne** me voir. I'd like him to come back to see me.
Son chien se promenait souvent loin de chez lui mais il **revenait** toujours. His dog often wandered far away from his house, but he'd always come back.

je/j' = I **tu** = you **il** = he/it **elle** = she/it **on** = we/one **nous** = we **vous** = you **ils/elles** = they

revenir

FUTURE

je	**reviendrai**
tu	**reviendras**
il/elle/on	**reviendra**
nous	**reviendrons**
vous	**reviendrez**
ils/elles	**reviendront**

CONDITIONAL

je	**reviendrais**
tu	**reviendrais**
il/elle/on	**reviendrait**
nous	**reviendrions**
vous	**reviendriez**
ils/elles	**reviendraient**

PAST HISTORIC

je	**revins**
tu	**revins**
il/elle/on	**revint**
nous	**revînmes**
vous	**revîntes**
ils/elles	**revinrent**

PLUPERFECT

j'	**étais revenu(e)**
tu	**étais revenu(e)**
il/elle/on	**était revenu(e)**
nous	**étions revenu(e)s**
vous	**étiez revenu(e)(s)**
ils/elles	**étaient revenu(e)s**

IMPERATIVE

reviens / revenons / revenez

EXAMPLE PHRASES

Je ne **reviendrai** jamais ici. I'll never come back here.

Il **revint** nous voir le lendemain. He came back to see us the next day.

Elle ne **reviendrait** pas si elle avait le choix. She wouldn't come back if she had the choice.

Ils **étaient revenus** le soir même avec leur fille. They had come back that same evening with their daughter.

je/j' = I **tu** = you **il** = he/it **elle** = she/it **on** = we/one **nous** = we **vous** = you **ils/elles** = they

rire (to laugh)

PRESENT

je	**ris**
tu	**ris**
il/elle/on	**rit**
nous	**rions**
vous	**riez**
ils/elles	**rient**

PRESENT SUBJUNCTIVE

je	**rie**
tu	**ries**
il/elle/on	**rie**
nous	**riions**
vous	**riiez**
ils/elles	**rient**

PERFECT

j'	**ai ri**
tu	**as ri**
il/elle/on	**a ri**
nous	**avons ri**
vous	**avez ri**
ils/elles	**ont ri**

IMPERFECT

je	**riais**
tu	**riais**
il/elle/on	**riait**
nous	**riions**
vous	**riiez**
ils/elles	**riaient**

PRESENT PARTICIPLE

riant

PAST PARTICIPLE

ri

EXAMPLE PHRASES

C'était juste pour **rire**. It was only for a laugh.
Elle **rit** toujours de mes plaisanteries. She always laughs at my jokes.
On **a** bien **ri**. We had a good laugh.
Ne **ris** pas, ce n'est pas drôle! Don't laugh, it's not funny!
Je n'aime pas qu'on **rie** derrière mon dos. I don't like it when people laugh behind my back.

rire

FUTURE		CONDITIONAL	
je	**rirai**	je	**rirais**
tu	**riras**	tu	**rirais**
il/elle/on	**rira**	il/elle/on	**rirait**
nous	**rirons**	nous	**ririons**
vous	**rirez**	vous	**ririez**
ils/elles	**riront**	ils/elles	**riraient**

PAST HISTORIC		PLUPERFECT	
je	**ris**	j'	**avais ri**
tu	**ris**	tu	**avais ri**
il/elle/on	**rit**	il/elle/on	**avait ri**
nous	**rîmes**	nous	**avions ri**
vous	**rîtes**	vous	**aviez ri**
ils/elles	**rirent**	ils/elles	**avaient ri**

IMPERATIVE

ris / rions / riez

EXAMPLE PHRASES

Tu ne **riras** pas tant quand ce sera ton tour. You won't be laughing so much when it's your turn.

Elle **rit** quand il lui raconta l'histoire. She laughed when he told her the story.

Il ne **rirait** pas s'il savait où tu es allé. He wouldn't be laughing if he knew where you've been.

Ils **avaient ri** quand elle leur avait raconté ce qui s'était passé. They had laughed when she had told them what had happened.

rompre (to break; to split up)

PRESENT

je	**romps**
tu	**romps**
il/elle/on	**rompt**
nous	**rompons**
vous	**rompez**
ils/elles	**rompent**

PRESENT SUBJUNCTIVE

je	**rompe**
tu	**rompes**
il/elle/on	**rompe**
nous	**rompions**
vous	**rompiez**
ils/elles	**rompent**

PERFECT

j'	**ai rompu**
tu	**as rompu**
il/elle/on	**a rompu**
nous	**avons rompu**
vous	**avez rompu**
ils/elles	**ont rompu**

IMPERFECT

je	**rompais**
tu	**rompais**
il/elle/on	**rompait**
nous	**rompions**
vous	**rompiez**
ils/elles	**rompaient**

PRESENT PARTICIPLE
rompant

PAST PARTICIPLE
rompu

EXAMPLE PHRASES

Elle **a rompu** le silence. She broke the silence.

Paul et Jo **ont rompu**. Paul and Jo have split up.

La corde s'est **rompue**. The rope broke.

rompre

FUTURE

je	**romprai**
tu	**rompras**
il/elle/on	**rompra**
nous	**romprons**
vous	**romprez**
ils/elles	**rompront**

CONDITIONAL

je	**romprais**
tu	**romprais**
il/elle/on	**romprait**
nous	**romprions**
vous	**rompriez**
ils/elles	**rompraient**

PAST HISTORIC

je	**rompis**
tu	**rompis**
il/elle/on	**rompit**
nous	**rompîmes**
vous	**rompîtes**
ils/elles	**rompirent**

PLUPERFECT

j'	**avais rompu**
tu	**avais rompu**
il/elle/on	**avait rompu**
nous	**avions rompu**
vous	**aviez rompu**
ils/elles	**avaient rompu**

IMPERATIVE

romps / rompons / rompez

EXAMPLE PHRASES

Il **rompit** le silence en entrant. He broke the silence when he came in.

Le charme **était rompu**. The spell was broken.

Il **avait** déjà **rompu** avec Alice quand il a rencontré Christine. He'd already split up with Alice when he met Christine.

savoir (to know)

PRESENT		PRESENT SUBJUNCTIVE	
je	**sais**	je	**sache**
tu	**sais**	tu	**saches**
il/elle/on	**sait**	il/elle/on	**sache**
nous	**savons**	nous	**sachions**
vous	**savez**	vous	**sachiez**
ils/elles	**savent**	ils/elles	**sachent**

PERFECT		IMPERFECT	
j'	**ai su**	je	**savais**
tu	**as su**	tu	**savais**
il/elle/on	**a su**	il/elle/on	**savait**
nous	**avons su**	nous	**savions**
vous	**avez su**	vous	**saviez**
ils/elles	**ont su**	ils/elles	**savaient**

PRESENT PARTICIPLE
sachant

PAST PARTICIPLE
su

EXAMPLE PHRASES

Tu **sais** ce que tu vas faire l'année prochaine? Do you know what you're going to do next year?
Je ne **sais** pas. I don't know.
Elle ne **sait** pas nager. She can't swim.
Je voulais qu'il le **sache**. I wanted him to know about it.
Tu **savais** que son père était enseignant? Did you know that her father was a teacher?

savoir

FUTURE

je	**saurai**
tu	**sauras**
il/elle/on	**saura**
nous	**saurons**
vous	**saurez**
ils/elles	**sauront**

CONDITIONAL

je	**saurais**
tu	**saurais**
il/elle/on	**saurait**
nous	**saurions**
vous	**sauriez**
ils/elles	**sauraient**

PAST HISTORIC

je	**sus**
tu	**sus**
il/elle/on	**sut**
nous	**sûmes**
vous	**sûtes**
ils/elles	**surent**

PLUPERFECT

j'	**avais su**
tu	**avais su**
il/elle/on	**avait su**
nous	**avions su**
vous	**aviez su**
ils/elles	**avaient su**

IMPERATIVE

sache / sachons / sachez

EXAMPLE PHRASES

Elle ne **saura** pas où on est. She won't know where we are.

Il ne le **sut** que beaucoup plus tard. He only knew about it a lot later.

Tous ces enfants **sauraient** lire si on leur apprenait. All these children would be able to read if they were taught.

Ils ne l'**avaient su** que beaucoup plus tard. They hadn't known about it until a lot later.

sentir (to smell; to feel)

PRESENT

je	**sens**
tu	**sens**
il/elle/on	**sent**
nous	**sentons**
vous	**sentez**
ils/elles	**sentent**

PRESENT SUBJUNCTIVE

je	**sente**
tu	**sentes**
il/elle/on	**sente**
nous	**sentions**
vous	**sentiez**
ils/elles	**sentent**

PERFECT

j'	**ai senti**
tu	**as senti**
il/elle/on	**a senti**
nous	**avons senti**
vous	**avez senti**
ils/elles	**ont senti**

IMPERFECT

je	**sentais**
tu	**sentais**
il/elle/on	**sentait**
nous	**sentions**
vous	**sentiez**
ils/elles	**sentaient**

PRESENT PARTICIPLE

sentant

PAST PARTICIPLE

senti

EXAMPLE PHRASES

Ça **sent** bon ici. It smells nice here.

Elle ne se **sent** pas bien. She's not feeling well.

Je n'**ai** rien **senti**. I didn't feel a thing.

Sens ces fleurs. Smell these flowers.

Ça **sentait** mauvais. It smelt bad.

sentir

FUTURE

je	**sentirai**
tu	**sentiras**
il/elle/on	**sentira**
nous	**sentirons**
vous	**sentirez**
ils/elles	**sentiront**

CONDITIONAL

je	**sentirais**
tu	**sentirais**
il/elle/on	**sentirait**
nous	**sentirions**
vous	**sentiriez**
ils/elles	**sentiraient**

PAST HISTORIC

je	**sentis**
tu	**sentis**
il/elle/on	**sentit**
nous	**sentîmes**
vous	**sentîtes**
ils/elles	**sentirent**

PLUPERFECT

j'	**avais senti**
tu	**avais senti**
il/elle/on	**avait senti**
nous	**avions senti**
vous	**aviez senti**
ils/elles	**avaient senti**

IMPERATIVE

sens / sentons / sentez

EXAMPLE PHRASES

Ne vous inquiétez pas: vous ne **sentirez** rien. Don't worry – you won't feel a thing.

Il **sentit** que ce n'était pas le bon moment. He felt that it wasn't the right time.

Elle se **sentirait** mieux si elle se reposait. She'd feel better if she rested.

Il n'**avait** rien **senti** pendant l'opération. He hadn't felt a thing during the operation.

servir (to serve)

PRESENT

je	**sers**
tu	**sers**
il/elle/on	**sert**
nous	**servons**
vous	**servez**
ils/elles	**servent**

PRESENT SUBJUNCTIVE

je	**serve**
tu	**serves**
il/elle/on	**serve**
nous	**servions**
vous	**serviez**
ils/elles	**servent**

PERFECT

j'	**ai servi**
tu	**as servi**
il/elle/on	**a servi**
nous	**avons servi**
vous	**avez servi**
ils/elles	**ont servi**

IMPERFECT

je	**servais**
tu	**servais**
il/elle/on	**servait**
nous	**servions**
vous	**serviez**
ils/elles	**servaient**

PRESENT PARTICIPLE
servant

PAST PARTICIPLE
servi

EXAMPLE PHRASES

On vous **sert**? Are you being served?
Ça **sert** à quoi ce bouton? What is this button for?
Servez-vous. Help yourself.
Il faut que je **serve** la soupe. I have to serve the soup.
Ça ne **servait** à rien de le supplier. It was no use begging him.

servir

FUTURE

je	**servirai**
tu	**serviras**
il/elle/on	**servira**
nous	**servirons**
vous	**servirez**
ils/elles	**serviront**

CONDITIONAL

je	**servirais**
tu	**servirais**
il/elle/on	**servirait**
nous	**servirions**
vous	**serviriez**
ils/elles	**serviraient**

PAST HISTORIC

je	**servis**
tu	**servis**
il/elle/on	**servit**
nous	**servîmes**
vous	**servîtes**
ils/elles	**servirent**

PLUPERFECT

j'	**avais servi**
tu	**avais servi**
il/elle/on	**avait servi**
nous	**avions servi**
vous	**aviez servi**
ils/elles	**avaient servi**

IMPERATIVE

sers / servons / servez

EXAMPLE PHRASES

Ces boîtes te **serviront** quand tu déménageras. You'll find these boxes useful when you move house.

Elle leur **servit** des profiteroles en dessert. She served them profiteroles for dessert.

Ça ne **servirait** à rien d'y aller maintenant. It would serve no purpose to go there now.

Cette valise n'**avait** pas **servi** depuis dix ans. This suitcase hadn't been used for ten years.

sortir (to go out; to take out)

PRESENT

je	**sors**
tu	**sors**
il/elle/on	**sort**
nous	**sortons**
vous	**sortez**
ils/elles	**sortent**

PRESENT SUBJUNCTIVE

je	**sorte**
tu	**sortes**
il/elle/on	**sorte**
nous	**sortions**
vous	**sortiez**
ils/elles	**sortent**

PERFECT

je	**suis sorti(e)**
tu	**es sorti(e)**
il/elle/on	**est sorti(e)**
nous	**sommes sorti(e)s**
vous	**êtes sorti(e)(s)**
ils/elles	**sont sorti(e)s**

IMPERFECT

je	**sortais**
tu	**sortais**
il/elle/on	**sortait**
nous	**sortions**
vous	**sortiez**
ils/elles	**sortaient**

PRESENT PARTICIPLE

sortant

PAST PARTICIPLE

sorti

In the perfect and the imperfect, use the auxiliary "avoir" when there is a direct object.

EXAMPLE PHRASES

Aurélie **sort** avec Bruno. Aurélie is going out with Bruno.

Je ne **suis** pas **sortie** ce week-end. I didn't go out this weekend.

Je n'**ai** pas **sorti** le chien parce qu'il pleuvait. I didn't take the dog out for a walk because it was raining.

Sortez en silence. Go out quietly.

Je ne veux pas que tu **sortes** habillée comme ça. I don't want you to go out dressed like that.

Il **sortait** quand c'est arrivé. He was going out when it happened.

sortir

FUTURE		CONDITIONAL	
je	**sortirai**	je	**sortirais**
tu	**sortiras**	tu	**sortirais**
il/elle/on	**sortira**	il/elle/on	**sortirait**
nous	**sortirons**	nous	**sortirions**
vous	**sortirez**	vous	**sortiriez**
ils/elles	**sortiront**	ils/elles	**sortiraient**

PAST HISTORIC		PLUPERFECT	
je	**sortis**	j'	**étais sorti(e)**
tu	**sortis**	tu	**étais sorti(e)**
il/elle/on	**sortit**	il/elle/on	**était sorti(e)**
nous	**sortîmes**	nous	**étions sorti(e)s**
vous	**sortîtes**	vous	**étiez sorti(e)(s)**
ils/elles	**sortirent**	ils/elles	**étaient sorti(e)s**

IMPERATIVE

sors / sortons / sortez

EXAMPLE PHRASES

Je **sortirai** la poubelle en partant. I'll take out the bin on my way out.

Il **sortit** une photo de sa poche. He took a photo out of his pocket.

Elle ne **sortirait** jamais de chez elle si son mari ne l'y obligeait pas. She'd never leave her house if her husband didn't force her.

Elle **était sortie** de l'hôpital la veille. She had come out of hospital the day before.

souffrir (to suffer; to be in pain)

PRESENT

je	**souffre**
tu	**souffres**
il/elle/on	**souffre**
nous	**souffrons**
vous	**souffrez**
ils/elles	**souffrent**

PRESENT SUBJUNCTIVE

je	**souffre**
tu	**souffres**
il/elle/on	**souffre**
nous	**souffrions**
vous	**souffriez**
ils/elles	**souffrent**

PERFECT

j'	**ai souffert**
tu	**as souffert**
il/elle/on	**a souffert**
nous	**avons souffert**
vous	**avez souffert**
ils/elles	**ont souffert**

IMPERFECT

j'	**souffrais**
tu	**souffrais**
il/elle/on	**souffrait**
nous	**souffrions**
vous	**souffriez**
ils/elles	**souffraient**

PRESENT PARTICIPLE
souffrant

PAST PARTICIPLE
souffert

EXAMPLE PHRASES

Il **souffre** beaucoup. He's in a lot of pain.

Elle **a** beaucoup **souffert** quand il l'a quittée. She suffered a lot when he left her.

Souffre en silence. Suffer in silence.

J'ai peur qu'il ne **souffre**. I'm scared he might be suffering.

Il **souffrait** de ne plus la voir. It pained him not to see her any more.

souffrir

FUTURE

je	**souffrirai**
tu	**souffriras**
il/elle/on	**souffrira**
nous	**souffrirons**
vous	**souffrirez**
ils/elles	**souffriront**

CONDITIONAL

je	**souffrirais**
tu	**souffrirais**
il/elle/on	**souffrirait**
nous	**souffririons**
vous	**souffririez**
ils/elles	**souffriraient**

PAST HISTORIC

je	**souffris**
tu	**souffris**
il/elle/on	**souffrit**
nous	**souffrîmes**
vous	**souffrîtes**
ils/elles	**souffrirent**

PLUPERFECT

j'	**avais souffert**
tu	**avais souffert**
il/elle/on	**avait souffert**
nous	**avions souffert**
vous	**aviez souffert**
ils/elles	**avaient souffert**

IMPERATIVE

souffre / souffrons / souffrez

EXAMPLE PHRASES

Je te promets que tu ne **souffriras** pas trop. I promise that you won't be in too much pain.

Ils **souffrirent** en silence. They suffered in silence.

Elle ne **souffrirait** pas tant si elle prenait son médicament. She wouldn't suffer so much if she took her medicine.

Elle **avait** beaucoup **souffert** durant son enfance. She had suffered a lot during her childhood.

je/j' = I **tu** = you **il** = he/it **elle** = she/it **on** = we/one **nous** = we **vous** = you **ils/elles** = they

se souvenir (to remember)

PRESENT		PRESENT SUBJUNCTIVE	
je	**me souviens**	je	**me souvienne**
tu	**te souviens**	tu	**te souviennes**
il/elle/on	**se souvient**	il/elle/on	**se souvienne**
nous	**nous souvenons**	nous	**nous souvenions**
vous	**vous souvenez**	vous	**vous souveniez**
ils/elles	**se souviennent**	ils/elles	**se souviennent**

PERFECT		IMPERFECT	
je	**me suis souvenu(e)**	je	**me souvenais**
tu	**t'es souvenu(e)**	tu	**te souvenais**
il/elle/on	**s'est souvenu(e)**	il/elle/on	**se souvenait**
nous	**nous sommes souvenu(e)s**	nous	**nous souvenions**
vous	**vous êtes souvenu(e)(s)**	vous	**vous souveniez**
ils/elles	**se sont souvenu(e)s**	ils/elles	**se souvenaient**

PRESENT PARTICIPLE
se souvenant

PAST PARTICIPLE
souvenu

EXAMPLE PHRASES

Je ne **me souviens** pas de son adresse. I can't remember his address.

Te souviens-tu du jour où Pierre s'est cassé le bras? Do you remember the day when Pierre broke his arm?

Souviens-toi: il neigeait ce jour-là. Remember – it was snowing that day.

Je ne crois pas qu'elle **s'**en **souvienne**. I don't think that she remembers it.

Il ne **se souvenait** pas où il avait mis ses clés. He couldn't remember where he'd put his keys.

se souvenir

FUTURE		CONDITIONAL	
je	**me souviendrai**	je	**me souviendrais**
tu	**te souviendras**	tu	**te souviendrais**
il/elle/on	**se souviendra**	il/elle/on	**se souviendrait**
nous	**nous souviendrons**	nous	**nous souviendrions**
vous	**vous souviendrez**	vous	**vous souviendriez**
ils/elles	**se souviendront**	ils/elles	**se souviendraient**

PAST HISTORIC		PLUPERFECT	
je	**me souvins**	je	**m'étais souvenu(e)**
tu	**te souvins**	tu	**t'étais souvenu(e)**
il/elle/on	**se souvint**	il/elle/on	**s'était souvenu(e)**
nous	**nous souvînmes**	nous	**nous étions souvenu(e)s**
vous	**vous souvîntes**	vous	**vous étiez souvenu(e)(s)**
ils/elles	**se souvinrent**	ils/elles	**s'étaient souvenu(e)s**

IMPERATIVE

souviens-toi / souvenons-nous / souvenez-nous

EXAMPLE PHRASES

Fais-lui une liste, sinon il ne **se souviendra** pas de ce qu'il doit acheter. Make him a list, otherwise he won't remember what he has to buy.

Elle **se souvint** qu'elle leur avait promis une surprise. She remembered that she'd promised them a surprise.

Si je ne prenais pas de notes, je ne **me souviendrais** pas de mes cours. If I didn't take notes, I wouldn't remember my lessons.

Il **s'était souvenu** un peu tard de son anniversaire. He had remembered her birthday a little late.

suffire (to be enough)

PRESENT

je	**suffis**
tu	**suffis**
il/elle/on	**suffit**
nous	**suffisons**
vous	**suffisez**
ils/elles	**suffisent**

PRESENT SUBJUNCTIVE

je	**suffise**
tu	**suffises**
il/elle/on	**suffise**
nous	**suffisions**
vous	**suffisiez**
ils/elles	**suffisent**

PERFECT

j'	**ai suffi**
tu	**as suffi**
il/elle/on	**a suffi**
nous	**avons suffi**
vous	**avez suffi**
ils/elles	**ont suffi**

IMPERFECT

je	**suffisais**
tu	**suffisais**
il/elle/on	**suffisait**
nous	**suffisions**
vous	**suffisiez**
ils/elles	**suffisaient**

PRESENT PARTICIPLE
suffisant

PAST PARTICIPLE
suffi

EXAMPLE PHRASES

Ça **suffit**! That's enough!

Ses jouets lui **suffisent**. His toys are enough for him.

Une séance avec l'ostéopathe **a suffi** pour me soulager. One session with the osteopath was enough to ease the pain.

Il **suffisait** de me le demander. You only had to ask.

suffire

FUTURE

je	**suffirai**
tu	**suffiras**
il/elle/on	**suffira**
nous	**suffirons**
vous	**suffirez**
ils/elles	**suffiront**

CONDITIONAL

je	**suffirais**
tu	**suffirais**
il/elle/on	**suffirait**
nous	**suffirions**
vous	**suffiriez**
ils/elles	**suffiraient**

PAST HISTORIC

je	**suffis**
tu	**suffis**
il/elle/on	**suffit**
nous	**suffîmes**
vous	**suffîtes**
ils/elles	**suffirent**

PLUPERFECT

j'	**avais suffi**
tu	**avais suffi**
il/elle/on	**avait suffi**
nous	**avions suffi**
vous	**aviez suffi**
ils/elles	**avaient suffi**

IMPERATIVE

suffis / suffisons / suffisez

EXAMPLE PHRASES

Ça te **suffira**, dix euros? Will ten euros be enough?

Sa promesse lui **suffit**: il lui faisait confiance. Her promise was enough for him – he trusted her.

Il **suffirait** de se dépêcher un peu pour le rattraper. We'd only have to hurry a little to catch up with him.

Il nous **avait suffi** d'aller à la bibliothèque municipale pour trouver le livre. We only had to go to the community library to find the book.

je/j' = I **tu** = you **il** = he/it **elle** = she/it **on** = we/one **nous** = we **vous** = you **ils/elles** = they

suivre (to follow)

PRESENT

je	**suis**
tu	**suis**
il/elle/on	**suit**
nous	**suivons**
vous	**suivez**
ils/elles	**suivent**

PRESENT SUBJUNCTIVE

je	**suive**
tu	**suives**
il/elle/on	**suive**
nous	**suivions**
vous	**suiviez**
ils/elles	**suivent**

PERFECT

j'	**ai suivi**
tu	**as suivi**
il/elle/on	**a suivi**
nous	**avons suivi**
vous	**avez suivi**
ils/elles	**ont suivi**

IMPERFECT

je	**suivais**
tu	**suivais**
il/elle/on	**suivait**
nous	**suivions**
vous	**suiviez**
ils/elles	**suivaient**

PRESENT PARTICIPLE
suivant

PAST PARTICIPLE
suivi

EXAMPLE PHRASES

Elle n'arrive pas à **suivre** en maths. She can't keep up in maths.

Mon chat me **suit** partout dans la maison. My cat follows me all around the house.

Il **a suivi** un cours d'allemand pendant six mois. He did a German course for six months.

Je n'aime pas qu'il me **suive** partout comme un petit chien. I don't like him following me everywhere like a dog.

Ils nous **suivaient** à vélo. They were cycling behind us.

suivre

FUTURE		**CONDITIONAL**	
je	**suivrai**	je	**suivrais**
tu	**suivras**	tu	**suivrais**
il/elle/on	**suivra**	il/elle/on	**suivrait**
nous	**suivrons**	nous	**suivrions**
vous	**suivrez**	vous	**suivriez**
ils/elles	**suivront**	ils/elles	**suivraient**

PAST HISTORIC		**PLUPERFECT**	
je	**suivis**	j'	**avais suivi**
tu	**suivis**	tu	**avais suivi**
il/elle/on	**suivit**	il/elle/on	**avait suivi**
nous	**suivîmes**	nous	**avions suivi**
vous	**suivîtes**	vous	**aviez suivi**
ils/elles	**suivirent**	ils/elles	**avaient suivi**

IMPERATIVE

suis / suivons / suivez

EXAMPLE PHRASES

Je vous **suivrai** de loin. I'll follow you at a distance.

Elle le **suivit** dans son bureau. She followed him into his office.

Il lui dit qu'il la **suivrait** en voiture. He told her that he would follow her in his car.

Je n'**avais** pas bien **suivi** les derniers événements. I hadn't really been following the latest events.

Suivez-moi. Follow me.

se taire (to stop talking)

PRESENT		PRESENT SUBJUNCTIVE	
je	**me tais**	je	**me taise**
tu	**te tais**	tu	**te taises**
il/elle/on	**se tait**	il/elle/on	**se taise**
nous	**nous taisons**	nous	**nous taisions**
vous	**vous taisez**	vous	**vous taisiez**
ils/elles	**se taisent**	ils/elles	**se taisent**

PERFECT		IMPERFECT	
je	**me suis tu(e)**	je	**me taisais**
tu	**t'es tu(e)**	tu	**te taisais**
il/elle/on	**s'est tu(e)**	il/elle/on	**se taisait**
nous	**nous sommes tu(e)s**	nous	**nous taisions**
vous	**vous êtes tu(e)(s)**	vous	**vous taisiez**
ils/elles	**se sont tu(e)s**	ils/elles	**se taisaient**

PRESENT PARTICIPLE
se taisant

PAST PARTICIPLE
tu

EXAMPLE PHRASES

Je préfère **me taire** quand ils se disputent. I prefer to keep quiet when they argue.

Il **s'est tu**. He stopped talking.

Sophie, **tais-toi**! Be quiet, Sophie!

Taisez-vous! Be quiet!

je/j' = I **tu** = you **il** = he/it **elle** = she/it **on** = we/one **nous** = we **vous** = you **ils/elles** = they

se taire

FUTURE

je	**me tairai**
tu	**te tairas**
il/elle/on	**se taira**
nous	**nous tairons**
vous	**vous tairez**
ils/elles	**se tairont**

CONDITIONAL

je	**me tairais**
tu	**te tairais**
il/elle/on	**se tairait**
nous	**nous tairions**
vous	**vous tairiez**
ils/elles	**se tairaient**

PAST HISTORIC

je	**me tus**
tu	**te tus**
il/elle/on	**se tut**
nous	**nous tûmes**
vous	**vous tûtes**
ils/elles	**se turent**

PLUPERFECT

je	**m'étais tu(e)**
tu	**t'étais tu(e)**
il/elle/on	**s'était tu(e)**
nous	**nous étions tu(e)s**
vous	**vous étiez tu(e)(s)**
ils/elles	**s'étaient tu(e)s**

IMPERATIVE

tais-toi / taisons-nous / taisez-vous

EXAMPLE PHRASES

Je **me tairai** si tu me laisses finir ma phrase. I'll stop talking if you let me finish my sentence.

Elle **se tut**. She stopped talking.

Je me **tairais** si j'étais sûr que tu n'allais pas inventer un mensonge. I'd stop talking if I were sure that you wouldn't invent some lie.

Il **s'était tu** et tout resta silencieux pendant quelques minutes. He had stopped talking and for a few minutes all was silent.

tenir (to hold)

PRESENT

je	**tiens**
tu	**tiens**
il/elle/on	**tient**
nous	**tenons**
vous	**tenez**
ils/elles	**tiennent**

PRESENT SUBJUNCTIVE

je	**tienne**
tu	**tiennes**
il/elle/on	**tienne**
nous	**tenions**
vous	**teniez**
ils/elles	**tiennent**

PERFECT

j'	**ai tenu**
tu	**as tenu**
il/elle/on	**a tenu**
nous	**avons tenu**
vous	**avez tenu**
ils/elles	**ont tenu**

IMPERFECT

je	**tenais**
tu	**tenais**
il/elle/on	**tenait**
nous	**tenions**
vous	**teniez**
ils/elles	**tenaient**

PRESENT PARTICIPLE

tenant

PAST PARTICIPLE

tenu

EXAMPLE PHRASES

Il **tient** de son père. He takes after his father.

Tiens-moi la main. Hold my hand.

Tiens, prends mon stylo. Here, have my pen.

Tiens-toi droit! Sit up straight!

Elle **tenait** beaucoup à son chat. She was really attached to her cat.

tenir

FUTURE	
je	**tiendrai**
tu	**tiendras**
il/elle/on	**tiendra**
nous	**tiendrons**
vous	**tiendrez**
ils/elles	**tiendront**

CONDITIONAL	
je	**tiendrais**
tu	**tiendrais**
il/elle/on	**tiendrait**
nous	**tiendrions**
vous	**tiendriez**
ils/elles	**tiendraient**

PAST HISTORIC	
je	**tins**
tu	**tins**
il/elle/on	**tint**
nous	**tînmes**
vous	**tîntes**
ils/elles	**tinrent**

PLUPERFECT	
j'	**avais tenu**
tu	**avais tenu**
il/elle/on	**avait tenu**
nous	**avions tenu**
vous	**aviez tenu**
ils/elles	**avaient tenu**

IMPERATIVE

tiens / tenons / tenez

EXAMPLE PHRASES

Vous ne pourrez pas tomber car je vous **tiendrai** le bras. There's no chance of you falling as I'll be holding your arm.

Il **tint** sa promesse. He kept his promise.

Il ne me **tiendrait** pas la main s'il voyait un de ses copains. He wouldn't hold my hand if he saw one of his friends.

Elle **avait tenu** à y aller. She insisted on going.

je/j' = I **tu** = you **il** = he/it **elle** = she/it **on** = we/one **nous** = we **vous** = you **ils/elles** = they

tomber (to fall)

PRESENT

je	**tombe**
tu	**tombes**
il/elle/on	**tombe**
nous	**tombons**
vous	**tombez**
ils/elles	**tombent**

PRESENT SUBJUNCTIVE

je	**tombe**
tu	**tombes**
il/elle/on	**tombe**
nous	**tombions**
vous	**tombiez**
ils/elles	**tombent**

PERFECT

je	**suis tombé(e)**
tu	**es tombé(e)**
il/elle/on	**est tombé(e)**
nous	**sommes tombé(e)s**
vous	**êtes tombé(e)(s)**
ils/elles	**sont tombé(e)s**

IMPERFECT

je	**tombais**
tu	**tombais**
il/elle/on	**tombait**
nous	**tombions**
vous	**tombiez**
ils/elles	**tombaient**

PRESENT PARTICIPLE
tombant

PAST PARTICIPLE
tombé

EXAMPLE PHRASES

Attention, tu vas **tomber**! Be careful, you'll fall!
Ça **tombe** bien. That's lucky.
Nicole **est tombée** de son cheval. Nicole fell off her horse.
Il **tombait** de sommeil. He was asleep on his feet.
Elle s'est fait mal en **tombant** dans l'escalier. She hurt herself falling down the stairs.

tomber

FUTURE		CONDITIONAL	
je	**tomberai**	je	**tomberais**
tu	**tomberas**	tu	**tomberais**
il/elle/on	**tombera**	il/elle/on	**tomberait**
nous	**tomberons**	nous	**tomberions**
vous	**tomberez**	vous	**tomberiez**
ils/elles	**tomberont**	ils/elles	**tomberaient**

PAST HISTORIC		PLUPERFECT	
je	**tombai**	j'	**étais tombé(e)**
tu	**tombas**	tu	**étais tombé(e)**
il/elle/on	**tomba**	il/elle/on	**était tombé(e)**
nous	**tombâmes**	nous	**étions tombé(e)s**
vous	**tombâtes**	vous	**étiez tombé(e)(s)**
ils/elles	**tombèrent**	ils/elles	**étaient tombé(e)s**

IMPERATIVE
tombe / tombons / tombez

EXAMPLE PHRASES

J'espère qu'il ne **tombera** pas de son cheval. I hope he won't fall off his horse.

La tasse **tomba** par terre et se cassa. The cup fell on the floor and broke.

Tu ne **tomberais** pas si souvent si tu regardais où tu marches. You wouldn't fall so often if you watched where you were going.

Il **était** mal **tombé** et s'était cassé le bras. He'd had a bad fall and had broken his arm.

je/j' = I **tu** = you **il** = he/it **elle** = she/it **on** = we/one **nous** = we **vous** = you **ils/elles** = they

traire (to milk)

PRESENT

je	**trais**
tu	**trais**
il/elle/on	**trait**
nous	**trayons**
vous	**trayez**
ils/elles	**traient**

PRESENT SUBJUNCTIVE

je	**traie**
tu	**traies**
il/elle/on	**traie**
nous	**trayions**
vous	**trayiez**
ils/elles	**traient**

PERFECT

j'	**ai trait**
tu	**as trait**
il/elle/on	**a trait**
nous	**avons trait**
vous	**avez trait**
ils/elles	**ont trait**

IMPERFECT

je	**trayais**
tu	**trayais**
il/elle/on	**trayait**
nous	**trayions**
vous	**trayiez**
ils/elles	**trayaient**

PRESENT PARTICIPLE

trayant

PAST PARTICIPLE

trait

EXAMPLE PHRASES

À la ferme, on a appris à **traire** les vaches. We learnt to milk cows on the farm.

Elle **trait** les vaches à six heures du matin. She milks the cows at six am.

Nous **avons trait** les vaches. We milked the cows.

Il faut qu'elle **traie** les vaches de bonne heure tous les matins. She has to milk the cows early every morning.

On **trayait** les vaches avant d'aller à l'école. We milked the cows before going to school.

je/j' = I **tu** = you **il** = he/it **elle** = she/it **on** = we/one **nous** = we **vous** = you **ils/elles** = they

traire

FUTURE

je	**trairai**
tu	**trairas**
il/elle/on	**traira**
nous	**trairons**
vous	**trairez**
ils/elles	**trairont**

CONDITIONAL

je	**trairais**
tu	**trairais**
il/elle/on	**trairait**
nous	**trairions**
vous	**trairiez**
ils/elles	**trairaient**

PAST HISTORIC

not used

PLUPERFECT

j'	**avais trait**
tu	**avais trait**
il/elle/on	**avait trait**
nous	**avions trait**
vous	**aviez trait**
ils/elles	**avaient trait**

IMPERATIVE

trais / trayons / trayez

EXAMPLE PHRASES

Je **trairai** les vaches pour toi quand tu seras parti. I'll milk the cows for you when you're away.

Je **trairais** les brebis si je savais comment faire. I'd milk the ewes if I knew what to do.

Cela faisait longtemps qu'elle n'**avait** pas **trait** une vache. She hadn't milked a cow for a long time.

vaincre (to defeat)

PRESENT

je	**vaincs**
tu	**vaincs**
il/elle/on	**vainc**
nous	**vainquons**
vous	**vainquez**
ils/elles	**vainquent**

PRESENT SUBJUNCTIVE

je	**vainque**
tu	**vainques**
il/elle/on	**vainque**
nous	**vainquions**
vous	**vainquiez**
ils/elles	**vainquent**

PERFECT

j'	**ai vaincu**
tu	**as vaincu**
il/elle/on	**a vaincu**
nous	**avons vaincu**
vous	**avez vaincu**
ils/elles	**ont vaincu**

IMPERFECT

je	**vainquais**
tu	**vainquais**
il/elle/on	**vainquait**
nous	**vainquions**
vous	**vainquiez**
ils/elles	**vainquaient**

PRESENT PARTICIPLE
vainquant

PAST PARTICIPLE
vaincu

EXAMPLE PHRASES

Il a réussi à **vaincre** sa timidité. He managed to overcome his shyness.
L'armée **a été vaincue**. The army was defeated.
La France **a vaincu** la Corée trois buts à deux. France beat Korea three goals to two.

vaincre

FUTURE

je	**vaincrai**
tu	**vaincras**
il/elle/on	**vaincra**
nous	**vaincrons**
vous	**vaincrez**
ils/elles	**vaincront**

CONDITIONAL

je	**vaincrais**
tu	**vaincrais**
il/elle/on	**vaincrait**
nous	**vaincrions**
vous	**vaincriez**
ils/elles	**vaincraient**

PAST HISTORIC

je	**vainquis**
tu	**vainquis**
il/elle/on	**vainquit**
nous	**vainquîmes**
vous	**vainquîtes**
ils/elles	**vainquirent**

PLUPERFECT

j'	**avais vaincu**
tu	**avais vaincu**
il/elle/on	**avait vaincu**
nous	**avions vaincu**
vous	**aviez vaincu**
ils/elles	**avaient vaincu**

IMPERATIVE

vaincs / vainquons / vainquez

EXAMPLE PHRASES

Tu ne **vaincras** pas ta peur en restant dans ta chambre. You won't overcome your fear if you stay in your bedroom.

Ils **vainquirent** l'armée ennemie après une bataille acharnée. They defeated the enemy army after a fierce battle.

Elle **avait** déjà **vaincu** cette adversaire. She'd already beaten this opponent.

je/j' = I **tu** = you **il** = he/it **elle** = she/it **on** = we/one **nous** = we **vous** = you **ils/elles** = they

valoir (to be worth)

PRESENT

je	**vaux**
tu	**vaux**
il/elle/on	**vaut**
nous	**valons**
vous	**valez**
ils/elles	**valent**

PRESENT SUBJUNCTIVE

je	**vaille**
tu	**vailles**
il/elle/on	**vaille**
nous	**valions**
vous	**valiez**
ils/elles	**vaillent**

PERFECT

j'	**ai valu**
tu	**as valu**
il/elle/on	**a valu**
nous	**avons valu**
vous	**avez valu**
ils/elles	**ont valu**

IMPERFECT

je	**valais**
tu	**valais**
il/elle/on	**valait**
nous	**valions**
vous	**valiez**
ils/elles	**valaient**

PRESENT PARTICIPLE

valant

PAST PARTICIPLE

valu

EXAMPLE PHRASES

Ça **vaut** combien? How much is it worth?

Ça ne **vaut** pas la peine de s'inquiéter. It's not worth worrying about.

Cette voiture **vaut** très cher. That car's worth a lot of money.

Il **valait** mieux ne pas y penser. It was best not to think about it.

valoir

FUTURE		CONDITIONAL	
je	**vaudrai**	je	**vaudrais**
tu	**vaudras**	tu	**vaudrais**
il/elle/on	**vaudra**	il/elle/on	**vaudrait**
nous	**vaudrons**	nous	**vaudrions**
vous	**vaudrez**	vous	**vaudriez**
ils/elles	**vaudront**	ils/elles	**vaudraient**

PAST HISTORIC		PLUPERFECT	
je	**valus**	j'	**avais valu**
tu	**valus**	tu	**avais valu**
il/elle/on	**valut**	il/elle/on	**avait valu**
nous	**valûmes**	nous	**avions valu**
vous	**valûtes**	vous	**aviez valu**
ils/elles	**valurent**	ils/elles	**avaient valu**

IMPERATIVE

vaux / valons / valez

EXAMPLE PHRASES

Ça **vaudra** sûrement la peine d'y aller. It will certainly be worth going.

Ça **vaudrait** la peine d'essayer. It would be worth a try.

Il **vaudrait** mieux que tu demandes la permission. You'd be best to ask for permission.

Son comportement lui **avait valu** une punition. His behaviour had earned him a punishment.

vendre (to sell)

PRESENT

je	**vends**
tu	**vends**
il/elle/on	**vend**
nous	**vendons**
vous	**vendez**
ils/elles	**vendent**

PRESENT SUBJUNCTIVE

je	**vende**
tu	**vendes**
il/elle/on	**vende**
nous	**vendions**
vous	**vendiez**
ils/elles	**vendent**

PERFECT

j'	**ai vendu**
tu	**as vendu**
il/elle/on	**a vendu**
nous	**avons vendu**
vous	**avez vendu**
ils/elles	**ont vendu**

IMPERFECT

je	**vendais**
tu	**vendais**
il/elle/on	**vendait**
nous	**vendions**
vous	**vendiez**
ils/elles	**vendaient**

PRESENT PARTICIPLE
vendant

PAST PARTICIPLE
vendu

EXAMPLE PHRASES

Elle voudrait **vendre** sa voiture. She would like to sell her car.

Est-ce que vous **vendez** des cartes SIM? Do you sell SIM cards?

Il m'**a vendu** son vélo pour cinquante euros. He sold me his bike for fifty euros.

Il **vendait** des glaces sur la plage. He sold ice creams on the beach.

je/j' = I **tu** = you **il** = he/it **elle** = she/it **on** = we/one **nous** = we **vous** = you **ils/elles** = they

vendre

FUTURE

je	**vendrai**
tu	**vendras**
il/elle/on	**vendra**
nous	**vendrons**
vous	**vendrez**
ils/elles	**vendront**

CONDITIONAL

je	**vendrais**
tu	**vendrais**
il/elle/on	**vendrait**
nous	**vendrions**
vous	**vendriez**
ils/elles	**vendraient**

PAST HISTORIC

je	**vendis**
tu	**vendis**
il/elle/on	**vendit**
nous	**vendîmes**
vous	**vendîtes**
ils/elles	**vendirent**

PLUPERFECT

j'	**avais vendu**
tu	**avais vendu**
il/elle/on	**avait vendu**
nous	**avions vendu**
vous	**aviez vendu**
ils/elles	**avaient vendu**

IMPERATIVE

vends / vendons / vendez

EXAMPLE PHRASES

Tu ne **vendras** rien à ce prix-là. You'll never sell anything at that price.

Elle **vendit** son appartement et partit vivre en Provence. She sold her flat and went to live in Provence.

Je ne **vendrais** pas ce piano pour rien au monde. I wouldn't sell this piano for anything in the world.

Il **avait** déjà **vendu** sa maison. He'd already sold his house.

venir (to come)

PRESENT		PRESENT SUBJUNCTIVE	
je	**viens**	je	**vienne**
tu	**viens**	tu	**viennes**
il/elle/on	**vient**	il/elle/on	**vienne**
nous	**venons**	nous	**venions**
vous	**venez**	vous	**veniez**
ils/elles	**viennent**	ils/elles	**viennent**

PERFECT		IMPERFECT	
je	**suis venu(e)**	je	**venais**
tu	**es venu(e)**	tu	**venais**
il/elle/on	**est venu(e)**	il/elle/on	**venait**
nous	**sommes venu(e)s**	nous	**venions**
vous	**êtes venu(e)(s)**	vous	**veniez**
ils/elles	**sont venu(e)s**	ils/elles	**venaient**

PRESENT PARTICIPLE
venant

PAST PARTICIPLE
venu

EXAMPLE PHRASES

Fatou et Malik **viennent** du Sénégal. Fatou and Malik come from Senegal.

Ils **sont venus** la voir ce matin. They came to see her this morning.

Viens avec moi! Come with me!

Elle aimerait que tu **viennes** à son mariage. She'd like you to come to her wedding.

Je **venais** de finir mes devoirs quand ils sont arrivés. I'd just finished my homework when they arrived.

venir

FUTURE		CONDITIONAL	
je	**viendrai**	je	**viendrais**
tu	**viendras**	tu	**viendrais**
il/elle/on	**viendra**	il/elle/on	**viendrait**
nous	**viendrons**	nous	**viendrions**
vous	**viendrez**	vous	**viendriez**
ils/elles	**viendront**	ils/elles	**viendraient**

PAST HISTORIC		PLUPERFECT	
je	**vins**	j'	**étais venu(e)**
tu	**vins**	tu	**étais venu(e)**
il/elle/on	**vint**	il/elle/on	**était venu(e)**
nous	**vînmes**	nous	**étions venu(e)s**
vous	**vîntes**	vous	**étiez venu(e)(s)**
ils/elles	**vinrent**	ils/elles	**étaient venu(e)s**

IMPERATIVE

viens / venons / venez

EXAMPLE PHRASES

Elle ne **viendra** pas cette année. She won't be coming this year.

Il **vint** nous voir après la messe. He came to see us after mass.

Elle **viendrait** avec nous si elle n'avait pas tant de travail. She'd come with us if she didn't have so much work.

Ils **étaient venus** nous annoncer leur fiançailles. They had come to tell us that they had got engaged.

vêtir (to dress)

PRESENT

je	**vêts**
tu	**vêts**
il/elle/on	**vêt**
nous	**vêtons**
vous	**vêtez**
ils/elles	**vêtent**

PRESENT SUBJUNCTIVE

je	**vête**
tu	**vêtes**
il/elle/on	**vête**
nous	**vêtions**
vous	**vêtiez**
ils/elles	**vêtent**

PERFECT

j'	**ai vêtu**
tu	**as vêtu**
il/elle/on	**a vêtu**
nous	**avons vêtu**
vous	**avez vêtu**
ils/elles	**ont vêtu**

IMPERFECT

je	**vêtais**
tu	**vêtais**
il/elle/on	**vêtait**
nous	**vêtions**
vous	**vêtiez**
ils/elles	**vêtaient**

PRESENT PARTICIPLE
vêtant

PAST PARTICIPLE
vêtu

EXAMPLE PHRASES

Il faut se lever, se laver et se **vêtir** en dix minutes. You have to get up, get washed and get dressed in ten minutes.

Vous n'**êtes** pas **vêtus** assez chaudement pour aller jouer dehors. You're not dressed warmly enough to go and play outside.

Tu **es** bizarrement **vêtu** aujourd'hui! You are strangely dressed today!

Nous vîmes une mariée tout de blanc **vêtue**. We saw a bride dressed all in white.

vêtir

FUTURE

je	**vêtirai**
tu	**vêtiras**
il/elle/on	**vêtira**
nous	**vêtirons**
vous	**vêtirez**
ils/elles	**vêtiront**

CONDITIONAL

je	**vêtirais**
tu	**vêtirais**
il/elle/on	**vêtirait**
nous	**vêtirions**
vous	**vêtiriez**
ils/elles	**vêtiraient**

PAST HISTORIC

je	**vêtis**
tu	**vêtis**
il/elle/on	**vêtit**
nous	**vêtîmes**
vous	**vêtîtes**
ils/elles	**vêtirent**

PLUPERFECT

j'	**avais vêtu**
tu	**avais vêtu**
il/elle/on	**avait vêtu**
nous	**avions vêtu**
vous	**aviez vêtu**
ils/elles	**avaient vêtu**

IMPERATIVE

vêts / vêtons / vêtez

EXAMPLE PHRASES

Il se **vêtira** tout seul. He'll get dressed himself.

Ses parents la **vêtirent** de rose pour la fête. Her parents dressed her in pink for the party.

Il s'**était vêtu** tout seul. He had got dressed himself.

vivre (to live)

PRESENT		PRESENT SUBJUNCTIVE	
je	**vis**	je	**vive**
tu	**vis**	tu	**vives**
il/elle/on	**vit**	il/elle/on	**vive**
nous	**vivons**	nous	**vivions**
vous	**vivez**	vous	**viviez**
ils/elles	**vivent**	ils/elles	**vivent**

PERFECT		IMPERFECT	
j'	**ai vécu**	je	**vivais**
tu	**as vécu**	tu	**vivais**
il/elle/on	**a vécu**	il/elle/on	**vivait**
nous	**avons vécu**	nous	**vivions**
vous	**avez vécu**	vous	**viviez**
ils/elles	**ont vécu**	ils/elles	**vivaient**

PRESENT PARTICIPLE
vivant

PAST PARTICIPLE
vécu

EXAMPLE PHRASES

Et ton grand-père? Il **vit** encore? What about your grandfather? Is he still alive?

Les gorilles **vivent** surtout dans la forêt. Gorillas mostly live in the forest.

Il **a vécu** dix ans à Lyon. He lived in Lyons for ten years.

Cela ne faisait pas longtemps qu'ils **vivaient** ensemble. They hadn't lived together for long.

vivre

FUTURE	
je	**vivrai**
tu	**vivras**
il/elle/on	**vivra**
nous	**vivrons**
vous	**vivrez**
ils/elles	**vivront**

CONDITIONAL	
je	**vivrais**
tu	**vivrais**
il/elle/on	**vivrait**
nous	**vivrions**
vous	**vivriez**
ils/elles	**vivraient**

PAST HISTORIC	
je	**vécus**
tu	**vécus**
il/elle/on	**vécut**
nous	**vécûmes**
vous	**vécûtes**
ils/elles	**vécurent**

PLUPERFECT	
j'	**avais vécu**
tu	**avais vécu**
il/elle/on	**avait vécu**
nous	**avions vécu**
vous	**aviez vécu**
ils/elles	**avaient vécu**

IMPERATIVE

vis / vivons / vivez

EXAMPLE PHRASES

Vivras-tu avec ta sœur quand tu feras tes études à Paris? Will you live with your sister when you're studying in Paris?

Elle **vécut** d'abord en Espagne, puis en Italie. She lived in Spain first and then in Italy.

S'ils n'avaient pas d'enfants, ils ne **vivraient** plus ensemble depuis longtemps. If they didn't have children they would have stopped living together long ago.

Ils n'**avaient** jamais **vécu** à la campagne. They'd never lived in the countryside.

voir (to see)

PRESENT

je	**vois**
tu	**vois**
il/elle/on	**voit**
nous	**voyons**
vous	**voyez**
ils/elles	**voient**

PRESENT SUBJUNCTIVE

je	**voie**
tu	**voies**
il/elle/on	**voie**
nous	**voyions**
vous	**voyiez**
ils/elles	**voient**

PERFECT

j'	**ai vu**
tu	**as vu**
il/elle/on	**a vu**
nous	**avons vu**
vous	**avez vu**
ils/elles	**ont vu**

IMPERFECT

je	**voyais**
tu	**voyais**
il/elle/on	**voyait**
nous	**voyions**
vous	**voyiez**
ils/elles	**voyaient**

PRESENT PARTICIPLE
voyant

PAST PARTICIPLE
vu

EXAMPLE PHRASES

Venez me **voir** quand vous serez à Paris. Come and see me when you're in Paris.

Est-ce que cette tache se **voit**? Does that stain show?

Est-ce que tu l'**as vu**? Have you seen him?

Il ne **voyait** rien sans ses lunettes. He couldn't see anything without his glasses.

voir

FUTURE

je	**verrai**
tu	**verras**
il/elle/on	**verra**
nous	**verrons**
vous	**verrez**
ils/elles	**verront**

CONDITIONAL

je	**verrais**
tu	**verrais**
il/elle/on	**verrait**
nous	**verrions**
vous	**verriez**
ils/elles	**verraient**

PAST HISTORIC

je	**vis**
tu	**vis**
il/elle/on	**vit**
nous	**vîmes**
vous	**vîtes**
ils/elles	**virent**

PLUPERFECT

j'	**avais vu**
tu	**avais vu**
il/elle/on	**avait vu**
nous	**avions vu**
vous	**aviez vu**
ils/elles	**avaient vu**

IMPERATIVE

vois / voyons / voyez

EXAMPLE PHRASES

Tu **verras** que je ne t'ai pas menti. You'll see that I didn't lie to you.

Il la **vit** arriver de loin. He saw her arrive from a long way off.

Il savait qu'il ne la **verrait** pas avant le lendemain. He knew that he wouldn't see her until the next day.

Ils ne l'**avaient** pas **vue** depuis son accident. They hadn't seen her since her accident.

vouloir (to want)

PRESENT

je	**veux**
tu	**veux**
il/elle/on	**veut**
nous	**voulons**
vous	**voulez**
ils/elles	**veulent**

PRESENT SUBJUNCTIVE

je	**veuille**
tu	**veuilles**
il/elle/on	**veuille**
nous	**voulions**
vous	**vouliez**
ils/elles	**veuillent**

PERFECT

j'	**ai voulu**
tu	**as voulu**
il/elle/on	**a voulu**
nous	**avons voulu**
vous	**avez voulu**
ils/elles	**ont voulu**

IMPERFECT

je	**voulais**
tu	**voulais**
il/elle/on	**voulait**
nous	**voulions**
vous	**vouliez**
ils/elles	**voulaient**

PRESENT PARTICIPLE
voulant

PAST PARTICIPLE
voulu

EXAMPLE PHRASES

Elle **veut** une tablette pour Noël. She wants a tablet for Christmas.
Veux-tu que je t'aide? Do you want me to help you?
Il n'**a** pas **voulu** te déranger. He didn't want to disturb you.
Ils **voulaient** aller au cinéma. They wanted to go to the cinema.

vouloir

FUTURE

je	**voudrai**
tu	**voudras**
il/elle/on	**voudra**
nous	**voudrons**
vous	**voudrez**
ils/elles	**voudront**

CONDITIONAL

je	**voudrais**
tu	**voudrais**
il/elle/on	**voudrait**
nous	**voudrions**
vous	**voudriez**
ils/elles	**voudraient**

PAST HISTORIC

je	**voulus**
tu	**voulus**
il/elle/on	**voulut**
nous	**voulûmes**
vous	**voulûtes**
ils/elles	**voulurent**

PLUPERFECT

j'	**avais voulu**
tu	**avais voulu**
il/elle/on	**avait voulu**
nous	**avions voulu**
vous	**aviez voulu**
ils/elles	**avaient voulu**

IMPERATIVE

veuille / veuillons / veuillez

EXAMPLE PHRASES

Ils ne **voudront** pas partir trop tard. They won't want to leave too late.

Elle ne **voulut** pas les inquiéter. She didn't want to worry them.

Tu **voudrais** une tasse de thé? Would you like a cup of tea?

Il n'**avait** pas **voulu** partir sans lui dire au revoir. He hadn't wanted to leave without saying goodbye to her.

se vouvoyer (to address each other as "vous")

PRESENT

on	**se vouvoie**
nous	**nous vouvoyons**
vous	**vous vouvoyez**
ils/elles	**se vouvoient**

PRESENT SUBJUNCTIVE

on	**se vouvoie**
nous	**nous vouvoyions**
vous	**vous vouvoyiez**
ils/elles	**se vouvoient**

PERFECT

on	**s'est vouvoyé**
nous	**nous sommes vouvoyé(e)s**
vous	**vous êtes vouvoyé(e)s**
ils/elles	**se sont vouvoyé(e)s**

IMPERFECT

on	**se vouvoyait**
nous	**nous vouvoyions**
vous	**vous vouvoyiez**
ils/elles	**se vouvoyaient**

PRESENT PARTICIPLE
se vouvoyant

PAST PARTICIPLE
vouvoyé

EXAMPLE PHRASES

Avec Hélène, on **se vouvoie** encore. Hélène and I are still addressing each other as "vous".

Vous **vous êtes** toujours **vouvoyés** avec Michel? Have you and Michel always addressed each other as "vous"?

Je préférerais qu'on **se vouvoie**. I'd rather we addressed each other as "vous".

Ils ne **se vouvoyaient** plus. They weren't addressing each other as "vous" any more.

se vouvoyer

FUTURE

on	**se vouvoiera**
nous	**nous vouvoierons**
vous	**vous vouvoierez**
ils/elles	**se vouvoieront**

CONDITIONAL

on	**se vouvoierait**
nous	**nous vouvoierions**
vous	**vous vouvoieriez**
ils/elles	**se vouvoieraient**

PAST HISTORIC

on	**se vouvoya**
nous	**nous vouvoyâmes**
vous	**vous vouvoyâtes**
ils/elles	**se vouvoyèrent**

PLUPERFECT

on	**s'était vouvoyé**
nous	**nous étions vouvoyé(e)s**
vous	**vous étiez vouvoyé(e)s**
ils/elles	**s'étaient vouvoyé(e)s**

IMPERATIVE

not used

EXAMPLE PHRASES

Je te parie qu'ils **se vouvoieront**. I bet they'll address each other as "vous".

Ils **se vouvoyèrent** les premiers jours. They addressed each other as "vous" for the first few days.

On **se vouvoierait** encore si je n'avais rien dit. We'd still be addressing each other as "vous" if I hadn't said anything.

Nous **nous étions vouvoyés** au début. We'd addressed each other as "vous" at the beginning.

Verb Index

How to use the Verb Index

The verbs in bold are the model verbs which you will find in the verb tables. All the other verbs follow one of these patterns, so the number next to each verb indicates which pattern fits this particular verb. For example, **aider** (*to help*) follows the same pattern as **donner** (number 274 in the verb tables). All the verbs are in alphabetical order. For reflexive verbs like **s'asseoir** (*to sit down*) or **se taire** (*to stop talking*), look under **asseoir** or **taire**, not under **s'** or **se**.

Superior numbers ([1], [2] etc) refer you to notes on page 446. These notes explain any differences between the verbs and their model.

With the exception of reflexive verbs which *always* take **être**, all verbs have the same auxiliary (**être** or **avoir**) as their model verb. There are a few exceptions which are indicated by a superior number [1] or [2]. An asterisk (*) means that the verb takes **avoir** when it is used with a direct object, and **être** when it isn't. For more information on verbs that take either **avoir** or **être**, see pages 113–116.

Notes

1 Auxiliary = **avoir**.

2 Auxiliary = **être**.

3 Only infinitive and 3rd persons of each tense used.

4 Past participle: **absous, absoute**.

5 Conjugated with either **avoir** or **être**.

6 No circumflex on: **j'accrois, tu accrois**, and **accru**.

7 Hardly used except in the infinitive and the 3rd persons of the present, future and conditional.

8 Past participle: **circoncis**.

9 Past participle: **confit**.

10 No circumflex on: **je décrois, tu décrois**, and **décru**.

11 When **demeurer** means *to live*, the auxiliary is **avoir**; when it means *to remain*, the auxiliary is **être**.

12 Past participle: **dissous, dissoute**.

13 Present participle: **faillissant**; past participle: **failli**; future: **je faillirai**, *etc*; conditional: **je faillirais**, *etc*. NB: **J'ai failli tomber** = I nearly fell.

14 When **fleurir** means *to prosper*, the present participle is **florissant**, and the imperfect is **florissait**.

15 Past participle: **frit**; used mainly in the present tense singular and in compound tenses.

16 Past participle: **inclus**.

17 Past participle: **mû, mue, mus, mues**.

18 Past participle: **nui**.

19 In questions, **je peux** can be replaced by **je puis**: **Puis-je vous aider?** May I help you?

20 Subjunctive: **je prévale**, *etc*.

21 Future: **je prévoirai**, *etc*; conditional: **je prévoirais**, *etc*.

22 Used only in the infinitive, present and past participles, and compound tenses.

23 Past participle: **relui**.

24 No past participle, no compound tenses.

25 Imperative 2nd person plural: **contredire – contredisez; dédire – dédisez; médire – médisez; prédire – prédisez**

Vocabulary

contents

how to use this section

This vocabulary section is divided into 50 topics, arranged in alphabetical order. This thematic approach enables you to learn related words and phrases together, so that you can become confident in using particular vocabulary in context.

Vocabulary within each topic is divided into nouns and useful phrases which are aimed at helping you to express yourself in idiomatic French. Vocabulary within each topic is graded to help you prioritize your learning. Essential words include the basic words you will need to be able to communicate effectively, important words help expand your knowledge, and useful words provide additional vocabulary which will enable you to express yourself more fully.

Nouns are grouped by gender: masculine ("le") nouns are given on the left-hand page, and feminine ("la") nouns on the right-hand page, enabling you to memorize words according to their gender. In addition, all feminine forms of adjectives are shown, as are irregular plurals and plurals of compound nouns.

At the end of the section you will find a list of supplementary vocabulary, grouped according to part of speech – adjective, verb, noun and so on. This is vocabulary which you will come across in many everyday situations.

Finally, there is an English index which lists all the essential and important nouns given under the topic headings for quick reference.

ABBREVIATIONS

adj	adjective
adv	adverb
conj	conjunction
f	feminine
inv	invariable
m	masculine
m+f	masculine and feminine form
n	noun
pl	plural
prep	preposition
qch	quelque chose
qn	quelqu'un
sb	somebody
sth	something
subj	subjunctive

The swung dash ~ is used to indicate the basic elements of the compound and appropriate endings are then added.

PHONETICS

i	as in	vie, lit
e	as in	blé, jouer
ɛ	as in	merci, très
a	as in	patte, plat
ɑ	as in	bas, gras
ɔ	as in	mort, donner
o	as in	mot, gauche
u	as in	genou, roue
y	as in	rue, tu
ø	as in	peu, deux
œ	as in	peur, meuble
ə	as in	le, premier
ɛ̃	as in	matin, plein
ɑ̃	as in	sans, vent
ɔ̃	as in	bon, ombre
œ̃	as in	brun, lundi
j	as in	yeux, pied
ɥ	as in	lui, huile
ɲ	as in	agneau, vigne
ŋ	as in	English **-ing**
ʃ	as in	chat, tache
ʒ	as in	je, gens
ʀ	as in	rue, venir

A colon : precedes words beginning with an aspirate **h** (**le :hibou** as opposed to **l'hippopotame**).

ESSENTIAL WORDS *(masculine)*

un **aéroport**	airport
un **aller-retour**	return ticket
un **aller simple**	single ticket
un **avion**	plane
les **bagages**	luggage
les **bagages à main**	hand luggage
le **billet (d'avion)**	(plane) ticket
le **départ**	departure
le **douanier**	customs officer
le **duty-free**	duty-free (shop)
l'**horaire**	timetable
le **numéro**	number
le **passager**	passenger
le **passeport**	passport
le **prix du billet**	fare
les **renseignements**	information
le **retard**	delay
le **sac**	bag
le **taxi**	taxi
le **touriste**	tourist
le **vol**	flight
le **voyage**	trip
le **voyageur**	traveller

USEFUL PHRASES

voyager par avion to travel by plane
retenir une place d'avion to book a plane ticket
enregistrer ses bagages to check in one's luggage
l'enregistrement en ligne online check-in
j'ai manqué la correspondance I missed my connection
l'avion a décollé/a atterri the plane has taken off/has landed
le tableau des arrivées/des départs the arrivals/departures board
le vol numéro 776 en provenance de Nice/à destination de Nice flight number 776 from Nice/to Nice

ESSENTIAL WORDS *(feminine)*

une	**agence de voyages**	travel agent's
une	**annulation**	cancellation
une	**arrivée**	arrival
la	**carte d'identité**	ID card
la	**carte d'embarquement**	boarding card
la	**correspondance**	connection
la	**douane**	customs
une	**entrée**	entrance
une	**hôtesse de l'air**	flight attendant
la	**location de voitures**	car hire
la	**passagère**	passenger
la	**porte d'embarquement**	departure gate
la	**réduction**	reduction
la	**réservation**	reservation
la	**sortie**	exit
la	**sortie de secours**	emergency exit
les	**toilettes**	toilets
la	**touriste**	tourist
la	**valise**	suitcase

USEFUL PHRASES

récupérer ses bagages to collect one's luggage
"livraison des bagages" "baggage reclaim"
passer la douane to go through customs
j'ai quelque chose à déclarer I have something to declare
je n'ai rien à déclarer I have nothing to declare
fouiller les bagages to search the luggage
voyager en classe affaires/économique to travel business/ economy class

IMPORTANT WORDS *(masculine)*

un	**accident d'avion**	plane crash
le	**billet électronique**	e-ticket
le	**chariot**	trolley
un	**escalier roulant**	escalator
un	**hélicoptère**	helicopter
le	**mal de l'air**	airsickness
le	**pilote**	pilot
le	**plan**	map

USEFUL WORDS *(masculine)*

un	**aiguilleur du ciel**	air-traffic controller
un	**atterrissage**	landing
un	**avion à réaction**	jet plane
un	**avion gros porteur**	jumbo jet
le	**contrôle de sécurité**	security check
le	**décollage**	take-off
les	**droits de douane**	customs duty
	l'**embarquement**	boarding
un	**équipage**	crew
un	**espace bébés**	mother and baby room
le	**:hublot**	window
le	**mur du son**	sound barrier
le	**parachute**	parachute
le	**portique de détection**	metal detector
le	**réacteur**	jet engine
le	**siège**	seat
le	**steward**	flight attendant
le	**tapis roulant**	moving walkway; luggage carousel
le	**trou d'air**	air pocket

USEFUL PHRASES

à bord on board
horaire prévu d'arrivée/de départ estimated time of arrival/departure
"attachez vos ceintures" "fasten your seat belts"
nous survolons Londres we are flying over London
j'ai le mal de l'air I am feeling airsick
détourner un avion to hijack a plane

IMPORTANT WORDS *(feminine)*

la **ceinture de sécurité**	seat belt
la **destination**	destination
la **durée**	length, duration
une **horloge**	clock
la **salle d'embarquement**	departure lounge
la **vitesse**	speed

USEFUL WORDS *(feminine)*

une **aérogare**	terminal
une **aile**	wing
l'**altitude**	altitude
la **boîte noire**	black box
la **boutique hors taxes**	duty-free shop
les **commandes**	controls
une **escale**	stop-over
une **étiquette**	label
la **:hauteur**	height
une **hélice**	propeller
la **compagnie aérienne**	airline
la **piste**	runway
la **soute**	baggage hold
la **tour de contrôle**	control tower
la **turbulence**	turbulence

USEFUL PHRASES

"vol AB251 pour Paris : embarquement immédiat, porte 51"
"flight AB251 to Paris now boarding at gate 51"

nous avons fait escale à New York we stopped over in New York

un atterrissage forcé an emergency landing

un atterrissage en catastrophe a crash landing

des cigarettes hors taxes duty-free cigarettes

ESSENTIAL WORDS *(masculine)*

un **agneau**	lamb
un **animal** (*pl* animaux)	animal
le **bœuf** [bœf] (*pl* ~s [bø])	ox
le **chat**	cat
le **chaton**	kitten
le **cheval** (*pl* chevaux)	horse
le **chien**	dog
le **chiot**	puppy
le **cochon**	pig
un **éléphant**	elephant
le **:hamster**	hamster
le **jardin zoologique**	zoo
le **lapin**	rabbit
le **lion**	lion
le **mouton**	sheep
un **oiseau** (*pl* -x)	bird
le **poisson**	fish
le **poulain**	foal
le **tigre**	tiger
le **veau**	calf
le **zoo**	zoo

USEFUL PHRASES

j'aime les chats, je déteste les serpents, je préfère les souris
I like cats, I hate snakes, I prefer mice
nous avons 12 animaux chez nous we have 12 pets (in our house)
nous n'avons pas d'animaux chez nous we have no pets (in our house)
les animaux sauvages wild animals
les animaux domestiques pets; livestock
mettre un animal en cage to put an animal in a cage
libérer un animal to set an animal free

ESSENTIAL WORDS *(feminine)*

la **chatte**	cat *(female)*
la **chienne**	dog *(female)*
la **souris**	mouse
la **tortue**	tortoise
la **vache**	cow

IMPORTANT WORDS *(feminine)*

la **cage**	cage
la **queue** [kø]	tail

USEFUL PHRASES

le chien aboie the dog barks; **il grogne** it growls
le chat miaule the cat miaows; **il ronronne** it purrs
j'aime faire du cheval *or* **monter à cheval** I like horse-riding
à cheval on horseback
"attention, chien méchant" "beware of the dog"
"chiens interdits" "no dogs allowed"
"couché!" *(to dog)* "down!"
les droits des animaux animal rights

USEFUL WORDS *(masculine)*

un	**âne**	donkey
le	**bouc**	billy goat
le	**cerf** [sɛʀ]	stag
le	**chameau** (*pl* -x)	camel
le	**cochon d'Inde**	guinea-pig
le	**crapaud**	toad
le	**crocodile**	crocodile
un	**écureuil**	squirrel
le	**:hérisson**	hedgehog
un	**hippopotame**	hippopotamus
le	**kangourou**	kangaroo
le	**lièvre**	hare
le	**loup**	wolf
le	**mulet**	mule
le	**museau** (*pl* -x)	snout
un	**ours** [uʀs]	bear
un	**ours blanc**	polar bear
le	**phoque**	seal
le	**piège**	trap
le	**poil**	coat, hair
le	**poney**	pony
le	**porc** [pɔʀ]	pig
le	**renard**	fox
le	**requin**	shark
le	**rhinocéros**	rhinoceros
le	**sabot**	hoof
le	**serpent**	snake
le	**singe**	monkey
le	**taureau** (*pl* -x)	bull
le	**zèbre**	zebra

USEFUL WORDS *(feminine)*

une **animalerie**	pet shop
la **baleine**	whale
la **bosse**	hump (*of camel*)
la **carapace**	shell (*of tortoise*)
la **chauve-souris** (*pl* ~s~)	bat
la **chèvre**	goat
la **corne**	horn
la **couleuvre**	grass snake
la **crinière**	mane
la **défense**	tusk
la **dinde**	turkey
la **fourrure**	fur
la **girafe**	giraffe
la **grenouille**	frog
la **griffe**	claw
la **gueule**	mouth (*of dog, cat, lion etc*)
la **jument**	mare
la **lionne**	lioness
la **mule**	mule
la **patte**	paw
la **poche**	pouch (*of kangaroo*)
les **rayures**	stripes (*of zebra*)
la **taupe**	mole
la **tigresse**	tigress
la **trompe**	trunk (*of elephant*)

bikes

ESSENTIAL WORDS *(masculine)*

le **casque**	helmet
le **cyclisme**	cycling
le **cycliste**	cyclist
le **frein**	brake
le **pneu**	tyre
le **Tour de France**	Tour de France cycle race
le **vélo**	bike
le **vélo tout terrain**	mountain bike
le **VTT**	mountain bike

USEFUL WORDS *(masculine)*

un **antivol**	padlock
le **catadioptre**	reflector
le **dérailleur**	derailleur
le **garde-boue** *(pl inv)*	mudguard
le **guidon**	handlebars
le **moyeu** (*pl* -x)	hub
le **pare-boue** *(pl inv)*	mudguard
le **phare**	front light
le **porte-bagages** *(pl inv)*	carrier
le **rayon**	spoke
le **réflecteur**	reflector
le **sommet**	top (*of hill*)

USEFUL PHRASES

aller à bicyclette, aller en vélo to go by bike
je suis venu(e) en vélo I came by bike
faire du cyclisme, faire du vélo to cycle
rouler to travel
à toute vitesse at full speed
changer de vitesse to change gears
s'arrêter to stop
freiner brusquement to brake sharply

ESSENTIAL WORDS *(feminine)*

la **bicyclette**	bicycle
la **lampe**	lamp

IMPORTANT WORDS *(feminine)*

la **crevaison**	puncture
la **roue**	wheel
la **vitesse**	speed; gear

USEFUL WORDS *(feminine)*

la **barre**	crossbar
la **chaîne**	chain
la **côte**	slope
la **descente**	descent
la **dynamo**	dynamo
la **montée**	climb
la **pédale**	pedal
la **pente**	slope
la **piste cyclable**	cycle path
la **pompe**	pump
la **sacoche**	saddlebag
la **selle**	saddle
la **sonnette**	bell
la **trousse pour crevaisons**	puncture repair kit
la **valve**	valve

USEFUL PHRASES

faire une promenade à *or* **en vélo** to go for a bike ride
avoir un pneu crevé to have a flat tyre
réparer un pneu crevé to mend a puncture
la roue avant/arrière the front/back wheel
gonfler les pneus to blow up the tyres
brillant(e), reluisant(e) shiny
rouillé(e) rusty
fluorescent(e) fluorescent

birds

ESSENTIAL WORDS *(masculine)*

le **canard**	duck
le **ciel**	sky
le **coq**	cock
le **dindon**	turkey
un **oiseau** (*pl* -x)	bird
le **perroquet**	parrot

USEFUL WORDS *(masculine)*

un **aigle**	eagle
le **bec**	beak
le **choucas**	jackdaw
le **coq de bruyère**	grouse
le **corbeau** (*pl* -x)	raven
le **coucou**	cuckoo
le **cygne** [siɲ]	swan
un **étourneau** (*pl* -x)	starling
le **faisan**	pheasant
le **faucon**	falcon
le **:hibou** (*pl* -x)	owl
le **martin-pêcheur** (*pl* ~s~s)	kingfisher
le **merle**	blackbird
le **moineau** (*pl* -x)	sparrow
le **nid**	nest
un **œuf**	egg
le **paon** [pɑ̃]	peacock
le **pic**	woodpecker
le **pigeon**	pigeon
le **pingouin**	penguin
le **rapace**	bird of prey
le **roitelet**	wren
le **rossignol**	nightingale
le **rouge-gorge** (*pl* ~s~s)	robin
le **serin**	canary
le **vautour**	vulture

ESSENTIAL WORDS *(feminine)*

une	**oie**	goose
la	**perruche**	budgie
la	**poule**	hen

USEFUL WORDS *(feminine)*

une	**aile**	wing
une	**alouette**	lark
une	**autruche**	ostrich
la	**cage**	cage
la	**caille**	quail
la	**cigogne**	stork
la	**colombe**	dove
la	**corneille**	crow
la	**grive**	thrush
une	**hirondelle**	swallow
la	**mésange bleue**	bluetit
la	**mouette**	seagull
la	**perdrix** [pɛʀdʀi]	partridge
la	**pie**	magpie
la	**plume**	feather

USEFUL PHRASES

voler to fly
s'envoler to fly away
faire son nid to build a nest
siffler to whistle
chanter to sing
mettre un oiseau en cage to put a bird in a cage
pondre un œuf to lay an egg
un oiseau migrateur a migratory bird

ESSENTIAL WORDS *(masculine)*

le	**bras**	arm
les	**cheveux**	hair
le	**cœur**	heart
le	**corps** [kɔʀ]	body
le	**doigt**	finger
le	**dos**	back
	l'**estomac** [ɛstɔma]	stomach
le	**genou** (*pl* -x)	knee
le	**nez**	nose
un	**œil** (*pl* yeux)	eye
le	**pied**	foot
le	**ventre**	stomach
le	**visage**	face
les	**yeux**	eyes

IMPORTANT WORDS *(masculine)*

le	**cou**	neck
le	**front**	forehead
le	**menton**	chin
le	**pouce**	thumb
le	**sang**	blood
le	**sourcil** [suʀsi]	eyebrow

USEFUL PHRASES

debout standing
assis(e) sitting
couché(e) lying
je vais me faire couper les cheveux I am going to have my hair cut

ESSENTIAL WORDS *(feminine)*

la	**bouche**	mouth
la	**dent**	tooth
la	**gorge**	throat
la	**jambe**	leg
la	**main**	hand
une	**oreille**	ear
la	**tête**	head

IMPORTANT WORDS *(feminine)*

la	**cheville**	ankle
une	**épaule**	shoulder
la	**figure**	face
la	**joue**	cheek
la	**langue**	tongue
la	**peau**	skin
la	**poitrine**	chest, bust
la	**voix**	voice

USEFUL PHRASES

grand(e) tall, big
petit(e) small, short
gros(se) fat
maigre skinny
mince slim
joli(e) pretty
laid(e) ugly
mignon(ne) cute

USEFUL WORDS *(masculine)*

le **cerveau**	brain
le **cil** [sil]	eyelash
le **coude**	elbow
le **derrière**	bottom
les **doigts de pied**	toes
le **foie**	liver
le **geste**	gesture
le **gros orteil**	the big toe
un **index**	forefinger
le **mollet**	calf (*of leg*)
le **muscle**	muscle
un **ongle**	nail
un **orteil**	toe
un **os** [ɔs] (*pl* ~ [o])	bone
le **poignet**	wrist
le **poing**	fist
le **poumon**	lung
le **rein**	kidney
le **sein**	breast
le **squelette**	skeleton
le **talon**	heel
le **teint**	complexion
les **traits**	features

USEFUL PHRASES

se moucher to blow one's nose
se couper les ongles to cut one's nails
se faire couper les cheveux to have one's hair cut
hausser les épaules to shrug one's shoulders
faire oui/non de la tête to nod/shake one's head
voir to see; **entendre** to hear; **se sentir** to feel;
sentir to smell; **toucher** to touch; **goûter** to taste;
serrer la main à qn to shake hands with sb
faire bonjour/au revoir de la main à qn to wave hello/goodbye to sb
montrer qch du doigt to point at sth

USEFUL WORDS *(feminine)*

une	**artère**	artery
la	**chair**	flesh
la	**colonne vertébrale**	spine
la	**côte**	rib
la	**cuisse**	thigh
la	**:hanche**	hip
la	**lèvre**	lip
la	**mâchoire**	jaw
la	**nuque**	nape of the neck
la	**paupière**	eyelid
la	**plante du pied**	sole of the foot
la	**prunelle**	pupil *(of the eye)*
la	**taille**	waist; size
la	**tempe**	temple
la	**veine**	vein

USEFUL PHRASES

tour de hanches hip measurement
tour de taille waist measurement
tour de poitrine chest measurement
sourd(e) deaf
aveugle blind
muet(te) dumb
handicapé(e) with a disability
il est plus grand que toi he is taller than you
elle a beaucoup grandi she has grown a lot
je me trouve trop gros I think I am overweight
elle a grossi/maigri she has put on/lost weight
elle fait 1,47 mètres she is 1.47 metres tall
il pèse 40 kilos he weighs 40 kilos

SEASONS

le **printemps**	spring
l'**été** *(m)*	summer
l'**automne** *(m)*	autumn
l'**hiver** *(m)*	winter

MONTHS

janvier	January	**juillet**	July
février	February	**août**	August
mars	March	**septembre**	September
avril	April	**octobre**	October
mai	May	**novembre**	November
juin	June	**décembre**	December

DAYS OF THE WEEK

lundi	Monday
mardi	Tuesday
mercredi	Wednesday
jeudi	Thursday
vendredi	Friday
samedi	Saturday
dimanche	Sunday

USEFUL PHRASES

au printemps in spring
en été/automne/hiver in summer/autumn/winter
en mai in May
le 10 juillet 2015 on 10 July 2015
nous sommes le 3 décembre it's 3 December
le samedi, je vais à la piscine on Saturdays I go to the swimming pool
samedi je suis allé à la piscine on Saturday I went to the swimming pool
samedi prochain/dernier next/last Saturday
le samedi précédent/suivant the previous/following Saturday

CALENDAR

le **calendrier**	calendar
le **jour**	day
la **saison**	season
la **semaine**	week
le **mois**	month
les **jours de la semaine**	days of the week
le **jour férié**	public holiday
le **weekend**	weekend

USEFUL PHRASES

le premier avril April Fools' Day
le premier mai May Day
le quatorze juillet Bastille Day (French national holiday)
le dimanche de Pâques Easter Sunday
le lundi de Pâques Easter Monday
mercredi des Cendres Ash Wednesday
vendredi saint Good Friday
le jour de l'An New Year's Day
le réveillon du jour de l'An New Year's Eve dinner *or* party
l'Avent *(m)* Advent
le Carême Lent
la Marseillaise the Marseillaise (French national anthem)
Noël *(m)* Christmas
à Noël at Christmas
le jour de Noël Christmas Day
la veille de Noël, la nuit de Noël Christmas Eve
Pâques *(fpl)* Easter
le jour de Pâques Easter Day
la Pâque juive Passover
le poisson d'avril April fool's trick
le Ramadan Ramadan
la Saint-Sylvestre New Year's Eve
la Saint-Valentin St Valentine's Day
la Toussaint All Saints' Day

ESSENTIAL WORDS *(masculine)*

un	**anniversaire**	birthday
un	**anniversaire de mariage**	wedding anniversary
le	**cadeau** (*pl* -x)	present
le	**mariage**	wedding
le	**rendez-vous** (*pl inv*)	appointment, date

IMPORTANT WORDS *(masculine)*

le	**festival**	festival
le	**feu d'artifice**	firework; firework display
le	**feu de joie**	bonfire

USEFUL WORDS *(masculine)*

le	**baptême**	christening
le	**cimetière**	cemetery
le	**décès**	death
le	**défilé**	procession; march
un	**enterrement**	funeral
le	**faire-part (de mariage)** (*pl inv*)	wedding invitation
le	**témoin**	witness

USEFUL PHRASES

fêter son anniversaire to celebrate one's birthday
ma sœur est née en 1995 my sister was born in 1995
elle vient d'avoir 17 ans she's just turned 17
il m'a offert ce cadeau he gave me this present
je te l'offre! I'm giving it to you!
je vous remercie thank you
divorcer to get divorced
se marier to get married
se fiancer (avec qn) to get engaged (to sb)
mon père est mort il y a deux ans my father died two years ago
enterrer, ensevelir to bury

ESSENTIAL WORDS *(feminine)*

la **date**	date
la **fête**	saint's day; festival; fair; party

IMPORTANT WORDS *(feminine)*

les **festivités**	festivities
la **fête foraine**	fun fair
les **fiançailles**	engagement
la **foire**	fair
la **mort**	death
la **naissance**	birth

USEFUL WORDS *(feminine)*

la **carte de vœux**	greetings card
la **cérémonie**	ceremony
la **demoiselle d'honneur**	bridesmaid
les **étrennes**	New Year's gift
la **fête folklorique**	folk festival
la **lune de miel**	honeymoon
les **noces**	wedding
la **retraite**	retirement

USEFUL PHRASES

les noces d'argent/d'or/de diamant silver/golden/diamond wedding anniversary
souhaiter la bonne année à qn to wish sb a happy New Year
faire une fête to have a party
inviter ses amis to invite one's friends
choisir un cadeau to choose a gift
joyeux Noël! Happy Christmas!
bon anniversaire! happy birthday!
tous mes vœux best wishes

ESSENTIAL WORDS *(masculine)*

le **bloc sanitaire**	washrooms
le **campeur**	camper
le **camping**	camping; campsite
le **canif**	penknife
le **couteau** (*pl* -x)	knife
le **dépôt de butane**	butane store
un **emplacement**	pitch, site
le **feu de camp**	campfire
le **gardien**	warden
le **gaz**	gas
le **lavabo**	washbasin
le **lit de camp**	camp bed
le **mobile home**	motorhome
le **supplément**	extra charge
le **terrain de camping**	campsite
le **véhicule**	vehicle
les **WC**	toilets

IMPORTANT WORDS *(masculine)*

le **barbecue**	barbecue
le **matelas pneumatique**	airbed
un **ouvre-boîtes**	tin-opener
le **réchaud**	stove
le **règlement**	rules
le **sac à dos**	rucksack
le **sac de couchage**	sleeping bag
le **tire-bouchon** (*pl* ~s)	corkscrew

USEFUL PHRASES

faire du camping to go camping
camper to camp
bien aménagé(e) well equipped
faire un feu to make a fire

ESSENTIAL WORDS *(feminine)*

une	**allumette**	match
une	**assiette**	plate
la	**boîte**	tin, can; box
les	**boîtes de conserve**	tinned food
la	**campeuse**	camper
la	**caravane**	caravan
la	**chaise longue**	deckchair
la	**cuiller, la cuillère**	spoon
la	**douche**	shower
	l'eau non potable	non-drinking water
	l'eau potable	drinking water
la	**fourchette**	fork
la	**glace**	mirror
la	**lampe électrique**	torch
la	**lampe de poche**	torch
la	**machine à laver**	washing machine
la	**nuit**	night
la	**piscine**	swimming pool
la	**poubelle**	dustbin
la	**salle**	room; hall
la	**table**	table
la	**tente**	tent
les	**toilettes**	toilets

IMPORTANT WORDS *(feminine)*

les	**installations sanitaires**	washing facilities
la	**laverie**	launderette
la	**lessive**	washing powder; washing
	l'ombre	shade; shadow
la	**prise de courant**	socket
la	**salle de jeux**	games room

USEFUL PHRASES

dresser *or* **monter une tente** to pitch a tent
griller des saucisses to grill some sausages

ESSENTIAL WORDS *(masculine)*

un **agent (de police)**	policeman
un **agriculteur**	farmer
un **artisan**	self-employed craftsman
le **boulot**	job
le **bureau** (*pl* -x)	office
le **caissier**	check-out assistant
le **chauffeur de taxi**	taxi driver
le **conseiller d'orientation**	careers adviser
le **designer web**	web designer
le **développeur**	developer
un **électricien**	electrician
un **employé**	employee
un **employeur**	employer
un **enseignant**	teacher
le **facteur**	postman
le **garagiste**	mechanic; garage owner
un **infirmier**	(male) nurse
un **informaticien**	computer scientist
le **mécanicien**	mechanic; engineer; train driver
le **médecin** *(m+f)*	doctor
le **métier**	trade
le **patron**	boss
le **pharmacien**	chemist
le **pompier**	firefighter
le **professeur**	teacher
le **programmeur**	programmer
le **salaire**	wages
le **soldat**	soldier
le **steward**	flight attendant
le **travail**	work
le **vendeur**	salesman, shop assistant

USEFUL PHRASES

intéressant(e)/peu intéressant(e) interesting/not very interesting
il est facteur he is a postman
il/elle est médecin he/she is a doctor
travailler to work
devenir to become

ESSENTIAL WORDS *(feminine)*

une	**agricultrice**	farmer
une	**ambition**	ambition
une	**artisane**	self-employed craftswoman
la	**banque**	bank
la	**caissière**	check-out assistant
la	**conseillère d'orientation**	careers adviser
la	**dactylo**	typist
la	**développeuse**	developer
une	**employée**	employee
une	**enseignante**	teacher
la	**factrice**	postwoman
une	**hôtesse de l'air**	flight attendant
une	**industrie**	industry
une	**infirmière**	nurse
une	**informaticienne**	computer scientist
la	**patronne**	boss
la	**professeur**	teacher
la	**profession**	profession
la	**programmeuse**	programmer
la	**réceptionniste**	receptionist
la	**retraite**	retirement
la	**secrétaire**	secretary
une	**usine**	factory
la	**vedette** *(m+f)*	star
la	**vendeuse**	shop assistant
la	**vie active**	working life

USEFUL PHRASES

travailler pour gagner sa vie to work for one's living
mon ambition est d'être juge it is my ambition to be a judge
que faites-vous dans la vie? what is your job?
postuler à un emploi to apply for a job

IMPORTANT WORDS *(masculine)*

un	**apprentissage**	apprenticeship
	l'**avenir**	future
le	**CDD**	fixed term contract
le	**CDI**	permanent contract
le	**chef**	boss
le	**chômage**	unemployment
le	**chômeur**	unemployed person
le	**coiffeur**	hairdresser
le	**collègue**	colleague
le	**commerçant**	shopkeeper
le	**commerce**	business
le	**concierge**	caretaker
le	**contrat**	contract
le	**décorateur**	decorator
un	**emploi**	job
un	**entretien (d'embauche)**	(job) interview
le	**gérant**	manager
un	**homme d'affaires**	businessman
un	**intérimaire**	temp
le	**marché du travail**	job market
un	**opticien**	optician
un	**ouvrier**	worker
le	**peintre**	painter
le	**pilote**	pilot
le	**plombier**	plumber
le	**président**	president; chairman
le	**salarié**	wage-earner
le	**sapeur-pompier** (*pl* ~s~s)	firefighter
le	**syndicat**	trade union

USEFUL PHRASES

être au chômage to be unemployed
licencier qn to make sb redundant
l'emploi saisonnier seasonal work
"offres d'emplois" "situations vacant"
être syndiqué to be in a union
gagner 150 livres par semaine to earn £150 a week

IMPORTANT WORDS *(feminine)*

les	**affaires**	business
une	**agence d'intérim**	temping agency
	l'ANPE	job centre
une	**augmentation**	rise
la	**candidature**	application
la	**carrière**	career
la	**coiffeuse**	hairdresser
la	**collègue**	colleague
la	**concierge**	caretaker
la	**cuisinière**	cook
une	**entrevue**	interview
la	**femme d'affaires**	businesswoman
la	**femme de ménage**	cleaner
la	**gérante**	manageress
la	**grève**	strike
une	**intérimaire**	temp
la	**lettre de motivation**	covering letter
une	**ouvrière**	worker
la	**peintre**	painter
la	**politique**	politics
la	**présidente**	president; chairwoman
la	**salariée**	wage-earner
la	**situation**	job; situation

USEFUL PHRASES

une augmentation de salaire a pay rise
se mettre en grève to go on strike
faire la grève to be on strike
travailler à plein temps/à mi-temps to work full-time/part-time
faire des heures supplémentaires to work overtime
la réduction du temps de travail reduction in working hours

USEFUL WORDS *(masculine)*

un **animateur**	activity leader
un **architecte**	architect
un **artiste**	artist
un **avocat**	lawyer
le **cadre**	executive
le **chercheur**	researcher
le **chirurgien**	surgeon
le **comptable**	accountant
le **couturier**	fashion designer
le **député**	MP
un **écrivain**	writer
le **fonctionnaire**	civil servant
un **homme politique**	politician
un **horaire**	schedule
un **ingénieur**	engineer
un **interprète**	interpreter
le **journaliste**	journalist
le **juge**	judge
le **maçon**	mason
le **mannequin** *(m+f)*	model *(person)*
le **marin**	sailor; seaman
le **menuisier**	joiner
le **notaire**	lawyer, solicitor
le **personnel**	staff
le **photographe**	photographer
le **présentateur télé**	TV presenter
le **président-directeur général, le PDG**	chairman and managing director
le **prêtre**	priest
le **rédacteur**	editor
le **représentant**	rep
le **stage en entreprise**	work placement
le **stage de formation**	training course
le **traducteur**	translator
le **vétérinaire** *(m+f)*	vet
le **vigneron**	wine grower
le **VRP**	sales rep

USEFUL WORDS *(feminine)*

une **animatrice**	activity leader
une **artiste**	artist
une **avocate**	lawyer
la **comptable**	accountant
la **couturière**	dressmaker
une **entreprise**	business
la **femme-agent**	policewoman
la **femme au foyer**	housewife
la **fonctionnaire**	civil servant
la **formation**	training
la **formation continue**	in-house training
la **grève du zèle**	work-to-rule
la **grève perlée**	go-slow
une **indemnité de chômage**	unemployment benefit
une **indemnité de licenciement**	redundancy payment
une **interprète**	interpreter
la **journaliste**	journalist
l'**orientation professionnelle**	careers guidance
la **présentatrice télé**	TV presenter
la **rédactrice**	editor
la **religieuse**	nun
la **représentante**	rep
la **société**	company
la **traductrice**	translator

USEFUL PHRASES

un emploi temporaire/permanent a temporary/permanent job
être engagé(e) to be taken on
être renvoyé(e) to be dismissed
mettre qn à la porte to give sb the sack
un emploi à mi-temps a part-time job
chercher du travail to look for work
faire un stage de formation to go on a training course
pointer to clock in *or* out
avoir un horaire flexible to work flexitime
travailler à son compte to be self-employed
travailler dans l'informatique/le tourisme to work in computing/tourism

ESSENTIAL WORDS *(masculine)*

un	**agent (de police)**	policeman
	l'**auto-stop**, le **stop**	hitch-hiking
un	**auto-stoppeur** (*pl* ~s)	hitch-hiker
le	**bouchon**	traffic jam
le	**camion**	lorry, truck
le	**carrefour**	crossroads
le	**chauffeur** *(m+f)*	driver; chauffeur
le	**conducteur**	driver
le	**cycliste**	cyclist
le	**diesel**	diesel
le	**feu rouge**	traffic lights, red light
les	**feux**	traffic lights
le	**frein**	brake
le	**garage**	garage
le	**garagiste**	mechanic; garage owner
le	**gas-oil**	diesel (oil)
le	**kilomètre**	kilometre
le	**litre**	litre
le	**mécanicien**	mechanic
le	**numéro**	number
le	**parking**	car park
le	**péage**	toll
le	**permis de conduire**	driving licence
le	**piéton**	pedestrian
le	**plan (de la ville)**	street map
le	**pneu**	tyre
le	**radar**	speed camera
le	**voyage**	journey

USEFUL PHRASES

faire du stop, **faire de l'auto-stop** to hitch-hike
s'arrêter au feu rouge to stop at the red light
freiner brusquement to brake sharply
100 kilomètres à l'heure, **100 kilomètres-heure** 100 kilometres an hour
crever, avoir un pneu crevé to have a puncture
as-tu ton permis? do you have a driving licence?

ESSENTIAL WORDS *(feminine)*

une **auto**	car
une **automobile**	car
une **autoroute**	motorway
une **autoroute à péage**	toll motorway
une **auto-stoppeuse** (*pl* ~s)	hitch-hiker
la **caravane**	caravan
la **carte grise**	(car) registration document
la **carte routière**	road map
la **carte verte**	insurance certificate
la **conductrice**	driver
la **déviation**	diversion
la **direction**	direction
la **direction assistée**	power steering
la **distance**	distance
l'**eau**	water
l'**essence**	petrol
l'**essence sans plomb**	unleaded petrol
l'**huile**	oil
la **police**	police
la **route**	road
la **route nationale**	main road
la **station-service** (*pl* ~s)	petrol station
la **voiture**	car

USEFUL PHRASES

on va faire une promenade en voiture we're going for a drive (in the car)
le plein, s'il vous plaît fill her up please!
prenez la route de Lyon take the road to Lyons
c'est un voyage de 3 heures it's a 3-hour journey
bonne route! have a good journey!
allez, en route! let's go!
en route nous avons vu ... on the way we saw ...
doubler *or* **dépasser une voiture** to overtake a car
se garer to park (the car)
réparer to fix

IMPORTANT WORDS *(masculine)*

un	**accident (de la route)**	(road) accident
un	**alcootest**	Breathalyzer® test
un	**automobiliste**	motorist
le	**camionneur**	lorry driver
le	**carburant**	petrol
le	**code de la route**	highway code
le	**coffre**	boot
le	**contrôle technique**	MOT test
un	**embouteillage**	traffic jam
	l'**embrayage**	clutch
un	**éthylotest**	Breathalyzer® kit
le	**gilet de sécurité**	high-vis vest
le	**klaxon**	horn
le	**lavage**	(car) wash
le	**moteur**	engine
les	**papiers**	official papers
le	**phare**	headlight
le	**pompiste**	petrol pump attendant
le	**rond-point** (*pl* ~s~s)	roundabout
le	**sens unique**	one-way street
le	**stationnement**	parking
le	**télépéage**	toll prepayment system
le	**triangle de pré-signalisation**	warning triangle

USEFUL PHRASES

d'abord on met le moteur en marche first you switch on the engine
le moteur démarre the engine starts up
la voiture démarre the car moves off
on roule we're driving along
accélérer to accelerate
continuer to continue
ralentir to slow down
s'arrêter to stop
stationner to park; to be parked
couper le moteur to switch off the engine
il y a eu un accident there's been an accident
vos papiers, s'il vous plaît may I see your papers please?

IMPORTANT WORDS *(feminine)*

une	**amende**	fine
une	**assurance**	insurance
une	**auto-école** (*pl* ~s)	driving school
une	**automobiliste**	motorist
la	**batterie**	battery
la	**carrosserie**	bodywork
la	**ceinture de sécurité**	seat belt
la	**circulation**	traffic
la	**collision**	collision
la	**crevaison**	puncture
la	**frontière**	border
la	**marque**	make (*of car*)
la	**panne**	breakdown
la	**pièce de rechange**	spare part
la	**police d'assurance**	insurance policy
la	**pompe à essence**	petrol pump
la	**portière**	(car) door
la	**priorité**	right of way
la	**roue**	wheel
la	**roue de secours**	spare wheel
la	**vitesse**	speed; gear
la	**voiture de dépannage**	breakdown van
la	**voiture éléctrique/hybride**	electric/hybrid car
la	**zone bleue**	restricted parking zone

USEFUL PHRASES

être en panne d'essence to run out of petrol
aux heures d'affluence at rush hour
il a eu 150 euros d'amende he got a 150-euro fine
êtes-vous assuré(e)? are you insured?
n'oubliez pas de mettre vos ceintures don't forget to put on your seat belts
à la frontière at the border
être *or* **tomber en panne** to break down
je suis tombé(e) en panne sèche I've run out of petrol
la roue avant/arrière the front/back wheel

USEFUL WORDS *(masculine)*

un **accélérateur**	accelerator
un **apprenti conducteur**	learner driver
un **arrêt d'urgence**	emergency stop
le **blessé**	casualty
le **capot**	bonnet
le **carburateur**	carburettor
le **clignotant**	indicator
le **compteur de vitesse**	speedometer
le **contractuel**	traffic warden
le **démarreur**	starter
le **détour**	detour
un **essuie-glace** *(pl inv)*	windscreen wiper
le **lavage auto**	car-wash
le **moniteur d'auto-école**	driving instructor
le **motard**	motorcycle policeman; motorcyclist
le **panneau** *(pl* -x)	road sign
le **parcmètre**	parking meter
le **pare-brise** *(pl inv)*	windscreen
le **pare-chocs** *(pl inv)*	bumper
le **périphérique**	ring road
le **pot catalytique**	catalytic converter
le **PV**	fine
le **rétroviseur**	rear-view mirror
le **routier**	long-distance lorry driver
le **starter**	choke
le **système de navigation GPS**	satellite navigation system; GPS
le **virage**	bend
le **volant**	steering wheel

USEFUL PHRASES

l'accident a fait 6 blessés/morts 6 people were injured/killed in the accident
il faut faire un détour we have to make a detour
une contravention pour excès de vitesse a fine for speeding
dresser un PV à un conducteur to book a driver

USEFUL WORDS *(feminine)*

une	**agglomération**	built-up area
une	**aire de services**	service area
une	**aire de stationnement**	lay-by
une	**apprentie conductrice**	learner driver
une	**auto-école**	driving school
la	**bande d'arrêt d'urgence**	hard shoulder
la	**bande médiane**	central reservation
la	**boîte de vitesses**	gearbox
la	**bretelle de raccordement**	slip road
la	**conduite accompagnée**	*driving as a learner accompanied by an experienced driver*
la	**consommation d'essence**	petrol consumption
la	**contractuelle**	traffic warden
la	**contravention**	traffic offence
la	**dépanneuse**	breakdown van
la	**file**	lane
la	**galerie**	roof rack
la	**leçon de conduite**	driving lesson
la	**limitation de vitesse**	speed limit
la	**pédale**	pedal
la	**plaque d'immatriculation** *or* **minéralogique**	number plate
la	**pression**	pressure
la	**remorque**	trailer
la	**routière**	long-distance lorry driver
la	**voie**	way, road; lane *(on road)*
la	**voie de raccordement**	slip road

USEFUL PHRASES

"priorité à droite" "give way to the right"
"serrez à droite" "keep to the right"
"accès interdit" "no entry"
"stationnement interdit" "no parking"
"travaux" "roadworks"

ESSENTIAL WORDS *(masculine)*

un **anorak**	anorak
le **bouton**	button
le **caleçon**	boxer shorts
le **chapeau** (*pl* -x)	hat
le **col**	collar
le **collant**	tights
le **complet**	suit
le **costume**	suit (*for man*); costume
un **imper(méable)**	raincoat
le **jean** [dʒin]	jeans
le **maillot (de bain)**	swimming trunks *or* swimsuit
le **manteau** (*pl* -x)	coat
le **mouchoir**	handkerchief
le **pantalon**	trousers
le **parapluie**	umbrella
le **pardessus**	overcoat
le **pull-over, le pull** [pyl(ɔvœʀ)]	jumper
le **pyjama**	pyjamas
le **sac**	bag
le **slip de bain**	swimming trunks
le **slip**	pants
le **soulier**	shoe
les **sous-vêtements**	underwear
le **T-shirt, le tee-shirt**	T-shirt
les **vêtements**	clothes

IMPORTANT WORDS *(masculine)*

le **blouson**	jacket
le **chemisier**	blouse
le **gant**	glove
le **sac à main**	handbag
le **short** [ʃɔʀt]	shorts
le **tricot**	jumper
un **uniforme**	uniform
le **veston**	jacket (*for man*)

ESSENTIAL WORDS *(feminine)*

la **capuche**	hood
la **chaussette**	sock
la **chaussure**	shoe
la **chemise**	shirt
la **chemise de nuit**	nightdress
la **cravate**	tie
la **culotte**	knickers
la **jupe**	skirt
la **mode**	fashion
la **parka**	parka
la **pointure**	(shoe) size
la **robe**	dress
la **sandale**	sandal
la **taille**	size; waist
la **veste**	jacket

IMPORTANT WORDS *(feminine)*

la **botte**	boot
la **ceinture**	belt
la **pantoufle**	slipper
la **poche**	pocket

USEFUL PHRASES

le matin je m'habille in the morning I get dressed
le soir je me déshabille in the evening I get undressed
porter to wear
mettre to put on
quand je rentre du lycée je me change when I get home from school I get changed
à la mode fashionable
démodé(e) old-fashioned
cela fait très chic that's very smart
cela vous va bien that suits you
quelle est votre taille? what size do you take?
quelle est votre pointure? what shoe size do you take?
je chausse du 38 I take size 38 in shoes

USEFUL WORDS *(masculine)*

les	**accessoires**	accessories
les	**bas**	stockings
les	**baskets**	trainers
le	**béret**	beret
le	**bermuda**	Bermuda shorts
le	**bibi**	fascinator
le	**bleu de travail**	overalls
le	**bonnet**	(woolly) hat
le	**chandail**	(thick) jumper
le	**chapeau** (*pl* -x) **melon**	bowler hat
le	**collant**	tights
le	**débardeur**	tank top
le	**défilé**	fashion show
le	**foulard**	scarf
le	**gilet de corps**	vest
le	**gilet**	waistcoat; cardigan
les	**:hauts talons**	high heels
le	**jupon**	underskirt
les	**lacets**	(shoe)laces
le	**linge**	washing
le	**nettoyage à sec**	dry-cleaning
le	**nœud papillon**	bow tie
le	**pantacourt**	three-quarter length trousers
le	**polo**	polo shirt
le	**ruban**	ribbon
le	**sac à bandoulière**	shoulder bag
le	**soutien-gorge** (*pl* ~s~)	bra
le	**survêtement**	tracksuit
le	**sweat** [swɛt]	sweatshirt
le	**sweat à capuche**	hooded top
le	**tablier**	apron
le	**tailleur**	woman's suit
les	**talons aiguilles**	stiletto heels
le	**tricot de corps**	vest

USEFUL WORDS *(feminine)*

la	**boutonnière**	buttonhole
les	**bretelles**	braces
la	**cabine d'essayage**	fitting room
la	**canne**	walking stick
la	**casquette**	cap
la	**combinaison**	slip
la	**doudoune**	down jacket
une	**écharpe**	scarf
une	**espadrille**	espadrille
la	**fermeture éclair**	zip
la	**:haute couture**	haute couture
la	**jupe-culotte** (*pl* ~s~s)	culottes
la	**manche**	sleeve
la	**polaire**	fleece
la	**robe de chambre**	dressing gown
la	**robe de mariée**	wedding dress
la	**robe du soir**	evening dress (*for woman*)
la	**salopette**	dungarees
la	**tong**	flip flop

USEFUL PHRASES

long(ue) long
court(e) short
une robe à manches courtes/longues a short-sleeved/long-sleeved dress
serré(e) tight
ample loose
une jupe serrée a tight skirt
rayé(e) striped
à carreaux checked
à pois spotted
les vêtements sport casual clothes
en tenue de soirée in evening dress
à la mode fashionable
branché(e) trendy
démodé(e) old-fashioned

colours

beige	beige
blanc (blanche)	white
bleu(e)	blue
bordeaux	maroon
brun(e)	brown
doré(e)	golden
fauve	fawn
gris(e)	grey
jaune	yellow
marron	brown
mauve	mauve
noir(e)	black
orange, orangé(e)	orange
rose	pink
rouge	red
turquoise	turquoise
vert(e)	green
violet (violette)	violet, purple
bleu clair	pale blue
bleu foncé	dark blue
rouge vif	bright red
bleu ciel	sky blue
bleu marine	navy blue
bleu roi	royal blue

USEFUL PHRASES

la couleur colour

de quelle couleur sont tes yeux/tes cheveux? what colour are your eyes/ is your hair?

le bleu te va bien blue suits you; the blue one suits you

peindre qch en bleu to paint sth blue

des chaussures bleues blue shoes

des chaussures bleu clair light blue shoes

elle a les yeux verts she has green eyes

changer de couleur to change colour

la Maison Blanche the White House

blanc comme neige as white as snow

Blanche-Neige Snow White

un steak bleu a very rare steak, an underdone steak

le Petit Chaperon rouge Little Red Riding Hood

rougir to turn red

rougir de honte to blush with shame

pâle comme un linge as white as a sheet

tout(e) bronzé(e) as brown as a berry

il était couvert de bleus he was black and blue

un œil au beurre noir a black eye

ESSENTIAL WORDS *(masculine)*

un **ordinateur**	computer
un **ordinateur portable**	laptop
le **PC**	PC, personal computer
le **programme**	program

USEFUL WORDS *(masculine)*

le **blogue**	blog
le **blogueur**	blogger
le **clavier**	keyboard
le **curseur**	cursor
le **document**	document
un **écran (tactile)**	(touch) screen
le **fichier**	file
le **gaming**	gaming
le **:haut débit**	broadband
l'**Internet**	internet
le **jeu vidéo**	computer game
le **livre électronique**	e-book
le **logiciel**	software
le **mail**	email
les **médias sociaux**	social media
le **menu**	menu
le **microblogue**	microblog
le **moniteur**	monitor
le **navigateur**	browser
le **nom d'utilisateur**	username
le **nuage de tags**	cloud
le **pirate**	hacker
le **post**	post (*on forum or blog*)
le **réseau**	network
le **sans-fil**	wireless
le **serveur**	server
le **site de réseautage**	social networking site
le **site Web**	website
le **système d'exploitation**	operating system
le **virus**	virus
le **Web**	web
le **webmail**	webmail
le **wifi**	wifi

ESSENTIAL WORDS *(feminine)*

une **imprimante**	printer
l'**informatique**	computer science; computer studies
la **souris**	mouse
la **tablette**	tablet

USEFUL WORDS *(feminine)*

une **adresse électronique**	email address
une **appli**	app
une **application**	program
la **base de données**	database
la **blogueuse**	blogger
la **cartouche d'encre**	ink cartridge
la **clé électronique**	dongle
la **clé USB**	USB key
la **connexion Internet**	internet connection
la **console de jeu**	games console
la **corbeille**	recycle bin
les **données**	data
la **fenêtre**	window
la **fonction**	function
une **icône**	icon
l'**informatique en nuage**	cloud computing
une **interface**	interface
une **internaute**	internet user
la **manette**	joystick
la **mémoire**	memory
la **page d'accueil**	home page
la **sauvegarde**	back-up
la **touche**	key
la **webcam**	webcam

USEFUL PHRASES

taper, saisir to key; **copier** to copy
effacer to delete; **enregistrer** to save
imprimer to print
surfer sur Internet to surf the internet
faire les achats en ligne to shop online
télécharger un fichier to download *or* upload a file

COUNTRIES

ESSENTIAL WORDS *(masculine)*

le	**Canada**	Canada
les	**États-Unis**	United States
le	**pays**	country
les	**Pays-Bas**	Netherlands
le	**pays de Galles**	Wales
le	**Royaume-Uni**	United Kingdom
les	**USA**	USA

USEFUL WORDS *(masculine)*

le	**Danemark**	Denmark
	l'**Hexagone**	France
le	**Japon**	Japan
le	**Maroc**	Morocco
le	**Pakistan**	Pakistan
le	**tiers-monde**	Third World

USEFUL PHRASES

mon pays natal my native country
la capitale de la France the capital of France
de quel pays venez-vous? what country do you come from?
je viens des États-Unis/du Canada I come from the United States/ from Canada
je suis né(e) en Écosse I was born in Scotland
je vais aux Pays-Bas I'm going to the Netherlands
je reviens des États-Unis I have just come back from the United States
les pays en voie de développement the developing countries

ESSENTIAL WORDS *(feminine)*

l'**Allemagne**	Germany
l'**Angleterre**	England
la **Belgique**	Belgium
l'**Écosse**	Scotland
l'**Espagne**	Spain
l'**Europe**	Europe
la **France**	France
la **Grande-Bretagne**	Great Britain
la **:Hollande**	Holland
l'**Irlande (du Nord)**	(Northern) Ireland
l'**Italie**	Italy
la **Suisse**	Switzerland

USEFUL WORDS *(feminine)*

l'**Afrique**	Africa
l'**Algérie**	Algeria
l'**Amérique**	America
l'**Amérique du Sud**	South America
les **Antilles**	West Indies
l'**Asie**	Asia
l'**Australie**	Australia
l'**Autriche**	Austria
la **Chine**	China
la **Finlande**	Finland
la **Grèce**	Greece
l'**Inde**	India
la **Norvège**	Norway
la **Nouvelle-Zélande**	New Zealand
la **Pologne**	Poland
la **Roumanie**	Romania
la **Russie**	Russia
la **Suède**	Sweden
la **Tunisie**	Tunisia
l'**Union européenne**, l'**UE**	European Union, EU

NATIONALITIES

ESSENTIAL WORDS *(masculine)*

un **Allemand**	a German
un **Américain**	an American
un **Anglais**	an Englishman
un **Belge**	a Belgian
un **Britannique**	a Briton
un **Canadien**	a Canadian
un **Écossais**	a Scot
un **Espagnol**	a Spaniard
un **Européen**	a European
un **Français**	a Frenchman
un **Gallois**	a Welshman
un **:Hollandais**	a Dutchman
un **Irlandais**	an Irishman
un **Italien**	an Italian
un **Pakistanais**	a Pakistani
un **Suisse**	a Swiss

USEFUL PHRASES

il est irlandais, c'est un Irlandais he is Irish
elle est irlandaise, c'est une Irlandaise she is Irish
le paysage irlandais the Irish countryside
une ville irlandaise an Irish town
un Canadien français a French Canadian

ESSENTIAL WORDS *(feminine)*

une **Allemande**	a German
une **Américaine**	an American
une **Anglaise**	an Englishwoman, an English girl
une **Belge**	a Belgian
une **Britannique**	a Briton, a British girl *or* woman
une **Canadienne**	a Canadian
une **Écossaise**	a Scot
une **Espagnole**	a Spaniard
une **Européenne**	a European
une **Française**	a Frenchwoman, a French girl
une **Galloise**	a Welshwoman, a Welsh girl
une **:Hollandaise**	a Dutchwoman, a Dutch girl
une **Irlandaise**	an Irishwoman, an Irish girl
une **Italienne**	an Italian
une **Pakistanaise**	a Pakistani
une **Suisse**	a Swiss girl *or* woman

USEFUL PHRASES

je suis écossais – je parle anglais I am Scottish – I speak English
une Canadienne française a French Canadian
je suis écossaise I am Scottish
un étranger (une étrangère) a foreigner
à l'étranger abroad; **la nationalité** nationality

USEFUL WORDS *(masculine)*

un **Africain**	an African
un **Algérien**	an Algerian
un **Antillais**	a West Indian
un **Arabe**	an Arab
un **Asiatique**	an Asian
un **Australien**	an Australian
un **Chinois**	a Chinese
un **Danois**	a Dane
un **Finlandais**	a Finn
un **Grec**	a Greek
un **Indien**	an Indian
un **Japonais**	a Japanese
un **Marocain**	a Moroccan
un **Néo-Zélandais** *(pl inv)*	a New-Zealander
un **Polonais**	a Pole
un **Russe**	a Russian
un **Tchèque**	a Czech
un **Tunisien**	a Tunisian

USEFUL WORDS *(feminine)*

une **Africaine**	an African
une **Algérienne**	an Algerian
une **Antillaise**	a West Indian
une **Arabe**	an Arab
une **Asiatique**	an Asian
une **Australienne**	an Australian
une **Chinoise**	a Chinese
une **Danoise**	a Dane
une **Finlandaise**	a Finn
une **Grecque**	a Greek
une **Indienne**	an Indian
une **Japonaise**	a Japanese
une **Marocaine**	a Moroccan
une **Néo-Zélandaise** (*pl* ~s)	a New-Zealander
une **Polonaise**	a Pole
une **Russe**	a Russian
une **Tchèque**	a Czech
une **Tunisienne**	a Tunisian

ESSENTIAL WORDS *(masculine)*

	l'**air**	air
un	**arbre**	tree
le	**bois**	wood
le	**bruit**	noise
le	**champ**	field
le	**chasseur**	hunter
le	**château** (*pl* -x)	castle
le	**chemin**	path, way
le	**fermier**	farmer
le	**marché**	market
le	**pays**	country; district
le	**paysan**	countryman, farmer
le	**paysage**	scenery
le	**pique-nique** (*pl* ~s)	picnic
le	**pont**	bridge
le	**ruisseau**	stream
le	**sentier**	track
le	**terrain**	ground
le	**touriste**	tourist
le	**village**	village

USEFUL PHRASES

en plein air in the open air
je connais le chemin du village I know the way to the village
faire un tour en bicyclette to go cycling
les gens du pays the locals
nous avons fait un pique-nique we went for a picnic

ESSENTIAL WORDS *(feminine)*

une	**auberge de jeunesse**	youth hostel
la	**barrière**	gate; fence
la	**camionnette**	van
la	**campagne**	country
la	**canne**	walking stick
la	**ferme**	farm, farmhouse
la	**forêt**	forest
la	**montagne**	mountain
la	**pierre**	stone, rock
la	**promenade**	walk
la	**randonnée**	hike
la	**rivière**	river
la	**route**	road
la	**terre**	earth, ground
la	**tour**	tower
la	**touriste**	tourist
la	**vallée**	valley

USEFUL PHRASES

à la campagne in the country
aller à la campagne to go into the country
habiter à la campagne/en ville to live in the country/in town
cultiver la terre to cultivate the land

IMPORTANT WORDS (*masculine*)

un **agriculteur**	farmer
les **campagnards**	country people
le **fleuve**	river
le **gendarme** (*m+f*)	policeman
le **lac**	lake
le **sommet**	top (*of hill*)

USEFUL WORDS (*masculine*)

le **bâton**	stick
le **blé**	corn; wheat
le **buisson**	bush
le **caillou** (*pl* -x)	pebble
un **étang**	pond
le **foin**	hay
le **fossé**	ditch
le **:hameau** (*pl* -x)	hamlet
le **marais**	marsh
le **moulin (à vent)**	(wind)mill
le **poteau** (*pl* -x) **indicateur**	signpost
le **poteau** (*pl* -x) **télégraphique**	telegraph pole
le **pré**	meadow
le **sentier**	path

USEFUL PHRASES

agricole agricultural
paisible, tranquille peaceful
au sommet de la colline at the top of the hill

IMPORTANT WORDS *(feminine)*

l'**agriculture**	agriculture
une **agricultrice**	farmer
une **auberge**	inn
la **botte (de caoutchouc)**	(wellington) boot
la **chaussée**	road surface
la **colline**	hill
la **feuille**	leaf
la **paysanne**	countrywoman
la **poussière**	dust
la **propriété**	property, estate
la **tranquillité**	peace

USEFUL WORDS *(feminine)*

la **boue**	mud
la **bruyère**	heather
la **carrière**	quarry
la **caverne**	cave
la **chasse**	hunting; shooting
la **chute d'eau**	waterfall
la **:haie**	hedge
les **jumelles**	binoculars
la **lande**	moor
la **mare**	pond
la **moisson**	harvest
la **plaine**	plain
la **récolte**	crop, harvest
la **rive**	bank (of river)
les **ruines**	ruins
la **source**	spring, source
les **vendanges**	grape harvest

USEFUL PHRASES

s'égarer, se perdre to lose one's way
faire la moisson to bring in the harvest
faire les vendanges to harvest the grapes

ESSENTIAL WORDS *(masculine)*

	l'**âge**	age
un	**air**	appearance
les	**cheveux**	hair
les	**yeux**	eyes

USEFUL PHRASES

affreux(euse) hideous
agité(e) agitated
aimable nice
amusant(e) amusing, entertaining
barbu(e) bearded, with a beard
beau handsome; **belle** beautiful
bête stupid
calme calm
chauve bald
court(e) short
dégoûtant(e) disgusting
désagréable unpleasant
drôle funny
dynamique dynamic
formidable great
gai(e) cheerful
gentil(le) kind
grand(e) tall
gros(se) fat
heureux(euse) happy
impoli(e) rude
intelligent(e) intelligent
jeune young
joli(e) pretty
laid(e) ugly
long(ue) long
maigre skinny
malheureux(euse) unhappy, unfortunate
méchant(e) naughty
mignon(ne) cute

ESSENTIAL WORDS *(feminine)*

la	**barbe**	beard
la	**couleur**	colour
les	**lentilles (de contact)**	(contact) lenses
les	**lunettes**	glasses
la	**moustache**	moustache
la	**personne**	person
la	**pièce d'identité**	ID
la	**taille**	height, size; waist

USEFUL PHRASES

mince slim
nerveux(euse) nervous, tense
optimiste/pessimiste optimistic/pessimistic
petit(e) small, little
poli polite
sage well-behaved
sérieux(euse) serious
timide shy
vieux, vieille old
elle a l'air triste she looks sad
il pleurait he was crying
il souriait he was smiling
il avait les larmes aux yeux he had tears in his eyes
un homme de taille moyenne a man of average height
je mesure/je fais 1 mètre 70 I am 1 metre 70 tall
de quelle couleur sont tes yeux/tes cheveux? what colour are your eyes/ is your hair?
j'ai les cheveux blonds I have fair hair
j'ai les yeux bleus/verts I have blue eyes/green eyes
les cheveux bruns dark *or* brown hair
les cheveux châtains chestnut-coloured hair
les cheveux frisés curly hair
les cheveux roux/noirs/blancs red/black/grey hair
les cheveux teints dyed hair

IMPORTANT WORDS *(masculine)*

le	**bouton**	spot
le	**caractère**	character, nature
le	**regard**	look
le	**sourire**	smile
le	**teint**	complexion

USEFUL WORDS *(masculine)*

le	**défaut**	fault
le	**dentier**	false teeth
le	**géant**	giant
le	**geste**	gesture
le	**grain de beauté**	mole, beauty spot
le	**poids**	weight

USEFUL PHRASES

il a bon caractère he is good-tempered
il a mauvais caractère he is bad-tempered
avoir le teint pâle to have a pale complexion
porter des lunettes/des lentilles to wear glasses/contact lenses

IMPORTANT WORDS *(feminine)*

la **beauté**	beauty
la **curiosité**	curiosity
une **expression**	expression
une **habitude**	habit
l'**humeur**	mood
la **laideur**	ugliness
la **qualité**	(good) quality
la **voix**	voice

USEFUL WORDS *(feminine)*

la **boucle**	curl
la **cicatrice**	scar
les **fossettes**	dimples
la **frange**	fringe
la **permanente**	perm
la **ressemblance**	resemblance
les **rides**	wrinkles
les **taches de rousseur**	freckles
la **timidité**	shyness

USEFUL PHRASES

je suis toujours de bonne humeur I am always in a good mood
il est de mauvaise humeur he is in a bad mood
il s'est mis en colère he got angry
elle ressemble à sa mère she looks like her mother
il se ronge les ongles he bites his nails

ESSENTIAL WORDS *(masculine)*

	l'**allemand**	German
	l'**alphabet**	alphabet
	l'**anglais**	English
	l'**apprentissage**	apprenticeship; learning
le	**cahier de texte(s)**	homework book
le	**camarade de classe**	school friend
le	**carnet**	notebook
le	**club**	club
le	**collège**	secondary school
le	**copain**	pal
les	**cours**	lessons
le	**crayon**	pencil
le	**dessin**	drawing
le	**devoir**	test
les	**devoirs**	homework
le	**directeur**	headmaster
le	**dortoir**	dormitory
un	**échange**	exchange
un	**écolier**	schoolboy
un	**élève**	pupil, schoolboy
un	**emploi du temps**	timetable
	l'**enseignement**	education, teaching
	l'**espagnol**	Spanish
un	**étudiant**	student
un	**examen**	exam
un	**examen blanc**	mock exam
un	**exposé**	presentation
le	**français**	French
le	**groupe**	group
le	**gymnase**	gym(nasium)
	l'**italien**	Italian
le	**laboratoire**	laboratory
le	**livre**	book
le	**lycée**	secondary school

ESSENTIAL WORDS *(feminine)*

la	**biologie**	biology
la	**camarade de classe**	school friend
la	**cantine**	dining hall, canteen
la	**carte**	map
la	**chimie**	chemistry
la	**classe**	class; year; classroom
la	**copine**	pal
la	**directrice**	headmistress
une	**école**	school
une	**école maternelle**	nursery school
une	**école primaire**	primary school
une	**écolière**	schoolgirl
	l'**éducation physique**	PE
	l'**électronique**	electronics
une	**élève**	pupil, schoolgirl
	l'**EPS**	PE
une	**erreur**	mistake
	l'**étude (de)**	study (of)
les	**études**	studies
une	**étudiante**	student
une	**excursion**	trip, outing
une	**expérience**	experiment
la	**faute**	mistake
la	**géographie**	geography
la	**gomme**	rubber
les	**grandes vacances**	summer holidays
la	**gymnastique**	gym(nastics)
	l'**histoire**	history; story
	l'**informatique**	computer studies
la	**journée**	day
les	**langues (vivantes)**	(modern) languages
la	**leçon**	lesson
la	**lecture**	reading
les	**mathématiques**	mathematics
les	**maths**	maths
la	**matière**	(school) subject
la	**musique**	music

ESSENTIAL WORDS *(masculine continued)*

le	**mot**	word
un	**ordinateur**	computer
le	**prix**	prize
le	**professeur**	teacher
le	**professeur des écoles**	primary schoolteacher
les	**progrès**	progress
le	**résultat**	result
le	**self**	cafeteria
le	**semestre**	semester
le	**stylo**	pen
le	**tableau (noir)**	blackboard
le	**travail**	work
les	**travaux manuels**	handicrafts
les	**travaux pratiques**	practical class
le	**trimestre**	term

USEFUL PHRASES

travailler to work
apprendre to learn
étudier to study
depuis combien de temps apprenez-vous le français? how long have you been learning French?
apprendre qch par cœur to learn sth off by heart
j'ai des devoirs tous les jours I have homework every day
ma petite sœur va à l'école – moi, je vais au collège my little sister goes to primary school – I go to secondary school
enseigner le français to teach French
le professeur d'allemand the German teacher
j'ai fait des progrès en maths I have made progress in maths
passer un examen to sit an exam
être reçu(e) à un examen to pass an exam
échouer à un examen to fail an exam
avoir la moyenne to get a pass mark

ESSENTIAL WORDS *(feminine continued)*

la	**natation**	swimming
la	**note**	mark
la	**phrase**	sentence
la	**physique**	physics
la	**piscine**	swimming pool
la	**professeur**	teacher
la	**professeur des écoles**	primary schoolteacher
la	**question**	question
la	**récréation**	break
la	**rentrée (des classes)**	beginning of term
la	**réponse**	answer
la	**salle de classe**	classroom
la	**salle des professeurs**	staffroom
les	**sciences**	science
une	**université**	university
les	**vacances**	holidays

USEFUL PHRASES

facile/difficile easy/difficult
intéressant(e) interesting
ennuyeux(euse) boring
lire to read; **écrire** to write
écouter to listen (to)
regarder to look at, watch
répéter to repeat
répondre to reply
parler to speak
elle est première/dernière de la classe she is top/bottom of the class
entrer en classe to go into the classroom
faire une erreur to make a mistake
corriger to correct
j'ai fait une faute de grammaire I made a grammatical mistake
j'ai eu une bonne note I got a good mark
répondez à la question! answer the question!

IMPORTANT WORDS *(masculine)*

le **baccalauréat, le bac**	French school-leaving certificate/exam
le **bulletin**	report
le **bureau**	office
le **certificat**	certificate
le **classeur**	folder, file
le **concours**	competitive exam
le **conseil de classe**	staff meeting *(to discuss progress of pupils)*
le **couloir**	corridor
le **cours magistral**	lecture
le **diplôme**	diploma
le **dossier**	file
un **écrit**	written exam
un **instituteur**	primary schoolteacher
le **livre électronique**	e-book
un **oral**	oral exam
le **papier**	paper
le **règlement**	rules

USEFUL PHRASES

mon ami prépare son bac my friend is sitting his school-leaving exam *(like A-levels)*

les Français n'ont pas classe le mercredi après-midi French children have Wednesday afternoons off

réviser ses leçons to revise

je vais réviser la leçon demain I'll go over the lesson again tomorrow

IMPORTANT WORDS *(feminine)*

une	**absence**	absence
une	**appréciation**	comment *(from teacher)*
la	**conférence**	lecture
la	**cour (de récréation)**	playground
une	**institutrice**	primary schoolteacher
les	**langues anciennes**	ancient languages
une	**LV1 (langue vivante 1)**	first foreign language studied
une	**LV2 (langue vivante 2)**	second foreign language studied
la	**mention**	grade
la	**règle**	rule; ruler
la	**traduction**	translation
la	**trousse**	pencil case
la	**version**	translation (from foreign language)

USEFUL PHRASES

en sixième in Year 7, in the first form
en cinquième in Year 8, in the second form
en quatrième in Year 9, in the third form
en troisième in Year 10, in the fourth form
en seconde in Year 11, in the fifth form
en première in lower sixth
en terminale in upper sixth

présent(e) present
absent(e) absent
punir un élève to punish a pupil
mettre une colle à qn to give sb detention
taisez-vous! be quiet!
levez la main! put your hand up!

USEFUL WORDS *(masculine)*

le **Bic®**	Biro®
le **brouillon**	rough copy
le **cahier**	exercise book, jotter
le **calcul**	sum
le **cartable**	satchel
le **collège technique**	technical college
le **correcteur (liquide)**	correction fluid
le **dictionnaire**	dictionary
un **examinateur**	examiner
un **exercice**	exercise
le **feutre**	felt-tip pen
le **grec**	Greek
un **inspecteur**	school inspector
un **internat**	boarding school
le **latin**	Latin
le **lycéen**	secondary school pupil
le **lycée professionnel**	vocational school
le **manuel**	textbook
le **pensionnaire**	boarder
le **principal**	headmaster (*of collège*)
le **professeur principal**	form tutor
le **proviseur**	headmaster (*of lycée*)
le **pupitre**	desk
le **rang**	row (*of seats etc*)
le **russe**	Russian
le **sac à dos**	backpack
le **stylo bille**	Biro®
le **stylo feutre**	felt-tip pen
le **surveillant**	supervisor
le **tableau interactif**	interactive whiteboard
le **taille-crayon** (*pl* ~s)	pencil sharpener
le **test**	test
le **thème**	prose translation
le **trimestre**	term
le **vestiaire**	cloakroom
le **vocabulaire**	vocabulary

USEFUL WORDS *(feminine)*

l'**algèbre**	algebra
l'**arithmétique**	arithmetic
la **calculatrice,** la **calculette**	calculator
la **colle**	detention; difficult question
la **composition**	essay; class exam
la **conduite**	behaviour
la **craie**	chalk
la **distribution des prix**	prize-giving
une **école maternelle**	nursery school
une **école normale**	College of Education
l'**écriture**	handwriting
l'**éducation civique**	civics
l'**encre**	ink
une **épreuve**	test
la **faculté,** la **fac**	university; faculty
la **feuille de présence**	absence sheet
la **géométrie**	geometry
la **grammaire**	grammar
une **inspectrice**	school inspector
la **lycéenne**	secondary school pupil
la **moyenne**	pass mark; average mark
l'**orthographe**	spelling
la **poésie**	poetry, poem
la **punition**	punishment
la **retenue**	detention
la **sacoche**	schoolbag, satchel
les **SVT (sciences de la vie et de la terre)**	environmental science
la **serviette**	briefcase
la **surveillante**	supervisor
la **tache**	blot
la **tâche**	task
la **technologie**	technology
les **TIC (technologies de l'information et de la communication)**	ICT

ESSENTIAL WORDS *(masculine)*

l'**air**	air
les **animaux**	animals
les **arbres**	trees
le **bois**	wood
un **écologiste**	environmentalist
l'**environnement**	environment
les **fruits**	fruit
le **gas-oil**	diesel
le **gaz**	gas
les **gaz à effet de serre**	greenhouse gases
les **gaz d'échappement**	exhaust fumes
les **habitants**	inhabitants
les **légumes**	vegetables
le **monde**	world
le **pays**	country
les **poissons**	fish
le **temps**	weather; time
les **Verts**	the Greens
le **verre**	glass

IMPORTANT WORDS *(masculine)*

l'**aluminium**	aluminium
l'**avenir**	future
le **biocarburant**	biofuel
le **changement climatique**	climate change
le **climat**	climate
le(s) **dégât(s)**	damage
le **détergent**	detergent
le **développement durable**	sustainable development
le **fleuve**	river
le **gouvernement**	government
le **lac**	lake
le **parc éolien**	wind farm
le **polluant**	pollutant
le **trou dans la couche d'ozone**	hole in the ozone layer

ESSENTIAL WORDS *(feminine)*

les **bouteilles**	bottles
la **carte**	map
la **côte**	coast
l'**eau**	water
l'**écologie**	ecology
l'**empreinte carbone**	carbon footprint
une **éolienne**	wind turbine
une **espèce**	species
l'**essence**	petrol
les **fleurs**	flowers
une **île**	island
la **mer**	sea
la **montagne**	mountain
la **plage**	beach
les **plantes**	plants
la **pluie**	rain
la **pollution**	pollution
la **question**	question
la **région**	region, area
la **rivière**	river
la **température**	temperature
la **terre**	earth
une **usine**	factory
la **voiture**	car

IMPORTANT WORDS *(feminine)*

la **centrale nucléaire**	nuclear plant
la **chaleur**	heat
la **crise**	crisis
la **forêt**	forest
la **lessive**	washing powder; washing
la **planète**	planet
la **solution**	solution
la **taxe**	tax
la **zone**	zone

USEFUL WORDS *(masculine)*

les	**aliments bio**	organic food
un	**aérosol**	aerosol
le	**canal** (*pl* canaux)	canal
les	**CFC**	CFC
le	**chercheur**	researcher
le	**combustible**	fuel
le	**commerce équitable**	fair trade
le	**continent**	continent
les	**déchets nucléaires/ industriels**	nuclear/industrial waste
le	**dépotoir**	dumping ground
le	**désert**	desert
le	**développement durable**	sustainable development
un	**écosystème**	ecosystem
un	**engrais (chimique)**	(artificial) fertilizer
un	**océan**	ocean
les	**OGM**	GMO
le	**panneau solaire** (*pl* ~x ~s)	solar panel
le	**pot catalytique**	catalytic converter
le	**produit**	product
les	**produits chimiques**	chemicals
le	**réchauffement planétaire**	global warming
le	**recyclage**	recycling
les	**scientifiques**	scientists
	l'**univers**	universe

USEFUL PHRASES

il est très écolo he's very environmentally-minded
un produit écologique an eco-friendly product
à l'avenir in the future
polluer to pollute; **détruire** to destroy
contaminer to contaminate
interdire to ban
sauver to save
recycler to recycle
hybride hybrid
vert(e) green

USEFUL WORDS *(feminine)*

la **biodiversité**	biodiversity
la **catastrophe**	disaster
l'**énergie éolienne**	wind power
l'**énergie nucléaire**	nuclear power
une **énergie renouvelable**	renewable energy
l'**énergie solaire**	solar energy
une **éruption**	eruption
la **forêt tropicale humide**	tropical rainforest
la **lune**	moon
la **marée noire**	oil slick
la **nocivité**	harmfulness
les **pluies acides**	acid rain
la **pollution sonore**	noise pollution
la **population**	population
les **vidanges**	sewage
la **voiture électrique/hybride**	electric/hybrid car

USEFUL PHRASES

biodégradable biodegradable
nocif(ive) pour l'environnement harmful to the environment
biologique organic
l'essence sans plomb unleaded petrol
les espèces en voie de disparition endangered species

ESSENTIAL WORDS *(masculine)*

les **adultes**	adults
l'**âge**	age
le **bébé**	baby
le **cousin**	cousin
un **enfant**	child
le **fiancé**	fiancé
le **fils** [fis]	son
le **frère**	brother
le **garçon**	boy
les **gens**	people
le **grand-père** (*pl* ~s~s)	grandfather
les **grands-parents**	grandparents
un **homme**	man
le **jeune homme**	youth, young man
les **jeunes**	young people
le **mari**	husband
le **nom**	name
le **nom de famille**	surname
le **nom de jeune fille**	maiden name
un **oncle**	uncle
le **papa**	daddy
le **parent**	relative
les **parents**	parents
le **père**	father
le **prénom**	first *or* Christian name

USEFUL PHRASES

quel âge avez-vous? how old are you?
j'ai 15 ans – il a 40 ans I'm 15 – he is 40
comment vous appelez-vous? what is your name?
je m'appelle Robert my name is Robert
il s'appelle Jean-Pierre his name is Jean-Pierre
fiancé(e) engaged
marié(e) married
divorcé(e) divorced
séparé(e) separated
épouser qn, se marier avec qn to marry sb
se marier to get married; **divorcer** to get divorced

ESSENTIAL WORDS *(feminine)*

la	**cousine**	cousin
une	**enfant**	child
la	**famille**	family
la	**femme**	woman; wife
la	**fiancée**	fiancée
la	**fille**	daughter; girl
la	**grand-mère** (*pl* ~s~s)	grandmother
les	**grandes personnes**	grown-ups
la	**maman**	mummy
la	**mère**	mother
la	**sœur**	sister
la	**tante**	aunt

USEFUL PHRASES

plus jeune/âgé que moi younger/older than me
as-tu des frères et sœurs? do you have any brothers *or* sisters?
j'ai un frère et une sœur I have one brother and one sister
je n'ai pas de frères/de sœurs I don't have any brothers/sisters
je suis enfant unique I am an only child
toute la famille the whole family
grandir to grow
vieillir to get old
je m'entends bien avec mes parents I get on well with my parents
ma mère travaille my mother works

IMPORTANT WORDS *(masculine)*

un **ado(lescent)**	teenager
un **arrière-grand-père** (*pl* ~s~s)	great-grandfather
les **arrière-grands-parents**	great-grandparents
le **beau-père** (*pl* ~x~s)	father-in-law; stepfather
le **célibataire**	bachelor
le **compagnon**	partner
l'**époux**	husband
le **mariage**	marriage; wedding
le **neveu**	nephew
le **PACS**	civil partnership
le **petit-fils** [pətifis] (*pl* ~s~)	grandson
les **petits-enfants** [pətizɑ̃fɑ̃]	grandchildren
le **veuf**	widower

USEFUL WORDS *(masculine)*

le **beau-fils** [bofis] (*pl* ~x~)	son-in-law; stepson
le **beau-frère** (*pl* ~x~s)	brother-in-law
le **couple**	couple
le **demi-frère** (*pl* ~s)	stepbrother
le **filleul**	godson
le **gendre**	son-in-law
le **gosse**	kid
les **jumeaux**	twins
le **marié**	bridegroom
les **nouveaux mariés**	newly-weds
un **orphelin**	orphan
le **parrain**	godfather
le **retraité**	pensioner
le **surnom**	nickname
les **triplés**	triplets
le **vieillard**	old man

USEFUL PHRASES

naître to be born
vivre to live
mourir to die
je suis né(e) en 2001 I was born in 2001
ma grand-mère est morte my grandmother is dead
elle est morte en 1995 she died in 1995

IMPORTANT WORDS *(feminine)*

une	**ado(lescente)**	teenager
les	**allocations familiales**	child benefit
un	**arrière-grand-mère** (*pl* ~s~s)	great-grandmother
la	**belle-mère** (*pl* ~s~s)	mother-in-law; stepmother
la	**célibataire**	single woman
la	**compagne**	partner
une	**épouse**	wife
la	**jeune fille au pair**	au pair girl
la	**jeunesse**	youth
la	**nièce**	niece
la	**petite-fille** (*pl* ~s~s)	granddaughter
la	**veuve**	widow

USEFUL WORDS *(feminine)*

la	**belle-fille** (*pl* ~s~s)	daughter-in-law; stepdaughter
la	**belle-sœur** (*pl* ~s~s)	sister-in-law
la	**demi-sœur** (*pl* ~s)	stepsister
la	**famille monoparentale**	single-parent family
la	**femme au foyer**	housewife
la	**filleule**	goddaughter
la	**gosse**	kid
la	**jeune mariée**	bride
les	**jumelles**	twins, twin sisters
la	**marraine**	godmother
la	**nurse**	nanny
une	**orpheline**	orphan
la	**retraitée**	pensioner
la	**vieillesse**	old age

USEFUL PHRASES

il/elle est célibataire he/she is single
il est veuf he is a widower
elle est veuve she is a widow
je suis le cadet (la cadette) I am the youngest
je suis l'aîné(e) I am the eldest
ma sœur aînée my older sister
mon petit frère my little brother

ESSENTIAL WORDS *(masculine)*

un	**agriculteur**	farmer
un	**animal** (*pl* animaux)	animal
le	**bœuf** [bœf] (*pl* -s [bø])	ox
le	**canard**	duck
le	**champ**	field
le	**chat**	cat
le	**cheval** (*pl* chevaux)	horse
le	**chien**	dog
le	**chien de berger**	sheepdog
le	**cochon**	pig
le	**dindon**	turkey
le	**fermier**	farmer
le	**mouton**	sheep
le	**poulet**	chicken
le	**veau** (*pl* -x)	calf
le	**village**	village

IMPORTANT WORDS *(masculine)*

un	**agneau** (*pl* -x)	lamb
le	**coq**	cock
le	**paysan**	countryman
le	**tracteur**	tractor

USEFUL PHRASES

l'agriculture biologique organic farming
l'agriculture intensive intensive farming
un champ de blé a cornfield
l'élevage en batterie battery farming
s'occuper des animaux to look after the animals
traire les vaches to milk the cows
rentrer la moisson to bring in the harvest

ESSENTIAL WORDS *(feminine)*

une	**agricultrice**	farmer
la	**barrière**	gate; fence
la	**brebis**	ewe
la	**camionnette**	van
la	**campagne**	country
une	**exploitation agricole**	farm
la	**ferme**	farm; farmhouse
la	**fermière**	farmer; farmer's wife
la	**forêt**	forest
la	**jument**	mare
la	**poule**	hen
la	**serre**	greenhouse
la	**terre**	earth, ground
la	**truie**	sow
la	**vache**	cow

IMPORTANT WORDS *(feminine)*

la	**colline**	hill
la	**paysanne**	countrywoman

USEFUL PHRASES

vivre à la campagne to live in the country
travailler dans une ferme to work on a farm
faire la récolte to bring in the crops
faire les foins to make hay
les poulets élevés en plein air free range chickens
les œufs de poules élevées en plein air free range eggs

USEFUL WORDS *(masculine)*

un	**âne**	donkey
le	**bélier**	ram
le	**berger**	shepherd
le	**bétail**	cattle
le	**blé**	corn; wheat
le	**chevreau** (*pl* -x)	kid
un	**élevage**	cattle farm
un	**engrais**	fertilizer
un	**épouvantail**	scarecrow
un	**étang**	pond
le	**foin**	hay
le	**fossé**	ditch
le	**fumier**	manure
le	**grain**	grain, seed
le	**grenier**	loft
le	**:hangar**	shed, barn
le	**maïs** [mais]	maize
le	**marché**	market
le	**moulin (à vent)**	(wind)mill
le	**paysage**	landscape
le	**porc** [pɔʀ]	pig
le	**poulailler**	henhouse
le	**poulain**	foal
le	**poussin**	chick
le	**pré**	meadow
le	**puits**	well
le	**raisin**	grape
le	**seigle**	rye
le	**sillon**	furrow
le	**silo**	silo
le	**sol**	ground, earth
le	**taureau** (*pl* -x)	bull
le	**troupeau** (*pl* -x)	(*sheep*) flock; (*cattle*) herd

USEFUL WORDS *(feminine)*

	l'**avoine**	oats
la	**basse-cour** (*pl* ~s~s)	farmyard
la	**boue**	mud
la	**céréale**	cereal crop
la	**charrette**	cart
la	**charrue**	plough
la	**chaumière**	(thatched) cottage
la	**chèvre**	goat
une	**échelle**	ladder
une	**écurie**	stable
une	**étable**	cow-shed, byre
la	**foire**	fair
la	**grange**	barn
la	**laine**	wool
la	**lande**	moor, heath
la	**meule de foin**	haystack
la	**moisson**	harvest
la	**moissonneuse-batteuse** (*pl* ~s~s)	combine harvester
une	**oie**	goose
	l'**orge**	barley
la	**paille**	straw
la	**porcherie**	pigsty
la	**récolte**	crop
les	**vendanges**	grape harvest, grape picking
la	**vigne**	vine

fish and insects

ESSENTIAL WORDS *(masculine)*

les **fruits de mer**	seafood
le **poisson**	fish
le **poisson rouge**	goldfish

IMPORTANT WORDS *(masculine)*

le **crabe**	crab
un **insecte**	insect

USEFUL WORDS *(masculine)*

un **aquarium**	aquarium
le **brochet**	pike
le **cafard**	cockroach
le **calmar**	squid
le **criquet**	cricket
le **frelon**	hornet
le **grillon**	cricket
le **:haddock**	haddock
le **:hareng**	herring
le **:homard**	lobster
le **merlan**	whiting
le **moucheron**	midge
le **moustique**	mosquito
le **papillon**	butterfly
le **papillon de nuit**	moth
le **poulpe**	octopus
le **requin**	shark
le **saumon**	salmon
le **têtard**	tadpole
le **thon**	tuna
le **ver**	worm
le **ver à soie**	silkworm

USEFUL PHRASES

nager to swim
voler to fly
nous allons à la pêche we're going fishing

ESSENTIAL WORDS *(feminine)*

l'**eau**	water

IMPORTANT WORDS *(feminine)*

la **mouche**	fly
la **sardine**	sardine
la **truite**	trout

USEFUL WORDS *(feminine)*

une **abeille**	bee
une **aile**	wing
une **anguille**	eel
une **araignée**	spider
la **chenille**	caterpillar
la **cigale**	cicada
la **coccinelle** [kɔksinɛl]	ladybird
la **crevette**	shrimp
la **fourmi**	ant
la **grenouille**	frog
la **guêpe**	wasp
une **huître**	oyster
la **langouste**	crayfish
les **langoustines**	scampi
la **libellule**	dragonfly
la **limande**	dab
la **méduse**	jellyfish
la **morue**	(salt) cod
la **moule**	mussel
la **pieuvre**	octopus
la **puce**	flea
la **punaise**	bug
la **sauterelle**	grasshopper
la **sole**	sole

USEFUL PHRASES

une piqûre de guêpe a wasp sting
une toile d'araignée a spider's web

ESSENTIAL WORDS *(masculine)*

l'**alcool**	alcohol
un **apéritif**	aperitif
le **bar**	bar
le **beurre**	butter
le **bifteck**	steak
le **bœuf**	beef
le **bol**	bowl
les **bonbons**	sweets
le **café**	coffee; café
le **café au lait**	milky coffee
le **café-crème**	coffee with milk
le **chocolat (chaud)**	(hot) chocolate
le **cidre**	cider
le **coca**	Coke®
le **couteau** (*pl* -x)	knife
le **croissant**	croissant
le **croque-monsieur** *(pl inv)*	ham and cheese toastie
le **cuisinier**	cook
le **déjeuner**	lunch
le **demi**	half-pint
le **dessert**	dessert
le **dîner**	dinner
le **fromage**	cheese
un **fruit**	piece of fruit
les **fruits**	fruit
les **fruits de mer**	seafood
le **garçon (de café)**	waiter
le **gâteau** (*pl* -x)	cake
le **:hamburger**	hamburger
les **:hors-d'œuvre**	hors d'œuvre, starters
le **jambon**	ham
le **jus de fruit**	fruit juice
le **lait**	milk
les **légumes**	vegetables
le **menu**	fixed-price menu
un **œuf** [œf] (*pl* -s [ø])	egg

ESSENTIAL WORDS *(feminine)*

l'**addition**	bill
une **assiette**	plate
la **baguette**	French loaf
la **bière**	beer
la **boisson**	drink
la **boîte**	tin, can; box
la **bouteille**	bottle
la **carte**	menu
les **céréales**	cereal
la **confiture**	jam
la **confiture d'oranges**	marmalade
la **conserve**	canned food
la **crêpe**	pancake
les **crudités**	mixed raw vegetables
la **cuiller, la cuillère**	spoon
l'**eau (minérale)**	(mineral) water
une **entrecôte**	(entrecôte) steak
une **entrée**	first course
la **faim**	hunger
la **fourchette**	fork
les **frites**	chips
la **glace**	ice cream
l'**huile**	oil
la **limonade**	lemonade
une **olive**	olive
une **omelette**	omelette
la **pâtisserie**	pastry; patisserie
la **poissonnerie**	fish shop
les **pommes frites**	chips
la **quiche**	quiche
la **salade**	salad
la **saucisse**	sausage
la **soif**	thirst
la **soucoupe**	saucer
la **soupe**	soup
la **table**	table
la **tasse**	cup

ESSENTIAL WORDS *(masculine continued)*

un **œuf à la coque**	soft-boiled egg
un **œuf dur**	hard-boiled egg
le **pain**	bread
le **pain grillé**	toast
le **pain au chocolat**	pain au chocolat
le **pâté**	pâté
le **patron**	owner
le **petit déjeuner**	breakfast
le **pique-nique** (*pl* ~s)	picnic
le **plat**	dish; course
le **plat du jour**	today's special
le **plateau** (*pl* ~x)	tray
les **plats cuisinés**	ready-made meals
le **poisson**	fish
le **porc** [pɔʀ]	pork
le **potage**	soup
le **poulet (rôti)**	(roast) chicken
le **quart**	quarter (*bottle/litre etc*)
le **repas**	meal
le **restaurant**	restaurant
le **riz**	rice
le **rôti**	roast
le **sandwich** [sɑ̃dwitʃ]	sandwich
le **saucisson**	salami
le **sel**	salt
le **self**	self-service restaurant
le **service**	service
le **steak** [stɛk]	steak
le **sucre**	sugar
le **thé**	tea
le **veau**	veal
le **verre**	glass
le **vin**	wine
le **vinaigre**	vinegar
le **yaourt**	yoghurt

ESSENTIAL WORDS *(feminine continued)*

la	**tranche (de)**	slice (of)
la	**vaisselle**	dishes
la	**viande**	meat

IMPORTANT WORDS *(feminine)*

la	**brasserie**	restaurant
la	**cafétéria**	cafeteria
la	**carafe**	carafe, jug
les	**chips**	crisps
la	**côte de porc**	pork chop
la	**crème**	cream
la	**cuiller à café/à dessert/ à soupe**	teaspoon/dessert spoon/ tablespoon
la	**farine**	flour
la	**grillade**	grilled meat
la	**mayonnaise**	mayonnaise
la	**merguez**	spicy sausage
la	**moutarde**	mustard
une	**odeur**	smell
la	**pizza**	pizza
la	**pression**	draught beer
la	**recette**	recipe
la	**serveuse**	waitress
la	**tarte**	tart
la	**terrine**	pâté
la	**théière**	teapot
la	**vanille**	vanilla

IMPORTANT WORDS *(masculine)*

l'**agneau**	lamb
l'**ail**	garlic
le **chariot**	trolley
le **chef** *(m+f)*	chef
le **choix**	choice
le **commerce équitable**	fair trade
le **couvert**	cover charge; place setting
les **escargots**	snails
le **goût**	taste
le **goûter**	snack
le **lapin**	rabbit
le **mouton**	mutton
le **parfum**	flavour
le **pichet**	jug
le **poivre**	pepper
le **pourboire**	tip
le **prix fixe**	set price
le **prix net**	inclusive price
le **serveur**	waiter
le **sirop**	syrup; cordial
le **supplément**	extra charge

USEFUL WORDS *(masculine)*

le **bouchon**	cork
le **cacao**	cocoa
le **casse-croûte** *(pl inv)*	snack
le **champagne**	champagne
le **citron pressé**	freshly-squeezed lemon juice
le **cognac**	brandy
le **foie**	liver
le **gibier**	game
le **glaçon**	ice cube
le **ketchup**	ketchup
le **lard**	bacon
les **lardons**	diced bacon
le **miel**	honey
un **ouvre-boîtes** *(pl inv)*	tin opener
le **panaché**	shandy

USEFUL WORDS *(feminine)*

une	**assiette anglaise**	selection of cold meats
la	**biscotte**	Melba toast
la	**brioche**	bun
la	**carte des vins**	wine list
la	**côtelette**	chop
la	**crème anglaise**	custard
la	**crème Chantilly**	whipped cream
la	**cruche**	jug
les	**cuisses de grenouille**	frogs' legs
la	**gelée**	jelly
une	**infusion**	herbal tea
la	**margarine**	margarine
la	**miette**	crumb
les	**moules**	mussels
la	**nappe**	tablecloth
la	**nourriture**	food
la	**paille**	straw
les	**pâtes**	pasta
la	**purée**	mashed potatoes
les	**rillettes**	potted meat (*made of pork or goose*)
la	**sauce**	sauce; gravy
la	**serviette**	napkin
la	**tartine**	piece of bread and butter
la	**tisane**	herbal tea
les	**tripes**	tripe
la	**vinaigrette**	vinaigrette dressing
la	**volaille**	poultry

USEFUL PHRASES

cuisiner to cook
manger to eat
boire to drink
avaler to swallow
mon plat préféré my favourite dish
qu'est-ce que tu bois? what are you having to drink?
c'est bon it's nice

USEFUL WORDS *(masculine continued)*

le	**petit pain**	roll
le	**ragoût**	stew
les	**rognons**	kidneys
le	**rosbif**	roast beef
le	**thermos**	flask
le	**tire-bouchon** (*pl* ~s)	corkscrew
un	**toast**	slice of toast
le	**whisky**	whisky

USEFUL PHRASES

déjeuner to have lunch
dîner to have dinner
goûter qch to taste sth
ça sent bon! that smells good!
le vin blanc/rosé/rouge white/rosé/red wine
un steak saignant/à point/bien cuit a rare/medium/well-done steak
avoir faim to be hungry
avoir soif to be thirsty
mettre le couvert, mettre la table to set the table
débarrasser to clear the table
faire la vaisselle to do the dishes
nous goûtons en rentrant de l'école we have a snack when we come back from school
prendre le petit déjeuner to have breakfast
délicieux(ieuse) delicious
dégoûtant(e) disgusting
bon appétit! enjoy your meal!
à votre santé! cheers!
l'addition, s'il vous plaît! the bill please!
est-ce que le service est compris? is service included?
"service (non) compris" "service (not) included"
manger au restaurant to eat out
inviter qn à déjeuner to invite sb to lunch
prendre l'apéritif to have drinks

SMOKING

le	**briquet**	lighter
le	**tabac**	tobacco; tobacconist's
le	**cendrier**	ashtray
le	**cigare**	cigar
un	**espace fumeur(s)**	smoking area
le	**timbre à la nicotine**	nicotine patch
une	**allumette**	match
la	**cigarette**	cigarette
la	**cigarette électronique**	e-cigarette
la	**pipe**	pipe
la	**zone fumeur(s)**	smoking area

USEFUL PHRASES

une boîte d'allumettes a box of matches
avez-vous du feu? do you have a light?
allumer une cigarette to light up
"défense de fumer" "no smoking"
je ne fume pas I don't smoke
j'ai arrêté de fumer I've stopped smoking
fumer est très mauvais pour la santé smoking is very bad for you
vapoter to vape, to smoke an e-cigarette

ESSENTIAL WORDS *(masculine)*

un	**appareil-photo** (*pl* ~s~s)	camera
	l'**argent de poche**	pocket money
le	**baby-sitting**	baby-sitting
le	**babyfoot**	table football
le	**baladeur**	personal stereo
le	**billet**	ticket
le	**CD**	CD
le	**chanteur**	singer
le	**cinéma**	cinema
le	**club**	club
le	**concert**	concert
les	**copains**	friends
le	**correspondant**	pen friend
le	**DVD**	DVD
les	**échecs**	chess
le	**film**	film
le	**:hobby**	hobby
	l'**Internet**	internet
le	**jeu** (*pl* -x)	game
le	**jeu vidéo**	video game, computer game
le	**journal** (*pl* journaux)	newspaper
le	**lecteur de CD/DVD/MP3**	CD/DVD/MP3 player
le	**magazine (people)**	(celebrity) magazine
le	**membre**	member
le	**musée**	museum; art gallery
un	**ordinateur**	computer
un	**ordinateur portable**	laptop
le	**passe-temps** (*pl inv*)	hobby
le	**programme**	programme
le	**roman**	novel
le	**roman policier**	detective novel
le	**spectacle**	show
le	**sport**	sports
le	**(téléphone) portable**	mobile (phone)
le	**temps libre**	free time
le	**théâtre**	theatre
le	**week-end** (*pl* ~s)	weekend

ESSENTIAL WORDS *(feminine)*

la	**bande dessinée**	comic strip
la	**brochure**	leaflet
les	**cartes**	cards
la	**chaîne de télévision**	TV channel
la	**chanson**	song; singing
la	**chanteuse**	singer
la	**console de jeu**	games console
les	**copines**	(girl)friends
la	**correspondante**	pen friend
la	**danse**	dance; dancing
la	**distraction**	entertainment
une	**excursion**	trip, outing
la	**fête**	party
les	**informations**	news
	l'**informatique**	computing
la	**lecture**	reading
la	**musique (pop/classique)**	(pop/classical) music
la	**patinoire**	skating rink
la	**photo**	photo
la	**presse**	the press
la	**promenade**	walk
la	**publicité**	publicity
la	**radio**	radio
la	**revue**	magazine
la	**tablette**	tablet
la	**télé(vision)**	TV, television
la	**vedette (de cinéma)** *(m+f)*	(film) star

USEFUL PHRASES

je sors avec mes amis I go out with my friends
je lis les journaux, je regarde la télévision I read the newspapers, I watch television
bricoler to do DIY
faire du baby-sitting to baby-sit
je joue au football/au tennis/aux cartes I play football/tennis/cards
je joue de la guitare I play the guitar
zapper to channel-hop

IMPORTANT WORDS *(masculine)*

un	**appareil-photo numérique**	digital camera
le	**caméscope**	camcorder
le	**concours**	competition
le	**dessin animé**	cartoon
le	**disque compact**	compact disc, CD
le	**feuilleton**	serial; soap
le	**graveur de CD/DVD**	CD/DVD writer
le	**jouet**	toy
les	**loisirs**	leisure activities
le	**PC**	PC, personal computer
le	**petit ami**	boyfriend
le	**rendez-vous**	date
le	**site web**	website
le	**SMS**, le **texto**	text message
le	**tricot**	knitting

USEFUL WORDS *(masculine)*

le	**blog**	blog
le	**chat** [tʃat]	chat; chatroom
un	**éclaireur**	scout
le	**fan** [fan]	fan
le	**forum**	forum
le	**:hit-parade**	charts
le	**jeu de société**	board game
les	**mots croisés**	crossword puzzle(s)
les	**people**	celebrities
le	**scout**	scout
le	**skate(board)**	skateboard
le	**vidéoclub**	video shop

USEFUL PHRASES

passionnant(e) exciting
ennuyeux(euse) boring
amusant(e) funny
pas mal not bad, quite good
faire des photos, prendre des photos to take photos
je m'ennuie I'm bored

IMPORTANT WORDS *(feminine)*

les	**actualités**	news
une	**affiche**	notice; poster
la	**carte mémoire**	memory card
la	**collection**	collection
une	**émission**	programme
une	**exposition**	exhibition
la	**maison des jeunes**	youth club
la	**peinture**	painting
la	**petite amie**	girlfriend
la	**petite annonce**	advert; small ad
la	**randonnée**	hike
la	**réunion**	meeting
la	**soirée**	evening

USEFUL WORDS *(feminine)*

la	**boîte de nuit**	night club
la	**chorale**	choir
la	**colonie de vacances**	holiday camp
la	**diapositive**	slide
une	**éclaireuse**	girl guide
la	**méchanique**	mechanics
la	**photographie**	photograph; photography
la	**planche de skate**	skateboard

USEFUL PHRASES

aller en boîte to go clubbing
danser to dance
on se réunit le vendredi we meet on Fridays
on se retrouve à vingt heures devant le cinéma see you at 8pm in front of the cinema
j'ai rendez-vous avec elle samedi I have a date with her on Saturday
je fais des économies pour m'acheter un lecteur de mp3 I'm saving up to buy an MP3 player
j'aimerais faire le tour du monde I'd like to go round the world

ESSENTIAL WORDS *(masculine)*

un **abricot**	apricot
un **ananas**	pineapple
le **citron**	lemon
un **fruit**	piece of fruit
les **fruits**	fruit
le **marron (grillé)**	(roasted) chestnut
le **pamplemousse**	grapefruit
le **raisin**	grape(s)
le **raisin sec**	raisin

IMPORTANT WORDS *(masculine)*

un **arbre fruitier**	fruit tree
le **melon**	melon

USEFUL WORDS *(masculine)*

un **avocat**	avocado
le **cassis**	blackcurrant
le **kiwi**	kiwi-fruit
le **noyau** (*pl* -x)	stone (*in fruit*)
le **pépin**	pip (*in fruit*)
le **pruneau** (*pl* -x)	prune

ESSENTIAL WORDS *(feminine)*

la	**banane**	banana
la	**cerise**	cherry
la	**fraise**	strawberry
la	**framboise**	raspberry
une	**orange**	orange
la	**peau**	skin
la	**pêche**	peach
la	**poire**	pear
la	**pomme**	apple
la	**tomate**	tomato

USEFUL WORDS *(feminine)*

la	**baie**	berry
la	**cacahuète**	peanut
la	**clémentine**	clementine
la	**datte**	date
la	**figue**	fig
la	**grenade**	pomegranate
la	**groseille**	redcurrant
la	**mandarine**	tangerine
la	**mûre**	blackberry
la	**myrtille**	blueberry
la	**noisette**	hazelnut
la	**noix**	nut; walnut
la	**noix de cajou**	cashew nut
la	**noix de coco**	coconut
la	**prune**	plum
la	**rhubarbe**	rhubarb
la	**vigne**	vine

USEFUL PHRASES

un jus d'orange/d'ananas an orange/a pineapple juice
une grappe de raisin a bunch of grapes
mûr(e) ripe
pas mûr(e) unripe
peler un fruit to peel a fruit
une peau de banane a banana skin

ESSENTIAL WORDS *(masculine)*

un **abat-jour**	lampshade
le **congélateur**	freezer
le **fauteuil**	armchair
le **freezer**	freezer compartment
le **frigidaire**, le **frigo**	fridge
le **lit**	bed
le **meuble**	piece of furniture
les **meubles**	furniture
le **miroir**	mirror
le **placard**	cupboard
le **radiateur**	heater
le **radio-réveil**	radio alarm
le **réfrigérateur**	fridge
le **téléphone**	telephone

IMPORTANT WORDS *(masculine)*

un **appareil (ménager)**	kitchen appliance
un **aspirateur**	vacuum cleaner
le **buffet**	sideboard
le **bureau** (*pl* -x)	desk
le **canapé**	sofa
le **canapé-lit**	sofa bed
le **coffre**	chest
le **four à micro-ondes**	microwave oven
le **lave-linge**	washing machine
le **lave-vaisselle**	dishwasher
le **lecteur de CD/DVD**	CD/DVD player
le **lecteur MP3**	MP3 player
le **livre électronique**	e-book
le **piano**	piano
le **portable**	mobile phone
le **sèche-linge**	tumble-dryer
le **tableau** (*pl* -x)	picture
le **téléphone sans fil**	cordless phone

ESSENTIAL WORDS *(feminine)*

une **armoire**	wardrobe
la **bouilloire**	kettle
la **chaîne (stéréo)**	stereo system
la **chaise**	chair
la **cuisinière (électrique/à gaz)**	(electric/gas) cooker
la **glace**	mirror
la **lampe**	lamp
la **ligne fixe**	landline
la **machine à laver**	washing machine
la **pendule**	clock
la **pièce**	room
la **radio**	radio
la **table**	table
la **télévision**	television

IMPORTANT WORDS *(feminine)*

la **bibliothèque**	bookcase
la **liseuse**	e-reader
la **peinture**	painting
la **radio numérique (DAB)**	digital radio
la **table basse**	coffee table
la **tablette tactile**	tablet

USEFUL WORDS *(masculine)*

le	**berceau** (*pl* -x)	cradle
le	**cadre**	frame
le	**caméscope**	camcorder
le	**camion de déménagement**	removal van
le	**casque**	headphones
le	**chargeur**	charger
le	**déménagement**	move
le	**déménageur**	removal man
les	**écouteurs**	earphones
le	**fer à repasser**	iron
le	**four**	oven
le	**GPS**	sat nav
le	**:home cinéma**	home cinema system
le	**lampadaire**	standard lamp
le	**lisseur (à cheveux)**	hair straighteners
le	**lit d'enfant**	cot
les	**lits superposés**	bunk beds
le	**matelas**	mattress
le	**mobilier**	furniture
le	**pèse-personne**	scales
le	**portemanteau** (*pl* -x)	coat hanger; coat rack; hat stand
le	**robot ménager**	food processor
le	**répondeur**	answering machine
le	**sèche-cheveux** *(pl inv)*	hair-dryer
le	**secrétaire**	writing desk
le	**siège**	seat
le	**store**	blind
le	**tabouret**	stool
le	**tapis**	rug
le	**tiroir**	drawer
le	**volets**	shutters
les	**vidéoprojecteur**	video projector

USEFUL PHRASES

un appartement meublé a furnished flat
allumer/éteindre le radiateur to switch on/off the heater
j'ai fait mon lit I've made my bed
s'asseoir to sit down
mettre qch au four to put sth in the oven

USEFUL WORDS *(feminine)*

une	**antenne**	aerial
une	**antenne parabolique**	satellite dish
la	**caméra vidéo**	video camera, camcorder
la	**chaîne compacte**	music centre
la	**clé USB**	USB stick
la	**coiffeuse**	dressing table
la	**commode**	chest of drawers
une	**enceinte**	speaker
une	**étagère**	shelves
la	**:hotte aspirante**	cooker hood
la	**lampe halogène**	halogen lamp
la	**machine à coudre**	sewing machine
la	**moquette**	fitted carpet
la	**planche à repasser**	ironing board
la	**table de chevet**	bedside table
la	**télécommande**	remote control

USEFUL PHRASES

tirer les rideaux to draw the curtains
fermer les volets to close the shutters
c'est un 4 pièces it's a 4-roomed flat

ESSENTIAL WORDS

les Alpes *(fpl)*	the Alps
l'Atlantique *(m)*	the Atlantic
Bordeaux	Bordeaux
la Bourgogne	Burgundy
la Bretagne	Brittany
Bruxelles	Brussels
la Côte d'Azur	the Cote d'Azur
Douvres	Dover
Édimbourg	Edinburgh
l'est *(m)*	the east
la Loire	the Loire
Londres	London
Lyon	Lyons
la Manche	the Channel
Marseille	Marseilles
le Massif Central	the Massif Central
la Méditerranée	the Mediterranean
la mer du Nord	the North Sea
le Midi	the South of France
le nord	the north
la Normandie	Normandy
l'ouest *(m)*	the west
Paris	Paris
les Pyrénées *(fpl)*	the Pyrenees
le Rhône	the Rhone
la Seine	the Seine
le sud	the south

IMPORTANT WORDS

Québec	Quebec *(city)*
le Québec	Quebec *(state)*
le Rhin	the Rhine
la Tamise	the Thames

USEFUL WORDS

Alger	Algiers
Anvers	Antwerp
Athènes	Athens
Barcelone	Barcelona
Berlin	Berlin
Le Caire	Cairo
la capitale	the capital
le chef-lieu	the main town
la Corse	Corsica
l'Extrême-Orient *(m)*	the Far East
Genève	Geneva
les îles *(fpl)* **anglo-normandes**	the Channel Islands
les îles *(fpl)* **Britanniques**	the British Isles
le Jura	the Jura Mountains
le lac Léman	Lake Geneva
Moscou	Moscow
le Moyen-Orient	the Middle East
le Pacifique	the Pacific
Pékin	Beijing
le Pôle nord/sud	the North/South Pole
le Proche-Orient	the Near East
la Sardaigne	Sardinia
Varsovie	Warsaw
Venise	Venice
Vienne	Vienna
les Vosges *(fpl)*	the Vosges Mountains

USEFUL PHRASES

aller à Londres/en Bourgogne to go to London/to Burgundy
aller dans le Midi to go to the South of France
je viens de Londres/du Massif Central I come from London/from the Massif Central
au nord in *or* to the north; **au sud** in *or* to the south
à l'est in *or* to the east; **à l'ouest** in *or* to the west

GREETINGS

bonjour hello
salut hi; goodbye
ça va? how are you?
ça va *(in reply)* fine
enchanté(e) pleased to meet you
allô hello *(on telephone)*
bonsoir good evening; good night
bonne nuit good night *(when going to bed)*
au revoir goodbye
à demain see you tomorrow
à bientôt see you soon
à tout à l'heure see you later
adieu farewell

BEST WISHES

bon anniversaire happy birthday
joyeux Noël merry Christmas
bonne année happy New Year
joyeuses Pâques happy Easter
meilleurs vœux best wishes
bienvenue welcome
félicitations congratulations
bon appétit enjoy your meal
bon courage all the best
bonne chance good luck
bon voyage safe journey
à tes (*or* vos) souhaits bless you *(after a sneeze)*
à la tienne (*or* la vôtre) cheers
à ta (*or* votre) santé cheers

SURPRISE

mon Dieu my goodness
comment?, hein?, quoi? what?
ah bon oh, I see
ça, par exemple well, well
sans blague(?) really(?)
ah oui?, c'est vrai?, vraiment? really?
tu rigoles, tu plaisantes you're kidding
quelle chance! what a stroke of luck!
tiens! well, well!

POLITENESS

excusez-moi I'm sorry, excuse me
s'il vous (*or* **te) plaît** please
SVP please
merci thank you
non merci no thank you; **oui merci** yes please
de rien, je vous en prie, il n'y a pas de quoi not at all, it's quite all right, don't mention it
volontiers gladly

AGREEMENT

oui yes
bien sûr of course
d'accord OK
bon fine

DISAGREEMENT

non no
mais non no *(contradicting a positive statement)*
si yes *(contradicting a negative statement)*
bien sûr que non of course not
jamais de la vie not on your life
pas du tout not at all
au contraire on the contrary
ça, par exemple well I never
quel culot what a cheek
mêlez-vous de vos affaires mind your own business

DIFFICULTIES

au secours help
au feu fire
aïe ouch
pardon (I'm) sorry, excuse me, I beg your pardon
je m'excuse I'm sorry
je regrette I'm sorry
désolé(e) I'm (really) sorry
c'est dommage, quel dommage what a pity
zut bother
j'en ai marre I'm fed up
je n'en peux plus I can't stand it any more
oh là là oh dear
quelle horreur how awful

ORDERS

attention! be careful!
hep *or* **eh, vous là-bas!** hey, you there!
fiche le camp! clear off!
chut! shhhh!
ça suffit! that's enough!
défense de fumer no smoking
allez go on, come on
allons-y let's go
allez-y, vas-y go ahead

OTHERS

aucune idée no idea
peut-être perhaps, maybe
je ne sais pas I don't know
vous désirez? can I help you?
voilà there, there you are
j'arrive just coming
ne t'en fais pas don't worry
ce n'est pas la peine it's not worth it
à propos by the way
dis donc (*or* **dites donc)** by the way
chéri(e) darling
le (*or* **la) pauvre** poor thing
tant mieux so much the better
ça m'est égal I don't mind
tant pis too bad
ça dépend that depends
que faire? what shall I (or we) do?
à quoi bon? what's the point?
ça m'embête it bothers me
ça m'agace it gets on my nerves

ESSENTIAL WORDS *(masculine)*

un **accident**	accident
le **dentiste** *(m+f)*	dentist
le **docteur** *(m+f)*	doctor
un **hôpital** (*pl* hôpitaux)	hospital
un **infirmier**	(male) nurse
le **lit**	bed
le **malade**	patient
le **médecin** *(m+f)*	doctor
le **rendez-vous** *(pl inv)*	appointment
le **ventre**	stomach

IMPORTANT WORDS *(masculine)*

un **antiseptique**	antiseptic
le **brancard**	stretcher
le **cabinet (de consultation)**	surgery
le **cachet**	tablet
le **comprimé**	tablet
le **coton hydrophile**	cotton wool
le **coup de soleil**	sunburn
le **médicament**	medicine, drug
le **pansement**	dressing; bandage
le **patient**	patient
le **pharmacien**	chemist
le **plâtre**	plaster (cast)
le **remède**	medicine
un **rhume**	cold
le **sang**	blood
le **sirop**	syrup
le **sparadrap**	sticking plaster

USEFUL PHRASES

il y a eu un accident there's been an accident
être admis(e) à l'hôpital to be admitted to hospital
vous devez rester au lit you must stay in bed
être malade, être souffrant(e) to be ill
je suis diabétique I am diabetic
se sentir mieux to feel better
soigner to look after

ESSENTIAL WORDS *(feminine)*

une	**aspirine**	aspirin
une	**infirmière**	nurse
la	**pastille**	lozenge
la	**pharmacie**	chemist's
la	**santé**	health
la	**température**	temperature

IMPORTANT WORDS *(feminine)*

une	**allergie**	allergy
une	**ambulance**	ambulance
une	**assurance**	insurance
la	**blessure**	injury, wound
la	**chambre d'hôpital**	hospital room
la	**clinique**	clinic, private hospital
la	**crème**	cream, ointment
la	**cuillerée**	spoonful
la	**diarrhée**	diarrhoea
la	**douleur**	pain
la	**grippe**	flu
la	**grippe porcine**	swine flu
une	**insolation**	sunstroke
la	**maladie**	illness
une	**opération**	operation
une	**ordonnance**	prescription
la	**patiente**	patient
la	**pilule**	pill; the Pill
la	**piqûre**	injection; sting
la	**réaction allergique**	allergic reaction
les	**urgences**	Accident and Emergency

USEFUL PHRASES

je me suis blessé(e), je me suis fait mal I have hurt myself
je me suis coupé le doigt I have cut my finger
je me suis foulé la cheville I have sprained my ankle
il s'est cassé le bras he has broken his arm
je me suis brûlé I have burnt myself
j'ai mal à la gorge/mal à la tête/mal au ventre I've got a sore throat/ a headache/a stomach ache
avoir de la température *or* **de la fièvre** to have a temperature

USEFUL WORDS *(masculine)*

un **abcès**	abscess
un **accès**	fit
le **bandage**	bandage
le **bleu**	bruise
le **cancer**	cancer
le **choc**	shock
le **dentier**	false teeth
le **fauteuil roulant**	wheelchair
le **fortifiant**	tonic
le **microbe**	germ
le **nerf**	nerve
les **oreillons**	mumps
le **poison**	poison
le **pouls** [pu]	pulse
les **premiers secours**	first aid
les **premiers soins**	first aid
le **préservatif**	condom
le **régime**	diet
le **repos**	rest
le **rhume des foins**	hayfever
le **SAMU**	emergency medical service
le **sida**	AIDS
le **stress**	stress
le **vertige**	dizzy spell

USEFUL PHRASES

j'ai mal au cœur I feel sick
maigrir to lose weight
grossir to put on weight
avaler to swallow
saigner to bleed
vomir to vomit
être en forme to be in good shape
se reposer to rest

USEFUL WORDS *(feminine)*

l'	**acné**	acne
une	**angine**	tonsillitis
une	**appendicite**	appendicitis
la	**béquille**	crutch
la	**carte européenne d'assurance maladie**	European health insurance card
la	**cicatrice**	scar
la	**coqueluche**	whooping cough
la	**crise cardiaque**	heart attack
une	**écharde**	splinter
une	**égratignure**	scratch
une	**épidémie**	epidemic
la	**grossesse**	pregnancy
la	**guérison**	recovery
la	**migraine**	migraine
la	**nausée**	nausea
la	**pandémie**	pandemic
la	**plaie**	wound
la	**pommade**	ointment
la	**radio**	X-ray
la	**rougeole**	measles
la	**rubéole**	German measles
la	**toux**	cough
la	**transfusion**	blood transfusion
la	**varicelle**	chickenpox
la	**variole**	smallpox

USEFUL PHRASES

guérir to cure; to get better
grièvement blessé(e) seriously injured
êtes-vous assuré(e)? are you insured?
je suis enrhumé(e) I have a cold
ça fait mal! that hurts!
respirer to breathe; **s'évanouir** to faint
tousser to cough; **mourir** to die
perdre connaissance to lose consciousness
avoir le bras en écharpe to have one's arm in a sling

ESSENTIAL WORDS *(masculine)*

un	**ascenseur**	lift
les	**bagages**	luggage
le	**balcon**	balcony
le	**bar**	bar
le	**bruit**	noise
le	**chèque**	cheque
le	**client**	guest
le	**confort**	comfort
le	**déjeuner**	lunch
le	**directeur**	manager
un	**escalier**	stairs
un	**étage**	floor; storey
le	**garçon**	waiter
le	**grand lit**	double bed
un	**hôtel**	hotel
les	**lits jumeaux**	twin beds
le	**numéro**	number
le	**passeport**	passport
le	**petit déjeuner**	breakfast
le	**porteur**	porter
le	**prix**	price
le	**réceptionniste**	receptionist
le	**repas**	meal
le	**restaurant**	restaurant
le	**rez-de-chaussée**	ground floor
le	**séjour**	stay
le	**tarif**	rates
le	**téléphone**	telephone
les	**WC**	toilets
le	**wifi**	wifi

USEFUL PHRASES

je voudrais réserver une chambre I would like to book a room
une chambre avec douche/avec salle de bains a room with a shower/with a bathroom
une chambre pour une personne a single room
une chambre pour deux personnes a double room

ESSENTIAL WORDS *(feminine)*

	l'**addition**	bill
les	**arrhes** [aʀ]	deposit
la	**carte bancaire**	bank card
la	**chambre**	room
la	**clé, clef**	key
la	**cliente**	guest
la	**date**	date
la	**directrice**	manageress
la	**douche**	shower
	l'**entrée**	entrance
la	**fiche**	form
la	**monnaie**	change
la	**note**	bill
la	**nuit**	night
la	**pension**	guesthouse
la	**pension complète**	full board
la	**piscine**	swimming pool
la	**réception**	reception
la	**réceptionniste**	receptionist
la	**réservation**	reservation, booking
la	**salle de bains**	bathroom
la	**serviette (de toilette)**	towel
la	**serveuse**	waitress
la	**sortie de secours**	fire escape
la	**télévision**	television
les	**toilettes**	toilets
la	**valise**	suitcase
la	**vue**	view

USEFUL PHRASES

nous avons réservé en ligne we made a booking online
avez-vous une pièce d'identité? do you have any ID?
à quelle heure est le petit déjeuner? what time is breakfast served?
faire la chambre to clean the room
"ne pas déranger" "do not disturb"

IMPORTANT WORDS *(masculine)*

un	**accueil**	welcome
le	**bouton**	switch
le	**cabinet de toilette**	toilet
le	**coffre-fort**	safe
le	**digicode**	entry code
les	**draps**	sheets
le	**guide**	guidebook
le	**pourboire**	tip
le	**prix net**	inclusive price
le	**reçu**	receipt

USEFUL WORDS *(masculine)*

le	**cuisinier**	cook
le	**forfait**	package (deal)
le	**:hall**	foyer
un	**hôtelier**	hotelier
le	**maître d'hôtel**	head waiter
le	**parking**	car park
le	**pensionnaire**	guest (at guesthouse)
le	**sommelier**	wine waiter

USEFUL PHRASES

occupé(e) occupied
libre vacant
propre clean
sale dirty
dormir to sleep
se réveiller to wake
"tout confort" "with all facilities"
pourriez-vous me réveiller à 7 heures demain matin? I'd like a 7 o'clock alarm call tomorrow morning, please
une chambre donnant sur la mer a room overlooking the sea

IMPORTANT WORDS *(feminine)*

une	**auberge**	inn
la	**carte magnétique**	electronic key card
la	**demi-pension** (*pl* ~s)	half-board
la	**femme de chambre**	chambermaid
la	**réclamation**	complaint
la	**pension de famille**	guesthouse
la	**pensionnaire**	guest (at guesthouse)

USEFUL PHRASES

chambre avec demi-pension room with breakfast and dinner provided
on se met à la terrasse? shall we sit outside?
on nous a servis à la terrasse we were served outside
un hôtel 3 étoiles a three-star hotel
TTC (toutes taxes comprises) inclusive of tax

house – general

ESSENTIAL WORDS *(masculine)*

un **appartement**	flat
un **ascenseur**	lift
le **balcon**	balcony
le **bâtiment**	building
le **chauffage central**	central heating
le **confort**	comfort
un **escalier**	stairs
un **étage**	floor; storey
l'**extérieur**	exterior
le **garage**	garage
un **grand ensemble**	housing estate
un **HLM (habitation à loyer modéré)**	council flat *or* house
un **immeuble**	block of flats
l'**intérieur**	interior
le **jardin**	garden
le **meuble**	piece of furniture
les **meubles**	furniture
le **mur**	wall
le **numéro de téléphone**	phone number
le **parking**	car park
le **rez-de-chaussée** *(pl inv)*	ground floor
le **salon**	living room
le **séjour**	living room
le **sous-sol** (*pl* ~s)	basement
le **terrain**	plot of land
le **village**	village

USEFUL PHRASES

quand je rentre à la maison when I go home
regarder par la fenêtre to look out of the window
chez moi/toi/nous at my/your/our house
déménager to move house
louer un appartement to rent a flat

ESSENTIAL WORDS *(feminine)*

une **adresse**	address
une **allée**	avenue, drive
une **avenue**	avenue
la **cave**	cellar
la **chambre (à coucher)**	bedroom
la **clé, clef**	key
la **cuisine**	kitchen
la **douche**	shower
l'**entrée**	entrance
la **fenêtre**	window
une **HLM (habitation à loyer modéré)**	council flat *or* house
la **maison**	house
la **pièce**	room
la **porte**	door
la **porte d'entrée**	front door
la **rue**	street
la **salle à manger**	dining room
la **salle de bains**	bathroom
la **salle de séjour**	living room
la **salle**	room
les **toilettes**	toilet
la **ville**	town
la **vue**	view

USEFUL PHRASES

j'habite un appartement/une maison I live in a flat/a house
en haut upstairs
en bas downstairs
au premier on the first floor
au rez-de-chaussée on the ground floor
à la maison at home

house – general

IMPORTANT WORDS *(masculine)*

l'**ameublement**	furniture
le **cabinet de toilette**	toilet
le **concierge**	caretaker
le **couloir**	corridor
le **débarras**	storage cupboard
le **déménagement**	move
l'**entretien**	upkeep
le **gîte**	holiday home
le **logement**	accommodation
le **loyer**	rent
le **meublé**	furnished flat
le **palier**	landing
le **propriétaire**	owner; landlord
le **toit**	roof
le **voisin**	neighbour

USEFUL WORDS *(masculine)*

le **bureau**	study
le **carreau** (*pl* -x)	tile; windowpane
le **décor**	decoration
le **grenier**	attic
le **locataire**	tenant; lodger
le **parquet**	parquet floor
le **pavillon**	house
le **plafond**	ceiling
le **plancher**	floor
le **seuil**	doorstep
le **store**	blind
le **studio**	studio flat
le **tuyau** (*pl* -x)	pipe
le **vestibule**	hall
le **volet**	shutter

USEFUL PHRASES

frapper à la porte to knock at the door

on a sonné the doorbell's just gone

IMPORTANT WORDS *(feminine)*

la **cheminée**	chimney; fireplace
la **concierge**	caretaker
la **cour**	yard
la **femme de ménage**	cleaner
la **fumée**	smoke
la **pelouse**	lawn
la **propriétaire**	owner; landlady
la **voisine**	neighbour

USEFUL WORDS *(feminine)*

une **antenne**	aerial
une **ardoise**	slate
la **chambre d'amis**	spare room
la **chaudière**	boiler
la **façade**	front (*of house*)
la **:haie**	hedge
la **locataire**	tenant; lodger
la **loge**	caretaker's room
la **lucarne**	skylight
la **mansarde**	attic
la **marche**	step
la **paroi**	partition
la **porte-fenêtre** (*pl* ~s~s)	French window
la **sonnette**	door bell
la **tuile**	roof tile
la **vitre**	window pane

USEFUL PHRASES

de l'extérieur from the outside
à l'intérieur on the inside
jusqu'au plafond up to the ceiling

ESSENTIAL WORDS *(masculine)*

le **bouton**	switch
le **cendrier**	ashtray
le **dentifrice**	toothpaste
le **drap**	sheet
un **essuie-mains** *(pl inv)*	hand towel
un **évier**	sink
le **gaz**	gas
le **lavabo**	washbasin
le **lecteur de DVD**	DVD player
le **ménage**	housework
le **miroir**	mirror
un **oreiller**	pillow
le **placard**	cupboard
le **plateau** (*pl* -x)	tray
le **poster** [pɔstɛʀ]	poster
le **radiateur**	heater
le **réveil**	alarm clock
les **rideaux**	curtains
le **robinet**	tap
le **savon**	soap
le **tableau**	picture
le **tapis**	rug
le **téléviseur**	television set

USEFUL PHRASES

prendre un bain, se baigner to have a bath
prendre une douche to have a shower
faire le ménage to do the housework
j'aime faire la cuisine I like cooking

ESSENTIAL WORDS *(feminine)*

une **armoire**	wardrobe
la **baignoire**	bath
la **balance**	scales
la **boîte aux lettres**	letterbox
la **brosse**	brush
la **cafetière**	coffee pot; coffee maker
la **casserole**	saucepan
la **chaîne hi-fi**	hi-fi
la **couverture**	blanket
la **cuisinière**	cooker
la **douche**	shower
l'**eau**	water
l'**électricité**	electricity
la **glace**	mirror
la **lampe**	lamp
la **lumière**	light
la **machine à laver**	washing machine
la **photo**	photo
la **poubelle**	dustbin
la **radio**	radio
la **serviette**	towel; napkin
la **télévision**	TV, television
la **vaisselle**	dishes

USEFUL PHRASES

regarder la télévision to watch television
à la télévision on television
allumer/éteindre la télévision to switch on/off the TV
jeter qch à la poubelle to throw sth in the dustbin
faire la vaisselle to do the dishes

IMPORTANT WORDS *(masculine)*

un **aspirateur**	vacuum cleaner
le **bidet**	bidet
le **four**	oven
le **lave-vaisselle** *(pl inv)*	dishwasher
le **linge**	bedclothes; washing

USEFUL WORDS *(masculine)*

le **balai**	broom
le **bibelot**	ornament
le **chiffon**	duster
le **cintre**	coat hanger
le **coussin**	cushion
le **couvercle**	lid
le **fer à repasser**	iron
le **four à micro-ondes**	microwave oven
le **grille-pain** *(pl inv)*	toaster
un **interrupteur**	switch
le **mixeur**	blender
le **moulin à café**	coffee grinder
le **papier peint**	wallpaper
le **seau** (*pl* -x)	bucket
le **torchon**	dishcloth
le **traversin**	bolster
le **vase**	vase

USEFUL PHRASES

brancher/débrancher to plug in/to unplug
passer l'aspirateur to hoover
faire la lessive to do the washing

IMPORTANT WORDS *(feminine)*

une	**ampoule électrique**	light bulb
la	**baignoire**	bath
la	**femme de ménage**	cleaner
la	**lessive**	washing powder; washing
la	**peinture**	paint; painting
la	**poêle** [pwal]	frying pan
la	**poussière**	dust
la	**prise de courant**	socket
la	**recette**	recipe
la	**serrure**	lock

USEFUL WORDS *(feminine)*

la	**bouilloire**	kettle
la	**cocotte-minute**® (*pl* ~s~)	pressure cooker
la	**corbeille à papier**	waste paper basket
la	**couette**	duvet
la	**couverture chauffante**	electric blanket
la	**descente de lit**	bedside rug
une	**échelle**	ladder
une	**éponge**	sponge
la	**moquette**	fitted carpet
les	**ordures**	rubbish
la	**planche à repasser**	ironing board
la	**poignée**	handle
la	**tapisserie**	wallpaper

USEFUL PHRASES

balayer to sweep (up)
nettoyer to clean
ranger ses affaires to tidy away one's things
laisser traîner ses affaires to leave one's things lying about

ESSENTIAL WORDS *(masculine)*

un	**abonnement (téléphonique)**	phone contract
un	**appel**	call
le	**billet**	ticket; banknote
le	**bureau** (*pl* -x) **de change**	bureau de change
le	**centime (d'euro)**	euro cent
le	**chèque**	cheque
le	**code postal**	postcode
le	**colis**	parcel
le	**courriel**	email
le	**cybercafé**	internet café
le	**DAB (distributeur automatique de billets)**	cashpoint, ATM
un	**employé**	counter clerk
un	**euro**	euro
le	**facteur**	postman
le	**franc suisse**	Swiss franc
le	**guichet**	counter
un	**indicatif**	dialling code
le	**justificatif**	written proof
un	**mail**	email
le	**numéro**	number
un	**office du tourisme**	tourist information office
un	**opérateur**	phone company
le	**paquet**	parcel
le	**passeport**	passport
le	**prix**	price
les	**renseignements**	information; directory enquiries
le	**répondeur**	answerphone
le	**SMS**	text message
le	**stylo**	pen
le	**syndicat d'initiative**	tourist information office
le	**tarif**	(postage) rate
le	**téléphone**	telephone
le	**(téléphone) fixe**	landline
le	**(téléphone) portable**	mobile (phone)
le	**timbre**	stamp

USEFUL PHRASES

la banque la plus proche the nearest bank

je voudrais encaisser un chèque/changer de l'argent I would like to cash a cheque/change some money

ESSENTIAL WORDS *(feminine)*

une	**adresse**	address
les	**arrhes**	deposit
la	**banque**	bank
la	**boîte aux lettres**	postbox
la	**boîte vocale**	voicemail
la	**caisse**	check-out
la	**carte d'identité**	ID card
la	**carte postale**	postcard
une	**enveloppe**	envelope
une	**erreur**	mistake
la	**factrice**	postwoman
la	**fiche**	form
la	**lettre**	letter
la	**livre sterling**	pound sterling
la	**monnaie**	change
la	**pièce d'identité**	ID
la	**poste**	post office
la	**réponse**	reply
la	**signature**	signature
la	**sonnerie**	ringtone
la	**tonalité**	dialling tone

USEFUL PHRASES

un coup de téléphone *or* **de fil** a phone call
téléphoner à qn to phone sb
décrocher to lift the receiver
composer le numéro to dial (the number)
allô – ici Jean *or* **c'est Jean à l'appareil** hello – this is Jean
la ligne est occupée the line is engaged
ne quittez pas hold the line
je me suis trompé(e) de numéro I got the wrong number
raccrocher to hang up
je voudrais appeler à l'étranger I'd like to make an international phone call

IMPORTANT WORDS *(masculine)*

un	**annuaire**	telephone directory
le	**carnet de chèques**	cheque book
le	**chèque de voyage**	traveller's cheque
le	**compte (en banque)**	(bank) account
le	**coup de téléphone**	phone call
le	**courrier**	mail
le	**crédit**	credit
le	**domicile**	home address
le	**formulaire**	form
le	**:haut débit**	broadband
le	**mail**	email
les	**objets trouvés**	lost property office
le	**paiement**	payment
le	**papier à lettres**	writing paper
le	**portefeuille**	wallet
le	**porte-monnaie** *(pl inv)*	purse
le	**supplément**	extra charge
le	**taux de change**	exchange rate
le	**télégramme**	telegram
le	**wifi**	wifi

USEFUL WORDS *(masculine)*

un	**accusé de réception**	acknowledgement of receipt
le	**combiné**	receiver
le	**destinataire**	addressee
l'	**expéditeur**	sender
un	**identifiant**	login
un	**imprimé**	printed matter
le	**mandat**	postal order
le	**mot de passe**	password
le	**numéro vert**	Freefone® number
le	**papier d'emballage**	wrapping paper
le	**récepteur**	receiver
le	**standardiste**	operator
le	**tampon**	stamp

IMPORTANT WORDS *(feminine)*

une	**adresse électronique**	email address
la	**cabine téléphonique**	callbox
la	**carte bancaire**	bank card
la	**Carte bleue®**	debit card
la	**carte SIM**	SIM card
la	**carte téléphonique**	phone card; top up card
la	**dépense**	expense
la	**fente**	slot
la	**levée**	collection
une	**opératrice**	operator
la	**pièce jointe**	attachment
la	**poste restante**	poste restante
la	**récompense**	reward
la	**taxe**	tax

USEFUL WORDS *(feminine)*

la	**boîte postale**	PO box
la	**communication interurbaine**	inter-city call
la	**communication locale**	local call
l'	**horloge parlante**	speaking clock
la	**lettre recommandée**	registered letter
la	**standardiste**	switchboard operator
la	**télécarte®**	phonecard

USEFUL PHRASES

j'ai perdu mon portefeuille I've lost my wallet
remplir une fiche to fill in a form
en majuscules in block letters
téléphoner en PCV to make a reverse charge call

GENERAL SITUATIONS

quelle est votre adresse? what is your address?
comment ça s'écrit? how do you spell that?
avez-vous la monnaie de 10 euros? do you have change of 10 euros?
écrire to write
répondre to reply
signer to sign
est-ce que vous pouvez m'aider? can you help me please?
pour aller à la gare? how do I get to the station?
tout droit straight on
à droite to *or* on the right; **à gauche** to *or* on the left

LETTERS

Cher Robert Dear Robert
Chère Anne Dear Anne
Monsieur Dear Sir
Madame (*or* Mademoiselle) Dear Madam
amitiés best wishes
bien affectueusement love from
bien amicalement *or* **cordialement** kind regards
grosses bises love and kisses
veuillez agréer mes (*or* nos) salutations distinguées yours faithfully
je vous prie d'agréer, Monsieur (*or* Madame), l'expression de mes sentiments les meilleurs yours sincerely
TSVP PTO

MOBILES

envoyer un SMS à qn to text sb
envoyer un MMS photo à qn to send a picture message
envoyer un MMS vidéo à qn to send a video message
télécharger une sonnerie to download a ringtone
Je ne te capte plus! You're breaking up!
Je n'ai plus de crédit. I'm out of credit.
Je n'ai pas de réseau. I can't get a network.

EMAIL

composer un mail to compose an email
envoyer un mail à qn to send an email to sb
faire suivre un mail to forward an email
joindre un fichier à un mail to attach a file to an email
répondre à un mail to reply to an email

ESSENTIAL WORDS *(masculine)*

un **accident**	accident
un **agent (de police)**	policeman
le **cambriolage**	burglary
le **commissariat de police**	police station
un **incendie**	fire
le **problème**	problem

IMPORTANT WORDS *(masculine)*

un **agresseur**	attacker
un **avocat**	lawyer
le **cambrioleur**	burglar
le **constat**	report
le **consulat**	consulate
le **coupable**	culprit
les **dégâts**	damage
le(s) **dommage(s)**	damage
un **espion**	spy
le **gendarme**	policeman
le **gouvernement**	government
les **impôts**	income tax
le **mort**	dead man
le **piratage**	hacking
le **porte-monnaie** *(pl inv)*	purse
le **portefeuille**	wallet
le **poste de police**	police station
le **propriétaire**	owner
le **témoin**	witness
le **viol**	rape
le **vol**	robbery
le **voleur**	thief

USEFUL PHRASES

voler to steal; to rob
cambrioler to burgle
on m'a volé mon portefeuille! someone has stolen my wallet!
contraire à la loi illegal
ce n'est pas de ma faute it's not my fault
au secours! help!

ESSENTIAL WORDS *(feminine)*

la **faute**	fault
l'**identité**	identity
la **pièce d'identité**	ID
la **vérité**	truth
la **victime**	victim

IMPORTANT WORDS *(feminine)*

une **agression**	assault
une **ambassade**	embassy
une **amende**	fine
une **armée**	army
une **avocate**	lawyer
la **bande**	gang
la **coupable**	culprit
la **fraude**	fraud
la **fraude fiscale**	tax evasion
la **gendarmerie**	police station
les **incivilités**	antisocial behaviour
la **manifestation**	demonstration
la **mort**	death
la **morte**	dead woman
la **permission**	permission
la **police d'assurance**	insurance policy
la **propriétaire**	owner
la **récompense**	reward
l'**usurpation d'identité**	identity theft
la **violence**	violence

USEFUL PHRASES

au voleur! stop thief!
au feu! fire!
braquer une banque to rob a bank
police-secours emergency services
incarcérer to imprison
innocent(e) innocent
s'évader to escape

USEFUL WORDS *(masculine)*

un **assassin**	murderer
le **butin**	loot
le **cadavre**	corpse
le **coup (de feu)**	(gun) shot
le **courage**	bravery
le **crime**	crime
le **criminel**	criminal
le **dealer**	drug dealer
le **détective privé**	private detective
le **détournement d'avion**	plane hijacking
le **drogué**	drug addict
un **enlèvement**	kidnapping
un **escroc** [ɛskʀo]	crook
le **flic**	cop
le **fusil** [fyzi]	gun
le **gangster**	gangster
le **garde**	guard
le **gardien**	guard; warden
le **:héros**	hero
le **:hold-up** *(pl inv)*	hold-up
le **juge**	judge
le **jury**	jury
le **meurtre**	murder
le **meurtrier**	murderer
un **otage**	hostage
le **palais de justice**	law courts
le **pirate de l'air**	hijacker
le **policier**	policeman
le **prisonnier**	prisoner
le **procès**	trial
le **PV**	fine
le **reportage**	report
le **revolver** [ʀevɔlvɛʀ]	revolver
le **sauvetage**	rescue
le **témoignage**	evidence
le **témoin**	witness
le **terrorisme**	terrorism
le **terroriste**	terrorist
le **tribunal**	court
le **voyou**	hooligan

USEFUL WORDS *(feminine)*

l'	**accusation**	the prosecution
une	**accusation**	charge; accusation
une	**arme**	weapon
une	**arrestation**	arrest
la	**bagarre**	fight
la	**bombe**	bomb
la	**cellule**	cell
la	**défense**	defence
la	**déposition**	statement
la	**dispute**	argument
la	**droguée**	drug addict
les	**drogues**	drugs
une	**émeute**	uprising
une	**enquête**	inquiry
une	**évasion**	escape
l'	**héroïne**	heroine; heroin
l'	**incarcération**	imprisonment
la	**loi**	law
une	**ordonnance**	police order
la	**preuve**	proof
la	**prison**	prison
la	**rafle**	raid
la	**rançon**	ransom
la	**tentative**	attempt

USEFUL PHRASES

une attaque à main armée a hold-up
enlever un enfant to abduct a child
se battre to fight
une bande de voyous a bunch of hooligans
en prison in prison
arrêter to arrest
inculper to charge
être en détention provisoire to be remanded in custody
mettre qn en examen to indict sb
prendre la fuite to run away

ESSENTIAL WORDS *(masculine)*

	l'**acier**	steel
	l'**argent**	silver
le	**bois**	wood
le	**coton**	cotton
le	**cuir**	leather
le	**fer**	iron
le	**gas-oil**	diesel
le	**gaz**	gas
le	**métal** (*pl* métaux)	metal
	l'**or**	gold
le	**plastique**	plastic
le	**tissu**	fabric
le	**verre**	glass

IMPORTANT WORDS *(masculine)*

	l'**acier inoxydable**	stainless steel
	l'**aluminium**	aluminium
le	**carton**	cardboard
	l'**état**	condition
le	**fer forgé**	wrought iron
le	**papier**	paper
le	**synthétique**	synthetics
le	**tissu**	fabric

USEFUL PHRASES

une chaise de *or* **en bois** a wooden chair
une boîte en plastique a plastic box
une bague d'or *or* **en or** a gold ring
en bon état in good condition
en mauvais état in bad condition

ESSENTIAL WORDS *(feminine)*

la **fourrure**	fur
la **laine**	wool
la **pierre**	stone

IMPORTANT WORDS *(feminine)*

la **brique**	brick
la **soie**	silk

USEFUL PHRASES

un manteau en fourrure a fur coat
un pull en laine a woolly jumper
rouillé(e) rusty

USEFUL WORDS *(masculine)*

l'**acrylique**	acrylic
le **béton**	concrete
le **bronze**	bronze
le **caoutchouc** [kautʃu]	rubber
le **caoutchouc mousse**	foam rubber
le **charbon**	coal
le **ciment**	cement
le **cristal**	crystal
le **cuivre**	copper
le **cuivre jaune**	brass
le **daim**	suede
l'**étain**	tin; pewter
le **fer-blanc**	tin, tinplate
le **fil**	thread
le **fil de fer**	wire
le **lin**	linen
le **liquide**	liquid
le **marbre**	marble
les **matériaux**	materials
l'**osier**	wickerwork
le **plâtre**	plaster
le **plomb**	lead
le **satin**	satin
le **velours**	velvet
le **velours côtelé**	corduroy

USEFUL WORDS *(feminine)*

l'**argile**	clay
la **cire**	wax
la **colle**	glue
la **dentelle**	lace
une **étoffe**	material
la **faïence**	ceramics
la **ficelle**	string
la **paille**	straw
la **porcelaine**	china
la **toile**	linen; canvas

ESSENTIAL WORDS *(masculine)*

le	**CD**	CD
le	**chef d'orchestre**	conductor
le	**groupe**	group, band
un	**instrument de musique**	musical instrument
le	**musicien**	musician
un	**orchestre**	orchestra
le	**piano**	piano
le	**violon**	violin

USEFUL WORDS *(masculine)*

un	**accord**	chord
un	**accordéon**	accordion
un	**alto**	viola
un	**archet**	bow
le	**basson**	bassoon
le	**biniou**	Breton bagpipes
les	**bois**	woodwind
le	**clairon**	bugle
le	**cor**	horn
les	**cuivres**	brass
un	**enregistrement numérique**	digital recording
un	**étui**	case
un	**harmonica**	harmonica
le	**:hautbois**	oboe
le	**jazz** [dʒaz]	jazz
le	**microphone**	microphone
un	**orgue**	organ
le	**pupitre**	music stand
le	**saxophone**	saxophone
le	**solfège**	music theory
le	**soliste**	soloist
le	**studio d'enregistrement**	recording studio
le	**tambour**	drum
le	**tambourin**	tambourine
le	**triangle**	triangle
le	**trombone**	trombone
le	**violoncelle**	cello

ESSENTIAL WORDS *(feminine)*

la **batterie**	drums, drum kit
la **clarinette**	clarinet
la **flûte**	flute
la **flûte à bec**	recorder
la **guitare**	guitar
la **musique**	music

USEFUL WORDS *(feminine)*

la **composition**	composition
la **contrebasse**	double bass
la **corde**	string
les **cordes**	brass
la **cornemuse**	bagpipes
les **cymbales**	cymbals
la **fanfare**	brass band; fanfare
la **grosse caisse**	bass drum
la **:harpe**	harpe
la **note**	note
la **soliste**	soloist
la **sono**	PA system
la **table de mixage**	(mixing) deck
la **touche**	(piano) key
la **trompette**	trumpet

USEFUL PHRASES

jouer *or* **interpréter un morceau** to play a piece
jouer fort/doucement to play loudly/softly
jouer juste/faux to play in tune/out of tune
jouer du piano/de la guitare to play the piano/the guitar
faire de la batterie to play drums
Luc à la batterie Luc on drums
travailler son piano to practise the piano
est-ce que tu joues dans un groupe? do you play in a band?
une fausse note a wrong note

CARDINAL NUMBERS

zéro	0	zero
un (*m*), une (*f*)	1	one
deux	2	two
trois	3	three
quatre	4	four
cinq	5	five
six	6	six
sept	7	seven
huit	8	eight
neuf	9	nine
dix	10	ten
onze	11	eleven
douze	12	twelve
treize	13	thirteen
quatorze	14	fourteen
quinze	15	fifteen
seize	16	sixteen
dix-sept	17	seventeen
dix-huit	18	eighteen
dix-neuf	19	nineteen
vingt	20	twenty
vingt et un	21	twenty -one
vingt-deux	22	twenty-two
vingt-trois	23	twenty-three
trente	30	thirty
trente et un	31	thirty-one
trente-deux	32	thirty-two
quarante	40	forty
cinquante	50	fifty
soixante	60	sixty
soixante-dix	70	seventy
soixante et onze	71	seventy-one
quatre-vingts	80	eighty
quatre-vingt-un	81	eighty-one
quatre-vingt-dix	90	ninety
quatre-vingt-onze	91	ninety-one
cent	100	one hundred

CARDINAL NUMBERS *(continued)*

cent un	**101**	a hundred and one
cent deux	**102**	a hundred and two
cent dix	**110**	a hundred and ten
cent quatre-vingt-deux	**182**	a hundred and eighty-two
deux cents	**200**	two hundred
deux cent un	**201**	two hundred and one
deux cent deux	**202**	two hundred and two
trois cents	**300**	three hundred
quatre cents	**400**	four hundred
cinq cents	**500**	five hundred
six cents	**600**	six hundred
sept cents	**700**	seven hundred
huit cents	**800**	eight hundred
neuf cents	**900**	nine hundred
mille	**1000**	one thousand
mille un	**1001**	a thousand and one
mille deux	**1002**	a thousand and two
deux mille	**2000**	two thousand
deux mille deux	**2002**	two thousand and two
dix mille	**10000**	ten thousand
cent mille	**100000**	one hundred thousand
un million	**1000000**	one million
deux millions	**2000000**	two million

USEFUL PHRASES

mille euros a thousand euros
un million de dollars one million dollars
trois virgule deux (3,2) three point two (3.2)

ORDINAL NUMBERS

premier(ière)	1er, 1ère	first
deuxième	2^{e}	second
troisième	3^{e}	third
quatrième	4^{e}	fourth
cinquième	5^{e}	fifth
sixième	6^{e}	sixth
septième	7^{e}	seventh
huitième	8^{e}	eighth
neuvième	9^{e}	ninth
dixième	10^{e}	tenth
onzième	11^{e}	eleventh
douzième	12^{e}	twelfth
treizième	13^{e}	thirteenth
quatorzième	14^{e}	fourteenth
quinzième	15^{e}	fifteenth
seizième	16^{e}	sixteenth
dix-septième	17^{e}	seventeenth
dix-huitième	18^{e}	eighteenth
dix-neuvième	19^{e}	nineteenth
vingtième	20^{e}	twentieth
vingt et unième	21^{e}	twenty-first
vingt-deuxième	22^{e}	twenty-second
trentième	30^{e}	thirtieth
trente et unième	31^{e}	thirty-first
quarantième	40^{e}	fortieth
cinquantième	50^{e}	fiftieth
soixantième	60^{e}	sixtieth
soixante-dixième	70^{e}	seventieth
quatre-vingtième	80^{e}	eightieth
quatre-vingt-dixième	90^{e}	ninetieth
centième	100^{e}	hundredth

ORDINAL NUMBERS *(continued)*

cent unième	**101e**	hundred and first
cent-dixième	**110e**	hundred and tenth
deux centième	**200e**	two hundredth
trois centième	**300e**	three hundredth
quatre centième	**400e**	four hundredth
cinq centième	**500e**	five hundredth
six centième	**600e**	six hundredth
sept centième	**700e**	seven hundredth
huit centième	**800e**	eight hundredth
neuf centième	**900e**	nine hundredth
millième	**1000e**	thousandth
deux millième	**2000e**	two thousandth
millionième	**1000000e**	millionth
deux millionième	**2000000e**	two millionth

FRACTIONS

un(e) demi(e)	$^{1}/_{2}$	a half
un(e) et demi(e)	$1^{1}/_{2}$	one and a half
deux et demi(e)	$2^{1}/_{2}$	two and a half
un tiers	$^{1}/_{3}$	a third
deux tiers	$^{2}/_{3}$	two thirds
un quart	$^{1}/_{4}$	a quarter
trois quarts	$^{3}/_{4}$	three quarters
un sixième	$^{1}/_{6}$	a sixth
trois et cinq sixièmes	$3^{5}/_{6}$	three and five sixths
un douzième	$^{1}/_{12}$	a twelfth
sept douzièmes	$^{7}/_{12}$	seven twelfths
un centième	$^{1}/_{100}$	a hundredth
un millième	$^{1}/_{1000}$	a thousandth

USEFUL PHRASES

une assiette de a plate of
une bande de a group of
beaucoup de lots of
une boîte de a tin *or* can of; a box of
un bol de a bowl of
une bouchée de a mouthful of
un bout de papier a piece of paper
une bouteille de a bottle of
cent grammes de a hundred grammes of
une centaine de (about) a hundred
une cuillerée de a spoonful of
un demi de bière half a litre of beer
une demi-douzaine de half a dozen
un demi-litre de half a litre of
tous (*f* toutes) les deux both of them
une dizaine de (about) ten
une douzaine de a dozen
une foule de loads of
un kilo de a kilo of
à quelques kilomètres de a few kilometres from
un litre de a litre of
une livre de a pound of
un mètre de a metre of

USEFUL PHRASES

à quelques mètres de a few metres from
des milliers de thousands of
la moitié de half of
un morceau de sucre a lump of sugar
un morceau de gâteau a piece of cake
une paire de a pair of
un paquet de a packet of
un peu de a little
une pile de a pile of
la plupart de *or* **des** most (of)
plusieurs several
une poignée de a handful of
une portion de a portion of
un pot de a pot *or* tub *or* jar of
une quantité de a lot of, many
un quart de a quarter of
un tas de a heap of, heaps of
une tasse de a cup of
un tonneau de a barrel of
une tranche de a slice of
trois quarts de three quarters of
un troupeau de a herd of (cattle); a flock of (sheep)
un verre de a glass of

ESSENTIAL WORDS *(masculine)*

le **bijou** (*pl* -x)	jewel
le **bracelet**	bracelet
le **dentifrice**	toothpaste
le **déodorant**	deodorant
le **gant de toilette**	face flannel
le **maquillage**	make-up
le **miroir**	mirror
le **parfum**	perfume
le **peigne**	comb
le **rasoir**	razor
le **shampooing** [ʃɑ̃pwɛ̃]	shampoo

USEFUL WORDS *(masculine)*

un **après-rasage**	after-shave
le **bigoudi**	curler
le **blaireau** (*pl* -x)	shaving brush
le **bouton de manchette**	cufflink
le **collier**	necklace
le **démaquillant**	make-up remover
le **diamant**	diamond
le **dissolvant**	nail varnish remover
les **effets personnels**	personal effects
le **fard**	make-up
le **fard à paupières**	eye-shadow
le **fond de teint**	foundation
le **gel de douche**	shower gel
le **kleenex®**	tissue
le **papier hygiénique**	toilet paper
le **pendentif**	pendant
le **porte-clefs** *(pl inv)*	key-ring
le **poudrier**	(powder) compact
le **rimmel®**	mascara
le **rouge à lèvres**	lipstick
le **sèche-cheveux**	hairdryer
le **vernis à ongles**	nail varnish

ESSENTIAL WORDS *(feminine)*

la	**bague**	ring
la	**brosse à dents**	toothbrush
la	**chaîne**	chain
la	**chaînette**	chain
la	**crème de beauté**	face cream
la	**crème hydratante**	moisturizer
une	**eau de toilette**	eau de toilette
la	**glace**	mirror
la	**montre**	watch

USEFUL WORDS *(feminine)*

une	**alliance**	wedding ring
la	**boucle d'oreille** (*pl* ~s d'oreille)	earring
la	**broche**	brooch
la	**coiffure**	hairstyle
la	**crème à raser**	shaving cream
une	**éponge**	sponge
la	**gourmette**	chain bracelet
la	**manucure**	manicure
la	**mousse à raser**	shaving foam
la	**perle**	pearl
la	**poudre**	face powder
la	**trousse de toilette**	toilet bag

USEFUL PHRASES

se maquiller to put on one's make-up
se démaquiller to take off one's make-up
se coiffer to do one's hair
se peigner to comb one's hair
se raser to shave
se brosser les dents to brush one's teeth

plants and gardens

ESSENTIAL WORDS *(masculine)*

un **arbre**	tree
le **jardin**	garden
le **jardinage**	gardening
le **jardinier**	gardener
les **légumes**	vegetables
le **soleil**	sun

IMPORTANT WORDS *(masculine)*

le **banc**	bench
le **bouquet de fleurs**	bunch of flowers
le **buisson**	bush
le **gazon**	lawn

USEFUL PHRASES

planter to plant
désherber to weed
offrir un bouquet de fleurs à qn to give sb a bunch of flowers
tondre le gazon to mow the lawn
"défense de marcher sur le gazon" "keep off the grass"
mon père aime jardiner my father likes gardening

ESSENTIAL WORDS *(feminine)*

une **abeille**	bee
la **branche**	branch
la **feuille**	leaf
la **fleur**	flower
l'**herbe**	grass
la **pelouse**	lawn
la **plante**	plant
la **pluie**	rain
la **rose**	rose
la **terre**	earth, ground

IMPORTANT WORDS *(feminine)*

la **barrière**	gate; fence
la **culture**	cultivation
la **guêpe**	wasp
les **mauvaises herbes**	weeds
l'**ombre**	shade; shadow
la **plate-bande** (*pl* ~s~s)	flowerbed
la **racine**	root

USEFUL PHRASES

les fleurs poussent the flowers are growing
par terre on the ground
arroser les fleurs to water the flowers
cueillir des fleurs to pick flowers
se mettre à l'ombre to go into the shade
rester à l'ombre to remain in the shade
à l'ombre d'un arbre in the shade of a tree

plants and gardens

USEFUL WORDS *(masculine)*

un **arbuste**	shrub, bush
un **arrosoir**	watering can
le **bassin**	(ornamental) pool
le **bourgeon**	bud
le **bouton-d'or** *(pl ~s~)*	buttercup
le **chèvrefeuille**	honeysuckle
le **chrysanthème**	chrysanthemum
le **coquelicot**	poppy
le **crocus**	crocus
le **feuillage**	leaves
l'**hortensia**	hydrangea
le **jardin potager**	vegetable garden
le **lierre**	ivy
le **lilas**	lilac
le **lis** [lis]	lily
le **muguet**	lily of the valley
un **œillet**	carnation
un **outil**	tool
le **papillon**	butterfly
le **parterre**	flowerbed
le **pavot**	poppy
le **perce-neige** *(pl inv)*	snowdrop
le **pissenlit**	dandelion
le **pois de senteur**	sweet pea
le **rosier**	rose bush
le **sol**	earth, soil
le **tournesol**	sunflower
le **tronc**	trunk *(of tree)*
le **tuyau d'arrosage**	hose
le **ver**	worm
le **verger**	orchard

USEFUL WORDS *(feminine)*

une	**allée**	path
la	**baie**	berry
la	**brouette**	wheelbarrow
la	**clôture**	fence
une	**épine**	thorn
les	**graines**	seeds
la	**:haie**	hedge
la	**jacinthe**	hyacinth
la	**jonquille**	daffodil
la	**marguerite**	daisy
une	**orchidée**	orchid
la	**pâquerette**	daisy
la	**pensée**	pansy
la	**pivoine**	peony
la	**primevère**	primrose
la	**rocaille**	rockery
la	**rosée**	dew
la	**serre**	greenhouse
la	**tige**	stalk
la	**tondeuse**	lawnmower
la	**tulipe**	tulip
la	**violette**	violet

seaside and boats

ESSENTIAL WORDS *(masculine)*

le **baigneur**	swimmer
le **bateau** (*pl* -x) **de pêche**	fishing boat
le **bikini**	bikini
le **bord de la mer**	seaside
le **maillot (de bain)**	swimming trunks *or* swimsuit
le **pêcheur**	fisherman
le **pique-nique** (*pl* ~s)	picnic
le **port**	port, harbour
le **quai** [ke]	quay
le **slip de bain**	swimming trunks

IMPORTANT WORDS *(masculine)*

le **château** (*pl* -x) **de sable**	sandcastle
le **coup de soleil**	sunburn
le **crabe**	crab
le **fond**	bottom
l'**horizon**	horizon
le **mal de mer**	seasickness
le **matelas pneumatique**	airbed, lilo®
le **sable**	sand
le **vacancier**	holiday-maker

USEFUL PHRASES

au bord de la mer at the seaside
à l'horizon on the horizon
il a le mal de mer he is sea-sick
nager to swim
se noyer to drown
je vais me baigner I'm going for a swim
plonger dans l'eau to dive into the water
flotter to float

ESSENTIAL WORDS *(feminine)*

la	**côte**	coast
	l'**eau**	water
une	**île**	island
les	**lunettes de soleil**	sunglasses
la	**mer**	sea
la	**natation**	swimming
la	**pierre**	stone
la	**plage**	beach
la	**promenade**	walk
la	**serviette**	towel

IMPORTANT WORDS *(feminine)*

la	**chaise longue**	deckchair
la	**crème solaire**	suncream
la	**planche à voile**	windsurfing (board)
la	**traversée**	crossing

USEFUL PHRASES

au fond de la mer at the bottom of the sea
à la plage on the beach; to the beach
faire la traversée en bateau to go across by boat
se bronzer to get a tan
être bronzé(e) to be tanned
il sait nager he can swim

USEFUL WORDS *(masculine)*

l'	**air marin**	sea air
un	**aviron**	oar
le	**bac**	ferry
le	**caillou** (*pl* -x)	pebble
le	**cap** [kap]	headland
le	**coquillage**	shell
le	**courant**	current
un	**équipage**	crew
les	**flots**	waves
le	**gouvernail**	rudder
le	**maître nageur**	lifeguard
le	**marin**	sailor
le	**mât**	mast
le	**matelot**	sailor
le	**naufrage**	shipwreck
les	**naufragés**	people who are shipwrecked
le	**navire**	ship
un	**océan**	ocean
le	**parasol**	parasol
le	**pavillon**	flag
le	**pédalo**	pedalo
le	**phare**	lighthouse
le	**port de plaisance**	marina
le	**radeau** (*pl* -x)	raft
le	**rivage**	shore
le	**rocher**	rock
le	**seau** (*pl* -x)	bucket
le	**vaisseau** (*pl* -x)	vessel

USEFUL WORDS *(feminine)*

les	**algues**	seaweed
une	**ancre**	anchor
la	**baie**	bay
la	**barque**	small boat
la	**bouée**	buoy
la	**cargaison**	cargo
la	**ceinture de sauvetage**	lifebelt
la	**croisière**	cruise
	l'**écume**	foam
une	**embouchure**	mouth *(of river)*
une	**épave**	wreck
la	**falaise**	cliff
une	**insolation**	sunstroke
la	**jetée**	pier
les	**jumelles**	binoculars
la	**marée**	tide
la	**marine**	navy
la	**mouette**	seagull
la	**passerelle**	gangway; bridge *(of ship)*
la	**pelle**	spade
la	**rame**	oar
la	**vague**	wave
la	**voile**	sail; sailing

USEFUL PHRASES

j'ai eu une insolation I had sunstroke
à marée basse/haute at low/high tide
faire de la voile to go sailing

ESSENTIAL WORDS *(masculine)*

un **achat**	purchase
un **achat en lignre**	online purchase
l'**argent**	money
le **billet de banque**	banknote
le **boucher**	butcher
le **boulanger**	baker
le **bureau** (*pl* -x) **de poste**	post office
le **bureau de tabac**	tobacconist's
le **Caddie®**	trolley
le **cadeau** (*pl* -x)	present
le **caissier**	check-out assistant
le **centime (d'euro)**	euro cent
le **centre commercial**	shopping centre
le **charcutier**	pork butcher
le **chariot**	trolley
le **chèque**	cheque
le **chéquier**	cheque book
le **client**	customer
un **épicier**	grocer
un **euro**	euro
le **fleuriste**	flower shop
le **franc**	franc
le **grand magasin**	department store
un **hypermarché**	supermarket
le **magasin**	shop
le **magasin de chaussures**	shoe shop
le **marché**	market; deal
le **panier**	basket
le **prix**	price
le **rayon**	department
les **soldes**	sales
le **souvenir**	souvenir
le **supermarché**	supermarket
le **tabac**	tobacconist's
le **vendeur**	shop assistant, salesman

ESSENTIAL WORDS *(feminine)*

une	**agence de voyages**	travel agent's
	l'alimentation	food
la	**banque**	bank
la	**boucherie**	butcher's
la	**boulangerie**	bakery
la	**boutique**	small shop
la	**boutique en ligne**	online shop
la	**caisse**	check-out
la	**caissière**	check-out assistant
la	**carte bancaire**	bank card
la	**Carte bleue®**	debit card
la	**carte de crédit**	credit card
la	**charcuterie**	pork butcher's
la	**cliente**	customer
une	**épicerie**	grocer's
la	**liste**	list
la	**monnaie**	change
la	**parfumerie**	perfume shop/department
la	**pâtisserie**	cake shop
la	**pharmacie**	chemist's
la	**pointure**	(shoe) size
la	**poste**	post office
la	**réduction**	reduction
la	**taille**	size
la	**vendeuse**	shop assistant

USEFUL PHRASES

acheter/vendre to buy/sell
ça coûte combien? how much does this cost?
ça fait combien? how much does that come to?
je l'ai payé(e) 5 euros I paid 5 euros for it
chez le boucher/le boulanger at the butcher's/baker's

IMPORTANT WORDS *(masculine)*

un **article**	article
le **coiffeur**	hairdresser
le **commerçant**	shopkeeper
le **commerce**	trade
le **commerce équitable**	fair trade
le **comptoir**	counter
le **cordonnier**	cobbler
un **escalier roulant**	escalator
le **gérant**	manager
le **marchand de fruits**	fruiterer
le **marchand de légumes**	greengrocer
le **marché aux puces**	flea market
le **portefeuille**	wallet
le **porte-monnaie** *(pl inv)*	purse
le **pressing**	dry-cleaner's
le **reçu**	receipt
le **remboursement**	refund
le **ticket de caisse**	receipt

USEFUL PHRASES

je ne fais que regarder I'm just looking
c'est trop cher it's too expensive
quelque chose de moins cher something cheaper
c'est bon marché it's cheap
"payez à la caisse" "pay at the check-out"
c'est pour offrir? would you like it gift-wrapped?
il doit y avoir une erreur there must be some mistake
la vendeuse m'a fait un paquet-cadeau the shop assistant gift-wrapped it for me

IMPORTANT WORDS *(feminine)*

la **bibliothèque**	library
la **brocante**	secondhand shop
la **calculette**	calculator
la **cordonnerie**	cobbler's
la **grande surface**	supermarket
la **librairie**	bookshop
la **marque**	brand
la **promotion**	special offer
la **réclamation**	complaint
la **vitrine**	shop window

USEFUL PHRASES

avec ça? anything else?
se faire rembourser to get a refund
ce pantalon est trop petit, je voudrais l'échanger these trousers are too small, I'd like to exchange them
créer un compte to create an account
"en vente ici" "on sale here"
une voiture d'occasion a used car
en promotion on special offer

USEFUL WORDS *(masculine)*

un **agent immobilier**	estate agent
un **avoir**	credit note
le **bijoutier**	jeweller
le **bon cadeau**	gift voucher
le **coloris**	colour
le **comparateur**	comparison site
le **confiseur**	confectioner
un **horloger**	watchmaker
le **libraire**	bookseller
le **magasin de jeux vidéo**	video games shop
le **marchand de journaux**	newsagent
un **opticien**	optician
le **poissonnier**	fishmonger
le **produit**	product; *(pl)* produce
le **quincaillier**	ironmonger
le **rabais**	discount
le **vidéoclub**	video shop
le **voyagiste**	travel agent

USEFUL PHRASES

faire du lèche-vitrines to go window shopping
heures d'ouverture opening hours
payer cash to pay cash
payer par carte bancaire to pay by card

USEFUL WORDS *(feminine)*

une	**agence immobilière**	estate agent's
la	**bijouterie**	jeweller's
la	**blanchisserie**	laundry
la	**caisse d'épargne**	savings bank
les	**commissions**	shopping
la	**confiserie**	sweetshop
une	**course**	errand
les	**courses**	shopping
la	**devanture**	shop window; display
la	**droguerie**	hardware shop
une	**encolure**	collar size
une	**horlogerie**	watchmaker's
les	**marchandises**	goods
la	**papeterie**	stationer's
la	**queue** [kø]	queue
la	**quincaillerie**	hardware shop
la	**remise**	discount
la	**succursale**	branch
la	**teinturerie**	dry-cleaner's
la	**vente**	sale

USEFUL PHRASES

en vitrine in the window
faire les courses to go shopping
dépenser to spend

sports

ESSENTIAL WORDS *(masculine)*

le **badminton**	badminton
le **ballon**	ball *(large)*
le **basket**	basketball
le **billard**	billiards
le **but** [byt]	goal
le **champion**	champion
le **championnat**	championship
le **cyclisme**	cycling
un **essai**	try
le **foot(ball)**	football
le **golf**	golf
le **:hand(-ball)**	handball
le **:hockey**	hockey
le **jeu** (*pl* -x)	game; play
le **joueur**	player
le **match**	match
le **point**	point
le **résultat**	result
le **rugby**	rugby
le **ski**	skiing; ski
le **ski nautique**	water skiing
le **sport**	sport
le **stade**	stadium
le **tennis**	tennis; tennis court
le **terrain**	ground; pitch
le **volley**	volleyball

USEFUL PHRASES

jouer au football/au tennis to play football/tennis
marquer un but/un point/un essai to score a goal/a point/a try
marquer les points to keep the score
le champion du monde the world champion
gagner/perdre un match to win/lose a match
faire match nul to draw
mon sport préféré my favourite sport

ESSENTIAL WORDS *(feminine)*

l'**aérobic**	aerobics
la **balle**	ball *(small)*
la **championne**	champion
une **équipe**	team
l'**équitation**	horse-riding
la **gymnastique**	gymnastics
la **joueuse**	player
la **natation**	swimming
la **partie**	game
la **piscine**	swimming pool
la **planche à voile**	windsurfing (board)
la **promenade**	walk
la **voile**	sailing

USEFUL PHRASES

égaliser to equalize
courir to run
sauter to jump
lancer, jeter to throw
battre qn to beat sb
s'entraîner to train
Liverpool mène (par) 2 à 1 Liverpool is leading by 2 goals to 1
une partie de tennis a game of tennis
il fait partie d'un club he belongs to a club
aller à la piscine to go to the swimming pool
sais-tu nager? can you swim?
faire du sport to do sport
faire une promenade en vélo to go cycling
faire de la voile to go sailing
faire du footing/de l'alpinisme to go jogging/climbing
faire de la marche/de la randonnée to go walking/hiking

USEFUL WORDS *(masculine)*

un **adversaire**	opponent
l'**alpinisme**	mountaineering
un **arbitre**	referee; (*tennis*) umpire
les **arts martiaux**	martial arts
l'**athlétisme**	athletics
l'**aviron**	rowing
le **catch**	wrestling
le **champ de course**	race course
le **championnat**	championship
le **chronomètre**	stopwatch
le **débutant**	beginner
le **détenteur du titre**	titleholder
un **entraîneur**	trainer, coach
le **filet**	net
le **footing**	jogging
le **gardien de but**	goalkeeper
l'**hippodrome**	race course
le **javelot**	javelin
les **Jeux olympiques**	Olympic Games
le **jogging**	jogging; tracksuit
le **judo**	judo
le **maillot**	(football) jersey
le **parapente**	paragliding
le **patin (à glace)**	(ice) skate; (ice) skating
le **ping-pong**	table tennis
le **quart de finale**	quarter final
les **rollers**	roller skates
le **saut en hauteur**	high jump
le **saut en longueur**	long jump
le **score**	score
le **spectateur**	spectator
le **squash**	squash
le **tir**	shooting
le **tir à l'arc**	archery
le **toboggan**	toboggan; water slide

IMPORTANT WORDS *(feminine)*

la **boule**	bowl; billiard ball
les **boules**	bowls
la **course**	race
les **courses**	horse-racing
la **défense**	defence
l'**escalade**	climbing
la **marche**	walking
la **piste**	ski slope; track
la **randonnée**	hiking
la **rencontre**	match

USEFUL WORDS *(feminine)*

les **baskets**	trainers
la **boxe**	boxing
la **compétition**	competition
la **coupe**	cup
la **demi-finale**	semi-final
une **éliminatoire**	heat
l'**escrime**	fencing
une **étape**	stage
la **finale**	final
la **gagnante**	winner
la **luge**	sledge; sledging
la **lutte**	wrestling
la **mêlée**	scrum
la **mi-temps** *(pl inv)*	half-time
la **patinoire**	skating rink
la **perdante**	loser
la **plongée**	diving
la **prolongation**	extra time
la **raquette**	racket
la **station de sports d'hiver**	winter sports resort
les **tennis**	tennis shoes
la **tribune**	stand

theatre and cinema

ESSENTIAL WORDS *(masculine)*

un **acteur**	actor
le **balcon**	dress circle
le **billet**	ticket
le **cinéma**	cinema
le **cirque**	circus
le **clip vidéo**	pop video
le **clown** [klun]	clown
le **comédien**	actor
le **comique**	comedian
le **costume**	costume
le **film**	film
le **guichet**	box office
un **opéra**	opera
un **orchestre**	orchestra; stalls
le **programme**	programme
le **public**	audience
le **rideau** (*pl* -x)	curtain
le **spectacle**	show
le **théâtre**	theatre
le **western**	western

USEFUL PHRASES

aller au théâtre/au cinéma to go to the theatre/to the cinema
réserver une place to book a seat
un fauteuil d'orchestre a seat in the stalls
mon acteur préféré/actrice préférée my favourite actor/actress
pendant l'entracte during the interval
entrer en scène to come on stage
jouer le rôle de to play the part of

ESSENTIAL WORDS *(feminine)*

une **actrice**	actress
une **ambiance**	atmosphere
la **comédienne**	actress
la **comique**	comedienne
la **musique**	music
la **pièce (de théâtre)**	play
la **place**	seat
la **salle**	auditorium; audience
la **séance**	performance; showing
la **sortie**	exit
la **vedette** *(m+f)* **de cinéma**	film star

USEFUL PHRASES

jouer to play
danser to dance
chanter to sing
tourner un film to shoot a film
"prochaine séance: 21 heures" "next showing: 9 o'clock"
"version originale" "in the original language"
"sous-titré" "subtitled"
"complet" "full house"
applaudir to clap
bis! encore!
bravo! bravo!
un film d'amour/de science-fiction a romance/a science fiction film
un film d'adventure/d'horreur an adventure/horror film

IMPORTANT WORDS *(masculine)*

	l'**acteur principal**	leading man
le	**ballet**	ballet
un	**entracte**	interval
le	**générique**	credits
le	**:héros**	hero
le	**maquillage**	make-up
un	**ouvreur**	usher
le	**pourboire**	tip
le	**sous-titre** (*pl* ~s)	subtitle
le	**titre**	title

USEFUL WORDS *(masculine)*

les	**applaudissements**	applause
un	**auteur dramatique** (*m+f*)	playwright
le	**décor**	scenery
un	**écran**	screen
le	**foyer**	foyer
le	**metteur en scène**	director
le	**parterre**	stalls
le	**personnage**	character (*in play*)
le	**poulailler**	the "gods"
le	**producteur**	producer
le	**projecteur**	spotlight
le	**réalisateur**	director
le	**régisseur**	stage manager
le	**rôle**	part
le	**scénario**	script
le	**souffleur**	prompter
le	**spectateur**	member of the audience
le	**texte**	script, lines
le	**vestiaire**	cloakroom

IMPORTANT WORDS *(feminine)*

l'	**actrice principale**	leading lady
une	**affiche**	notice; poster
la	**bande-annonce**	trailer
la	**comédie**	comedy
la	**critique**	review; critics
une	**héroïne**	heroine
la	**location**	booking; box office
une	**ouvreuse**	usherette

USEFUL WORDS *(feminine)*

la	**comédie musicale**	musical
la	**corbeille**	circle
les	**coulisses**	wings
la	**distribution**	cast *(on programme)*
une	**estrade**	platform
la	**farce**	farce
la	**fosse d'orchestre**	orchestra pit
une	**intrigue**	plot
les	**jumelles de théâtre**	opera glasses
la	**loge**	box
les	**lunettes 3D**	3D glasses
la	**metteuse en scène**	director
la	**mise en scène**	production
la	**première**	first night
la	**rampe**	footlights
la	**réalisatrice**	director
la	**répétition**	rehearsal
la	**répétition générale**	dress rehearsal
la	**représentation**	performance
la	**scène**	stage; scene
la	**tragédie**	tragedy

time

ESSENTIAL WORDS *(masculine)*

un	**an**	year
un	**après-midi** *(pl inv)*	afternoon
un	**instant**	moment
le	**jour**	day
le	**matin**	morning
le	**mois**	month
le	**moment**	moment
le	**quart d'heure**	quarter of an hour
le	**réveil**	alarm clock
le	**siècle**	century
le	**soir**	evening
le	**temps**	time
le	**week-end** (*pl* ~s)	weekend

USEFUL PHRASES

à midi at midday
à minuit at midnight
après-demain the day after tomorrow
aujourd'hui today
avant-hier the day before yesterday
demain tomorrow
hier yesterday
il y a 2 jours 2 days ago
dans 2 jours in 2 days
huit jours a week
quinze jours a fortnight
tous les jours every day
quel jour sommes-nous? what day is it?
le combien sommes-nous? what's the date?
en ce moment at the moment
3 heures moins le quart a quarter to 3
3 heures et quart a quarter past 3
au 21ème siècle in the 21st century
hier soir last night, yesterday evening

ESSENTIAL WORDS *(feminine)*

une **année**	year
une **après-midi** *(pl inv)*	afternoon
une **demi-heure** (*pl* ~s)	half an hour
une **heure**	hour
l'**heure**	time *(in general)*
la **journée**	day
la **matinée**	morning
la **minute**	minute
la **montre**	watch
la **nuit**	night
la **pendule**	clock
la **quinzaine**	fortnight
la **seconde**	second
la **semaine**	week
la **soirée**	evening

USEFUL PHRASES

l'année dernière/prochaine last/next year
dans une demi-heure in half an hour
une/deux/trois fois once/twice/three times
plusieurs fois several times
3 fois par an 3 times a year
9 fois sur 10 9 times out of 10
il était une fois once upon a time there was
10 à la fois 10 at the same time
quelle heure est-il? what time is it?
avez-vous l'heure? have you got the time?
il est 6 heures/6 heures moins 10/6 heures et demie it is 6'clock/10 to 6/ half past 6
il est 14 heures pile it is 2 o'clock exactly
tout à l'heure *(past)* a short while ago; *(future)* soon
tôt, de bonne heure early; **tard** late
cette nuit *(past)* last night; *(to come)* tonight

IMPORTANT WORDS *(masculine)*

l'**avenir**	future
le **lendemain**	next day
le **retard**	delay; lateness

USEFUL WORDS *(masculine)*

le **cadran**	face (*of clock*)
le **calendrier**	calendar
le **chronomètre**	stopwatch
le **futur**	future; future tense
le **Moyen-Âge**	Middle Ages
le **passé**	past; past tense
le **présent**	present (time); present tense

USEFUL PHRASES

après-demain the day after tomorrow
avant-hier the day before yesterday
le surlendemain two days later
la veille the day before
à l'avenir in the future
un jour de congé a day off
un jour férié a public holiday
un jour ouvrable a weekday
par un jour de pluie on a rainy day
au lever du jour at dawn
le lendemain matin/soir the following morning/evening
à présent now
vous êtes en retard you are late

USEFUL WORDS *(feminine)*

une **aiguille**	hand (*of clock*)
une **année bissextile**	leap year
la **décennie**	decade
une **époque**	era; time
l'**horloge**	(large) clock
une **horloge normande**	grandfather clock

USEFUL PHRASES

vous êtes an avance you are early
cette montre avance/retarde this watch is fast/slow
arriver à temps, arriver à l'heure to arrive on time
combien de temps? how long?
le 3e millénaire the third millennium
faire la grasse matinée to have a lie-in
d'une minute à l'autre any minute now
aujourd'hui en huit a week today
la veille au soir the night before
à cette époque at that time

ESSENTIAL WORDS *(masculine)*

un **atelier**	workshop
le **bricolage**	DIY
le **bricoleur**	handyman
un **outil**	tool

USEFUL WORDS *(masculine)*

le **cadenas**	padlock
le **chantier**	construction site
le **ciseau** (*pl* -x)	chisel
les **ciseaux**	scissors
le **clou**	nail
un **échafaudage**	scaffolding
un **élastique**	rubber band
un **escabeau** (*pl* -x)	stepladder
le **fil de fer (barbelé)**	(barbed) wire
le **foret**	drill
le **marteau** (*pl* -x)	hammer
le **marteau-piqueur** (*pl* ~x~s)	pneumatic drill
le **pic**	pickaxe
le **pinceau** (*pl* -x)	paintbrush
le **ressort**	spring
le **scotch®**	Sellotape®
le **tournevis**	screwdriver

USEFUL PHRASES

faire du bricolage to do odd jobs
enfoncer un clou to hammer in a nail
"attention peinture fraîche" "wet paint"
peindre to paint; **tapisser** to wallpaper

ESSENTIAL WORDS *(feminine)*

la **clé, clef**	key; spanner
la **corde**	rope
la **machine**	machine

USEFUL WORDS *(feminine)*

une **aiguille**	needle
la **bêche**	spade
la **boîte à outils**	toolbox
la **clef anglaise**	spanner
la **colle**	glue
une **échelle**	ladder
la **fourche**	(garden) fork
la **lime**	file
la **pelle**	shovel
la **perceuse**	drill
la **pile**	battery
les **pinces**	pliers
la **pioche**	pickaxe
la **planche**	plank
la **punaise**	drawing pin
la **scie**	saw
la **serrure**	lock
la **vis** [vis]	screw

USEFUL PHRASES

"chantier interdit" "construction site: keep out"
pratique handy
couper to cut; **réparer** to mend
visser to screw (in); **dévisser** to unscrew

ESSENTIAL WORDS *(masculine)*

un	**agent (de police)**	policeman
un	**arrêt de bus**	bus stop
le	**bâtiment**	building
le	**bureau** (*pl* -x) **de poste**	post office
le	**bureau** (*pl* -x)	office
le	**centre-ville** (*pl* ~s~s)	town centre
le	**cinéma**	cinema
le	**coin**	corner
le	**commissariat**	police station
les	**environs**	surroundings
un	**habitant**	inhabitant
un	**HLM (habitation à loyer modéré)**	council flat
un	**hôtel**	hotel
un	**hôtel de ville**	town hall
un	**immeuble**	block of flats
le	**jardin public**	park
le	**magasin**	shop
le	**marché**	market
le	**métro**	underground, subway
le	**musée**	museum; art gallery
le	**parc**	park
le	**parking**	car park
le	**piéton**	pedestrian
le	**pont**	bridge
le	**quartier**	district
le	**restaurant**	restaurant
le	**sens interdit**	one-way street
le	**taxi**	taxi
le	**théâtre**	theatre
le	**tour**	tour
le	**touriste**	tourist

ESSENTIAL WORDS *(feminine)*

une	**auto**	car
la	**banlieue**	suburbs
la	**banque**	bank
la	**boutique**	(small) shop
la	**cathédrale**	cathedral
une	**église**	church
la	**gare**	train station
la	**gare routière**	bus station
une	**HLM (habitation à loyer modéré)**	council flat
la	**laverie automatique**	launderette
la	**mairie**	town hall
la	**piscine**	swimming pool
la	**place**	square
la	**police**	police
la	**pollution**	air pollution
la	**poste**	post office
la	**route**	road
la	**rue**	street
la	**station de taxis**	taxi rank
la	**station-service** (*pl* ~s~)	petrol station
la	**tour**	tower
une	**usine**	factory
la	**ville**	town, city
la	**voiture**	car
la	**vue**	view

USEFUL PHRASES

je vais en ville I'm going into town
au centre-ville in the town centre
sur la place in the square
une rue à sens unique a one-way street
traverser la rue to cross the street
au coin de la rue at the corner of the street
habiter en banlieue to live in the suburbs

IMPORTANT WORDS *(masculine)*

le	**carnet de tickets**	book of tickets
le	**carrefour**	crossroads
le	**château** (*pl* -x)	castle
le	**DAB (distributeur automatique de billets)**	cashpoint, ATM
un	**embouteillage**	traffic jam
un	**endroit**	place
le	**jardin zoologique**	zoo
le	**kiosque (à journaux)**	newspaper stall
le	**lieu** (*pl* -x)	place
le	**maire**	mayor
le	**monument**	monument
le	**parcmètre**	parking meter
le	**passant**	passer-by
le	**sens unique**	one-way street
le	**temple**	Protestant church
le	**trottoir**	pavement
le	**zoo**	zoo

USEFUL PHRASES

marcher to walk
prendre le bus/le métro to take the bus/the underground
acheter un carnet de tickets to buy a book of 10 tickets
composter to punch (*ticket*)

IMPORTANT WORDS *(feminine)*

une **affiche**	notice; poster
la **bibliothèque**	library
la **chaussée**	road
la **circulation**	traffic
la **déviation**	diversion
la **mosquée**	mosque
la **rue principale**	main street
la **synagogue**	synagogue
la **vieille ville**	old town
la **zone bleue**	restricted parking zone
la **zone industrielle**	industrial estate
la **zone piétonne**	pedestrian precinct

USEFUL PHRASES

industriel(le) industrial
historique historic
joli(e) pretty
laid(e) ugly
propre clean
sale dirty

USEFUL WORDS *(masculine)*

un	**Abribus®**	bus shelter
un	**arrondissement**	district
un	**autobus**	bus
le	**bistrot**	café
le	**bus**	bus
le	**cimetière**	cemetery
le	**citadin**	town dweller
le	**citoyen**	citizen
le	**conseil municipal**	town council
le	**défilé**	parade
un	**édifice**	building
un	**égout**	sewer
le	**faubourg**	suburb
le	**gratte-ciel** *(pl inv)*	skyscraper
le	**panneau** (*pl* -x)	roadsign
le	**passage clouté**	pedestrian crossing
le	**pavé**	cobblestone
le	**refuge**	traffic island
les	**remparts**	ramparts
le	**réverbère**	street lamp
le	**square**	square
le	**virage**	bend

USEFUL WORDS *(feminine)*

une	**agglomération**	built-up area
la	**camionnette de livraison**	delivery van
la	**caserne de pompiers**	fire station
la	**cité universitaire**	halls of residence
les	**curiosités**	sights, places of interest
la	**flèche**	arrow; spire
la	**foule**	crowd
la	**galerie**	art gallery
la	**grand-rue**	main street
une	**impasse**	dead end
la	**piste cyclable**	cycle path
la	**population**	population
la	**poussette**	pushchair
la	**prison**	prison
la	**queue** [kø]	queue
la	**statue**	statue

ESSENTIAL WORDS *(masculine)*

un	**aller-retour**	return ticket
un	**aller simple**	single ticket
les	**bagages**	luggage
le	**billet**	ticket
le	**buffet**	station buffet
le	**compartiment**	compartment
le	**départ**	departure
le	**douanier**	customs officer
le	**frein**	brake
le	**guichet**	ticket office
	l'**horaire**	timetable
le	**mécanicien**	engine-driver
le	**métro**	underground, subway
le	**numéro**	number
les	**objets trouvés**	lost property office
le	**passeport**	passport
le	**plan**	map
le	**pont**	bridge
le	**porteur**	porter
le	**prix du billet**	fare
le	**prix du ticket**	fare
le	**quai** [ke]	platform
les	**renseignements**	information
le	**retard**	delay
le	**sac**	bag
le	**supplément**	extra charge
le	**taxi**	taxi
le	**TGV**	high-speed train
le	**ticket**	ticket
le	**train**	train
le	**train express**	fast train
le	**train rapide**	express train
le	**vélo**	bike
le	**voyage**	journey
le	**voyageur**	traveller

ESSENTIAL WORDS *(feminine)*

une	**arrivée**	arrival
la	**bicyclette**	bicycle
la	**classe**	class
la	**consigne**	left-luggage office
la	**consigne automatique**	left-luggage locker
la	**correspondance**	connection
la	**direction**	direction
la	**douane**	customs
une	**entrée**	entrance
la	**gare**	station
la	**ligne**	line
la	**place**	seat
la	**réduction**	reduction
la	**réservation**	reservation
la	**salle d'attente**	waiting room
la	**sortie**	exit
la	**station de métro**	underground station
la	**station de taxis**	taxi rank
la	**valise**	suitcase
la	**voie**	track, line
la	**voiture**	carriage

USEFUL PHRASES

réserver une place to book a seat
payer un supplément to pay an extra charge
faire/défaire ses bagages to pack/unpack
prendre le train to take the train
manquer son train to miss the train
monter dans le train/bus to get onto the train/bus
descendre du train/bus to get off the train/bus
c'est libre? is this seat free?
composter son billet to punch one's ticket

IMPORTANT WORDS *(masculine)*

le	**chemin de fer**	railway
le	**conducteur**	driver
le	**contrôleur**	ticket collector
un	**escalier roulant**	escalator
le	**pourboire**	tip
le	**tarif**	fare
le	**wagon-lit** (*pl* ~s~s)	sleeping car
le	**wagon-restaurant** (*pl* ~s~s)	dining car

USEFUL WORDS *(masculine)*

le	**chef de gare**	stationmaster
le	**chef de train**	guard
le	**cheminot**	railwayman
le	**coup de sifflet**	whistle
le	**déraillement**	derailment
un	**indicateur**	timetable
le	**passage à niveau**	level crossing
les	**rails**	rails
le	**signal d'alarme**	alarm
le	**train de marchandises**	goods train
le	**trajet**	journey
le	**wagon**	carriage

USEFUL PHRASES

le train est en retard the train is late

un compartiment fumeur/non-fumeur a smoking/non-smoking compartment

"défense de se pencher au dehors" "do not lean out of the window"

IMPORTANT WORDS *(feminine)*

la **barrière**	barrier
la **couchette**	sleeping car
la **destination**	destination
la **durée**	length (of time)
la **frontière**	border
la **portière**	carriage door
la **SNCF**	French Railways

USEFUL WORDS *(feminine)*

la **banquette**	seat
la **carte d'abonnement**	season ticket
la **carte jeune**	young persons' discount card
une **étiquette**	label
la **locomotive**	locomotive
la **malle**	trunk
la **salle d'attente**	waiting room
la **sonnette d'alarme**	alarm
la **voie ferrée**	(railway) line *or* track

USEFUL PHRASES

je t'accompagnerai à la gare I'll go to the station with you
je viendrai te chercher à la gare I'll come and pick you up at the station
le train de 10 heures à destination de Paris/en provenance de Paris
the 10 o'clock train to/from Paris

ESSENTIAL WORDS *(masculine)*

un **arbre**	tree
le **bois**	wood

USEFUL WORDS *(masculine)*

un **abricotier**	apricot tree
un **arbre fruitier**	fruit tree
le **bouleau** (*pl* -x)	birch
le **bourgeon**	bud
le **buis**	box tree
le **buisson**	bush
le **cerisier**	cherry tree
le **châtaignier**	chestnut tree
le **chêne**	oak
un **érable**	maple
le **feuillage**	foliage
le **figuier**	fig tree
le **frêne**	ash
le **:hêtre**	beech
le **:houx**	holly
un **if**	yew
le **marronnier**	chestnut tree
le **noyer**	walnut tree
un **oranger**	orange tree
un **orme**	elm
le **pêcher**	peach tree
le **peuplier**	poplar
le **pin**	pine
le **platane**	plane tree
le **poirier**	pear tree
le **pommier**	apple tree
le **rameau** (*pl* -x)	branch
le **sapin**	fir tree
le **saule pleureur**	weeping willow
le **tilleul**	lime tree
le **tronc**	trunk
le **verger**	orchard
le **vignoble**	vineyard

ESSENTIAL WORDS *(feminine)*

la **branche**	branch
la **feuille**	leaf
la **forêt**	forest

USEFUL WORDS *(feminine)*

l'**aubépine**	hawthorn
la **baie**	berry
l'**écorce**	bark
la **racine**	root

vegetables

ESSENTIAL WORDS *(masculine)*

le	**champignon**	mushroom
le	**chou** (*pl* -x)	cabbage
le	**chou-fleur** (*pl* ~x~s)	cauliflower
le	**:haricot**	bean
le	**:haricot vert**	French bean
les	**légumes**	vegetables
un	**oignon** [ɔɲɔ̃]	onion
les	**petits pois**	peas

USEFUL WORDS *(masculine)*

	l'**ail** [aj]	garlic
un	**artichaut**	artichoke
le	**brocoli**	broccoli
le	**céleri**	celery
les	**choux de Bruxelles**	Brussels sprouts
le	**concombre**	cucumber
le	**cresson**	watercress
le	**maïs**	corn
les	**épinards**	spinach
le	**navet**	turnip
le	**persil** [pɛrsi]	parsley
le	**poireau** (*pl* -x)	leek
le	**poivron**	(sweet) pepper
le	**radis**	radish

USEFUL PHRASES

cultiver des légumes to grow vegetables
un épi de maïs corn on the cob

ESSENTIAL WORDS *(feminine)*

la	**carotte**	carrot
les	**crudités**	mixed raw vegetables
la	**pomme de terre** (*pl* ~s de terre)	potato
la	**salade (verte)**	(green) salad
la	**tomate**	tomato

USESFUL WORDS *(feminine)*

les	**asperges**	asparagus
une	**aubergine**	aubergine
la	**betterave**	beetroot
la	**chicorée**	endive
la	**courge**	marrow
la	**courgette**	courgette
une	**endive**	chicory
la	**laitue**	lettuce

USEFUL PHRASES

des carottes râpées grated carrot
biologique organic
végétarien(ne) vegetarian

ESSENTIAL WORDS *(masculine)*

l'**arrière**	back
un **autobus**	bus
un **autocar**	coach
l'**avant**	front
un **avion**	plane
le **bateau** (*pl* -x)	boat
le **bateau à rames/à voile**	rowing/sailing boat
le **bus**	bus
le **camion**	lorry
le **car**	coach
le **casque**	helmet
le **ferry**	ferry
un **hélicoptère**	helicopter
un **hovercraft**	hovercraft
le **métro**	underground
le **mobile home**	motorhome
le **moyen de transport**	means of transport
le **poids lourd**	heavy goods vehicle
le **prix du billet**	fare
le **risque**	risk
le **scooter**	scooter
le **taxi**	taxi
le **train**	train
les **transports publics**	public transport
le **véhicule**	vehicle
le **vélo**	bike
le **vélomoteur**	moped

USEFUL PHRASES

voyager to travel
il est allé à Paris en avion he flew to Paris
prendre le bus/le métro/le train to take the bus/the subway/the train
faire de la bicyclette to go cycling
on peut y aller en voiture you can go there by car

ESSENTIAL WORDS *(feminine)*

la	**bicyclette**	bicycle
la	**camionnette**	van
la	**caravane**	caravan
la	**distance**	distance
la	**moto**	motorbike
la	**voiture**	car

IMPORTANT WORDS *(feminine)*

une	**ambulance**	ambulance
la	**dépanneuse**	breakdown van
la	**voiture de pompiers**	fire engine

USEFUL PHRASES

dépanner qn to repair sb's car
une voiture de location a hire car
une voiture de sport a sports car
une voiture de course a racing car
une voiture de fonction a company car
"voitures d'occasion" "used cars"
démarrer to start, to move off

USEFUL WORDS *(masculine)*

un **aéroglisseur**	hovercraft
le **bac**	ferry
le **bateau-mouche** (*pl* ~x~s)	tour boat in Paris
le **break** [bʀɛk]	estate car
le **bulldozer** [byldozɛʀ]	bulldozer
le **camion-citerne** (*pl* ~s~s)	tanker
le **canoë** [kanɔe]	canoe
le **canot**	rowing boat
le **canot de sauvetage**	lifeboat
le **char (d'assaut)**	tank
le **cyclomoteur**	moped
un **hydravion**	seaplane
le **navire**	ship
un **ovni (objet volant non identifié)**	UFO (unidentified flying object)
le **paquebot**	passenger liner
le **pétrolier**	oil tanker (*ship*)
le **planeur**	glider
le **porte-avions** (*pl inv*)	aircraft carrier
le **remorqueur**	tug
le **semi-remorque** (*pl* ~s)	articulated lorry
le **sous-marin** (*pl* ~s)	submarine
le **téléphérique**	cable car
le **télésiège**	chairlift
le **tram(way)**	tram
le **vaisseau** (*pl* -x)	vessel
le **vélomoteur**	moped
le **yacht** [jɔt]	yacht

USEFUL WORDS *(feminine)*

la **camionnette de livraison**	delivery van
la **charrette**	cart
la **fusée**	rocket
la **jeep®**	Jeep®
la **locomotive**	locomotive
la **mobylette**	moped
la **péniche**	barge
la **remorque**	trailer
la **soucoupe volante**	flying saucer
la **vedette**	speedboat

ESSENTIAL WORDS *(masculine)*

l'**air**	air
l'**automne**	autumn
le **brouillard**	fog
le **bulletin de la météo**	weather report
le **ciel**	sky
le **climat**	climate
le **cyclone**	cyclone
le **degré**	degree
l'**est**	east
l'**été**	summer
le **froid**	cold
l'**hiver**	winter
le **nord**	north
le **nuage**	cloud
l'**ouest**	west
le **parapluie**	umbrella
le **printemps**	spring
le **soleil**	sun; sunshine
le **sud**	south
le **temps**	weather
le **tsunami**	tsunami
le **vent**	wind

USEFUL PHRASES

quel temps fait-il? what's the weather like?
il fait chaud/froid it's hot/cold
il fait beau it's a lovely day
il fait mauvais (temps) it's a horrible day
en plein air in the open air
il y a du brouillard it's foggy
30° à l'ombre 30° in the shade
écouter la météo *or* **les prévisions** to listen to the forecast
pleuvoir to rain
neiger to snow
il pleut it's raining
il neige it's snowing

ESSENTIAL WORDS *(feminine)*

la	**glace**	ice
une	**inondation**	flood
la	**météo**	weather forecast
la	**neige**	snow
la	**pluie**	rain
la	**région**	region, area
la	**saison**	season
la	**température**	temperature

USEFUL PHRASES

le soleil brille the sun is shining
le vent souffle the wind is blowing
il gèle it's freezing
geler to freeze
fondre to melt
ensoleillé(e) sunny
orageux(euse) stormy
pluvieux(euse) rainy
frais (fraîche) cool
variable changeable
humide humid
le ciel est couvert the sky is overcast

USEFUL WORDS *(masculine)*

un	**arc-en-ciel** (*pl* arcs-en-ciel)	rainbow
le	**baromètre**	barometer
le	**changement**	change
le	**chasse-neige** (*pl inv*)	snowplough
le	**clair de lune**	moonlight
le	**coucher de soleil**	sunset
le	**courant d'air**	draught
le	**crépuscule**	twilight
le	**dégel**	thaw
le	**déluge**	downpour
un	**éclair**	flash of lightning
le	**flocon de neige**	snowflake
le	**gel**	frost
le	**givre**	frost
le	**glaçon**	icicle
un	**orage**	thunderstorm
un	**ouragan**	hurricane
le	**paratonnerre**	lightning conductor
le	**rayon de soleil**	ray of sunshine
le	**tonnerre**	thunder
le	**verglas**	black ice

IMPORTANT WORDS *(feminine)*

une	**amélioration**	improvement
une	**averse**	shower
la	**chaleur**	heat
une	**éclaircie**	sunny spell
la	**fumée**	smoke
la	**poussière**	dust
les	**précipitations**	rainfall
les	**prévisions (météorologiques)**	(weather) forecast
la	**tempête**	storm
la	**visibilité**	visibility

USEFUL WORDS *(feminine)*

	l'**atmosphère**	atmosphere
	l'**aube**	dawn
la	**brise**	breeze
la	**brume**	mist
la	**canicule**	heatwave
la	**chute de neige**	snowfall
la	**congère**	snowdrift
la	**flaque d'eau**	puddle
la	**foudre**	lightning
la	**gelée**	frost
la	**goutte de pluie**	raindrop
la	**grêle**	hail
une	**inondation**	flood
la	**rafale**	gust of wind
la	**rosée**	dew
la	**sécheresse**	drought
les	**ténèbres**	darkness
la	**vague de chaleur**	heatwave

ESSENTIAL WORDS *(masculine)*

le	**bureau** (*pl* -x)	office
le	**dortoir**	dormitory
le	**drap**	sheet
le	**lit**	bed
les	**lits superposés**	bunk beds
le	**petit déjeuner**	breakfast
le	**repas**	meal
le	**séjour**	stay
le	**silence**	silence
le	**tarif**	rate(s)
le	**visiteur**	visitor
les	**WC**	toilets

IMPORTANT WORDS *(masculine)*

le	**guide**	guidebook
le	**linge**	bedclothes; washing
le	**règlement**	rules
le	**sac à dos**	rucksack
le	**sac de couchage**	sleeping bag

ESSENTIAL WORDS *(feminine)*

une	**AJ**	youth hostel
une	**auberge de jeunesse**	youth hostel
la	**carte**	map; card
la	**cuisine**	kitchen; cooking
la	**douche**	shower
la	**nuit**	night
la	**poubelle**	dustbin
la	**salle à manger**	dining room
la	**salle de bains**	bathroom
la	**salle de jeux**	games room
les	**toilettes**	toilets
les	**vacances**	holidays

IMPORTANT WORDS *(feminine)*

la	**carte d'adhérent**	membership card
la	**randonnée**	hike

USEFUL PHRASES

passer une nuit à l'auberge de jeunesse to spend a night at the youth hostel

je voudrais louer un sac de couchage I would like to hire a sleeping bag

il n'y a plus de place there's no more room

The vocabulary items on pages 204 to 233 have been grouped under parts of speech rather than topics because they can apply in a wide range of circumstances. Use them just as freely as the vocabulary already given.

CONJUNCTIONS

> **What is a conjunction?**
> A **conjunction** is a word such as *and*, *but*, *or*, *so*, *if* and *because*, that links two words or phrases, or two parts of a sentence, for example, *Diane <u>and</u> I have been friends for years; I left <u>because</u> I was bored.*

alors que while
aussi ... que as ... as
avant de + *infinitive* before
car because
cependant however
c'est-à-dire that is to say
comme as
comment how
depuis que since
dès que as soon as
donc so; then
et and
et alors? so what!
lorsque when
maintenant que now (that)
mais but
ne ... que only
ni ... ni neither ... nor
or now
ou or
ou ... ou either ... or
ou bien or
parce que because
pendant que while
pourquoi why
pourvu que + *subj* provided that, so long as
puisque since, because
quand when
que that; than
si if
sinon otherwise
tandis que whilst
tant que so long as
vu que in view of the fact that

ADJECTIVES

What is an adjective?
An **adjective** is a 'describing' word that tells you more about a person or thing, such as their appearance, colour, size or other qualities, for example, *pretty, blue, big*.

abordable affordable
abrégé(e) shortened
absurde absurd
accueillant(e) welcoming
actif, active active
actuel(le) present
aérien(ne) aerial
affectueux(euse) affectionate
affreux(euse) dreadful
âgé(e) old
agité(e) restless; stormy (*sea*)
agréable pleasant
agricole agricultural
aigu, aiguë acute; piercing
aimable kind, nice
aîné(e) elder, eldest
amer, amère bitter
amoureux(euse) in love
amusant(e) entertaining
ancien(ne) old, former
animé(e) busy
annuel(le) annual
anonyme anonymous
anxieux(euse) anxious, worried
appliqué(e) diligent
apte capable
arrière: siège *m* **arrière** back seat
assis(e) sitting, seated
aucun(e) no, not any
automatique automatic
autre other
avant: siège *m* **avant** front seat
avantageux(euse) good value
barbu bearded
bas(se) low
beau (bel), belle beautiful
bête silly
bien fine, well; comfortable
bienvenu(e) welcome
bizarre strange, odd
blessé(e) injured
bon(ne) good
bon marché *inv* cheap
bordé(e) de lined with
bouillant(e) boiling
bouleversé(e) upset
bref, brève brief
brillant(e) bright, brilliant; shiny
bruyant(e) noisy
calme calm
capable capable
carré(e) square
catholique Catholic
célèbre famous
certain(e) sure
chaque each
chargé(e) de loaded with; responsible for

charmant(e) delightful
chaud(e) warm, hot
cher, chère dear; expensive
chic smart
choquant(e) shocking
chouette brilliant
chrétien(ne) Christian
clair(e) clear; light
classique classical
climatisé(e) air-conditioned
commode convenient
complet, complète complete; full
compliqué(e) complicated
composé(e) de comprising
compréhensif(ive) understanding
compris(e) understood; included
confortable comfortable
constipé(e) constipated
contemporain(e) contemporary
content(e) happy
continuel(le) continuing
convenable suitable
correct(e) correct
couché(e) lying down
courageux(euse) brave, courageous
court(e) short
couvert(e) de covered with
créé(e) created, established
cruel(le) cruel
cuit(e) cooked
culturel(le) cultural
curieux(euse) curious, strange
dangereux(euse) dangerous
debout standing (up)
décevant(e) disappointing
déchiré(e) torn
découragé(e) discouraged
déçu(e) disappointed
défendu(e) forbidden
dégoûté(e) disgusted
délicat(e) delicate
délicieux(euse) delicious
dernier, dernière last, latest
désagréable unpleasant
désert(e) deserted
désespéré(e) desperate
désolé(e) desolate, sorry
détestable ghastly
détruit(e) destroyed
différent(e) different
difficile difficult
digne worthy
direct(e) direct
disponible available
distingué(e) distinguished
distrait(e) absent-minded
divers(e) different
divertissant(e) entertaining
divin(e) divine
divisé(e) divided
doré(e) golden; gilt
doux, douce gentle; sweet; soft
droit(e) straight; right(hand)
drôle funny
dur(e) hard
économique economic; economical
effrayé(e) frightened
égal(e) equal; even
électrique electric
élégant(e) elegant
élevé(e) high; **bien élevé(e)** well-mannered
embêtant(e) annoying

enchanté(e) delighted
énervé(e) irritated; nervous
ennuyé(e) bothered
ennuyeux(euse) boring
énorme huge
ensoleillé(e) sunny
entendu(e) agreed
entier, entière whole
épais(se) thick
épouvantable terrible
épuisé(e) exhausted
essentiel(le) essential
essoufflé(e) out of breath
étendu(e) stretched out
étonnant(e) astonishing
étonné(e) astonished
étrange strange
étranger, étrangère foreign
étroit(e) narrow
éveillé(e) awake
évident(e) obvious
exact(e) exact
excellent(e) excellent
expérimenté(e) experienced
extraordinaire extraordinary
fâché(e) angry
facile easy
faible weak
fatigant(e) tiring
fatigué(e) tired
faux, fausse false, wrong
favori(te) favourite
fermé(e) closed
féroce fierce
fier, fière proud
fin(e) fine; thin
final(e) final
fondé(e) founded
formidable tremendous
fort(e) strong; hard
fou, folle mad
fragile fragile; frail
frais, fraîche fresh, cool
froid(e) cold
furieux(euse) furious
futur(e) future
gai(e) cheerful
gauche left(hand)
général(e) general
généreux(euse) generous
génial(e) brilliant
gentil(le) kind, nice
gonflé(e) swollen
gracieux(euse) graceful
grand(e) big; tall
gratuit(e) free
grave serious
gros(se) big; fat
habile skilful
habitué(e) à used to
habituel(le) usual
haut(e) high; tall
heureux(euse) happy
historique historical
honnête honest
identique identical
illuminé(e) lit; floodlit
illustré(e) illustrated
imaginaire imaginary
immense huge
immobile motionless
important(e) important

impossible impossible
impressionnant(e) impressive
imprévu(e) unforeseen
inattendu(e) unexpected
incapable (de) incapable (of)
inconnu(e) unknown
incroyable unbelievable
indispensable indispensable
industriel(le) industrial
inondé(e) flooded
inquiet, inquiète worried
insouciant(e) carefree
insupportable unbearable
intelligent(e) intelligent
interdit(e) prohibited
intéressant(e) interesting
interminable endless
international(e) international
interrompu(e) interrupted
inutile useless
irrité(e) annoyed
isolé(e) isolated
jeune young
jaloux(ouse) jealous
joli(e) pretty
joyeux(euse) merry, cheerful
juif, juive Jewish
juste just; correct
lâche cowardly
laid(e) ugly
large wide; broad
léger, légère light
lent(e) slow
leur/leurs their
libre free
local(e) local
long(ue) long
lourd(e) heavy
magique magical
magnifique magnificent
maigre thin
malade ill
malheureux(euse) unhappy, unfortunate
malhonnête dishonest
mauvais(e) bad
mécanique mechanical
méchant(e) naughty
mécontent(e) unhappy
médical(e) medical
meilleur(e) better, best
même same
merveilleux(euse) marvellous
militaire military
minable pathetic
mince slim
mobile mobile; moving; movable
moche ugly
moderne modern
moindre least
mon/ma/mes my
montagneux(euse) mountainous
mort(e) dead
mouillé(e) wet
mouvementé(e) lively
moyen(ne) average
mû, mue (par) moved (by)
multicolore multicoloured
muni(e) de provided with
municipal(e) municipal, town
mûr(e) ripe
musclé(e) muscular
musical(e) musical

musulman(e) Muslim
mystérieux(euse) mysterious
natal(e) native
national(e) national
naturel(le) natural
né(e) born
nécessaire necessary
négatif(ive) negative
nerveux(euse) nervous
net(te) clear
neuf, neuve new
nombreux(euse) numerous
normal(e) normal
notre/nos our
nouveau (nouvel), nouvelle new
noyé(e) drowned
obligatoire compulsory
obligé(e) de obliged to
occupé(e) taken; busy; engaged
officiel(le) official
ordinaire ordinary
original(e) original
orné(e) de decorated with
outré(e) outraged
ouvert(e) open
paisible peaceful
pâle pale
pareil(le) similar, same
paresseux(euse) lazy
parfait(e) perfect
particulier, particulière particular; private
passionnant(e) exciting
passionné(e) passionate
patient(e) patient
pauvre poor
pénible painful
permanent(e) permanent
perpétuel(le) perpetual
personnel(le) personal
petit(e) small, little
pittoresque picturesque
plat(e) flat
plein(e) (de) full (of)
plusieurs several
pneumatique inflatable
poli(e) polite; polished
populaire popular
portatif(ive) portable
positif(ive) positive
possible possible
pratique practical; handy
précédent(e) previous
précieux(euse) precious
précis(e) precise
préféré(e) favourite
premier, première first
pressant(e) urgent
pressé(e): être pressé(e) to be in a hurry
prêt(e) ready
primaire primary
privé(e) private
privilégié(e) privileged
prochain(e) next
proche nearby; close
profond(e) deep
propre own; clean
protestant(e) Protestant
prudent(e) cautious
public, publique public
publicitaire publicity
quel(le) what
quelque(s) some

rafraîchissant(e) refreshing
rangé(e): bien rangé(e) neat and tidy
rapide fast
rare rare
ravi(e) delighted
récent(e) recent
reconnaissant(e) grateful
rectangulaire rectangular
réel(le) real
religieux(euse) religious
réservé(e) reserved
responsable (de) responsible (for)
rêveur(euse) dreamy
riche rich
ridicule ridiculous
rond(e) round
rusé(e) cunning
sage well-behaved; wise
sain et sauf safe and sound
sale dirty
sanitaire sanitary
satisfait(e) (de) satisfied (with)
sauvage wild
scolaire school (*year etc*)
sec, sèche dry
second(e) second
secondaire secondary
secret, secrète secret
semblable similar
sensible sensitive
sérieux(euse) serious
serré(e) tight
seul(e) alone
sévère severe
simple simple
sincère sincere
sinistre sinister
situé(e) situated
social(e) social
solennel(le) solemn
solide solid
sombre dark
son/sa/ses his, her, its, one's
soudain(e) sudden
souriant(e) smiling
sous-marin(e) underwater
spécial(e) special
suivant(e) following
suivi(e) de followed by
super super
superbe magnificent
supérieur(e) upper; advanced
supplémentaire extra
sûr(e) sure
surprenant(e) surprising
sympa(thique) nice, likeable
technique technical
tel(le) such
temporaire temporary
terrible terrible
théâtral(e) theatrical
tiède lukewarm
timide shy
ton/ta/tes your
touristique tourist (*area etc*)
tout/toute/toutes all
traditionnel(le) traditional
tranquille quiet, peaceful
trempé(e) soaked
triste sad
troublé(e) disturbed
typique typical

uni(e) plain
unique only; unique
urbain(e) urban
urgent(e) urgent
utile useful
valable valid
varié(e) varied; various
vaste vast
véritable real
vide empty
vieux (vieil), vieille old
vif, vive bright
vilain(e) naughty; ugly;nasty
violent(e) violent
vivant(e) alive; lively
voisin(e) neighbouring
votre/vos your
vrai(e) real, true

ADVERBS AND PREPOSITIONS

What is an adverb?
An **adverb** is a word used with verbs to give information on where, when or how an action takes place, for example, *here, today, quickly*. An adverb can also add information to adjectives and other adverbs, for example, *extremely quick, very quickly*.

What is a preposition?
A preposition is one word such as *at, for, with, into* or *from*, or words such as *in front of* or *near to*, which are usually followed by a noun or a pronoun.

Prepositions show how people and things relate to the rest of the sentence, for example, *She's at home; It's for you; You'll get into trouble; It's in front of you.*

à to, at
abord: d'abord first, at first;
tout d'abord first of all;
aux abords de alongside
absolument absolutely
actuellement at present
admirablement admirably
afin de so as to
ailleurs elsewhere;
d'ailleurs moreover
ainsi thus;
ainsi que as well as
alors then
anxieusement anxiously
après after;
après-demain the day after tomorrow;
d'après according to
assez fairly, quite;
assez de enough
aujourd'hui today
auparavant previously
auprès de next to
aussi also, too; as
aussitôt at once
autant (de) as much; as many;
d'autant plus (que) all the more (since)
autour (de) around
autrefois formerly
autrement otherwise; differently;
autrement dit in other words;
autrement que other than
avance: à l'avance in advance;
d'avance in advance
avant (de) before
avec with
bas: en bas downstairs, at the bottom

beaucoup a lot; much;
beaucoup de a lot of; many
bien well;
bien entendu of course
bientôt soon
bord: à bord (de) on board;
au bord de beside
bout: au bout de after; at the end of
bref in short
brusquement suddenly
cependant however
certainement certainly
chez at (*or* to) the house;
chez moi/toi/lui/elle at my/your/his/her house
combien (de) how much, how many
comme as, like;
comme d'habitude as usual;
comme toujours as usual
comment how
complètement completely
compris: y compris including
conséquent: par conséquent as a result
continuellement continually
contraire: au contraire on the contrary
contre against;
ci-contre opposite;
par contre on the other hand
côté: à côté de next to, beside;
de ce côté (de) on this side (of);
de l'autre côté (de) on the other side (of);
juste à côté next door
couramment fluently
cours: au cours de during
dans in, into
davantage (de) more
de of, from
debout standing
dedans inside
dehors outside
déjà already
demain tomorrow;
après-demain the day after tomorrow
depuis since, for
derrière behind
dès from; **dès que** as soon as
dessous underneath;
ci-dessous below;
en dessous (de) below
dessus on top;
au-dessus (de) above;
ci-dessus above
devant in front (of)
doucement gently
droit: tout droit straight (on)
droite: à droite on the right, to the right
dur hard
effet: en effet indeed
également also; equally
encore still; again;
encore une fois once again
enfin at last
énormément (de) a lot (of)
ensemble together
ensuite then
entièrement entirely
entre between
environ about
éventuellement possibly

évidemment obviously
exactement exactly
exprès on purpose
extérieur: à l'extérieur (de) outside
extrêmement extremely
face à faced with;
en face (de) opposite
facilement easily
façon: de façon à so as to
fidèlement faithfully
finalement in the end; after all
fort hard
franchement frankly
gauche: à gauche on the left, to the left
général: en général usually
généralement generally
gentiment nicely
grâce à thanks to
gravement gravely; seriously
guère: ne ... guère hardly
habitude: d'habitude usually;
comme d'habitude as usual
hasard: par hasard by chance;
au hasard at random
haut: en haut (de) at the top (of);
de haut en bas from top to bottom
heure: à l'heure on time;
de bonne heure early
heureusement fortunately
hier yesterday;
avant-hier the day before yesterday
ici here
immédiatement immediately
importe: n'importe où anywhere
intellectuellement intellectually
intérieur: à l'intérieur (de) inside
jadis formerly, once
jamais ever;
ne ... jamais never
jusque: jusqu'à until;
jusqu'ici so far, until now;
jusque-là until then
justement exactly
là there; **là-bas** over there;
là-haut up there
légèrement slightly
lendemain:
le lendemain the next day;
le lendemain matin the next morning
lentement slowly
loin (de) far (from)
long: le long de along
longtemps for a long time
lourdement heavily
maintenant now
mal badly
malgré in spite of
malheureusement unfortunately
manuellement manually
maximum: au maximum at the maximum
même same; even;
même pas not even;
quand même even so
mentalement mentally
mieux better; **le mieux** best
milieu: au milieu de in the middle of
moins less, minus;
moins de less than, fewer than;
au moins at least;
du moins at least

mystérieusement mysteriously
naturellement of course, naturally
nerveusement nervously
normalement normally
notamment especially
nouveau: de nouveau again
nulle part nowhere
ne ... nullement in no way
où where;
n'importe où anywhere
outre: en outre furthermore
paisiblement peacefully
par by; through;
par terre on the ground;
par-dessous under;
par-dessus over
parfaitement perfectly
parfois sometimes
parmi among
part: à part apart (from);
nulle part nowhere;
quelque part somewhere
particulier: en particulier in particular
particulièrement particularly
partiellement partially
partir: à partir de from
partout everywhere
pas: pas du tout not at all;
pas loin de not far from;
pas mal de a lot of
patiemment patiently
peine: à peine scarcely, hardly, barely
pendant during, for
peu: peu à peu little by little;
à peu près about, approximately
peut-être perhaps, maybe
poliment politely
plus [plys]:
deux plus deux two plus two;
en plus moreover;
de plus moreover;
de plus en plus [dəplyzɑ̃ply] more and more;
plus [ply]:
plus de (pommes) no more (apples);
plus de (dix) more than (ten);
ne ... plus no more, no longer;
plus tard later;
non plus neither, either;
moi non plus! nor me!
plutôt rather
pour for; in order to
pourtant yet, nevertheless
près de near
présent: à présent at present
presque almost, nearly
proximité: à proximité de near to
puis then
quand when;
quand même however, even so, nevertheless
quant à (moi) as for (me)
quelquefois sometimes
quelque part somewhere
rapidement quickly
rarement rarely
récemment recently
régulièrement regularly
retard: en retard late
sans without;
sans cesse incessantly

sauf except
selon according to
sérieusement seriously
seulement only
simplement simply
soigneusement carefully
soudain suddenly
sous under
souvent often
sur on
sûrement certainly
sur-le-champ at once
surtout especially
tant de so much, so many
tard late;
  plus tard later;
  trop tard too late
tellement so; so much
temps: de temps en temps from time to time;
  de temps à autre from time to time;
  en même temps at the same time
tôt early;
  trop tôt too soon, too early;
  le plus tôt possible as soon as possible
toujours always; still
tout: en tout in all;
  tout d'abord first of all;
  tout à coup suddenly;
  tout à fait completely, quite;
  tout près (de) very near;
  tout de suite at once
travers: à travers through
très very
trop too; too much;
  trop de too much, too many
uniquement only
un à un one by one
vers towards; about (*of time*)
vite quickly, fast
vraiment really
y there, to that place, in that place

SOME EXTRA NOUNS

What is a noun?
A **noun** is a naming word for a living being, a thing, or an idea, for example, *woman, Andrew, desk, happiness.*

un accent accent
un accord agreement
un accueil reception
une action action
une activité activity
les affaires *fpl* things
l'âge *m* age
l'air *m* air
une ambition ambition
une âme soul
un ami friend
une amie friend
l'amour *m* love
l'angoisse *f* anguish, distress
une annonce advertisement
une antenne parabolique satellite dish
l'argent *m* silver; money
l'arrière *m* back, rear
un article article
l'attention *f* attention; **à l'attention de** for the attention of
un attrait attraction
un avantage advantage
une aventure adventure
un avis notice; opinion; **à mon avis** in my opinion
le bain bath
la barrière gate; fence
la bataille battle
le bâton stick
la beauté beauty
la bêtise stupidity
le bien good
la bise kiss
le bonheur happiness
le bonhomme de neige snowman
la boue mud
la bousculade bustle
le bout end
le bruit noise
le but aim; goal
le calme peace, calm
le candidat candidate
le canif penknife
le caractère character, nature
la carte d'identité ID card
le cas case; **en cas de** in case of; **en tout cas** in any case
la catastrophe disaster
le/la catholique Catholic
la cause cause; **à cause de** because of
le CD-ROM CD-ROM
le centimètre centimetre
le centre centre
le cercle circle
le chagrin distress
la chance luck
la chapelle chapel

le chapitre chapter
le charme charm
le chef boss
le chiffre figure
le choix choice
la chose thing
le/la chrétien(ne) Christian
le chuchotement whispering
la civilisation civilization
le classement classification
la cloche bell
le clocher steeple
le coin corner
la colère anger
la colonne column
le commencement beginning
la compagne companion; partner
le compagnon companion; partner
la comparaison comparison
le compte calculation
la confiance confidence
le confort comfort
la conscience conscience
le conseil advice
la construction construction
le contraire the opposite
la copie copy
la corbeille basket
la corde rope
lecorrecteur orthographique spellchecker
le/la correspondant(e) correspondent
le côté side
le coup blow, bang, knock
le courage courage, bravery
le cours course, lesson
la coutume custom
le couvent convent
la crainte fear
le cri cry
la croix cross
la cuisine kitchen; cookery
la culture culture
le curé vicar, priest
la curiosité curiosity
le danger danger
les débris *mpl* wreckage
le début beginning
la décision decision
les dégâts *mpl* damage
le délai time limit
le déodorant deodorant
le désarmement disarmament
le désastre disaster
le désir wish
le désordre disorder
le destin destiny
le détail detail
la détresse distress
Dieu God
la différence difference; **quelle est la différence entre X et Y?** what is the difference between X and Y?
la difficulté difficulty
la dimension dimension
la direction direction
la discipline discipline
la dispute argument
ledisque dur hard disk
la distance distance
le distributeur dispenser
le documentaire documentary

la documentation documentation
le doute doubt;
sans doute no doubt; probably
le drapeau flag
le droit right
la droite the right
la durée time
un échange exchange;
en échange de in exchange for
une échelle ladder
l'économie *f* economy; saving
un effet effect
un effort effort
un électeur elector
une élection election
l'élégance *f* elegance
un endroit place
l'énergie *f* energy
l'enfance *f* childhood
un ennemi enemy
l'ennui *m* boredom; problem
une enseigne sign
un ensemble group
l'enthousiasme *m* enthusiasm
un entretien conversation; interview
les environs *mpl* surrounding district
l'épaisseur *f* thickness
une erreur mistake
l'espace *m* space
une espèce sort; species;
en espèces in cash
un espoir hope
l'essentiel *m* the main thing
une étape stage; stopping point
un état state
l'étendue *f* extent
une étoile star
l'étonnement *m* astonishment
un événement event
un excès excess
un exemple example;
par exemple for example
l'exil *m* exile
une expérience experience; experiment
un expert expert
une explication explanation
une exposition exhibition
un extrait extract
la fabrication manufacture
la façon way;
de cette façon in this way
le fait fact
la famille family
la fanfare brass band; fanfare
la faute fault;
c'est de ma faute it's my fault
la fermeture closure
le feu fire
la fin end
la flèche arrow
la foi faith
la fois time
la folie madness
le fond background; bottom
la force strength
la forme shape
la foule crowd
la fraîcheur freshness
les frais *mpl* expenses
le franc franc
la gaieté, la gaîté gaiety

la gauche the left
le genre type, kind, sort
la gentillesse kindness
le goût taste; **chacun ses goûts** each to his own
le gouvernement government
la grandeur size
le gros lot first prize
le groupe group
la guerre war
le guide guide
l'habileté *f* skill
une habitude habit
l'harmonie *f* harmony
le :haut-parleur (*pl* haut-parleurs) loudspeaker
la :hauteur height
l'honneur *m* honour
les honoraires *mpl* fees
la :honte shame
l'humeur *f* mood
l'humour *m* humour
l'hygiène *f* hygiene
une idée idea
un/une idiot(e) idiot
une image picture
l'imagination *f* imagination
un/une imbécile idiot
un/une immigré(e) immigrant
l'importance *f* importance
un/une inconnu(e) stranger
un inconvénient disadvantage
les informations *fpl* news
un inspecteur inspector
les instructions *fpl* instructions
l'intérêt *m* interest
une interruption break, interruption
une interview interview
une invitation invitation
la jalousie jealousy
la joie joy
le jouet toy
le jour day
le journal (*pl* journaux) newspaper
le/la juif/juive Jew
la largeur width
la larme tear
le lecteur reader
le lecteur de disquettes disk drive
la légende legend, caption
le lever de soleil sunrise
le lieu place; **au lieu de** instead of
la ligne line
la limite boundary, limit
la liste list
la littérature literature
la livre (sterling) pound (sterling)
la location rental
le loisir leisure
la longueur length
la Loterie nationale National Lottery
la lumière light
la lune moon
la lutte struggle
le machin thing, contraption
le magazine magazine
la malchance bad luck
le malheur misfortune
la manière way
le manque (de) lack (of)
lematériel hardware
le maximum maximum

la médecine medicine (*science*)
le mélange mixture
le membre member
la mémoire memory
le mensonge lie
la messe mass
la méthode method
le mieux best
le milieu middle
le minimum minimum
le Ministère de the Ministry of
le mot word; message
le moyen (de) the means (of);
au moyen de by means of
le/la musulman(e) Muslim
le mystère mystery
le niveau (*pl* -x) level
le nom name
le nombre number
la nourriture food
la nouvelle (piece of) news
un objet object
l'obscurité *f* darkness
une observation remark
une occasion opportunity; occasion
un octet byte
une œuvre work
une ombre shadow
une opinion opinion
un ordre order
l'orgueil *m* pride
l'ouverture *f* opening
la page page
la paire pair
la paix peace
le panier basket
le panneau (*pl* -x) sign, notice
le pari bet
la parole word
la part part; **de la part de** from
la partie part
le pas footstep
la patience patience
le pays country
la peine difficulty; sentence
la pensée thought
la permission permission
la perruque wig
la personne person
le pétrole oil, petroleum; paraffin
le peuple nation
la phrase sentence
la pile battery
la plaisanterie joke
le plaisir pleasure
le plan plan; map;
au premier plan in the foreground;
à l'arrière plan in the background
le plateau (*pl* -x) tray; plateau
la plupart de most (of)
le poids weight
le point point, mark; full stop
le point de vue point of view
la politesse politeness
la politique politics
le pont bridge, deck
portée: à portée de la main within arm's reach
le portrait portrait
la position position

la possibilité possibility, opportunity
la poupée doll
la poussière dust
le pouvoir power
les préparatifs *mpl* preparations
la préparation preparation
la présence presence
le pressentiment feeling
le principe principle;
  en principe in principle
le problème problem
le produit product; produce
la profondeur depth
le projet plan
la propreté cleanliness
la prospérité prosperity
les provisions provisions
la prudence caution
la publicité publicity
la qualité quality
la question question
la queue tail
le raccourci short cut
la raison reason
le rapport connection
la reine queen
la religion religion
les remerciements *mpl* thanks
le remue-ménage commotion
la rencontre meeting
le rendez-vous appointment
les renseignements *mpl* information
la réponse reply
la reprise resumption
la réputation reputation
le rescapé survivor
le réseau (*pl* -x) network
la résolution resolution
le respect respect
les restes *mpl* remains
le résultat result
le résumé summary
le retour return;
  de retour back
la réussite success
le rêve dream
la révolution revolution
le roi king
le ruisseau stream
le rythme rhythm
la saleté dirtiness
le salon de beauté beauty parlour
le sang-froid calm
le sanglot sob
le schéma diagram
le seau bucket
le secours help
le secret secret
la section section
la sécurité security
le séjour stay
la sélection selection
la semaine week
le sens sense
la sensation feeling
la série series
le service service;
  de service on duty
le signe sign
le silence silence
la situation situation
la société society

la solution solution
la somme sum
le son sound
le sort fate
la sorte sort, kind
le soupçon suspicion
le sourire smile
le souvenir souvenir; memory
le spectateur spectator
le/la stagiaire trainee
le style style
le succès success
la sueur sweat
le sujet subject; **au sujet de** about
la surprise surprise
la surveillance supervision; watch
le système system
la tache stain
la tâche task
le talent talent
le tas heap, pile
le taux de change exchange rate
la taxe tax
le téléscope telescope
le/la téléspectateur(trice) viewer
la tentative attempt
le terme term, expression
le texte text
la théorie theory
la timidité shyness
le tour turn; trick; **c'est ton tour** it's your turn
le tournoi tournament
la tragédie tragedy
le traitement treatment; salary
le tremblement de terre earthquake
la tristesse sadness
le tube tube; hit song
le type type; guy
le va-et-vient comings and goings
la valeur value
la vapeur steam
la veine luck
la version version
le verso back (of page)
la victoire victory
la vie life
les vœux *mpl* wishes
le voyage journey
la vue view; **de vue** bysight; **en vue de** with a view to

VERBS

> **What is a verb?**
> A **verb** is a 'doing' word which describes what somebody or something does, what they are, or what happens to them, for example, *play, be, disappear*.

abandonner to abandon
abîmer to spoil, to damage
aboutir to end
s'abriter to shelter
accepter to accept
accompagner to go with
accomplir to accomplish
s'accoutumer à to become accustomed to
accrocher to hang (up); to catch (*à* on)
accueillir to welcome
accuser to accuse
acheter to buy
achever to finish
admettre to admit
admirer to admire
adorer to adore
s'adresser à to apply to; to speak to
afficher to display
affirmer to maintain, to assert
agacer to irritate
agir to act, to behave;
  il s'agit de it is a question of
s'agrandir to grow
aider qn à to help sb to
aimer to like, to love;
  aimer bien to like;
  aimer mieux to prefer
ajouter to add
aller to go;
  aller chercher qn to go and meet sb;
  s'en aller to go away
allumer to switch on; to light
amener to bring
s'amuser to enjoy oneself
annoncer to announce
annuler to cancel
s'apercevoir de to notice
appartenir (à) to belong (to)
appeler to call;
  s'appeler to be called
apporter to bring
apprécier to appreciate
apprendre (à faire qch) to learn (to do sth);
  apprendre qch à qn to teach sb sth
s'approcher de to approach
approuver to approve
appuyer to press;
  s'appuyer to lean
arracher to pull out; to snatch; to tear
s'arranger: cela s'arrangera it will be all right
arrêter to stop; to arrest;
  s'arrêter to stop
arriver to arrive; to happen
s'asseoir to sit down

assister à to attend, to be present at, to go to
assurer to assure; to insure
attacher to tie, to fasten
attaquer to attack
atteindre to reach
attendre to wait (for)
attirer to attract
attraper to catch
augmenter to increase
(s')avancer to go forward
avoir to have;
 avoir l'air to seem;
 avoir besoin de to need;
 avoir chaud/froid to be hot/cold;
 avoir envie de to want to; **avoir l'habitude de** to be in the habit of;
 avoir honte (de) to be ashamed (of);
 avoir l'intention de to intend to;
 avoir lieu to take place;
 avoir du mal à to have difficulty in;
 en avoir marre to be fed up;
 avoir peur to be afraid;
 avoir raison/tort to be right/ wrong
avouer to confess
baisser to lower
balbutier to stammer
barrer to block
bâtir to build
battre to beat;
 se battre to fight
bavarder to chat
bloquer to block
bouger to move
bouleverser to upset
bricoler to potter about, to do odd jobs
briller to shine
briser to break
brûler to burn
(se) cacher to hide
(se) calmer to calm down
casser to break
causer to cause; to chat
cesser (de) to stop
changer to change;
 changer d'avis to change one's mind
chanter to sing
charger to load
chasser to chase (off); to get rid of
chauffer to heat up
chercher to look for
choisir to choose
chuchoter to whisper
circuler to move
cirer to polish
cocher to tick
collaborer to collaborate
collectionner to collect
coller to stick
commander to order
commencer (à) to begin (to)
compenser to compensate for
comporter to comprise
composer to compose; to make up; to dial
composter to date-stamp; to punch
comprendre to understand
compter to count; to intend to
concerner to concern
conclure to conclude

condamner to condemn; to sentence
conduire to drive; **se conduire** to behave
confectionner to make
confirmer to confirm
connaître to know
consacrer to devote
conseiller to advise
conserver to keep
considérer to consider
consister to consist
consommer to consume
constater to establish
constituer to make up
construire to build
consulter to consult
contacter to get in touch with
contempler to contemplate
contenir to contain
continuer to continue
convenir to be suitable
copier to copy
corriger to correct
se coucher to go to bed; to lie down
coudre to sew
couler to flow
couper to cut (off)
courir to run
coûter to cost
couvrir to cover
craindre to fear
créer to create
creuser to dig
crier to shout
critiquer to criticize
croire to believe
cueillir to pick
cultiver to grow
danser to dance
se débrouiller to manage
décevoir to disappoint
déchirer to tear
décider (de) to decide (to); **se décider (à)** to make up one's mind (to)
déclarer to declare
découper to cut up
se décourager to become discouraged
découvrir to discover
décrire to describe
défendre to forbid; to defend
dégager to clear
se déguiser to dress up
demander to ask; **demander à qn de faire qch** to ask sb to do sth; **se demander** to wonder
demeurer to live
démolir to demolish
dépasser to overtake
se dépêcher to hurry
dépendre de to depend on
déplaire: cela me déplaît I don't like it
déposer to put down
déranger to disturb
désapprouver to disapprove of
descendre to come *or* go down; to get off; to take down
déshabiller to undress
désirer to desire, to want

désobéir to disobey
dessiner to draw
détester to hate
détourner to divert
détruire to destroy
développer to develop
devenir to become
deviner to guess
devoir to have to (*must*)
différer (de) to be different (from)
diminuer to reduce
dire to say, to tell
diriger to direct;
  se diriger vers to go towards
discuter to discuss
disparaître to disappear
se disputer to argue
distinguer to distinguish
distribuer to distribute
diviser to divide
dominer to dominate
donner to give
donner sur to overlook
dormir to sleep
se doucher to have a shower
douter (de) to doubt
dresser to set up;
  se dresser to stand (up)
durer to last
échanger to exchange
s'échapper (de) to escape (from)
éclairer to light (up)
éclater de rire to burst out laughing
économiser to save
écouter to listen (to)
écraser to crush;
  s'écraser to crash
s'écrier to cry out
écrire to write;
  s'écrire to write to each other;
  ça s'écrit comment? how do you spell it?
effacer to erase
effectuer to carry out
effrayer to frighten
s'élancer to rush forward
élever to erect; to bring up;
  s'élever to rise
emballer to wrap (up)
embrasser to kiss
emmener to take
empêcher (de) to prevent (from)
employer to use
emporter to take
emprunter qch à qn to borrow sth from sb
encourager qn à faire to encourage sb to do
s'endormir to fall asleep
enfermer to imprison
s'enfuir to flee
enlever to take away; to take off
s'ennuyer to be bored
enregistrer to record
entasser to stack
entendre to hear;
  qu'entendez-vous par...? what do you mean by ...?;
  entendre parler de to hear about;
  s'entendre to agree
entourer (de) to surround (with)
entrer (dans) to go *or* come in(to)
envahir to invade
envelopper to wrap (up)

envoyer to send
épeler to spell
éprouver to experience
espérer to hope
essayer (de faire qch) to try (to do sth)
essuyer to wipe
établir to establish, to set up
étaler to spread out
éteindre to put out; to switch off
s'étendre to stretch out
étonner to astonish;
s'étonner to be astonished
étouffer to suffocate
être to be;
être d'accord to agree;
être assis(e) to be sitting;
être obligé(e) de to be obliged to;
être sur le point de to be just about to;
être de retour to be back;
être en train de faire qch to be doing sth
étudier to study
(s')éveiller to wake up
éviter (de faire) to avoid (doing)
exagérer to exaggerate
examiner to examine
s'excuser (de) to apologize (for)
exister to exist
expliquer to explain
exprimer to express
fabriquer to make
se fâcher to become angry
faillir: il a failli tomber he almost fell
faire to do; to make;
faire attention to be careful;
faire la bise à qn to kiss sb on the cheek;
faire chaud/froid to be hot/cold;
faire la connaissance de to meet;
faire entrer quelqu'un to let somebody in;
se faire couper les cheveux to have one's hair cut;
faire halte to stop;
faire du mal (à) to harm;
faire partie de to belong to;
faire la queue to queue;
faire de son mieux (pour) to do one's best (to);
faire une promenade to go for a walk;
faire semblant de to pretend to;
faire signe to signal, to wave; **faire un stage** to go on a training course
falloir to be necessary;
il faut one must
féliciter to congratulate
fermer to close, to shut;
fermer à clef to lock
se figurer to imagine
finir to finish
fixer to stare at; to fix
flâner to stroll
fonctionner to work;
faire fonctionner to operate
former to form
fouiller to search
fournir to provide
frapper to hit, to knock
fréquenter to frequent; to see
gagner to win; to earn
garantir to guarantee

garder to keep
gâter to spoil;
  se gâter to go wrong
gémir to groan
gêner to bother
glisser to slip, to slide
gratter to scratch
grimper to climb
guetter to watch
habiter to live (in)
s'habituer à to get used to
hésiter to hesitate
heurter to bump into
ignorer not to know
imaginer to imagine
imprimer to print
indiquer qch à qn to inform sb of sth
s'inquiéter to worry
inscrire to note down;
  s'inscrire to register
installer to put in;
  s'installer to settle
s'instruire to educate oneself
insulter to insult
interdire to prohibit;
  "interdit de fumer" "no smoking"
intéresser to interest;
  s'intéresser à qch to be interested in sth
interroger to question
interrompre to interrupt
interviewer to interview
introduire to introduce
inventer to invent
inviter to invite
jeter to throw (away)
joindre to join
jurer to swear
laisser to leave; to let; to allow;
  laisser tomber to drop
lancer to throw
(se) laver to wash
lever to lift; to raise;
  se lever to get up; to stand up
lire to read
loger (chez) to live (with)
louer to hire, to rent
lutter to struggle
manœuvrer to operate
manquer to miss; to be lacking
marcher to walk; to work
se marier (avec qn) to marry (sb)
marquer to mark; to write down; to score
mêler to mix; **se mêler (à qch)** to get involved (in sth)
menacer to threaten
mener to lead
mentir to lie
mériter to deserve
mesurer to measure
mettre to put (on); to take;
  mettre qch au point to finalize sth; to perfect sth;
  mettre qn à la porte to throw sb out;
  se mettre à l'abri to take shelter;
  se mettre en colère to get angry;
  se mettre en route to set off
monter to come *or* go up; to get into
montrer to show

se moquer de to make fun of
mordre to bite
multiplier to multiply
noter to write down; to mark
nourrir to feed
obliger qn à faire to force sb to do
observer to observe; to keep
obtenir to obtain, to get
s'occuper de to attend to
offrir to give
s'opposer à to be opposed to
ordonner to order
organiser to organize
orner (de) to decorate (with)
oser (faire qch) to dare (to do sth)
oublier to forget
ouvrir to open
paraître to appear
parier (sur) to bet (on)
parler to speak, to talk
partager to share
participer (à) to take part (in)
partir to leave, to go away
passer to pass; to spend (*time*);
passer un examen to sit an exam;
se passer to happen
passionner to fascinate
payer to pay
peindre to paint
pénétrer (dans) to enter
penser (à) to think (about)
perdre to lose;
perdre qn de vue to lose sight of sb
permettre (à qn de faire) to allow (sb to do)
persuader to persuade
peser to weigh
photographier to photograph
placer to place, to put
se plaindre (de) to complain (about)
plaire (à) to please;
cela me plaît I like that
plaisanter to joke
pleurer to cry
plier to fold
porter to carry; to wear; to take
poser to put (down);
poser des questions to ask questions
posséder to own
poursuivre to pursue
pousser to push; to grow
pouvoir to be able to
pratiquer to play; to practise
précipiter to hurl;
se précipiter dans to rush into
prédire to predict
préférer to prefer
prendre to take;
prendre qch à qn to take sth from sb;
prendre part à to take part in;
prendre soin (de) to take care (to)
préparer to prepare
présenter to present; to introduce;
se présenter to appear; to introduce oneself
prêter qch à qn to lend sb sth
prévoir to foresee
prier to request;
je vous en prie please, don't mention it
priver qn de qch to deprive sb of sth

produire to produce;
se produire to happen
profiter (de) to take advantage (of)
se promener to go for a walk
promettre (à qn de faire qch) to promise (sb to do sth)
prononcer to pronounce
proposer (de faire) to suggest (doing)
protéger to protect
protester to protest
prouver to prove
provoquer to cause
se quereller to quarrel
quitter to leave
raccommoder to mend
raconter to tell
ralentir to slow down
ramasser to pick up
ramener to bring *or* take back
ranger to tidy
se rappeler to remember
rapporter to report; to bring back
rassurer to reassure
rater to miss; to fail
rattraper qn to catch up with sb
recevoir to receive
réchauffer to warm (up)
recommander to recommend; to register
recommencer to begin again
reconnaître to recognize
recouvrir (de) to cover (with)
reculer to move back; to reverse
redescendre to come *or* go down again
refaire to do again
refermer to close again
réfléchir to think
refuser (de) to refuse (to)
regagner to go back to
regarder to look (at)
régler to adjust; to settle
regretter (que) to be sorry (that)
rejoindre to join; to catch up
se relever to get up again
relier to connect
relire to read again
remarquer to notice
rembourser to refund
remercier (de) to thank (for)
remettre to put back; to postpone
remplacer to replace
remplir (de) to fill (with)
remuer to stir
rencontrer to meet;
se rencontrer to meet
rendre to give back;
rendre visite à to visit;
se rendre to give oneself up;
se rendre à to visit;
se rendre compte to realize
renseigner to inform;
se renseigner (sur) to inquire (about)
rentrer to go back (in)
renverser to run over; to spill; to knock over
renvoyer to expel, to dismiss; to send back
réparer to repair
repasser to iron
répéter to repeat
répondre to answer

se reposer to rest
reprendre to resume
représenter to represent
réserver to book
résoudre to solve
respecter to respect
ressembler à to look like
rester to stay
retenir to book
retourner to return;
  se retourner to turn round
retrouver to meet; to find (again)
se réunir to meet
réussir (à faire) to succeed (in doing)
réveiller to wake up;
  se réveiller to wake up
révéler to reveal
revenir to come back
rêver to dream
revoir to see again;
  au revoir goodbye
rire to laugh
risquer (de) to risk
rougir to blush
rouler to drive (along)
saisir to grasp
salir to dirty
saluer to greet
sauter to jump
sauver to save;
  se sauver to run off
savoir to know
sécher to dry
secouer to shake
sélectionner to select
sembler to seem
sentir to smell; to feel;
  se sentir (mal) to feel (ill)
séparer to separate
serrer to tighten;
  se serrer la main to shake hands
se servir to help oneself;
  se servir de qch to use sth
siffler to whistle
signaler to point out
signer to sign
soigner to look after
sonner to ring
sortir to go *or* come out; to take out
se soucier de to worry about
souffrir to suffer
souhaiter to wish
soulager to relieve
soulever to lift
soupçonner to suspect
soupirer to sigh
sourire to smile
se souvenir de qch to remember sth
sucer to suck
suffire to be sufficient
suggérer to suggest
suivre to follow
supposer to suppose
surprendre to surprise
sursauter to jump
se taire to be quiet;
  taisez-vous! be quiet!
téléphoner (à) to phone
tendre to hold out
tenir to hold
tenter de to attempt to
(se) terminer to finish

tirer to pull; to shoot
tomber to fall;
  laisser tomber to drop;
  tomber en panne to break down
toucher to touch
tourner to turn; to shoot;
  se tourner vers to turn towards
traduire to translate
trahir to betray
traîner to drag
travailler to work
traverser to cross; to go through; to go over
trembler to shake
tricher to cheat
tromper to deceive;
  se tromper to be mistaken
troubler to worry
trouver to find;
  se trouver to be situated
tuer to kill
unir to unite
utiliser to use
vaincre to conquer
valoir to be worth
vendre to sell
venir to come;
  venir de faire qch to have just done sth
vérifier to check
verser to pour
visiter to visit
vivre to live
voir to see
voler to steal; to fly
vouloir to want;
  vouloir bien faire to be happy to do;
  vouloir dire to mean
voyager to travel

Notes

Notes

Notes

Notes

Notes

Notes

Notes

Notes

Notes